# ARBITRATION ADVOCACY

THIRD EDITION

# Arbitration Advocacy

Third Edition

Ariana R. Levinson

Steven Lubet

NITA®

National Institute for Trial Advocacy

Address inquiries to:
Reprint Permission
National Institute for Trial Advocacy
325 W. South Boulder Rd., Ste. 1
Louisville, CO 80027-1130
Phone: (800) 225-6482
Email: publications@nita.org

ASPEN PUBLISHING

Official co-publisher of NITA.
aspenpublishing.com/NITA

ISBN 979-8-88669-0-590
FBA 2059
eISBN 979-8-88669-0-606
eFBA 2060

Library of Congress Cataloging-in-Publication Data

Names: Levinson, Ariana R., author. | Lubet, Steven, author.
Title: Arbitration advocacy / Ariana R. Levinson, Steven Lubet.
Description: Third Edition. | Louisville : National Institute for Trial Advocacy, 2024. | Series: NITA practical guide series | Includes index.
Identifiers: LCCN 2024017315 (print) | LCCN 2024017316 (ebook) | ISBN 9798886690590 (paperback) | ISBN 9798886690606 (ebook)
Subjects: LCSH: Arbitration and award--United States.
Classification: LCC KF9085 .C643 2024 (print) | LCC KF9085 (ebook) | DDC 347.73/9--dc22
LC record available at https://lccn.loc.gov/2024017315
LC ebook record available at https://lccn.loc.gov/2024017316

Printed in the United States of America

# • About the Authors •

**Ariana R. Levinson** is the Frost, Brown, Todd Professor of Law at the University of Louisville, Louis D. Brandeis School of Law where she teaches Arbitration Practice, Dispute Resolution, Evidence, Labor Law, and Employment Law. She is the faculty advisor for the mock arbitration team. Prior to teaching at Brandeis School of Law, Professor Levinson taught at USC Gould School of Law and at UCLA School of Law where she co-taught trial advocacy with Professor Al Moore. She practiced law for eight years before entering academia, including handling many arbitrations as a union-side attorney and clerking for the Honorable John G. Davies (United States District Court, Central District of California).

Professor Levinson is a fellow in the Rutgers School of Management & Labor Relations Institute for the Study of Employee Ownership & Profit Sharing. She has published five law review articles about arbitration and is a co-author, with Steve Ware, of the West handbook *Principles of Arbitration Law*. She is a reviewer for the *Journal of Participation and Employee Ownership* and the *American Business Law Journal*. She is often called upon by the press for expertise and has been quoted by the *New York Times*, the *ABA Journal*, Bloomberg BNA Daily Labor Report, and CNN. Professor Levinson regularly provides CLE for attorneys. She graduated *magna cum laude* from the University of Michigan Law School.

**Steven Lubet** is a professor of law at Northwestern University. As director of the Law School's Program on Advocacy and Professionalism, he teaches courses on Legal Ethics, Trial Advocacy, Pretrial Litigation, and Negotiation. In addition to over fifty books and articles on legal ethics and litigation, he has published widely in the areas of international criminal law and dispute resolution. Professor Lubet is the author of *Modern Trial Advocacy* (currently in its sixth edition, which is co-authored by J.C. Lore), which has also been published in Canadian and Israeli editions. Professor Lubet is co-author of *Judicial Conduct and Ethics* (Lexis, 2000) (also currently in its sixth edition), which has been called the nation's leading authority on judicial ethics. Professor Lubet's other books include *Nothing but the Truth: Why Trial Lawyers Don't, Can't and Shouldn't Have to Tell the Whole Truth* (NYU Press, 2001), as well as *Exercises and Problems in Professional Responsibility* (NITA) and *Problems and Materials in Evidence and Trial Advocacy* (NITA), both co-authored with Northwestern University School of Law Professors Robert Burns and Thomas Geraghty. In conjunction with the National Institute for Trial Advocacy, he has organized litigation programs in the United States, the United Kingdom, Canada, Israel, New Zealand, Australia, Singapore, and Hong Kong.

# • Dedications •

In memory of John W. Cooley who co-authored the first edition of this book and whose work remains its foundation.

*For Andrew Petti.*
*A. R. L.*

*To Robert Burns, my colleague, teacher, guide, and friend.*
*S. L.*

# CONTENTS

# • PREFACE •

## THE EVER-EXPANDING ARTISTIC ROLE OF THE EFFECTIVE ADVOCATE

What is your favorite movie/streaming show? Probably one that is well-written and seamlessly produced with fantastic actors. Effective advocacy requires practitioners to produce interesting and seamless stories with which to convince the factfinder to rule in your favor. As an arbitration advocate, you—the attorney—are screenwriter, director, and an actor all in one.

Advocates (effective ones, anyway) are artists and scientists, whether we wish to be or not. We can't help it. As lawyers, we train in the science of advocacy, i.e., thinking and reasoning, and find comfort there. Analytical thinking lulls us into expecting results that are objective, predictable, stable, and secure.

And then real life launches us into the art of advocacy, which is subjective, ambiguous, unpredictable, and risky. The intuitive-creative aspects of advocacy require us to use our imaginations and see things not only as they are but as they could be, and attempt things in ways we have never tried before. When first encountered, this side of advocacy seems governed by charisma alone. In reality, you can master it with the skills in this book.

In addition to teaching the intuitive-analytical model of effective advocacy, this book uses what we call a "pracademic" approach, blending practice and theory throughout. Organized into eleven chapters and an appendix section of arbitration checklists, the book provides a full range of features to help the arbitration advocate represent their client competently and efficiently. Chapter 1 introduces uninitiated advocates to the two principal ADR processes, arbitration and mediation, and provides basic information regarding the nature of the two processes and their advantages and disadvantages in relation to the court adjudication process. Chapters 2 through 7 provide useful information and practice tips for advocates regarding every stage of representation in the arbitration process. Each of these chapters has a related checklist in the appendices detailing key actions to take at critical stages of the arbitration process. Chapter 8 addresses the hybrid ADR processes (mini-trial, summary jury trial, etc.) and describes successful applications. Chapters 9 and 10 address the topic of effective advocacy in online arbitration. Chapter 11 provides an overview of a sample arbitration proceeding. The appendices also contain a listing of ADR providers and a listing of online dispute resolution (ODR) providers.

We wrote *Arbitration Advocacy* with several audiences in mind. First, we have written for alternative dispute resolution (ADR) practitioners—advocates representing clients who have either opted or who have been mandated to have their disputes resolved through an ADR process. Our second audience consists of the organizers of and participants in continuing legal education (CLE) programs around the country. The step-by-step approach, analyses of critical process and advocacy issues, and succinct presentations of useful information in chart form make it an ideal teaching tool for arbitration seminars.

A third audience we have geared this publication to is the teachers and students of law school courses on arbitration advocacy. At this writing, there are very few, if any, law student textbooks providing detailed, hands-on instruction in effective representation of clients in arbitration. This book seeks to fill that gap in ADR literature currently available for law school instruction.

Finally, ADR neutrals, especially arbitrators, may find that chapters 5, 6, and 10 on effective advocacy in arbitration sessions provide insight into how the advocates appearing before them can most effectively present information and bring the dispute to closure.

A section of this book deserves special mention. Parts of chapters 5 and 6 concerning advocacy during the arbitration hearing are adapted from J.C. Lore and Steve Lubet's book, *Modern Trial Advocacy*, 6th ed. (NITA 2020). These chapters present, in an abbreviated form, many of the useful trial advocacy principles directly applicable to an arbitration hearing. Space limitations prevent inclusion of the in-depth explanations and the many helpful examples contained in the *Modern Trial Advocacy* book. Chapters 5 and 6 cross-reference *Modern Trial Advocacy* so you can quickly find those explanations and examples. Throughout the text, these references will be made parenthetically as (Lubet & Lore, *MTA*), followed by the chapter or section number in that book, if appropriate.

In conclusion, we would like to make a few observations about the style and architecture of this book. At our editor's good suggestion, we have made every effort to use a personable and personalized writing style, as if we were having a face-to-face conversation with you. We hope you find this style to be friendly and engaging as intended. At various locations throughout several chapters, you will happen onto anecdotes—some funny, some not; some about famous people; some about ordinary people. We have done this for several reasons. First, anecdotes enliven and invigorate instructional passages that would otherwise be hortatory and didactic. Second, we consider anecdotes to be the "origin of all teaching," helping readers not only understand the teaching points, but also remember when and how to apply them later in practice. Third, CLE and law school instructors can use the anecdotes as teaching devices in ADR advocacy seminars and courses. Additionally, advocates can use them (particularly the ones appearing in chapter 4) to explain to their clients the "dos and don'ts" of client conduct during arbitration hearings.

We sincerely hope this book will significantly enhance the quality of arbitration advocacy, both nationally and internationally, for many years to come.

John W. Cooley & Steven Lubet, 1997, 2003

Steven Lubet & Ariana R. Levinson, 2024

# Acknowledgments


### Ariana R. Levinson

I thank Professor William A. Hilyerd, the Legal Reference Services Coordinator at the Louis D. Brandeis School of Law, and Virginia Judd, Legal Editor at the National Institute for Trial Advocacy (NITA), for invaluable research and editorial assistance. I thank the research assistants who also helped with this update—Andie Mooradian, David DeKold, Briana Berry, Michael A Ballard, Kyra Henry, and Evan Mitchell. I thank Rachel J. Goedken for sharing her experience using the book and my colleagues who responded to my listserv inquiries, Rick Bales, Christopher Shulman, Amy Schmitz, Dwight Golann, Lainey Feingold, Katherine Simpson, Jean Sternlight, and Sarah Cole. The number of people from whom I have learned about arbitration, dispute resolution, trial advocacy, and evidence is too long to list. I am grateful for each of you. These include my colleagues, students, and attorneys who serve as guest class panelists at, and graduates of, the University of Louisville Brandies School of Law, where I have had the opportunity and support to write and teach for many years. They also include my colleagues at other institutions and on listservs who write and teach in the areas of employment law, labor law, evidence, dispute resolution, trial advocacy, and arbitration, as well as my mentors, coworkers, and clients from my time as a practicing attorney.

### Steven Lubet

I am grateful for the support of a great academic institution: the Northwestern University School of Law. In particular, I am indebted to two fine colleagues, Bob Burns and Tom Geraghty, and to two supportive deans, Robert Bennett and David Van Zandt.

# • Chapter One •

# General Description of Arbitration in the ADR Context

*MARIA: Do you know anything about art restitution?*
*RANDY: Not a thing.*
*MARIA: Well, it's never too late to learn.*[1]

*Woman in Gold* is a movie about art restitution in which a Los Angeles attorney trained in litigation learns instead to arbitrate. He also learns about history, family, and friendship. In the decade since *Woman in Gold* was released, alternatives both to litigation and, within litigation, to trial have enjoyed increasing popularity. Innovative methods abound for resolving disputes when the court process is not the best procedural alternative to satisfy our clients' emotional, economic, and psychological needs and interests.

Among the many dispute resolution alternatives available today, the most prominent are arbitration and mediation. This book principally focuses on arbitration, viewing it initially in the context of other dispute resolution processes, particularly mediation. A companion book, *Mediation Advocacy*, Second Edition (NITA 2002), provides in-depth treatment of the art and science of mediation advocacy.

This chapter addresses foundational topics necessary to develop a working knowledge of both processes. We define arbitration and mediation and view them in the context of other dispute resolution mechanisms; consider the differences between the two processes; compare the relative advantages and disadvantages of litigation, arbitration, and mediation; and gain an understanding of the distinctions between mandatory and voluntary arbitration and mediation. In addition, we introduce the two basic steps to initiating alternative dispute resolution.

## 1.1 Overview of the Processes

Arbitration and mediation are two principal processes in a broad spectrum of dispute resolution methods, collectively called alternative dispute resolution

1. *Woman in Gold* (Origin Pictures and BBC Films, 2015) (https://www.scripts.com/script-pdf/41).

or ADR.[2] In arbitration, one or more neutrals (a disinterested third party) render a decision after reviewing evidence and hearing arguments. During mediation, a neutral assists the disputants in reaching a voluntary settlement of their differences through an agreement that defines their future behavior. The essential distinction between the two processes lies in who makes the resolution decision for the parties. In arbitration, the parties relinquish decision making to the neutral, who decides for them. By pre-agreement, the neutral's decision is either binding or nonbinding. If binding, the neutral's decision is final and the winning party may enforce it against the losing party; if nonbinding, the neutral's decision is advisory in aid of settlement. In mediation, the parties participate in a joint decision-making process and make the decision themselves.

The wide variety of ADR solutions between pure negotiation and court adjudication are demonstrated in the following chart:

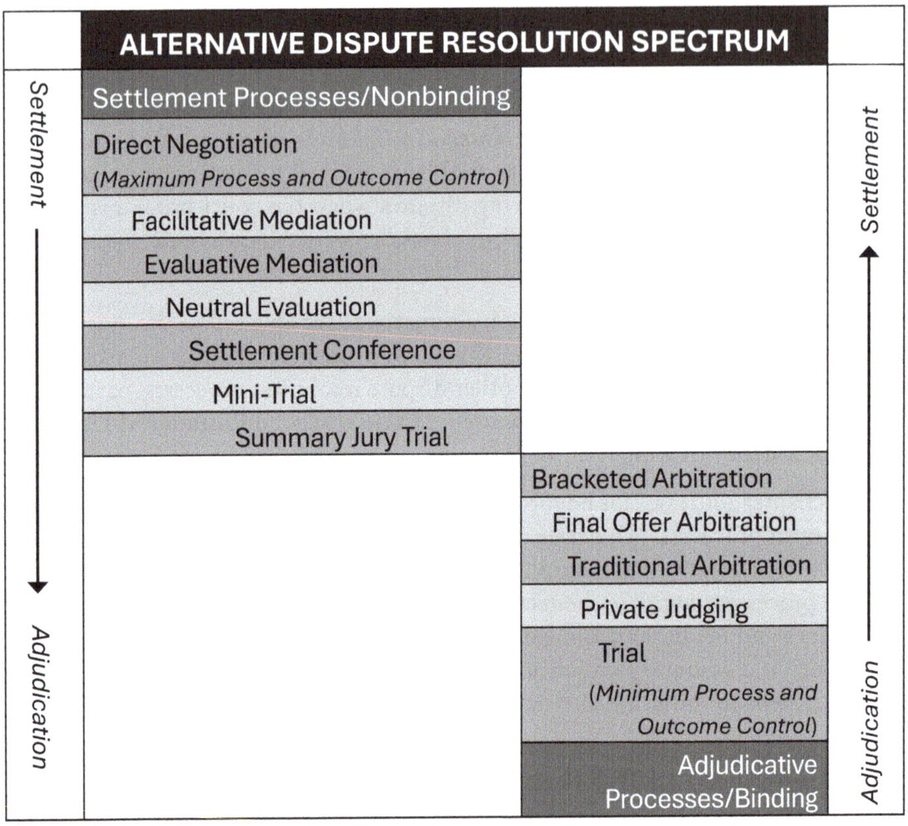


2. *See generally* Stephen B. Goldberg et al., Dispute Resolution: Negotiation, Mediation, and Other Processes (7th ed. 2020); Leonard L. Riskin et al., Dispute Resolution and Lawyers: A Contemporary Approach (6th ed. 2019).

These different forms of ADR will be explained in the course of this book.

## 1.2 Important Differences Between Arbitration and Mediation

As previously noted, the most basic difference between arbitration and mediation is that arbitration involves a decision by the intervening third party (or neutral) after an evidentiary hearing, while mediation does not. Another way to distinguish arbitration and mediation is to compare the neutral's mental functions under each process. In arbitration, the neutral uses primarily "left brain" or rational mental processes—analytical, mathematical, logical, technical, and administrative. In mediation, the neutral additionally employs "right brain" or creative mental processes—conceptual, intuitive, artistic, holistic, symbolic, and emotional. Furthermore, an arbitrator deals largely with the *objective*, whereas a mediator deals primarily with the *subjective.* Typically, the arbitrator is typically a passive participant whose role is to determine right or wrong; the mediator, by contrast, is an active participant who attempts to move the parties to reconciliation and agreement, regardless of who or what is right or wrong.

The mediator's role involves instinctive reactions, intuition, keen interpersonal skills, and sensitivity to subtle psychological and behavioral indicators, in addition to applying logic and rational thinking. This complexity of interactions means that some people find it much more difficult to perform effectively in the role of mediator as opposed to in the role of arbitrator.

The two processes are typically employed to resolve different types of disputes. Parties use mediation when they believe they can reach an agreement with the assistance of a disinterested third party. Parties that will have an ongoing relationship after they resolve the conflict also tend to use mediation. On the other hand, parties generally use arbitration when they have failed to reach a negotiated settlement or no reasonable likelihood of a negotiated settlement exists, and when time constraints, the need for an expert decision-maker, or other arbitration attributes make it preferable to litigation. If the parties use the two processes in sequence, mediation normally occurs first; if it is unsuccessful, the parties resort to arbitration. Viewed in terms of the judicial process, arbitration is comparable to a trial, while mediation is akin to a judicial settlement conference.

Although mediation and arbitration differ substantially, they both have the underlying structure of a decision-making process. The following chart depicts the interrelationship of their various stages. Section 2.1 discusses the stages of arbitration in more detail.

| STAGES OF MEDIATION AND ARBITRATION | |
|---|---|
| MEDIATION PROCESS | ARBITRATION PROCESS |
| Initiation | |
| Preparation | |
| Introduction | Prehearing conference |
| Problem statement<br>Problem clarification<br>Generation and evaluation of alternatives | Hearing |
| Selection of alternatives | Decision-making |
| Agreement | Award |

## 1.3 Advantages and Disadvantages of Arbitration, Mediation, and Court Adjudication

Most trial advocates are well aware of the advantages and disadvantages of litigation culminating in a court adjudication. Many are also knowledgeable about mediation. They are not always as knowledgeable, however, about the advantages and disadvantages of arbitration and how to assess it in relation to court adjudication. This section describes the advantages and disadvantages of these three processes by analyzing the nature of the forum, the nature of the procedures, and cost. Of course, an advantage in one type of dispute, or for one party, may be a disadvantage in a different type of dispute, or for another party.

### *1.3.1 Advantages of the Processes*

***The nature of the forum.*** Court adjudication occurs in a public forum where judges are randomly assigned cases to supervise and decide and are held accountable for their decisions. Both mediation and arbitration are nonpublic, a trait advantageous to the resolution of certain types of disputes where the parties desire privacy of both the proceedings and the outcome. Furthermore, in both mediation and arbitration, by mutual agreement the parties select qualified neutrals, who sometimes have specific expertise relevant to the dispute. Also, in arbitration, but more so in mediation, the parties usually have significant control over the resolution process. Representation by counsel is advisable but not necessary in some instances.

***The nature of the procedure.*** In court adjudication, procedures are highly structured and institutionalized, typified by detailed rules and numerous compliance mechanisms. Rules of evidence enhance the reliability of proof of claims and defenses. Court adjudication yields results that are appealable and ultimately final, binding, and enforceable, making absolute closure a real possibility.

In disputes not requiring such stringent procedures, mediation and arbitration offer measurable advantages. Arbitration, while having some of the evidentiary and procedural regularity of court adjudication, is conducted in a less formal and less rigorous setting, enhancing the potential for a more expeditious resolution. Applying legal and equitable norms and creating remedies often tailor-made to the situation, arbitrators issue decisions as awards that can be enforced through the judicial process, bringing finality to the conflict. A party has no right to a jury trial in arbitration, providing flexibility to hold a hearing virtually or conducting the arbitration process online.

Some disputes are best resolved in settings having few, if any, procedural restraints. Mediation offers several advantages in those instances. With minimal procedural requirements, mediation provides an unlimited opportunity for flexibility in communicating the parties' underlying concerns and priorities. It can educate the parties on alternative solutions, empower them to improve and strengthen their relationship in future interactions, and stimulate them to explore and reach creative solutions affording mutual gain and a high rate of compliance.

***The cost of the process.*** Court adjudication is publicly funded—tax dollars pay the cost of the judges' services and other court administrative services. In mediation and arbitration, the parties usually share the expense of the neutrals' fees and certain administrative costs. Depending on the nature of a particular dispute, however, the fees and costs associated with the mediation and arbitration process are normally less than those associated with a case that traverses the course of the court adjudication process.

### 1.3.2 Disadvantages of the Processes

Each of the three processes also has disadvantages.

***Forum disadvantages.*** The complex court adjudication process routinely mystifies parties, who usually need to be represented by legal counsel. Moreover, a judge randomly assigned to hear a particular case may not have the necessary substantive or technical expertise to appreciate fully the intricacies of legal counsel's arguments. Also, the crush of court caseloads sometimes results in substantial delay in processing individual cases. Parties often find that the court adjudicative process significantly disrupts their personal lives over long periods of time and ultimately produces a result that leaves them even more polarized than they were when they began the process.

Arbitration and mediation similarly have forum disadvantages. Private arbitration often lacks quality control since the arbitrators are independently selected in individual cases and are not generally accountable to any supervisory authority. Repeat players—parties who use arbitration regularly to resolve disputes with an individual using arbitration for the first time—often have an advantage. In the absence of uniform multiparty arbitration agreements, arbitration will not completely resolve a multiparty dispute. In mediation, the neutrals have little power or authority over the parties and certainly no power to impose unwanted outcomes on them. Consequently, one or more parties can significantly influence settlements in some situations by the power they possess and exercise behind the scenes. Moreover, in mediation there is no application or development of public standards.

***Procedural disadvantages.*** The court adjudication process has a limited range of possible remedies. The rigidity of the procedural structure means compromise is difficult. Arbitration, a process increasingly encumbered by "legalization," has its own drawbacks, which include the lack of public norms, the lack of binding precedent, insufficient opportunity for full discovery, relaxed rules of evidence, sometimes no written reasons for decisions, no uniformity of decisions, no right to a jury trial, typically no class action mechanism, and usually no opportunity for appeal. Similarly, mediation has several procedural disadvantages: no real due process safeguards exist, participation by the parties cannot be compelled by subpoena or otherwise, access to information may be severely constricted, and outcomes need not be principled. Closure to mediated outcomes is weak in the sense that they are nonbinding and unenforceable, except as provided by relevant contract law.

***Cost disadvantages.*** Though the public substantially funds the administration of the court adjudication process, it can be extremely expensive to use. The cumbersome discovery process and delays sometimes cause huge investments in attorneys' time and therefore increased attorney fees. Some complex arbitration hearings can spread over weeks and months, costing the parties much more than they had initially projected. Unsuccessful pre-adjudication or pre-arbitration mediations can add to the overall cost of securing closure of a dispute.

For quick reference, the charts that follow present the advantages and disadvantages of the three processes.

| ADVANTAGES OF THE PROCESSES | | |
|---|---|---|
| COURT ADJUDICATION | ARBITRATION | MEDIATION |
| Public forum | Privacy | Privacy |
| Already institutionalized | Parties control forum | Parties control forum |
| Neutrals are accountable | Expertise | Process educates disputants |
| Independence | Parties select neutrals | Parties select neutrals |
| Rules of evidence<br>Precedent | Written procedures | Flexible |

| | | |
|---|---|---|
| Announces and applies public norms | Choice of applicable norms | Reflects concerns and priorities of disputants |
| Uniformity | Tailors remedy to situation | Addresses underlying problem<br>Often results in creative solutions |
| Binding/closure<br>Decision appealable | Binding/closure | |
| Enforceability | Enforceability | High rate of compliance |
| Publicly funded | Expeditious<br>Relatively inexpensive | Relatively inexpensive |
| Subpoena power | | |
| Deterrence | | |
| | Virtual/online options | |

| DISADVANTAGES OF THE PROCESSES | | |
|---|---|---|
| **COURT ADJUDICATION** | **ARBITRATION** | **MEDIATION** |
| Lack of special substantive or technical expertise | Neutrals less accountable | Neutrals have no power to impose settlement |
| No control over selection of judges | Sometimes no power to compel multiparty participation | No power to compel participation |
| | Repeat-player advantage | Powerful party can influence outcome |
| Discovery can be expensive and burdensome | Limited or no discovery | Limited access to information |
| Delay<br>Expensive<br>Time consuming | Becoming increasingly encumbered by legalization | Extra cost if doesn't result in settlement |
| | Relaxed rules of evidence<br>No precedent | No due process safeguards |

| | | |
|---|---|---|
| | No public norms | No application/ development of public standards |
| Appeals can delay final outcome, damaging financially precarious parties | Usually, no appeal | Weak closure<br>Not binding |
| Mystifying | Sometimes no written reasons for decision | |
| Limited range of remedies | No uniformity | Outcome need not be principled |
| | Lack of quality control<br>No jury<br>Usually, no class action | |
| Requires lawyers<br>Polarizes, disruptive<br>Compromise difficult | | |

## 1.4 Court-Annexed Arbitration and Mediation

Traditionally, arbitration and mediation have been voluntary in the sense that the parties agree, either before or after the dispute arises, to submit it to one or both resolution methods. There has been an increasing trend, however, toward the creation of statutes and court rules providing for court-annexed arbitration and mediation, both to ease the backlog of cases and to reduce the time and money parties spend resolving their disputes. The rules governing these programs vary significantly from jurisdiction to jurisdiction; learn the specific requirements of the jurisdiction in which you are representing a client. For example, with respect to mandatory mediation, some jurisdictions require that parties submit all cases of a particular type to mediation as a prerequisite to litigating in the system. Some rules permit defendants to waive the mediation requirement, others do not. In some jurisdictions, mediations are facilitative; in others, evaluative. In some states, judges can independently determine whether a case should be submitted to one of any number of ADR processes for treatment, and others require neutrals to report back to judges on settlement progress. Some mandatory ADR programs require the parties to share the cost of the neutral, while others appoint the neutrals and pay them a nominal session fee. Some mandatory arbitration programs impose penalties, in the form of court costs and fees, on parties who reject the arbitration award, go to trial, and fare worse than they did in the arbitration proceeding.

Some people have criticized these programs for their coercive nature, pressuring parties who are sometimes unrepresented into forgoing substantial due process rights they would otherwise enjoy in a traditional trial proceeding. Courts, however, consider early settlement of cases to be in the parties' and the courts' best interests, and some courts require arbitration of disputes under a certain dollar amount.

## 1.5 Initiating the Processes

How you initiate the arbitration and mediation processes depends on the circumstances. In a court with a mandatory ADR program, the court schedules your case for a mediation conference or an arbitration hearing, as appropriate. If your client's dispute arises out of a contract that contains a mediation and/or arbitration clause, then the terms of that clause determine the steps to initiate the process. If the contract clause contains no specific guidance, or if the dispute is one not based in contract, you have wide latitude in initiating the appropriate ADR process. But several hurdles stand between you and initiation. You must: 1) tentatively decide the most appropriate process for your dispute; 2) convince opposing counsel that this process is the appropriate one; and 3) with opposing counsel, jointly decide on the provider of neutral services that you will engage. These three hurdles must be addressed by the attorney who negotiates a contract containing an arbitration clause as well.

### *1.5.1 Choosing Between Mediation and Arbitration*

Assuming you have narrowed your dispute resolution options to mediation and arbitration, consider the following criteria in choosing whether to mediate and whether, should mediation fail, to arbitrate or to litigate through trial. (Section 2.4 discusses additional criteria.)

- Most critically, mediation and advisory arbitration only resolve the dispute if the parties reach an agreement, whereas binding arbitration substitutes for litigation and a trial and provides finality and closure.
- If the parties to the dispute anticipate future dealings with each other and want to preserve a continuing relationship, mediation is likely to be productive.
- If one party is considerably more powerful than the other, the party with less power may benefit from the fairness-determining aspects of arbitration.

- If one or more parties need to avoid a published, precedential opinion that might enforce undesirable rights and/or duties into the future, arbitration is the favored choice. Large corporate clients, for example, engaged as defendants in a high volume of low-dollar disputes, where there is also a premium on speed of decision, privacy, and closure, may be well advised to opt for arbitration over mediation and trial.
- If your client has no clear legal entitlement, choose mediation so that you can concentrate on favorable facts in the process and reach a resolution prior to trial or an arbitration hearing.
- A case having multiple parties and/or multiple issues may be better suited for mediation than arbitration because a greater opportunity for beneficial trade-offs exists in such a facilitated bargaining process.
- If a fair resolution of the dispute requires that certain witnesses be compelled to be present, choose arbitration or litigation over mediation.

The following chart organizes and highlights some of these important criteria to consider when choosing between mediation and arbitration.

| IMPORTANT CRITERIA FOR SELECTING BETWEEN MEDIATION, ARBITRATION, AND LITIGATION | | |
|---|---|---|
| **MEDIATION WITH BACKUP LITIGATION** | **ARBITRATION WITHOUT MEDIATION** | **MEDIATION WITH BACKUP ARBITRATION** |
| | Need to offset power imbalance | Desire to preserve continuing relations |
| Emphasis on future dealings | Need for decision on past events | Emphasis on future dealings |
| | High volume of disputes | |
| Disputants desire total control of process | Need to compel participation | Need to avoid win-lose decision |
| Dispute has multiple parties and issues | Premium on speed and privacy | Premium on speed and privacy |
| Absence of clear legal entitlement | Premium on closure | Premium on closure |

### 1.5.2 Persuading Opposing Counsel to Participate

After selecting mediation or arbitration and convincing yourself of the wisdom of your choice, you must convince opposing counsel that your choice of process is a reasonable one. This is not always easy. Lawyers who have never used or been involved in an arbitration, for example, are reluctant to try it for the first time. This is just human nature. If they have never experienced it, they feel uncomfortable about recommending it to their clients. What if their clients ask questions about the process? Those lawyers will inevitably be embarrassed when unable to provide their clients with an explanation. Or worse yet, they may provide information that is incomplete, inaccurate, or derogatory of the arbitration process altogether. Resultingly, arbitration often arises from a pre-dispute decision to include an arbitration clause in the parties' contract.

If confronted with opposing counsel who is uneducated in ADR, try the following. Agree to meet with them to explain your experiences with arbitration, for example, and answer any questions counsel may have, or offer to provide a video of an arbitration of the type of dispute in which you are engaged. Viewing the video may be enough to quell counsel's jitters. Another option may be even better: contact the dispute resolution organization that you propose to engage to administer the arbitration and have one of its case managers call opposing counsel. Case managers spend a great deal of their time explaining ADR processes to lawyers, and they can answer opposing counsel's questions about arbitration.

### 1.5.3 Selecting the Appropriate Type of Neutral Services

Decide, with opposing counsel, whether to hire a particular neutral directly or to use a dispute resolution organization. Use an internet search to locate neutrals experienced in the relevant legal field who are in your area or provide virtual arbitration hearings. You can then ask other attorneys with whom you work or know through professional organizations about the neutral's reputation.

If you decide the cost of using a dispute resolution organization is worth having a vetted neutral and help with the logistics of the process, use a dispute resolution organization. The two primary organizations in the U.S. for arbitration are the American Arbitration Association and JAMS.[3] For labor arbitration, the FMCS (Federal Mediation and Conciliation Service) provides arbitrator lists.[4] There are also regional and local dispute resolution organizations that offer mediation services, which you can locate online.

---

3. For more information on these organizations, see the websites of the American Arbitration Association (www.adr.org) and JAMS (https://www.jamsadr.com/). JAMS was previously an acronym for Judicial Arbitration and Mediation Services, Inc., but is now a stand-alone name.
4. Find a Mediator, Fed. Mediation & Conciliation Serv., https://www.fmcs.gov/aboutus/locations/find-a-mediator/?wpbdp_view=search (last visited Jun. 2024).

# • Chapter Two •

## Preliminary Pre-Arbitration Considerations

*We cannot freely and wisely choose the right way for ourselves unless we know both good and evil.*

—*Helen Keller*[1]

Arbitration, in this country, goes back to procedures imported to the colonies from mercantile England. George Washington put an arbitration clause in his last will and testament to resolve disputes among his heirs. Abraham Lincoln urged lawyers to keep their clients out of court and arbitrated many controversies, including a boundary dispute between two farmers.[2] Today we use arbitration to resolve a broad range of disputes in various industries and in myriad areas of law. This chapter addresses specific considerations when initiating arbitration. We will explore the stages of the arbitration process and differences in the application of the arbitration process depending on the area of the law involved. We will also discuss drafting agreements to arbitrate, selecting cases for arbitration, choosing the appropriate arbitrator or arbitration panel, considering bifurcation and other procedural alternatives, choosing site inspections and audiovisual aids, and deciding whether to mediate first. As the opening quote suggests, to make these important choices wisely, you must distinguish between good and bad, between effective and ineffective, between efficient and inefficient, between economical and uneconomical.

These choices are further complicated because the rules for choosing change depending on the circumstances, similar to the card game Blackjack. The goal in Blackjack is for your cards to reach a total of 21 points without exceeding that score. This requires strategy and deciding whether it's worth the risk of taking one more card. Most of the time, if your hand totals 17 points, you stay—the risk of a high card is too great. But if you have been paying attention, counting cards, and a high probability suggests that the next card is likely to be a 4, you take your chances and draw.[3]

---

1. Helen Keller, My Religion, 181 (1956).
2. *See* John W. Cooley, *Arbitration vs. Mediation—Explaining the Differences*, 69 Judicature 263, 264 (February–March 1986).
3. Thank you to Ariana's GenZ son Zachary Petti for this timeless analogy.

Likewise in arbitration, even the most revered and time-honored rules must give way to situational needs and common sense. A good choice in one situation may be a very bad choice in another, depending on the nature of the dispute; the applicable law; and the identity of the parties, counsel, and the arbitrator(s). In making these initial choices, advocates draw heavily on our inner functions as artists and scientists—and, in particular, as architects. Good structural design begins with good initial choices. This chapter will help you make the right initial choices about the architecture of arbitration, regardless of the circumstances of the dispute.[4]

## 2.1 Stages of the Arbitration Process

The arbitration process normally consists of six stages: initiation, preparation, prehearing conferences, hearing, decision-making, and award.[5] We discuss these stages briefly in this section and in more detail in succeeding chapters.

| STAGES OF ARBITRATION |
|---|
| Initiation |
| Preparation |
| Prehearing conference |
| Hearing |
| Decision-making |
| Award |

### *2.1.1 Initiation*

There are four principal ways by which an arbitration proceeding is initiated: by a submission; by a "demand" or "notice" pursuant to a pre-dispute agreement; by a court order granting a motion to compel arbitration; and, in the case of a court-annexed proceeding, by court rule or court order.

#### 2.1.1.1 Submission

Parties initiate by submission where no prior agreement to arbitrate exists. First, both parties decide whether other parties need to be involved in the arbitration and whether the entire dispute is appropriate for arbitration. If not, decide with opposing

4. For additional guidance, *see* Martin Domke et al., Domke on Commercial Arbitration (3d ed. 2003).

5. Cooley, *supra* note 2 at 264–66.

counsel what aspects of the dispute will be arbitrated. Next, decide whether the arbitration will be administered by an agency or will be nonadministered. You can choose an arbitrator, for example, from a panel of a national dispute resolution organization or you and opposing counsel can agree to use an independent arbitrator.

If the arbitration is administered, the dispute resolution organization may schedule an administrative conference to coordinate the exchange of information, and to consider other matters that will expedite the arbitration process. If the arbitration is nonadministered, decide how you and opposing counsel will split up the administrative functions. Eventually, all parties to the dispute must sign the submission. At a minimum, it names the arbitrator(s) or method of appointment and describes the arbitrator's authority, the procedure to be used at the hearing, a statement of the matter in dispute, the amount of money in controversy, and the remedy sought.

Initiating arbitration by submission is very difficult because it requires parties already in dispute to cooperate in designing a process and procedures, choosing the neutrals, and administering the process. Because it is unrealistic to expect parties who are emotionally at odds to cooperate in this way, many advocates avert these problems by incorporating an arbitration clause into a contract, which locks in these parameters before the fact. This provides a vehicle through which arbitration can automatically be initiated by demand or notice, as next described.

#### 2.1.1.2 Demand or Notice

Where a contract clause requires the parties to arbitrate disputes arising out of the contract, one party may initiate arbitration unilaterally by serving upon the other party or parties a written demand or notice to arbitrate under the terms of that clause. When demanding arbitration pursuant to a contract clause, send a copy of the demand to the administering agency if the arbitration is being administered. Be careful to comply with all the procedural requirements in the arbitration clause to avoid losing arbitration rights on any issues. Though an opposing party may submit an answer to a demand, an answer is ordinarily not required, and a claim usually will be assumed to be denied in the absence of an answer. The arbitrator will read the demand and, if filed, the answer prior to the beginning of the hearing; these will often frame their decision, so set out the issues of the dispute as completely as possible.[6]

#### 2.1.1.3 Motion to Compel Arbitration Granted

Sometimes, although a party is bound by a contractual arbitration clause, they may not know, such as in the instance of an employee or consumer, or may believe the clause is unenforceable and instead file a lawsuit. Filing a lawsuit involves filing

---

6. *See* sections 3.1 and 3.2 for more detailed information on drafting an arbitration demand and answer.

a complaint, which is similar to a demand for arbitration but must comply with court formatting and substantive requirements.[7] The defense will then file a motion to compel arbitration. If the court rules for the defense, it will compel arbitration. The claimant can then simply use the complaint, modified to comply with any administrating agency requirements, as the demand for arbitration.

#### 2.1.1.4 Court Rule or Court Order

In court-annexed arbitration, the court initiates arbitration by order or rule. Court-annexed arbitration is usually nonbinding, unless the parties agree otherwise. Depending on the court-annexed system, an arbitrator or panel of arbitrators is chosen by the parties or is appointed by the judge or court administrator to preside over the arbitration process.

### *2.1.2 Preparation*

Understand and thoroughly prepare your case for arbitration as if you were proceeding to trial. Depending on the case's nature, prehearing discovery may be necessary, and the arbitrator normally determines its permissible extent. Your goals are simplicity and utility, which weigh against extensive discovery. Stipulate facts where possible. Ordinarily, court-annexed arbitration forbids discovery after the arbitration panel is assigned, though much discovery may have occurred before the panel assignment, while the case was pending on the court's docket.

### *2.1.3 Prehearing*

In more complex arbitration, the arbitrator often conducts a preliminary hearing (or prehearing conference) to clarify any pre-arbitration issues; discuss scheduling matters to expedite the arbitration process; and to handle any procedural, discovery, or evidentiary issues. At this hearing, make any necessary motions or objections, which can either be ruled upon during the hearing or scheduled for briefing. Conduct all pertinent communication at the preliminary hearing—arbitration, unlike mediation, does not permit ex parte conversations between the arbitrator and a party or a party's counsel.

### *2.1.4 Hearing*

Parties may waive oral hearing and have the dispute determined based on documents only. Some evidence suggests that reading a full transcript or affidavit provides a better basis to assess credibility than live testimony, which can lead to behavior miscues. In most cases, an arbitrator conducts an evidentiary-type hearing,

---

7. For a small but useful guide on drafting complaints, *see* Janet S. Kole, Pleading Your Case: Complaints and Responses (2011).

often online via videoconference. Because arbitration is a private proceeding, the hearing is not open to the public, but persons having a direct interest in the case are normally entitled to attend. Other persons may attend by agreement of the parties and with the arbitrator's permission. When a necessary party fails to appear in person or through counsel, the arbitrator may enter a default award against that party, although normally only after hearing the evidence presented by the party making an appearance.

A formal written record of the hearing is not usually necessary, and the use of a court reporter is the exception rather than the general practice. The arbitrator may record a virtual arbitration or a live arbitration, making the recording available to the parties. A party requiring an interpreter has the duty to arrange for one. Witnesses appearing at the hearing are normally required to speak under oath.

Counsel for each party customarily makes an opening statement designed to acquaint the arbitrator with the party's view of what the dispute is about and what the party expects to prove by the evidence. Occasionally, a respondent may opt to wait and make their opening statement immediately prior to presenting initial evidence, although doing so gives up the opportunity to persuasively frame the claimant's evidence.

Counsel for the complaining party normally presents their evidence first, and counsel for the parties may introduce any evidence they choose, subject to procedural, fairness, and relevance objections. Unless otherwise agreed, counsel need not comply with the strict rules of evidence, though the arbitrator may rely on principles underlying those rules for guidance when ruling on objections to evidence. Be aware, however, that certain court-annexed arbitration programs require that evidentiary rules be applied to some, if not all, the evidence introduced. Unlike the court setting, the arbitrator may direct that evidence be introduced that has not been previously advanced by either party. When authorized by rule or by law, the arbitrator may also subpoena witnesses or documents upon their own initiative or by request of counsel. In the appropriate case, an arbitrator may exercise the right to inspect the premises, accident location, or construction site in question.

### *2.1.5 Decision-Making*

When the issues are not complex, an arbitrator may render a decision immediately after the hearing ends and normally no later than thirty days from the hearing's closing date. When there are multiple arbitrators, however, and the case has several issues, the arbitrators usually take the case under advisement. Sometimes they direct post-hearing memoranda to be filed and meet later to thoroughly discuss the issues in the case, reach their decision, and commit it to writing. In very complex cases, these tasks may occur over several weeks.

### 2.1.6 Award

The arbitrator's decision is rendered in the form of an award. It may be given orally, but more commonly it is in written form and signed by all the arbitrators. Awards are normally short, definite, and final as to all matters under submission. Occasionally, particularly in labor and in international investment cases, they are accompanied by a short, well-reasoned opinion. Depending on the parties' pre-arbitration agreement, the award will be binding or nonbinding. If binding, it will be judicially enforceable and, to a limited extent, reviewable. In court-annexed arbitration, the award is usually nonbinding, and if either party rejects it, the parties proceed to a trial de novo in court.

## 2.2 Application of Arbitration to Various Types of Disputes

### 2.2.1 Business Disputes

Including arbitration clauses in contracts and arbitrating commercial disputes allows counsel to choose their neutral decision-makers. Arbitrators knowledgeable about the specific industry will understand technical terms and subtle nuances of the dispute that might escape a jury or a judge with no experience in the particular business field in question.

For example, technology disputes bring their own unique problems. These disputes often involve multiple parties and contain difficult technical or scientific issues to comprehend and decide. Decisions in such disputes also may impact other businesses, including publishing, cable, entertainment, telecommunications, and manufacturing. Arbitration can provide a useful, tailored mechanism to resolve these intricate problems and save parties both time and expense.

### 2.2.2 Construction Disputes

Construction claims are particularly suited to arbitration (or arbitration after attempted mediation). Construction disputes are characteristically technically complex, involve a unique vocabulary, and require the testimony of numerous experts. Often, the number of documents associated with these disputes is formidable, but arbitration can usually effect discovery voluntarily and much more quickly than a court case. Also, arbitration's lower formality and increased flexibility can accommodate the schedules of parties and witnesses, take witnesses out of turn, and design the process to meet the needs of the particular dispute and of the disputants.

### 2.2.3 Insurance Disputes

Arbitration has been used for many years to resolve all types of disputes that arise from insurance policies. These disputes can involve disagreements between insurance companies and their policyholders; between two or more insurance companies over liability; and between a third-party claimant and an insurance company over that claimant's right to be reimbursed under another person's policy. Personal injury, medical malpractice, legal malpractice, and property damage claims are just a few of the many types of cases that fall into this insurance dispute category. Other types of insurance-related claims that are routinely arbitrated include workers' compensation; title insurance; toxic tort and other environmental claims; architectural and engineering professional negligence claims; and flood, earthquake, and other natural disaster claims.

### 2.2.4 Healthcare Disputes

Although the healthcare industries have been slow to accept ADR for resolving disputes, ADR, and particularly arbitration, is well suited for the conflicts that arise in those industries. The industries define a broad spectrum of potential ADR users, including hospitals, physicians, health insurers, medical equipment manufacturers and distributors, pharmaceutical companies, nursing homes, various managed care and health maintenance organizations, dental clinics, independent laboratories, etc. Arbitration and other ADR processes have been used successfully to resolve disputes between healthcare institutions and providers, intellectual property disputes, disputes between insurers and subscribers, and contract disputes between medical product manufacturers and medical providers.

### 2.2.5 Securities Disputes

The securities industry has used arbitration since the early 1800s to resolve complaints between brokerage firms themselves, between a firm and a broker, or between brokers. The industry is self-regulated by a nonprofit organization, the Financial Industry Regulatory Authority (FINRA), with oversight by the U.S. Securities and Exchange Commission, a government entity. Several opinions by the U.S. Supreme Court in the 1990s upheld arbitration of disputes between investors and brokerage firms or brokers, and FINRA requires arbitration of these disputes when their account opening agreements require arbitration.

Specific rules govern the FINRA arbitration, including those describing what information must be in a claim, the amount of filing fees that will be charged, and how notification must be made to the other party. Consult the FINRA webpage and carefully read the rules before proceeding.

### 2.2.6 Customer Disputes

Many businesses, such as cell phone companies, car dealers, credit card issuers, music streaming services, and product manufacturers, bind customers to arbitration. The Better Business Bureau has for years administered arbitration programs that handle and resolve large volumes of small to mid-sized customer claims efficiently and cost effectively. Growing evidence suggests, however, that many consumers forgo arbitration, and that mandatory arbitration may adversely impact consumers' ability to vindicate their rights.

### 2.2.7 Employment Disputes

Since the 1990s, parties have increasingly used both arbitration and mediation in resolving employment disputes not involving collective bargaining issues. Some executive-level employees negotiate individual employment contracts that provide for arbitration. These contractual disputes sometimes concern wages, promotion, termination, benefits, covenants not to compete, confidentiality clauses, and scope of function. In many of these situations, parties use arbitration after mediation proves unsuccessful. Many employers mandate—as a condition of employment, in applications, policies, manuals, or a take-it-or-leave-it agreement—that employees use arbitration to settle any future employment disputes. These disputes include statutory claims, such as discrimination based on race, sex, religion, or sexual orientation; disability discrimination claims; and wage and hour claims. Like consumer arbitration, growing evidence suggests that many employees forgo arbitration, and that mandatory arbitration adversely impacts workers' ability to vindicate their rights.

### 2.2.8 Labor Union Disputes

When negotiations break down, arbitration is the leading mechanism for resolving labor disputes involving unionized workers and has been since the 1940s. The union and the employer negotiate a contract, termed a collective bargaining agreement, that sets out the terms and conditions of employment. The collective bargaining agreement normally provides that, rather than strike to resolve grievances, the parties negotiate and, if unable to reach negotiated agreement, proceed to arbitration. The parties benefit from the speed of the process and expertise of the arbitrator or arbitrators and receive an award, resolving the dispute, and an opinion to provide guidance when similar future disputes arise.

### 2.2.9 Real Estate Disputes

ADR has become common in the real estate industry. The disputants' desire to save time and money and to preserve confidentiality is driving this increased use. Real estate disputes commonly submitted for mediation and arbitration include home purchase and sale agreements, listing agreements, leases, real estate partnerships and joint ventures, and real estate valuation.

ADR may not always satisfy the needs of parties to real estate contracts, particularly when those contracts pertain to foreclosure; enforcement of a deed of trust, mortgage, or land contract; and mechanics' liens, all of which are more appropriately resolved by judicial means. When drafting buy/sell agreements, advocates should seriously consider excluding from arbitration these and other related procedures and remedies, which the court system is better equipped to handle.

### 2.2.10 Family Disputes

Because of the sheer number of disputes involving family law, the courts and parties are increasingly turning to private dispute resolution organizations for administrative relief. Before beginning the arbitration process, both sides sign an arbitration agreement that details the issues to be arbitrated, names the arbitrators, and confirms the parties' understanding that the arbitrators' decision will be binding. Although mediation is normally the preferred process in family disputes, particularly with respect to custody and visitation issues, arbitration is often quite helpful with respect to property division issues where mediation has been ineffective, and the parties desire a speedy, economical resolution. Many divorce settlement agreements include arbitration clauses to settle any post-divorce disputes. This helps minimize the possibility that one party will attempt to harass the other through a prolonged court battle. The mere presence of such an arbitration clause in a divorce decree encourages the parties to negotiate settlement of post-decree disputes rather than submit to the uncertainty of decision by a neutral arbitrator.

### 2.2.11 International Disputes

Arbitration has been the preferred method for settling international disputes for decades. Companies doing business internationally routinely include arbitration or other ADR-type clauses in their contracts to avoid problems that can arise when dealing with a foreign legal system. Also, many foreign companies feel more comfortable with the arbitration process than they do with litigation. Parties can choose nonadministered arbitration, but pursuing international arbitration through an organization has several advantages, including well-established rules and lists of highly qualified individuals to act as arbitrators. Besides the American Arbitration Association, JAMS, and the International Chamber of Commerce, other organizations that administer international arbitration or provide procedural rules include the London Court of International Arbitration, the United Nations Commission on International Trade Relations and Law, the International Bar Association, the International Centre for Settlement of Investment Disputes, and the World Intellectual Property Organization, which offers many arbitration services.

A recurring challenge when initiating international arbitration is agreeing with the opponents on a site to hold the arbitration proceedings. Try to choose a neutral location where professional and technical support are available. Consider how politically stable the area is, how local laws might affect the enforcement of the arbitration clause, and the degree of difficulty in enforcing an arbitral award once obtained. Other important challenges include determining where the other party's assets are held and whether the host jurisdiction adheres to the New York Convention on the Recognition and Enforcement of Foreign Arbitral Awards.[8]

## 2.3 Drafting the Arbitration Agreement

There are essentially two types of arbitration agreements: 1) a future dispute arbitration agreement, normally called an "arbitration clause," which is contained in a broader contract between the parties (for goods, services, etc.) and which anticipates arbitration procedures to follow should a dispute arise under that broader contract; and 2) a present-dispute arbitration agreement, called a "submission agreement," which counsel for the parties craft when the parties desire to arbitrate a dispute, but where there is no preexisting contract clause. In either type of agreement, the parties may provide that a dispute resolution organization administer the arbitration. You can use a submission agreement to initiate an arbitration either before commencing litigation or after a lawsuit has been filed, but before trial. Occasionally, when a dispute arises and counsel deems that the arbitration clause inadequately addresses the situation's needs, they supplement the arbitration clause by entering into a submission agreement.

There are at least two schools of thought about how detailed the first type of arbitration agreement—the arbitration clause—should be. Some lawyers draft the arbitration clause in an abbreviated format, indicating the parties' desire to arbitrate any and all contract disputes, designating a dispute resolution organization, adopting its procedural rules, and choosing the jurisdiction whose laws are to govern the legal issues. Any specific technical or procedural issues are worked out later, should a dispute arise. Other lawyers draft the arbitration clause with as much detail as possible to minimize the time involved in getting an eventual dispute to an arbitration hearing and receiving a timely decision by an arbitration panel. The most suitable drafting solution probably falls somewhere in the middle. Each contract, each set of contracting parties, and each set of lawyers presents a unique configuration of possibilities you must carefully analyze in deciding on the appropriate arbitration clause. Do not believe that simple, familiar language will satisfy every situation. Consider the not uncommon situation where Kentucky colleagues in Nashville and Louisville agree to a 4:00 p.m. phone call. The Louisvillian calls promptly at 4:00, but the Nashvillian doesn't pick up. Instead, the Nashvillian texts that they are in a meeting but will be available at 4:00 p.m. The failure to specify the time zone caused the confusion.

---

8. The New York Convention is available at "Convention on the Recognition and Enforcement of Foreign Arbitral Awards," June 10, 1958, 330 U.N.T.S. 3, https://www.newyorkconvention.org/english (last visited Jun. 2024).

In this section, we will explore the types of provisions to consider for inclusion in a submission agreement and an expanded arbitration clause.[9] You can find sample arbitration clauses for commercial disputes, both domestic and international, from JAMS on their webpage at https://www.jamsadr.com/clauses/. You can find sample arbitration clauses for a variety of types of disputes from the AAA on their webpage at https://www.adr.org/Clauses (both last visited 6/2024).

### 2.3.1 *Intent to Arbitrate*

When you draft an arbitration clause, you must communicate unequivocally the circumstances under which the parties intend to arbitrate any dispute between them. Most arbitration clauses allow the parties equal access to arbitration—that is, each party has a separate right to invoke arbitration and no party has a right to sue the other in court over disputes the agreement defines as arbitrable. Some arbitration clauses reserve to one party (usually the drafter of the agreement) the option to sue in court. Presumably, such agreements are enforceable if the parties to the arbitration agreement had equal bargaining power when they entered into the agreement. However, if there is a bargaining power imbalance, as in the situation of a *Fortune* 500 company and an individual consumer, a court may find the consumer's obligation to arbitrate to be unenforceable either because of duress or misunderstanding.

### 2.3.2 *Arbitrable Disputes*

Future-dispute arbitration clauses contain language committing the parties to arbitrate "any controversy or claim arising out of or relating to this contract." One would think that such broad language would include all possible disputes between the contracting parties within its sweep. This is not always so. Enterprising, creative lawyers who want to litigate in court find ways to argue that a particular dispute does not "arise out of or relate to" the contract in question. The present dispute, they might argue, arises out of a separate contract, not having an arbitration clause; or the dispute relates to a *service* related to the purchase of products and therefore not to the product sales contract containing an arbitration clause. Therefore, draft future-dispute arbitration clauses to anticipate as many future possibilities as you can imagine. Also review other contracts between the parties and even reference them, as necessary, in the clause, so there is no confusion about what kinds of disputes the parties intend to arbitrate—but don't be surprised when a clever lawyer claims to find a loophole.

On the other hand, disputes may arise during the contract's term that the parties agree should not be arbitrated, but rather litigated in court. As discussed in

---

9. *See generally* 10 James L. Branton & Jim D. Lovett, Alternative Dispute Resolution 2–61 to 2–63 (1995); Whitmore Gray, *Drafting the Dispute Resolution Clause*, in Commercial Arbitration for the 1990s 150–52 (Richard J. Medalie, ed., 1991).

section 2.2.9, certain real estate disputes must be carved out of an agreement to arbitrate, particularly those relating to foreclosures and enforcement of mortgages, liens, etc. In service contracts or joint ventures with increased risks of personal injuries, consider excluding from the arbitration clause's coverage any dispute regarding compensation for a contract-related injury. The point is, expend your effort at the drafting stage to enumerate the disputes that are arbitrable under the contract and you will spend less time later arguing which of the claimant's issues are arbitrable and which are not.

### *2.3.3 Joinder of Claims or Parties*

In drafting an arbitration clause or a submission agreement, consider the question of joinder of claims or parties. If you are drafting a submission agreement, the parties may already have claims pending in litigation that, although not technically arising out of the same contract, are related to an ongoing business arrangement and would more efficiently be resolved in a single forum. In such a case, consider discussing with opposing counsel the possibility of resolving those claims, along with others arising out of the contract, in arbitration.

If you represent a guarantor of a contract, and the parties to the underlying transaction agree to arbitrate any future disputes, make clear in any contract in which the guarantor is a signatory whether or not they agree to arbitrate any claim arising out of their status as guarantor. Perhaps you represent a corporate client that routinely contracts with members of the public (e.g., an investment broker) and that may be a future target of multiple lawsuits by separate plaintiffs or even a class action. If so, give serious thought to including in each contract's arbitration clause a provision clearly stating your client does not agree in advance to either a consolidated arbitration procedure or a class-action arbitration procedure, regardless of whether the rules of the preselected arbitration forum provide for such proceedings.

### *2.3.4 Designation of Dispute Resolution Organization*

Whether drafting an arbitration clause or a submission agreement, consider designating a dispute resolution organization to administer the arbitration process. Does this organization have on its roster neutrals with the experience and expertise pertinent to your dispute and to the legal, technical, and business issues? We discuss factors to consider in selecting an appropriate dispute resolution organization or arbitration forum in section 2.6.1.

### *2.3.5 Location of Arbitration*

If the parties to a contract are in different parts of the country or of the world, the location of the arbitration hearing may become an important drafting consideration. If the arbitration clause does not deal with the location of a hearing, this can develop into a major issue—particularly if an inconvenienced party asserts that the suggested location does not appropriately account for its logistical and economic limitations. Usually, if the arbitration clause names a particular office of a dispute resolution organization to administer the arbitration, the parties by implication are agreeing to the arbitration's location. Office selection may also determine the region in which that organization's affiliated arbitrators live and perform their neutral services. If you are choosing a dispute resolution firm in advance, consider the most convenient location for all the parties and witnesses, etc., to attend an arbitration hearing should a future dispute arise—in addition to where your preferred neutrals work and reside. If you are not naming a dispute resolution organization to administer the arbitration process, it is even more important for your arbitration clause to include an agreed-upon location for holding an arbitration. If, after the dispute arises, you and opposing counsel realize that the preselected location is inconvenient, then you can agree to change the location.

### *2.3.6 Virtual, Live, or Hybrid Hearing*

All the issues surrounding location are solved if you agree instead to a virtual hearing. Much arbitration is conducted online, and online arbitration is discussed in detail in Chapter 10. A virtual hearing can significantly lower costs and be more efficient than a live hearing, especially when parties and witnesses come from different geographic areas. You might also consider a live hearing where certain witnesses appear virtually, sometimes known as a hybrid hearing. Draft your arbitration clauses to address whether hearings will be in person, online, or a hybrid.

### *2.3.7 Procedure to Initiate Arbitration*

If you preselect a dispute resolution organization to administer the arbitration process and adopt its procedural rules, those rules will dictate how and when an aggrieved party can initiate an arbitration. Nonetheless, include in the arbitration clause the details of that organization's procedure for initiating arbitration. This has several benefits. First, it saves you the trouble of locating the organization's rules if you need to initiate arbitration in an emergency, or if you need to advise the client of the procedure when access to the rules is inconvenient—e.g., on the holidays, weekend, or while you are on vacation. Second, should a dispute arise, it provides clout for negotiating an early resolution. You can direct opposing counsel's attention to the arbitration provision and quote chapter and verse how and when you will initiate the arbitration process should you fail to resolve the dispute consensually. Finally, if a dispute arises in which your client has, in your view, breached the contract but their anger precludes them from acknowledging it, you can review the arbitration initiation procedure in the clause and use it as leverage to coax them to consider the advantages of a negotiated solution over the more expensive arbitrated one.

### 2.3.8 Pre-Arbitration ADR

Before you draft any arbitration agreement, discuss with your client the possible advantages of including pre-arbitration methods of dispute resolution, particularly mediation. Mediation-first arbitration clauses are becoming more popular because of their proven cost benefits. Usually, after just a few hours of mediation, counsel and parties can determine whether a mediated resolution is possible, whether the mediation should continue, or whether the parties are irreversibly deadlocked and arbitration should proceed. Usually, parties attempt mediation before investing the time and money to have their counsel prepare for an arbitration hearing.

### 2.3.9 Time Limits

The typical arbitration clause contains a time limit within which a party must initiate arbitration. Usually, the period is thirty days and is measured from the date the parties reach an impasse in their negotiations to resolve a dispute. Some arbitration agreements—particularly submission agreements—contain a provision setting time limits for each of the parties to present their case. This type of provision attempts to set some reasonable limit on the length, and therefore the cost, of the entire arbitration process. This is very important when multiple parties are involved. Arbitration agreements may also specify the time period within which the arbitration panel is to render its decision. Ordinarily, this period is thirty days after the close of the evidence. In especially complex cases, longer periods are specified.

### 2.3.10 Arbitrator Selection Procedures

If the arbitration agreement designates a dispute resolution organization, that organization's procedures will govern the selection of arbitrators unless specified otherwise. Where the arbitration is administered by the disputants, however, spell out in detail the method of selecting the arbitrators. Specify the number of arbitrators to be appointed and include a procedure for selecting arbitrators if the parties are unable to agree. A common method is to have each party select one arbitrator and then let those two arbitrators mutually select a third, neutral arbitrator. Some agreements designate the arbitrator or arbitrators by name. Also, if the arbitrators must have special qualifications, specify them in the agreement. Section 2.6 covers arbitrator selection in more detail.

### 2.3.11 Scope of Arbitrator's Authority and Jurisdiction

Another important aspect of any arbitration agreement is the parties' written understanding of the arbitrator's authority and jurisdiction. For example, what action will the arbitrator be authorized to take if a respondent or their counsel fails to appear at a hearing or if a claimant fails to prosecute? Some dispute resolution organizations have specific rules to guide arbitrators in such instances, but if your arbitration is to be nonadministered, draft clear provisions to cover these eventualities. Also, if you want to limit the arbitrator's jurisdiction—for example, no subject matter jurisdiction to hear or decide punitive damage claims or claims related to matters pending before a judge for decision—describe those limitations in the arbitration agreement.

### 2.3.12 *Pleadings and Discovery*

Normally, a dispute resolution organization's rules let the arbitrator specify the nature and type of pleadings and discovery permitted in arbitration proceedings. If, however, your arbitration agreement specifies permissible pleadings and the nature and scope of discovery, the arbitrators must honor that agreement. You can, therefore, specify in the arbitration agreement whether the parties desire fact or notice pleading for the claim, and you can agree to the required detail for the answer or possible counterclaim.

If you believe that contract disputes between the contracting parties will require more discovery than is normally permitted in arbitration, you and counsel for the other side can agree in advance to the form and extent of discovery that each party might initiate. For example, you might agree in advance to a limited number of interrogatories, requests to produce, and depositions of a specified length. You might also agree to procedures governing experts and their reports.

Although tempting, think long and hard before simply adopting the federal discovery rules for the typical arbitrated dispute. This could prove to be unnecessarily costly and burdensome to your client and turn into a situation where a discovery tail is wagging a small dog of a dispute.

### 2.3.13 *Confidentiality*

In arbitration clauses, particularly in submission agreements, there may be good reason to include a confidentiality provision. If the dispute involves sensitive business, technological, or financial information, draft specific prohibitory provisions, with associated automatic sanctions, preventing the disclosure of information exchanged in or introduced during the arbitration proceeding. Also consider requiring the return of all such confidential information to the producing party at the end of the arbitration proceeding.

In some types of contracts or documents mandating arbitration, the law prohibits including nondisclosure agreements (NDAs). Federal law prohibits enforcement of predispute NDAs in sexual assault and harassment cases, and some state laws prohibit NDAs in employment disputes.

### 2.3.14 Evidence

Although rules of evidence apply in some court-annexed arbitrations, they do not customarily apply in private arbitration. In private arbitrations, hearsay evidence is usually admissible, and other types of evidence ordinarily excluded in court may be deemed admissible, with the arbitrators' caveat that they will give the evidence "the weight they deem appropriate." This reduces the number of evidence objections and related lawyer squabbling, making the proceedings more efficient overall. The disadvantage of proceeding without rules of evidence is that your opponent may introduce information that has no foundation in fact, is unauthenticated, and that may be very prejudicial to your case. Even when no evidence rules apply, make objections to alert the arbitrator to any weakness in the offered evidence, rather than with any realistic hope of exclusion. Arbitrators can normally rule on these objections very quickly without extensive argument by counsel. Make note of this objectionable evidence and in your closing argument ask arbitrators to provide low weight, if any, to such evidence.

In drafting an arbitration agreement, consider whether you want the rules of evidence to apply to all the evidence in the case or only to certain types of evidence. Realize that if you agree, for example, to have the Federal Rules of Evidence apply in the arbitration proceeding, the arbitrators you choose should know how to make appropriate evidentiary rulings based on them. A panel of scientific experts, without a member who is a lawyer, may have difficulty applying evidentiary rules. Consequently, if you draft an arbitration agreement with a provision requiring evidentiary rules to apply to arbitration evidence, also propose that at least one of the panel arbitrators be a present or former litigator or former judge.

### 2.3.15 Court Reporter and Recording

When drafting an arbitration agreement, consider including a provision allowing the parties an option to hire a court reporter or record the proceedings. Most arbitrations do not need a court reporter to make a record of the proceedings, especially given the widespread availability of audio and video recording technology. In certain circumstances, however, you will want a professionally created record of the proceedings. The parties may agree to hire a court reporter and share the cost for a complex case where the hearing will extend over several days or weeks; a transcript of the hearing will aid in preparing post-hearing briefs.

You may also want to use a court reporter when one or more witnesses who will be testifying under oath in the arbitration proceeding is also testifying in a court case involving the same subject matter. Witnesses who testify in court can be impeached by any prior statement made under oath, even if made in a confidential arbitration proceeding.

The videoconferencing platform for virtual arbitration normally has an option to record. Commercial firms can create and link a written transcript to the video. Even for a live hearing, an audio or video recording can be made. Sometimes the arbitrator will record the hearing for later reference when writing the award and crafting an opinion. Often in arbitration, though, no recording is needed.

### 2.3.16 Interpreters and Accommodations

If working in a field where multiple languages will be spoken by witnesses or where witnesses may need accommodations to address disabilities or other needs, such as emotional support, including a clause to address these contingencies may be helpful. The clause should specify which party or parties will pay for an interpreter or accommodation in which circumstances. Specify whether a family member or coworker can serve as the interpreter or whether a certified interpreter must be hired. Provide that any interpreter must swear or affirm to provide accurate translation.

The clause may also address the permissibility of non-parties and non-witnesses' attendance at the hearing. For instance, sometimes a party will desire their significant other be present for emotional support or sometimes non-parties with an interest in the outcome of the dispute will request to send a representative to a hearing.

### 2.3.17 Nature, Effect, and Enforceability of Award

Draft your arbitration agreement to specify the nature, effect, and enforceability of an award or awards issued by an arbitration panel. The parties should agree whether they desire the customary short award without a statement of reasons or whether they desire the award to incorporate a reasoned opinion.

If you opt for the reasoned opinion, that opinion will be a basis to challenge the award by way of a motion for reconsideration. This may be fine if you are the one who wants to do the challenging, but if your opponents are unhappy with the arbitrators' reasoning, their motions for reconsideration may extend the proceedings, cause additional costly briefing, and delay the award's enforcement. In the rare case, the opinion may even provide the basis for a court challenge on the grounds that the arbitrators exceeded their authority or jurisdiction or that the award was manifestly unjust—whether or not there is actual merit to such challenges. Under such circumstances, the award's enforceability would be even further delayed.

When you draft an arbitration agreement, also consider whether to give the arbitrators the authority to issue partial awards. In certain cases, it may be crucial that your client obtain a preliminary award directing a respondent to protect or preserve certain assets. In construction situations, for example, you may want to allow for the opportunity to request the arbitrators to order that construction of a building continue. Or in a commercial situation, you may want the option of requesting, even before the arbitration hearing, that the arbitrators direct a manufacturer to continue shipping products to a distributor. Depending on your client's needs, these considerations deserve your very close attention in the arbitration agreement drafting stage.

With respect to the award's enforceability, the agreement should make clear when the award will be enforceable. Normally, an award is not enforceable until it is confirmed in court. However, if some other time better suits the parties' needs, state this explicitly in the agreement.

### 2.3.18 Appeal Procedures

In recent years, certain dispute resolution organizations have added to their ADR rules provisions allowing parties to preselect a second panel of arbitrators to hear any appeals from the first arbitration panel's decision. This appellate procedure is used in cases involving huge damage claims where the stakes are so high that the parties are unwilling to risk having a single arbitration panel issue an unchallengeable, binding award. If you are involved in such a case, consider proposing an appeal procedure, whether or not a dispute resolution organization will administer the arbitration.

### 2.3.19 Designation of Law to Govern the Arbitration Agreement

Specify in the arbitration agreement which jurisdiction's law controls the agreement. This sometimes warrants substantial thought. The jurisdiction whose law governs the arbitration agreement may differ from the jurisdiction whose law controls all or some of the legal issues in the underlying contract. A state's law of contract may, for example, govern several of the legal issues arising out of a contract for goods and services, but because interstate commerce is involved, the Federal Arbitration Act may govern some of the procedural and even substantive issues related to the arbitration and the arbitration clause itself. These drafting problems become even thornier when one or more of the parties are incorporated or reside in foreign countries. Sometimes you will need to do substantial legal research before satisfying yourself that the arbitration clause you are drafting best meets your client's interests regarding choice of law.

### 2.3.20 Court to Have Jurisdiction to Enforce Agreement and Award

The jurisdiction whose law governs the underlying contract may also be different than the one whose law will govern or will be convenient for controlling the proceedings or enforcing an award. Parties' circumstances may change significantly—even to the extent of relocation or reincorporation of companies—between the time that the arbitration clause becomes effective and the time that a dispute arises. Draft such provision as broadly as possible, permitting the filing of motions or the enforcing of awards "in any court having jurisdiction" at the pertinent time.

### 2.3.21 Payment of Arbitration Fees and Expenses

If your arbitration clause preselects a dispute resolution organization, your client will be obligated to pay the organization's administrative costs and the arbitrator fees. Some organizations vary the fee amount depending upon the number of parties to the dispute and the claim's complexity. Parties customarily pay an equal share of the arbitrators' fees. Also, arbitrators, in rendering their award, often require that the losing party pay the winning party's administrative costs.

### 2.3.22 Checklist: Advantages to Using a Dispute Resolution Organization

This checklist outlines areas that can be ensured by adopting the clause and rules of a dispute resolution organization.

| THE ADVANTAGES TO USING A DISPUTE RESOLUTION ORGANIZATION |
|---|
| ❑ **It makes clear that all disputes are arbitrable,** minimizing dilatory court actions to avoid the arbitration process. |
| ❑ **It is self-enforcing.** Arbitration can continue despite an objection from a party, unless the proceedings are stayed by court order or by agreement of the parties. |
| ❑ **It provides a complete set of rules and regulations,** eliminating the need to spell out rules and regulations in the parties' agreement. |
| ❑ **It provides for the appointment of an impartial neutral.** Adopting the rules of a dispute resolution organization may ensure procedure is available to disqualify an arbitrator for bias. |
| ❑ **It settles disputes over the locale of the proceeding.** The dispute resolution organization, rather than the courts, determines locale when the parties disagree. |
| ❑ **It can provide for administrative conferences.** If the clause adopts the rules of a dispute resolution organization, the rules may provide for an administrative conference to expedite the arbitration proceedings. |
| ❑ **It can provide for preliminary hearings.** A preliminary hearing can be arranged in large and complex cases to specify the issues to be resolved, clarify claims and counterclaims, provide for an exchange of information, and consider other matters that will expedite the arbitration proceedings. |
| ❑ **Mediation is available.** Mediation conferences can be arranged to facilitate a mutual settlement, without additional administrative cost to the parties. |
| ❑ **It establishes time limits to assure prompt disposition of disputes.** Arbitration clauses should specify time limits, especially to expedite smaller cases. |
| ❑ **It insulates the arbitrator from the parties.** Using a dispute resolution organization to facilitate communications between the parties and the arbitrator can serve to protect the continued neutrality of the arbitrator and the process. |

**THE ADVANTAGES TO USING A DISPUTE RESOLUTION ORGANIZATION**

- ❑ **It establishes a procedure for the serving of notices.** Depending on the rules used and the type of the case, notices can be served by regular mail, electronic mail, or through an online filing system of a dispute resolution organization.
- ❑ **It gives the arbitrator the power to decide matters equitably and to fashion any appropriate relief, including specific performance.** The rules can allow the arbitrator to grant any remedy or relief that the arbitrator deems just and equitable and within the scope of the agreement of the parties, including, but not limited to, specific performance of a contract.
- ❑ **It provides for enforcement of the award.** The award can be enforced in any court having jurisdiction, with only limited grounds for resisting the award.

## 2.4 Selecting Cases for Arbitration

### *2.4.1 Favorable Indications for Arbitration*

Where no arbitration clause governs the dispute resolution process, and a complaint has not been filed in court, look for a reason to suggest arbitration. Perhaps the dispute qualifies for compulsory arbitration under local court rule. Or, depending on the nature of the dispute, the relative costs, and the condition of the court docket, private arbitration might be an attractive alternative to languishing in a beleaguered, unresponsive court system.

A case's facts and law may weigh in favor of arbitration. Arbitration can be ideal for cases where

- the parties desire confidentiality;
- the parties need an expert in a particular field or type of dispute;
- a substantial power imbalance exists;
- the parties seek a more flexible process, such as a virtual or hybrid hearing;
- the parties agree that nontraditional relief, such as an apology or reprimand of an agent, will be necessary; or
- the parties have deadlocked after mediation.

Finally, with respect to finality and precedent considerations, arbitration is indicated where either party wants to avoid establishing a judicial precedent or they need an immediate decision to protect the interests of a third party or the public.

Also, if sufficient discovery has occurred while a case is pending on the court's docket, arbitration may be appropriate. When the lawyers have taken all their necessary discovery, they can take advantage of the speed and reduced expense of arbitration. Essentially, they can have their cake and eat it too.

### *2.4.2 Unfavorable Indications for Arbitration*

Arbitration is unsuitable where a disputant cannot effectively represent their best interests and will not be represented by counsel at the arbitration sessions. Such a dispute is best resolved in court, where a judge can appoint counsel or an appropriate representative, guardian, etc., and where the person will have available the full panoply of due process rights. And if your case is pending before a judge who is mutually acceptable to the parties and who could hear and decide the case sooner than you could select arbitrators and hold an arbitration hearing, proposing arbitration would be ridiculous, if not malpractice.

Other cases not suitable for arbitration would include those where a party is seeking an unusual remedy or creative resolution that is not available in arbitration, where the neutral's decision will require monitoring, or where the best resolution can result only if the neutral has access to confidential information not disclosable to the other side. Cases where the stakes are too high to risk a binding unappealable award or where judicial precedent is needed to explain the application of a new or rarely construed statute are unsuitable for arbitration, as are cases requiring substantial formal discovery. Cases of unequal bargaining power where one party, such as an employer, has mandated arbitration pre-dispute are less suitable for arbitration because arbitration is more likely to result in a loss or lower damage award for the weaker party.

Some cases have pivotal, emotional aspects that are best presented to and considered by a jury. Those cases are ordinarily unsuitable for arbitration.

## 2.5 Indicator Guide for Selecting Cases for Arbitration

### *2.5.1 Favorable Indicators Chart*

The following guide lists indicators favorable to an arbitrated resolution of a dispute. The presence of only one of these indicators (and the absence of any unfavorable indicators) may be sufficient to trigger an arbitration.

| FAVORABLE INDICATORS FOR ARBITRATION | |
|---|---|
| Parties and counsel agree to participate in the arbitration process and desire a prompt resolution | Nontraditional relief, not normally available in litigation, is sought |
| Pre-agreement exists to arbitrate disputes arising out of an underlying contract | Parties want to minimize litigation costs |
| An immediate decision by a third-party neutral is needed to protect the interests of a disputant or the public | Parties wish to avoid establishing a judicial precedent, or they wish to establish an arbitration precedent that will guide their future conduct |
| Parties want an expert in their field as the decision-maker | Parties want a flexible process, such as a virtual hearing |
| Sufficient discovery has occurred, or information has been developed to permit counsel to present their clients' claims and defenses cogently | Parties are still deadlocked after an attempted negotiated and/or mediated settlement |
| Parties want the matter settled confidentially | Parties have dramatically differing appraisals of the case's facts and of the applicable law |
| Dispute qualifies for compulsory arbitration under local court rules | |

### 2.5.2 *Unfavorable Indicators Chart*

The following guide lists indicators unfavorable to arbitration. The presence of one of these indicators could be a sufficient basis to decline arbitration.

| UNFAVORABLE INDICATORS FOR ARBITRATION | |
|---|---|
| A party cannot effectively represent its best interests and will not be represented by counsel at the arbitration sessions | A party seeks an unusual remedy or creative resolution that is not available in arbitration |
| The resolution will require monitoring | Major constitutional issues are involved |
| The best resolution requires disclosure of information to the decision-maker, but such information cannot be disclosed to the other side | Substantial formal discovery is needed to provide a party with the information necessary to support a claim or defense |
| Stakes are too high to risk a binding, unappealable award | A judicial precedent is needed to explain application of a new or rarely construed statute |
| Case has some pivotal emotional aspects that would best be presented to and considered by a jury | Case is currently pending in court before a judge who is mutually acceptable to the parties and who could hear and decide the case sooner than arbitration could begin |

## 2.6 Choosing the Appropriate Arbitration Forum and Panel

When you select an arbitration panel, you and opposing counsel will be required to agree to 1) an arbitration forum, 2) the number of arbitrators who will serve on your panel, and 3) the individual(s) who will serve as your arbitrator(s). The considerations related to these three topics are discussed below.

### *2.6.1 Choosing the Appropriate Arbitration Forum*

If you and opposing counsel decide not to administer the arbitration process yourselves, depending on the nature of the dispute, you may have several alternative arbitration forums, both nonprofit and for profit, from which to choose. Some of these alternatives follow.

#### 2.6.1.1 Court-Annexed Arbitration Programs

Some local jurisdictions have ADR programs that require all cases under a certain amount to be arbitrated. Others give the judges discretion to determine which cases are suitable for a particular dispute resolution process and to direct counsel to participate in it. In some of these programs, the only out-of-pocket expenses for using the arbitration services are the filing fees and other routine court costs. In other programs, the parties pay for the neutral's services. While many of these programs provide for nonbinding arbitration with an assessment to the party who rejects an arbitration award, you and opposing counsel can circumvent these potential additional costs by having your clients agree in advance to be bound by the arbitrators' decision. Thus, if you decide to arbitrate your dispute, you may want to investigate whether any court-annexed programs can provide inexpensive administrative support services of which you can take advantage.

Be aware, however, that there may be disadvantages to using the court-annexed arbitration forum. First, in some of the court-annexed programs, the arbitrators are lawyers who are appointed randomly to serve on panels, and the users have no control over who will be their arbitrators, except where there are grounds for disqualification based on bias or conflict of interest. In addition, in most of the court-annexed programs, the parties do not control the proceedings. The court normally sets the hearing's time and place, and there is no guarantee of confidentiality of the proceedings or of the award.

#### 2.6.1.2 Bar Association Arbitration Programs

Some bar associations have ADR programs that offer arbitration services. Normally, because of volunteer attorney support, disputing parties can access these services at minimal expense. Parties usually have more control over the arbitration process than in the court-annexed programs, and the association's staff or volunteers handle administrative details.

#### 2.6.1.3 Nonprofit ADR Organizations

Several nonprofit organizations offer ADR services and administer arbitration programs. Examples are the American Arbitration Association (AAA), the Center for Public Resources, and the Better Business Bureau. These organizations vary drastically in the costs they charge for use of their services. If you decide to go this route, carefully analyze and compare the costs and fees charged for your type of dispute.

#### 2.6.1.4 For-Profit Organizations

Several for-profit or "private" dispute resolution organizations offer arbitration services, some on a national basis, some regionally or locally. Some specialize in certain types of disputes; others service a wide range of disputes. Some have only attorneys on their panel of neutrals; others have attorneys and retired judges. Standard fees and costs vary from one company to another, and some companies will negotiate costs and fees depending on the case's size. If you and opposing counsel decide to use a private ADR firm to administer your arbitration, it may be a good idea to shop around to compare prices.[10]

### 2.6.2 Deciding on the Number of Arbitrators

The selection of the arbitrator(s) may be the most important aspect of the entire arbitration process. In most cases, a single arbitrator will satisfy your needs; in other cases—particularly those that are complex and that require both legal and technical expertise—multiple arbitrators will be needed.

If you and opposing counsel decide not to use a dispute resolution organization, you should set time limits for selecting an arbitration panel to prevent one party from unduly delaying a case. If together you cannot agree on an arbitrator panel, a court may have to appoint the arbitrators for you. In such situations, courts attempt to follow the criteria specified by the parties if possible.

#### 2.6.2.1 Single Arbitrator Panel

There are several advantages to having a single arbitrator. A single arbitrator can normally render a decision more quickly than several arbitrators reviewing all the evidence, conducting a post-hearing conference, and jointly reaching a decision. With a single arbitrator, there are usually fewer scheduling delays and there is obviously less cost. Also, it will be easier to choose a single arbitrator who fits your case's expertise and qualifications needs, rather than trying to find several arbitrators who are all well qualified, available, and willing to serve on a panel. Furthermore, the proceedings will run more efficiently because you will deal with only one person.

There can also be some disadvantages. One arbitrator might not have all the required qualifications, whereas a panel of arbitrators can cover all contingencies. Also, if a case deals with more than one area of law, you could have experts in several areas. It would be nearly impossible to have the same kind of coverage with one person.

If the case is administered, the organization will usually submit a list of arbitrators' names to each party. If the parties can't agree on an arbitrator, the organization will appoint one. The parties strike off an allowed number of arbitrators they do not want and note the rest in order of preference. The organization then appoints an arbitrator based on the parties' choices from the remaining names. The parties can also use the strike method until only one person is left on the list. This works well when parties are arbitrating more than one dispute because the parties can alternate who strikes first. The downside is that one side will get its choice because it was last to strike, and the other party may be unhappy with this choice. Even then, it may

---

10. See Appendix H for a listing of nonprofit and private ADR organizations.

be less expensive to have the organization produce the list and use the strike method than having the organization select the arbitrator.

Because there is a cost to using an organization to provide a list of arbitrators or to select an arbitrator for the parties, some parties list the arbitrators from whom to choose in their contract. In this instance, each party researches the background of the arbitrator candidates and agrees on the list from which they will select if a dispute arises. When a dispute does arise, they employ the strike-off mechanism.

As pointed out in section 2.3, the option of administered arbitration can be included in the arbitration clause, or it can be specified later when the parties decide to arbitrate, independent of a clause. If you mutually decide not to have the arbitration administered, you can still purchase a list of arbitrators from an organization, such as AAA, from which you can select. If a contract designates an organization that no longer exists, then you and your opponent can choose another one, or a court can substitute an appropriate organization.

You and opposing counsel can draft an arbitration clause that names a specific person to act as arbitrator, such as a well-known expert in your client's business field. There are risks associated with this technique. If the arbitrator is unavailable, lengthy, costly, and unnecessary disputes can arise over selecting an alternative. Beware, also, specifying arbitrator attributes in a contract, because if made too narrow, it can become difficult or impossible to find someone who meets the specific qualifications. This tactic can also be used by the opposing party to delay the case.

#### 2.6.2.2 Multiple Arbitrator Panels

Most multiple arbitrator panels consist of three arbitrators. You can choose panels in several ways. Each party can pick an arbitrator and those two arbitrators can pick a third (sometimes called an umpire). If the two arbitrators can't decide on the third, an organization can pick a neutral third person to serve on the panel. The organization can also pick three neutrals from their list of qualified arbitrators. They can tailor their choices to your needs and specifications while streamlining the process. You can also choose the panel through the strike method used to choose a single arbitrator. A court can also appoint multiple arbitrators to a panel, and a party can request the court to appoint arbitrators as well.

Some of your clients may want to opt for the umpire system of arbitrator selection because they like the idea of having a "friend" on the panel. Even the friendliest of arbitrators, however, must abide by the procedural rules and the arbitrator ethical norms. The arbitrator appointed by the party may overcompensate for the appearance of bias by being harsher to the appointing party than the arbitrator appointed by the opposing side. Inform your client of this phenomenon before they agree to use the umpire system. While the umpire system is still widely used in international arbitrations, in other arbitration situations fully neutral panels are much more common. Because of the increasingly perceived advantages of impartial decision-makers and the fact that the umpire system can often lead to delay if one party refuses to cooperate, the umpire system is being used less frequently.

### 2.6.3 Choosing Individuals to Serve as Arbitrators

Whether an arbitrator is selected by a party, an organization, the court, or other arbitrators, the most important attribute for an arbitrator to possess is impartiality. Other attributes an arbitrator should possess include patience, intelligence, common sense, the ability to decide with an open mind, and the firmness to control the proceedings. Although some arbitrators are lawyers, many arbitrators are chosen from different business fields based on their professional experience. Regardless of an arbitrator's background, however, all should be trained in the arbitration process.

An arbitrator need not be trained in every minute aspect of law. In fact, many effective arbitrators are not lawyers and have no legal training whatsoever. Functionally, it is much more important that an arbitrator is reasonable, flexible, and willing to conduct the proceeding to achieve a fair outcome. An effective arbitrator is actively involved in the management of the dispute before them. An arbitrator who sits on the sidelines and lets two parties fight it out does not qualify as an effective arbitrator.

When choosing an arbitrator, screen potential candidates as carefully as possible to determine their experience, level of education, and personality. If you are selecting an arbitrator from a list provided by a dispute resolution organization, you will normally be provided a brief curriculum vitae for each potential arbitrator. You can often research their background further online and even locate prior arbitration awards through legal databases such as Lexis. You can also ask the administering organization for more information about particular arbitrators. Ask friends and professional associates who may know of the arbitrators' suitability from previous cases or by reputation in particular fields. You may greatly minimize your research time by calling a few people you know. Do not underestimate the value of other advocates' experience with individual arbitrators.

Aristotle said, "[T]he arbitrator keeps equity in view, whereas the [judge] looks only to the law, and the reason why arbitrators were appointed was that equity might prevail."[11] This statement is true of many arbitrators even today. Take this into account when choosing arbitrators. If you have a situation where the equities are in your favor, but your position on the law is weak, then search out an arbitrator who will decide on a more equitable basis. Conversely, if you have a strong case on

---

11. 22 Aristotle, Art of Rhetoric 1.13.19 (J.H. Freese trans. Harvard Univ. Press. 1926). http://www.perseus.tufts.edu/hopper/text?doc=Perseus%3Atext%3A1999.01.0060%3Abook%3D1%3Achapter%3D13%3Asection%3D19 (last visited Jun. 2024). The original quote uses the word "dicast" instead of the word "judge." A dicast was one of 6000 ancient Athenian citizens chosen annually to try cases, combining the role of both judge and juror. 4 The Oxford English Dictionary 618 (2d ed. 1989).

the law, identify and select an arbitrator who has a reputation for taking a more legalistic approach to decision-making.

The attributes you will be looking for in an arbitrator may therefore vary dramatically depending on the dispute. If a dispute is highly technical, you will probably want an arbitrator who is well versed in the technical or scientific area in issue. If complex legal issues predominate in your dispute, and if more than one area of law is involved in a dispute, you may want your panel of experts to include one or more arbitrators competent in the pertinent areas of law.

Exercise care, however, in these selection situations. Sometimes an expert is so focused on one area that they miss other aspects of the dispute or bring assumptions to the dispute that color the outcome. In many disputes, a well-rounded arbitrator with a wide base of experience will be more than qualified.

Also, if you are unsure of what attributes you are looking for, are unable to obtain advice from others, or are unsure about which of several candidates you should select, you may be wise to let an organization pick an arbitrator for you. Many case administrators have years of experience working with arbitrators in the administrative phases of cases, know how other parties and counsel have evaluated arbitrators' service, and can pick someone who is well qualified to decide your dispute.

If you relinquish your right to choose your panel, however, do not blame the organization if the arbitration's result is not as good as you desired. No one can guarantee how an arbitrator will rule in any case. Your perception of what is fair may be much different from that of the arbitrator. The only measure that the organization has to determine an arbitrator's effectiveness is user evaluations. If the organization appoints an effective arbitrator and you are unhappy with the result, the chances are good that any effective arbitrator you selected would have arrived at a similar, if not identical, result.

Finally, but certainly not of least importance in your selection process, is consideration of the ethics of your arbitrator candidates. Arbitrators are held to a code of ethics that defines the limits of what they can and cannot do in performing their function.[12] An arbitrator must keep confidential everything told to them during the arbitration proceeding. They must also keep confidential the nature of any award given. An arbitrator must uphold the integrity and fairness of the arbitration process and must disclose any interest or relationship which could lead to partiality or bias. An arbitrator is further required to avoid any appearance of impropriety and to conduct proceedings fairly and diligently, ultimately rendering decisions in a just, independent, and deliberate manner. Any arbitrator you select should comply,

---

12. The Code of Ethics for Arbitrators in Commercial Disputes—Revised 2004 is available on the ABA website at https://www.americanbar.org/groups/dispute_resolution/resources/ethics/code-of-ethics-for-arbitrators-commercial-disputes/ (last visited Jun. 2024).

at a minimum, with these prescribed norms of ethical conduct and other norms described in section 2.12.

One important postscript here is that even after you select an arbitration panel, your job may not be finished. Arbitrators may be disqualified from serving on a particular arbitration panel for a variety of reasons. Disqualifications can occur on your motion or on the arbitrator's own motion. For example, you or opposing counsel may have had past dealings with the arbitrator, or the arbitrator may have been employed in the past in a position that would give the appearance of having interests conflicting with those of your client or the interests of the other party. Arbitrators are required to disclose potential conflicts of interests, and if there is any doubt, they normally recuse themselves, concluding that it is better to err on the side of caution rather than to have an award later overturned on grounds of prejudice or bias. Arbitrators can also recuse themselves if the timeframe for the proceedings is incompatible with their schedule or if they do not feel qualified enough to handle a dispute. A financial interest in any dispute is also a ground for disqualifying an arbitrator.

## 2.7 Attorney Ethics

Codes of professional conduct for lawyers vary from state to state but all are at least in part based on the ABA Model Rules of Professional Conduct (Model Rules or Mod. R.). The discussion that follows addresses the lawyer's ethical duties in an advisory and advocate role in an adjudicative process, such as arbitration, and includes references to the 2023 version of the Model Rules. This discussion is divided into subsections related to lawyers' duties to the client, to the tribunal, and to opposing parties, opposing counsel, and third parties. The following discussion is merely an overview of the Model Rules; for guidance in a specific situation, consult the text of the Model Rules and the rules applicable in the relevant jurisdiction(s). Many bar associations offer an ethics hotline; call if you are unable to ascertain your ethical obligations from the rules.

### *2.7.1 Duties to Client*

Attorney duties to clients are covered in the Model Rules of Professional Conduct, Rules 1.1–2.1. These rules are paraphrased and explained in the following subsections.

#### 2.7.1.1 Competence and Allocation of Authority Between Client and Lawyer

A lawyer must provide competent representation to the client. Competent representation means that the lawyer is required to have the legal knowledge, skill, thoroughness, and preparation reasonably necessary for the specific representation undertaken (Mod. R. 1.1). The client normally has the ultimate authority to determine the purposes to be served by the legal representation, within limits imposed by law and by the lawyer's professional obligations. A lawyer may limit the scope of representation if the limitation is reasonable under the specific circumstances and the client gives informed consent (Mod. R. 1.2).

#### 2.7.1.2 Diligence and Communication

A lawyer must represent a client with reasonable diligence. This requires a lawyer to control their workload so that each matter can be handled competently (Mod. R. 1.3). A lawyer must keep the client reasonably informed about the status of the matter and must explain the matter to the extent necessary to permit the client to make informed decisions regarding the representation (Mod. R. 1.4).

#### 2.7.1.3 Confidentiality of Information

In general, a lawyer must not reveal information relating to the representation of a client unless the client gives informed consent or unless the disclosure is impliedly authorized to carry out the representation. There are several exceptions to this rule, however. A lawyer may reveal information relating to the representation of a client where the disclosure is reasonably necessary to avoid death or serious bodily injury; prevent the client from committing a fraud or crime that is reasonably certain to result in substantial injury to property interest, or to mitigate or rectify substantial injury to the financial interests or property of another that has resulted from the client's commission of a crime or fraud in furtherance of which the client has used the lawyer's services; to secure legal advice about the lawyer's compliance with the Model Rules; to establish a claim or defense on behalf of the lawyer in a controversy between the lawyer and the client; to comply with other law or court order; or to resolve conflicts of interest related to changes in employment or firm composition (Mod. R. 1.6).

#### 2.7.1.4 Conflicts of Interest

A lawyer must not represent a client if the representation involves a concurrent conflict of interest. Such conflict of interest exists if representing one client will be directly adverse to another client or if the representation of one or more clients will be materially limited by the lawyer's responsibilities to another client, a former client, or a third person, or by a personal interest of the lawyer. Notwithstanding the existence of a concurrent conflict of interest, a lawyer may represent a client if the lawyer reasonably believes that they will be able to provide competent and diligent representation to each affected client, the representation is not prohibited by law, the representation does not involve the assertion of a claim by one client against another client represented by the lawyer in the same litigation or other proceeding before a tribunal, and each affected client gives written informed consent (Mod. R. 1.7; 1.8). The rules concerning concurrent conflicts of interest have extensive comments and they should be consulted if an apparent concurrent conflict of interest arises.

The Model Rules have requirements regarding other types of conflicts of interest that relate to representation adverse to a former client (Mod. R. 1.9); lawyers who are associated in a firm or who have terminated an association with a firm (Mod. R. 1.10); lawyers who are former and concurrent government officers and employees (Mod. R. 1.11); and lawyers who are former judges, or who serve as arbitrators, mediators, or other third-party neutrals (Mod. R. 1.12). Under Model Rule 1.12, in general, a lawyer may not represent anyone in connection with a matter in which the lawyer participated personally and substantially as a judge or other adjudicative officer, or law clerk to such a person, or as an arbitrator, mediator, or other third-party neutral, unless all parties to the proceeding give written informed consent. Unless qualifying for an exception to the provisions of Model Rule 1.12, no lawyer from a disqualified lawyer's firm may knowingly undertake or continue representation in a matter. The rule also prohibits a lawyer from negotiating for employment with any person who is involved as a party or as lawyer for a party in a matter in which the lawyer is participating personally and substantially as a judge or other adjudicative officer or an arbitrator, mediator, or other third-party neutral.

#### 2.7.1.5 Organization as Client

A lawyer employed or retained by an organization represents the organization acting through its authorized constituents (Mod. R. 1.13). Under this rule, a lawyer has special duties if they know that an officer, employee, or other person associated with the organization is engaged in an action, intends to act, or refuses to act in a matter related to the representation that is in violation of a legal obligation to the organization, or a violation likely to result in substantial injury to the organization. Subject to certain conflict of interest prohibitions of Model Rule 1.7, a lawyer representing an organization may also represent any of its directors, officers, employees, members, shareholders, or other constituents.

#### 2.7.1.6 Client with Diminished Capacity

When a lawyer reasonably believes that the client has diminished capacity; is at risk of substantial physical, financial, or other harm unless action is taken; and cannot adequately act in their own interest, the lawyer may take protective action, including consulting with individuals or entities that have the ability to take action to protect the client, and in certain cases, seeking the appointment of a guardian ad litem, conservator, or guardian. Information relating to the representation of such client is protected from disclosure, except that the lawyer is impliedly authorized to reveal information about the client to the extent reasonably necessary to protect the client's interest (Mod. R. 1.14).

#### 2.7.1.7 Declining or Terminating Representation

A lawyer may not represent a client and must withdraw from representation of a client where the representation will result in a violation of the Model Rules, the lawyer's physical or mental condition materially impairs the lawyer's ability to represent the client, or the lawyer is discharged. Upon termination of representation, a lawyer must take appropriate steps to protect a client's interests, such as giving reasonable notice to the client, allowing time for employment of other counsel, surrendering papers and property to which the client is entitled, and refunding any advance payment of fee or expense that has not been earned or incurred (Mod. R. 1.16).

#### 2.7.1.8 Lawyer as Advisor

A lawyer must exercise independent professional judgment and render candid advice on behalf of a client. In rendering advice, a lawyer may refer not only to law, but to other considerations such as moral, economic, social, and political factors that may be relevant to the client's situation (Mod. R. 2.1).

### *2.7.2 Duties to Tribunal*

Attorney duties to tribunals are covered in Model Rules 3.1–8.5. These rules are paraphrased and explained in the following subsections.

#### 2.7.2.1 Meritorious Claims and Contentions

The Model Rules define a tribunal as "a court, an arbitrator in a binding arbitration proceeding, or a legislative body, administrative agency, or other body acting in an adjudicative capacity" (Mod. R. 1.0). Quite simply, a lawyer may not bring or defend a proceeding, or assert or controvert an issue before a tribunal, unless there is a basis in law and fact for doing so that is not frivolous, which includes a good faith argument for an extension, modification, or reversal of existing law. A lawyer has a duty not to abuse legal procedure (Mod. R. 3.1).

#### 2.7.2.2 Expediting Litigation

A lawyer must make reasonable efforts to expedite litigation consistent with the interests of the client. Acquiring financial or other benefit from otherwise improper delay in litigation is not a legitimate interest of the client (Mod. R. 3.2).

#### 2.7.2.3 Candor Toward the Tribunal

A lawyer may not knowingly make a false statement of fact or law to a tribunal or fail to correct a false statement of material fact or law previously made to the tribunal by the lawyer. Furthermore, a lawyer may not knowingly fail to disclose to the tribunal legal authority in the controlling jurisdiction known to the lawyer to be directly adverse to the position of the client and not disclosed by opposing counsel. Also, a lawyer may not knowingly offer evidence that the lawyer knows to be false. A lawyer who represents a client in an adjudicative proceeding and who knows that a client or person intends to engage, is engaging, or has engaged in criminal or fraudulent conduct related to the proceeding shall take reasonable remedial measures, including, if necessary, disclosure to the tribunal (Mod. R. 3.3).

#### 2.7.2.4 Impartiality and Decorum of the Tribunal

Many forms of improper influence of proceedings before tribunals are proscribed by the Model Rules. For example, Model Rule 3.5 prohibits a lawyer from influencing a judge, juror, prospective juror, or other official by means prohibited by law or from engaging in conduct intended to disrupt a tribunal. Furthermore, it prohibits a lawyer from communicating ex parte with such a person during the proceeding unless authorized to do so by law or court order.

#### 2.7.2.5 Unauthorized Practice of Law

A lawyer may not practice law in a jurisdiction in violation of the regulation of the legal profession in that jurisdiction or assist another in doing so. Arbitration advocates should pay careful attention to this Model Rule. Some states have laws prohibiting lawyers not licensed in their particular jurisdictions from representing clients in arbitrations conducted in those jurisdictions. These prohibitions also extend in some states to paralegals who assist lawyers serving as advocates in arbitrations (Mod. R. 5.5). Lawyers may be subject to the disciplinary authority of more than one jurisdiction for the same conduct (Mod. R. 8.5).

#### 2.7.2.6 Misconduct

A lawyer may not violate or attempt to violate the Model Rules, knowingly assist or induce another to do so, or do so through the acts of another. Furthermore, a lawyer may not commit a criminal act that reflects adversely on the lawyer's honesty, trustworthiness, or fitness as a lawyer in other respects; engage in conduct involving dishonesty, fraud, deceit, or misrepresentation; engage in conduct that is prejudicial to the administration of justice; state or imply an ability to influence improperly a government agency or official or to achieve results by means that violate the Model Rules or other law; knowingly assist a judge or judicial officer in conduct that is a violation of applicable rules of judicial conduct or other law; or engage in conduct the lawyer should reasonably know is harassment or discrimination on enumerated bases (Mod. R. 8.4).

### *2.7.3 Duties to Opposing Parties and Counsel and Third Persons*

Attorney duties to opposing parties and counsel and third persons are covered in Model Rules 3.4–7.3. These rules are paraphrased and explained in the following subsections.

### 2.7.3.1 Fairness to Opposing Party and Counsel

Fair competition in an adversary proceeding contemplates prohibitions against destruction or concealment of evidence, improperly influencing witnesses, obstructive tactics in discovery procedure, and the like. Under Model Rule 3.4, a lawyer may not unlawfully obstruct another party's access to evidence, nor may a lawyer unlawfully alter, destroy, or conceal a document or other material having potential evidentiary value, or counsel or assist another person to do so. Furthermore, a lawyer may not falsify evidence, counsel or assist a witness to testify falsely, or offer a witness an inducement that is prohibited by law. A lawyer may not knowingly disobey a tribunal's rules, except in a situation where the lawyer can assert that no valid obligation exists. In a pretrial procedure, a lawyer may not make a frivolous discovery request or fail to make reasonably diligent effort to comply with a legally proper discovery request by an opposing party. Finally, a lawyer may not request a person, other than a client, to refrain from voluntarily giving relevant information to another party unless 1) that person is a relative or an employee or other agent of a client, and 2) the lawyer reasonably believes that the person's interests will not be adversely affected by refraining from giving such information.

### 2.7.3.2 Truthfulness in Statements to Others

A lawyer generally has no affirmative duty to inform an opposing party of relevant facts, but a lawyer is deemed to be engaging in a misrepresentation if they incorporate or affirm a statement of another person that the lawyer knows is false. Improper misrepresentation also arises in situations where a lawyer provides partially true information by misleading statements or omissions that are the equivalent of affirmative false statements. Specifically, Model Rule 4.1 prohibits a lawyer, in the course of representing a client, from knowingly making a false statement of material fact or law to a third person and from failing to disclose a material fact when disclosure is necessary to avoid assisting a criminal or fraudulent act by a client unless such disclosure is prohibited by another Model Rule. Whether a particular statement of a lawyer should be regarded as one of fact depends on the circumstances in which the statement is made. For example, under generally accepted conventions in negotiation, certain types of statements ordinarily are not taken as statements of material fact. Examples of these types of statements made during the course of a negotiation are estimates of price or value placed on the subject of a transaction, a party's intentions as to an acceptable settlement of a claim, and the existence of an undisclosed principal except where nondisclosure of the principal would constitute fraud.

### 2.7.3.3 Communication with Person Represented by Counsel

Under Model Rule 4.2, a lawyer representing a client may not communicate about the subject matter of the representation with a person the lawyer knows to be represented by another lawyer in the matter, unless the lawyer has the consent of the other lawyer or is authorized to engage in the communication by law or court order. This rule applies even though the person represented by another lawyer initiates or consents to the communication. The rule requires a lawyer to immediately terminate a conversation with such represented person as soon as the lawyer learns that person is represented by another lawyer. There are exceptions to this rule, however. The rule does not preclude a lawyer from communicating with a represented person, or an employee or agent of such person, concerning matters outside the representation. Thus, the existence of a controversy between a government agency and a private party, or between two corporations, does not prohibit a lawyer for either party from communicating with nonlawyer representatives of the other regarding a separate matter. Nor does the rule prohibit a lawyer from communicating with a represented person who is seeking advice from a lawyer who is not otherwise representing a client in the matter. And most importantly, a lawyer may not engage in a communication prohibited by the rule through the acts of another person. The rule, however, does not prohibit parties to a matter from communicating with each other, and a lawyer is not prohibited from advising a client concerning such communication. A lawyer who is uncertain whether a particular communication is precluded by the rule may seek a court order regarding the ethical propriety of the proposed communication. Many jurisdictions have an ethics hotline that attorneys may call for advice.

#### 2.7.3.4 Dealing with Unrepresented Persons and Prospective Clients

Model Rule 4.3 addresses the circumstances in which a lawyer may communicate with an unrepresented person, and it distinguishes between situations involving unrepresented persons whose interests may be adverse to those of the lawyer's client and those in which the person's interests are not in conflict with those of the client. When representing a client and when dealing with an unrepresented person, a lawyer may neither state nor imply that the lawyer is not an interested party. When the lawyer knows or reasonably should know that the unrepresented person misunderstands the lawyer's role in the matter, the lawyer must make reasonable efforts to correct the misunderstanding. A lawyer may not give legal advice to an unrepresented person, other than the advice to obtain counsel, where the lawyer knows or reasonably should know that the interests of such person are or have a reasonable possibility of conflicting with those of their client. The rule does not prohibit a lawyer from negotiating the terms of a transaction or settlement with an unrepresented person so long as the lawyer has explained that they represent an adverse party and is not representing the person. The lawyer may explain to such person the terms on which the lawyer's client will enter into an agreement or settle a matter, prepare documents for the person's signature, and explain the lawyer's own view of the meaning of the document or the lawyer's view of the underlying obligations. It is wise for the lawyer to advise the unrepresented person to seek legal review of the documents before signing them.

Model Rule 7.3 addresses a lawyer's communications with a particular type of unrepresented person—a prospective client. Under that rule, generally a lawyer may not by in-person, live telephone, or real-time electronic contact solicit professional employment from a prospective client when a significant motive for the lawyer's doing so is the lawyer's pecuniary gain. Exceptions to this general rule include situations where the person contacted is a lawyer, or has a family, close personal, or prior professional relationship with the contacting lawyer.

Similarly, a lawyer may not solicit professional employment from a prospective client if that prospective client has made known to the lawyer a desire not to be solicited; or if the solicitation involves coercion, duress, or harassment. Written, recorded, or electronic communication from a prospective client known to need legal services in a particular matter must include the words "Advertising Material" on the outside envelope, if any, and at the beginning and ending of any recorded or electronic communication, unless the intended recipients are members of the excepted categories of persons identified immediately above in this paragraph. Exceptions to this rule apply to a lawyer who participates with a prepaid or group legal service plan operated by an organization not owned or directed by the lawyer that uses in-person or telephone contact to solicit memberships or subscriptions for the plan from persons who are not known to need legal services in a particular matter covered by the plan.

#### 2.7.3.5 Respect for Rights of Third Parties

Model Rule 4.4 addresses the ethical restrictions on methods of obtaining evidence from third persons and unwarranted intrusions into privileged relationships, such as the lawyer-client relationship. Under that rule, when representing a client, a lawyer may not use means that have no substantial purpose other than to embarrass, delay, or burden a third person, or use methods of obtaining evidence that violate the legal rights of such a person. Furthermore, a lawyer who receives a document relating to the representation of another lawyer's client and knows or reasonably should know that the document was inadvertently sent shall promptly notify the sender.

## 2.8 Considering Procedural Alternatives

When a dispute has arisen and arbitration is going forward, either by virtue of an arbitration clause or by a negotiated submission agreement, consider whether there are procedural alternatives available to make the arbitration hearing process more efficient, less time consuming, and less expensive. Depending on the dispute's nature and the parties involved, consider, very early in the preliminary planning process, the usefulness of 1) videotaped or telephone testimony, 2) a bifurcated hearing, 3) consolidation of claims, 4) phasing the arbitration, 5) a class-action procedure, or 6) a virtual or hybrid hearing.

### 2.8.1 Recorded or Telephone Testimony

Witnesses or experts may be unavailable at the arbitration hearing, even via videoconferencing. Opposing counsel may agree to having the testimony—both direct and cross-examination—recorded in advance and then played back at the hearing. The disadvantage is that the arbitrators cannot question the witness. A remedy for this is to have the witness available on speakerphone after the recording is shown so that they can answer any questions from the arbitrators.

Also, if witnesses are unable at the last minute to attend the hearing, counsel can agree, with the approval of the arbitrator(s), to have them testify by videoconference or phone.

### 2.8.2 Bifurcation

Consider whether to ask the arbitrators to bifurcate the hearing into two parts. In the initial part, the parties present their respective evidence on the liability issues. After hearing the evidence and counsels' arguments on liability, the arbitrators recess to decide the liability issues and then return and announce their decision. If they determine there was no liability on the part of any respondent, they enter an award to that effect and adjourn the hearing. If they determine one or more of the respondents is liable, the hearing proceeds, addressing the damage issues in relation to only those respondents. This procedure can reduce a hearing's length in the appropriate case.

In many situations, however, counsel cannot separate evidence related to liability from that related to damages. Thus, they tend to err on the side of inclusiveness, so that where the apportionment of a witness's testimony is unclear, counsel normally attempts to introduce all the testimony under a liability label. Also, where certain witnesses' testimony can clearly be apportioned between liability and damage issues, witnesses might have to testify once in the liability portion and then return to testify again in the damage portion. This can greatly inconvenience witnesses and cause considerable expense to the parties. In short, bifurcation is probably best suited to cases in which the damage evidence is in the form of the testimony of expert witnesses who need not be called to testify on liability issues.

### 2.8.3 Consolidating Claims

When at least one party is common to separate disputes, there may be several reasons why you might propose that claims be consolidated for arbitration before the same panel. These include 1) reducing the risk of conflicting arbitration awards, 2) reducing the expense to the parties, and 3) minimizing the time spent by parties and witnesses in providing testimony. Depending on the circumstances, there may be very good reasons to object to consolidation if opposing counsel favors it. For example, if your respondent client has a minor dispute with the common party, but that common party has multiple disputes with a respondent third party, your client would not be happy about paying your fees to observe the other two parties battle out their dispute before the arbitrators. Also, your client may not want to be tainted by what the arbitrators may perceive as much more egregious conduct committed by the third party.

If parties cannot agree to consolidation, the party desiring it may file an action in court to compel it. Although courts are not uniform in their decisions, it is safe to say that where the issues to be resolved are substantially the same and no party will be prejudiced by consolidation, courts will usually order arbitrations to be consolidated.

### 2.8.4 Phasing the Arbitration

Phasing the arbitration combines consolidation and bifurcation. It can be quite useful in complex multiparty arbitrations. In this procedure, after several cases are consolidated for hearing, the arbitrators divide the proceedings into three parts: 1) determining the liability of the various parties; 2) awarding damages and interest; and 3) allocating arbitration costs among the parties. The key to this procedure's success is the arbitrator subdividing the liability determination proceedings into phases. The first phase involves hearings in which the principal parties present their cases against each other. These may include both claims and counterclaims. The second phase consists of the hearings of the multiple-respondent claims against each other, and the third and fourth phases, if needed, consist of hearing the claims of a third group of claimants against the parties already described and the third group's claims against each other. Although this procedure seems quite complicated when described in words, as applied it expedites the procedure. The arbitrators' decisions in the first liability phase directly impact on issues raised by the parties subsequently presenting their liability claims and defenses. As the arbitrators decide these issues, those parties learn how the arbitrators would most likely rule on similar claims or defenses in their cases. This streamlines the subsequent cases, with parties dropping or settling certain claims once they see the "writing on the wall."

### 2.8.5 Class-Action Procedure

If the number of potential plaintiffs is known and finite and the potential damages reasonably predictable, a respondent or respondents in arbitration may agree to a class-action procedure. In many multiple-claimant situations where several arbitrations may be pending, however, the class-action procedure will require that notice be issued to individuals who have no present formal claim against respondents, but who may have such a claim. This could expose respondents to the possibility of defending themselves before a single arbitration panel with authority to impose an award of an unknown high value, and without the right to an appeal. Respondents, faced with such a prospect, will normally oppose the class-action procedure, opting instead to take their chances in separate arbitrations before different panels. Nonetheless, it is possible that, despite a respondent's objection, a court may order class-wide arbitration if an arbitration clause can be construed to authorize it or, in cases where state law governs, such a class arbitration procedure is authorized by state law.

## 2.9 Considering Site Inspection and Audiovisual Aids

In some arbitrations, your preparations begin far in advance of the arbitration hearing—sometimes even before you select the arbitrators in the case. Two prime examples are preparations for cases that may involve site inspections by the arbitrator(s) and cases that require a long lead time to prepare presentational aids.

Site inspections are most common in construction and accident cases, particularly catastrophic accidents. Exhibits and audiovisual aids are essential to the effective presentation of any case, but they are particularly important in cases where proof requires the demonstration of the condition of physical objects as they were at the time of or immediately before or after a particular event.

Visit the pertinent site as soon after the event as possible. Arrange for photographs and/or video to be taken, and, if applicable, for accident reconstruction experts to examine the site and prepare their reports. If relevant, investigate whether any available photographs or video of the site were taken before the pertinent event occurred. If you determine that a model or mock-up of the site would be useful during the arbitration hearing, have it built or fabricated so it will be available at the arbitration hearing. Remember, arbitrations often proceed to hearing faster than court cases ordinarily do. The lead time for preparing for an arbitration may be short.

If effective presentation of your case requires the arbitrators to make an on-site inspection, visit the site in advance and think through how to conduct the arbitrators' visit. Consider how the parties and the arbitrator will travel to the site and if any travel costs are involved. In the rare situation involving multiple clients and a site distant from the arbitration's location, you may even have to arrange for bus transportation in advance of the visit. Sometimes the testimony of witnesses is taken on-site. If this is the situation in your case, you may have to arrange for the presence of recording equipment or a stenographer.

With the arbitrators' permission, you may also want to arrange for photographs and/or video of the site to be taken during the arbitrators' site visit for use when you resume the hearing. Photographs and/or video not only preserve the scene as the arbitrators saw it, but also serve as a valuable visual aid for you in demonstrating to the arbitrators a view of the site which either they did not see or saw but did not appreciate the relevance of at the time. Thus, during the site inspection, have photographs and/or video taken from several angles to get a total perspective. Depending on the case, you may want to engage the services of a professional photographer or videographer to do this. It is also often helpful to have both black and white and color versions of photos. If you are not using litigation software and/or a computer to project photographs, enlarge them to 8 by 10 inches so that they can be easily reviewed during the arbitration proceedings. Even if you are projecting them, it can also be helpful to have printed copies for the arbitrator(s) to reference later.

## 2.10 Selecting Expert Witnesses

Begin considering what experts your case needs very early in your arbitration preparations. In arbitration, expert opinions are necessary where the matter in question is highly technical and only a person with specialized skills can clarify the issue for an arbitrator. Expert testimony is almost always necessary where your opponent intends to call an expert to testify.

If you determine that experts are necessary, it is seldom prudent for multiple experts to testify on the same technical issue. Rarely does cumulative expert evidence provide any tactical advantage. In fact, it can be dangerous to your case because a skilled cross-examiner can draw out conflicts in your experts' separate testimony.

In selecting an expert witness, you may wish to consider the following criteria.

### *Qualifications*

- Does the expert have the appropriate background to testify?
- Is the expert well qualified and knowledgeable in the relevant subject area?

### *Professionalism*

- Is the expert a person of integrity?
- Does the expert fit the cultural norms around expected appearance of someone in their field?
- Does the expert speak with authority?

### *Communication*

- Can the expert boil down complicated processes to easily understood language?
- Can the expert create readily understandable analogies or illustrative examples?

### *Personality*

- Does the expert articulate their thoughts well?
- Have you had an opportunity to observe the expert testify previously?
- Would you believe the expert's opinion?

When selecting an expert, exercise both insight and caution. Your expert must be measured, reliable, and careful. They must explain their positions without rambling or exaggeration. Your expert must know when to speak and when to stop speaking.

## 2.11 Considering Whether to Mediate First

Even if your arbitration clause does not provide for mediation before resorting to arbitration, consider that option very seriously when a dispute arises under your contract. Also consider the mediation-first option when you and opposing counsel negotiate the provisions of a submission agreement. Many cases that would require days or even weeks of arbitration resolve in a few hours with the help of a skillful mediator. There is much benefit and very little risk of harm in trying mediation first. Even if a successful mediation lasted a full day, your client would come out far ahead financially by paying your fees and half of a mediator's fees compared to your fees for spending a day or more preparing for the arbitration and the time spent at the arbitration hearing itself. Even if mediation did not resolve the dispute, it might result in the informal disclosure of information that obviates the need to take any discovery for the subsequent arbitration. Mediation might also drain anger and hostility from the dispute, permitting the arbitration to proceed more efficiently and guarantee a less costly arbitration. In most dispute situations where an attempt at a negotiated resolution fails, make mediation your next choice of process.

## 2.12 Arbitrator Ethics

In this chapter, we have discussed factors to consider when selecting an arbitrator. This section briefly reviews the ethical code that governs the conduct of arbitrators. Be aware of the ethical restraints on arbitrator behavior so that you will know when it is appropriate for an arbitrator to disqualify or recuse themselves from a case, for you to file a motion for recusal, or for you to file a post-hearing court challenge to the award should you learn of the ethical problem after the hearing. The Code of Ethics for Arbitrators in Commercial Disputes—Revised 2004 (Code),[13] prepared jointly by a special committee of the American Arbitration Association (AAA) and a Task Force of the American Bar Association (ABA), consists of ethical guidelines for many types of arbitration, but it does not apply to labor arbitration, which is generally conducted under the Code of Professional Responsibility for Arbitrators of Labor-Management Disputes.[14]

---

13. *Code of Ethics for Arbitrators in Commercial Disputes*, Am. Arb. Assoc. (eff. Mar. 1, 2004), https://www.adr.org/sites/default/files/document_repository/Commercial_Code_of_Ethics_for_Arbitrators_2010_10_14.pdf (last visited Jun. 2024) [hereinafter *Arbitrator Code of Ethics*].

14. Code of Professional Responsibility for Arbitrators of Labor-Management Disputes of the National Academy of Arbitrators, Am. Arb. Ass'n, & Fed. Mediation & Conciliation Serv. (As amended Sept. 2007), https://www.adr.org/sites/default/files/document_repository/Code%20of%20Professional%20Responsibility%20for%20Arbitrators%20of%20Labor-Management%20Disputes_0.pdf (last visited Jun. 2024).

The Code addresses ethical norms applying to arbitrators whether they are selected or designated by the parties or other individuals as "neutrals" or appointed by the parties, acting alone, with those two party-appointed arbitrators then selecting a neutral arbitrator. Neutral arbitrators have a responsibility to serve competently and impartially. Before accepting a case, they must disclose 1) any known direct or indirect financial or personal interest in the outcome of the arbitration; 2) any known existing or past financial, business, professional, or personal relationships which might reasonably affect impartiality; 3) the nature and extent of any prior knowledge about the dispute; and 4) any other matters, relationships, or interests they are obligated to disclose by rules, practices, law, or the parties' agreement.[15] They must avoid conduct and statements that give the appearance of partiality toward or against any party and keep confidential all matters relating to the arbitration proceedings and decision.[16] Ex parte communications are prohibited with limited exceptions, including discussion of logistical matters and proceeding with a duly noticed hearing in the absence of one party.[17]

## 2.13 Lawyer Serving as Third-Party Neutral

In the last decade, alternative dispute resolution has come to be a substantial and important aspect of our public and private systems for resolving disputes. Apart from advocating on behalf of clients in arbitration, lawyers now often serve as arbitrators, either individually or as members of three-arbitrator panels. This role of arbitrator (and other third-party, neutral functions) is not unique to lawyers. Nonlawyers can also serve as arbitrators and as other third-party neutrals. When lawyers and nonlawyers serve in the neutral role, they may be subject to court rules or other laws that apply to third-party neutrals generally. Lawyer-neutrals, however, may also be subject to lawyer-specific court rules and rules of professional conduct. The American Bar Association added one such rule to the Model Rules of Professional Conduct to clarify and distinguish a lawyer's duties in a neutral role versus duties owed when serving in an advocate role. That rule, Model Rule 2.4, defines a lawyer's service in a neutral role as occurring "when the lawyer assists two or more persons who are not clients of the lawyer to reach resolution of a dispute or other matter that has arisen between them." It further provides that service as a third-party neutral "may include service as an arbitrator, a mediator or in such other capacity as will enable the lawyer to assist the parties to resolve the matter" (Mod. R. 2.4 (a)). When serving as a third-party neutral, a lawyer has two important initial duties to perform with respect to parties. The lawyer-neutral must first inform unrepresented parties that they are not representing the parties. Second, when a lawyer-neutral knows or reasonably should know that a party does not understand the lawyer-neutral's role in the matter, they must explain the difference between a lawyer's role as a third-party neutral and a lawyer's role as one who represents a client (Mod. R. 2.4(b)).

---

15. *Arbitrator Code of Ethics*, *supra* note 19, at Canon II.
16. *Id.* at Canon VI.
17. *Id.* at Canon III.

Today, some lawyers represent clients in some matters and serve as third-party neutrals in others. This broadening of the lawyer's role requires lawyers to be especially vigilant of the ethical requirements imposed by the requirements of each role. For example, a party in an arbitrated matter may subsequently ask the lawyer who served as a neutral to represent that party as a client in the same matter.

The ABA Model Rules of Professional Conduct forbid such representation unless all the parties to the proceedings give their written informed consent (Mod. R. 1.12(a)). Other laws or codes of ethics governing third-party neutrals may impose more stringent standards of personal or imputed disqualification in such situations. The conflicts of a lawyer who is personally disqualified under Model Rule 1.12(a) will be imputed to other lawyers in a law firm unless 1) the disqualified lawyer is timely screened from any participation in the matter and is apportioned no part of the fee generated by the firm's representation, and 2) the firm provides prompt written notice to the parties and any appropriate tribunal to enable them to determine compliance with the provisions of Model Rule 1.12 (Mod. R. 1.12(c)).

Lawyers who represent clients in alternative dispute resolution processes are typically governed by the Model Rules of Professional Conduct. Those ethical requirements are addressed above in this chapter in section 2.7. When advocating on behalf of a client before a tribunal, as in binding arbitration, the lawyer's duty of candor is governed by Model Rule 3.3. Otherwise, a lawyer's duty of candor toward both the third-party neutral and other parties is governed by Model Rule 4.1.

## 2.14 Civility Guidelines

In 1998, the American Bar Association's litigation section issued a set of guidelines for litigation conduct to address what it viewed as a decline in professionalism and civility among lawyers.[18] Modeled on the Standards of Professional Conduct adopted by the U.S. Court of Appeals for the Seventh Circuit, the ABA section of litigation's guidelines are purely aspirational and are not used as a basis for liability or discipline. Draw these guidelines to the attention of other arbitration advocates, as necessary, when inappropriate or unprofessional behavior of lawyers tends to threaten the intended purpose, the integrity, or the character of the arbitration process. Guidelines that directly pertain to the arbitration process address lawyers' duties to other counsel and to the arbitrators. Toward other counsel, among other guidelines, lawyers should:

- Not reflect any ill feelings of our clients toward opposing counsel's client.
- Be civil and courteous in all written and oral communications.

18. A full copy of the guidelines can be obtained at: *Guidelines for Conduct.* A.B.A. (June 2, 2020), https://www.njd.uscourts.gov/sites/njd/files/AppR.pdf or https://law.indiana.edu/instruction/tanford/web/reference/abatrialcode.html (both last visited Jun. 2024).

- Refrain from making disparaging personal remarks or acting with acrimony toward anyone involved with the arbitration.
- Treat adverse parties and witnesses with fair consideration.
- Should refrain from acting on or manifesting bias or prejudice toward anyone involved with the arbitration.
- Adhere to all agreements made with opposing counsel.
- Stipulate to relevant matters if they are undisputed and if no good-faith advocacy basis exists for not stipulating
- Refrain from litigation harassment, including via discovery and discovery scheduling and via requesting time extensions solely for the purpose of delay.
- Carefully craft document production requests so they are limited to those documents we reasonably believe are necessary, and appropriate, for the prosecution or defense of an action.
- Respond to document requests reasonably and not strain to interpret requests in an artificially restrictive manner to avoid disclosure of relevant and non-privileged documents.
- Engage only in conduct during a deposition that would be appropriate in the presence of an arbitrator.
- Expect the same level of conduct from our agents and authorized persons.

Toward the arbitrator, among other guidelines, lawyers should:

- Speak and write civilly and respectfully in all communications with the arbitrator.
- Be punctual and prepared for all . . . appearances so that all conferences and hearings may commence on time.
- If delayed, notify the arbitrator.
- Refrain from any conduct that brings disorder or disruption to the hearing.
- Advise our clients and witnesses appearing at the hearing of the proper conduct expected and required and, to the best of our ability, prevent our clients and witnesses from creating disorder or disruption.
- Refrain from knowingly misrepresenting, mischaracterizing, misquoting, or misciting facts or authorities in any oral or written communication to the arbitrator. (Do not rely solely on GenAI.)
- Before dates for hearings are set, or if that is not feasible, immediately after such date has been set, attempt to verify the availability of necessary witnesses and participants and promptly notify the arbitrator of any likely problems.

# • Chapter Three •

## Prehearing Advocacy

*[Y]ou should be able to tell when you yourself write something, is this really interesting? Or am I just putting a lot of words on paper? Would I want to read this myself if I weren't me?*

—*Stan Lee*[1]

The key to a successful arbitration is to prepare both your client and your case for the arbitration hearing far in advance of its scheduled date (Lore & Lubet, *MTA*). Similar to trial advocacy, you must prepare a persuasive trial story; but even more so than for a jury trial, you must match the story to the governing law and/or contract provisions. If you are a claimant, prehearing advocacy begins in earnest when you draft your arbitration demand and incorporated claims or when you draft your submission agreement. If you are a respondent, prehearing advocacy commences when you draft your answer. These pleadings provide sketches of the respective client's stories and define the general limits of the stories that ultimately play out before the arbitrator. These initial story designs provide the basic templates against which the arbitrators will measure questions of relevance. These important documents should not just be drafted, but well crafted, or as Stan Lee might say, interesting and easy to read. Take similar care in preparing motions, responses, position statements, discovery requests, and other pleadings during the arbitration's prehearing stage.

In addition, the preliminary hearing is a useful strategic tool to aid you in your prehearing preparation. Use information you gather there to organize the documents of the case and prepare your client and other witnesses to present their testimony at the hearing. In essence, it will aid you in performing your screenwriter and theatrical director functions, described in more detail in Chapters 4 and 5.

It is to these subjects that we now turn.[2]

---

1. Joey Esposito, *Stan Lee Reflects on 70 Years in Comics*, IGN (Jan. 24, 2012, 5:35 PM), https://www.ign.com/articles/2012/01/24/stan-lee-reflects-on-70-years-in-comics (last visited Jun. 2024).

2. *See generally*, Bette J. Roth et al., The Alternative Dispute Resolution Practice Guide, Ch. 8–11 (2022); Jay Folberg et al., Resolving Disputes: Theory, Practice, and Law, Ch. 17–24 (2022).

## 3.1 Drafting the Arbitration Demand

Arbitration is initiated by demand or by submission agreement. If the arbitration is triggered by a contract's arbitration clause, draft the demand in accordance with that clause. The demand for arbitration is a written notice by one party to the other(s) of that party's intent to initiate the arbitration process. When arbitration is initiated by submission agreement, the disputants sign an agreement or, if the case is administered, a submission form agreeing to participate in the arbitration.

Pay close attention to any time limitations within which a claimant must present or file a demand. These time constraints may appear in the arbitration clause itself, in a court rule, or in a statute. If a demand is not timely filed with a dispute resolution organization or served on the other parties, the claimant may lose the right to have claims adjudicated in any forum, private or public. If you file a demand with a dispute resolution organization, be prepared to deposit a filing or administrative fee at that time.

To be arbitrable, the nature of the controversy must be within the parameter of the arbitration clause.[3] Even when the parties have designated a particular dispute resolution organization to administer the arbitration, the clause's language controls over the language of the organization's published rules if there is an issue whether certain claims are arbitrable or whether certain procedures should be followed in relation to the demand.

Draft the demand clearly and succinctly, incorporating all the case's pertinent facts. There is no set structure or format for a demand, although it is prudent to include, at a minimum, the following information: 1) the names of all parties involved in the dispute; 2) a succinct, straightforward statement of facts, in chronological order; 3) a quote containing the exact language of the arbitration clause, or an attachment with a copy of the clause; 4) a statement of the claim or claims, and how they relate to the contract and the arbitration clause; and 5) a statement of the relief sought. In complex cases, claimants commonly attach to the demand a pleading in the form of a complaint that would be filed in court. Indeed, some dispute resolution organizations permit a court-filed complaint to serve as the demand and claims in arbitration when the parties opt to have their dispute resolved through arbitration rather than in the court system or when a court has compelled arbitration.[4]

---

3. *See generally* Stephen J. Ware & Ariana R. Levinson, Principles of Arbitration Law § 26 (2d ed. 2023); Brayman v. KeyPoint Gov't Sols., Inc., 83 F.4th 823, 833 (10th Cir. 2023) ("questions of arbitrability encompass . . . whether a particular . . . dispute is arbitrable because it is within the scope of a valid arbitration agreement. . . .").

4. *See e.g.*, *JAMS Comprehensive Arbitration Rules and Procedures: Rule 9: Notice of Claims*, JAMS, (eff. June 1, 2021), https://www.jamsadr.com/rules-comprehensive-arbitration/#Rule-9 (last visited Jun. 2024).

After drafting a demand, serve it on the other party or parties. This may usually be done in any manner of service that is acceptable for initiating a lawsuit in the court system. If you use the postal system, effect service by certified or registered mail. Under the rules of some dispute resolution organizations, the demand is first filed with the organization, which then serves it on the respondents. The organizations also have rules as to how many copies of the demand must be filed and served.

A checklist for drafting an arbitration demand appears in Appendix B.

## 3.2 Drafting the Response to the Demand

Once the claimant has filed the demand, the respondent can normally choose to answer or otherwise respond to the demand. Unlike the litigation setting, respondents are not usually required to file an answer. In fact, lack of an answer will not be construed as an admission of liability but rather as a denial of the claim(s) presented in the demand. One important exception to these principles relates to securities cases. FINRA has promulgated rules requiring respondents to answer demands with specificity. Failure to be specific in your answer may prevent you from introducing evidence for defenses not disclosed in the answer.[5]

When you can file an answer, it is in the respondent's best interest to respond to the demand to familiarize the arbitrator(s) with the case before the hearing. This avoids giving the arbitrators the impression that your client is being disrespectful to them or is taking a cavalier attitude toward the arbitration proceeding. Also, some dispute resolution organizations routinely require respondents to file an answer; still others require that an answer be filed if a claimant makes a demand for an answering statement. If a claimant makes such a demand, the respondent must file an answer or risk being barred from presenting any defense.

### *3.2.1 Drafting the Answer*

If the arbitration is taking place pursuant to the rules of a dispute resolution organization, the organization will notify the respondent of the proceedings. In such case, the respondent will usually have seven to ten days to answer or acknowledge the claim. Again, a failure to answer will normally be considered a denial.

To put the respondent's position, defenses, and contentions on the record, your answer should at a minimum:

---

5. *13308. Loss of Defenses Due to Untimely or Incomplete Answer*, FINRA (eff. Dec. 15, 2008), https://www.finra.org/rules-guidance/rulebooks/finra-rules/13308 (last visited Jun. 2024).

1) deny all the claims, as appropriate;
2) deny each separate claim with a short explanation of your version of the facts, and if some of the claimant's allegations are true, acknowledge the truth of the claims;
3) protest the relief being sought; and
4) make, if applicable, an unparticularized statement of the affirmative defenses.

By not providing the particularized facts supporting your affirmative defenses, you keep your defense options open during any discovery and through the course of the actual hearing. But be sure to read any pertinent arbitration rules very carefully. Some may require you to include particularized affirmative defenses in your answer or waive them. Regardless of the existence of any such rules, be aware that an arbitrator, acting at their own discretion, may simply bar proof of an affirmative defense of which the claimant had no prehearing notice.

Typical affirmative defenses appear in the chart that follows.

| TYPICAL AFFIRMATIVE DEFENSES | | | |
|---|---|---|---|
| Accord and Satisfaction | Duress | Statute of Frauds | Set-off |
| Assumption of Risk | Estoppel | Statute of Limitations | Waiver |
| Collateral Estoppel | Breach of Contract | Comparative Negligence | Contributory Negligence |
| Failure of Consideration | Failure to Exhaust Contractual Remedies | Condition Precedent | Failure to Mitigate Damages |
| Failure to State a Claim | Fraud | Illegality | Privilege |
| Frustration of Purpose | Impossibility | Release | Unclean Hands |
| Nonarbitrable Issue | Res Judicata | | |

Although not required, an answer may request a specific place for the hearing to be conducted, and it may reveal the name of the attorney or other party who will represent the respondent. An answer can also contain a request for a bill of particulars if the demand contains insufficient information for the respondent to be able to prepare a defense.

If the respondent chooses not to respond, the claimant can continue the arbitration process, selecting an arbitrator and scheduling the hearing. If the respondent fails to answer or appear, the claimant must prove the case based on proper evidence. The arbitrators will then determine an appropriate award based solely on the claimant's evidence.

### 3.2.2 Drafting Counterclaims

In addition to answering the demand, the respondent may also file a counterclaim. A counterclaim is usually separate from the answer and any affirmative defenses. File this claim at the same time as the answer, and include the same elements required in a demand. Also, the service and fee requirements are usually the same as filing a demand. Normally, a respondent's answer requires no fee; a fee is required only when filing a claim of some sort—even if that is a counterclaim.

Filing a counterclaim is the only opportunity for a respondent to present a new claim in the matter to be arbitrated. Under the Commercial Rules of the American Arbitration Association, for example, after the arbitrator has been appointed no new or different claims may be advanced without the arbitrator's consent.[6] Therefore, raise these claims in a counterclaim when filing the response. A counterclaim that arises out of a different and separate agreement that did not provide for arbitration cannot be alleged at this time.

### 3.2.3 Strategies for Answering a Demand

Here are a few general strategies for answering a demand in arbitration:

| GENERAL STRATEGIES |
|---|
| Be general—not technical. |
| Include only the facts pertinent to the explanation and understanding of your denials. |
| State your responses in a logical, precise manner. |
| If some of claimant's allegations are true, acknowledge the truth of the claims; if not, deny claimant's version and set forth your version of the facts. |
| State affirmative defenses in a general way, but touch on all of them. |

6. *Commercial Arbitration Rules and Mediation Procedures Including Procedures for Large, Complex Commercial Disputes*, Rule E-2, "Changes of Claim or Counterclaim," Am. Arb. Ass'n. (Sept. 1, 2022), https://www.adr.org/sites/default/files/Commercial-Rules_Web.pdf (last visited Jun. 2024).

## 3.3 Drafting Motions and Responses

Written motions are the exception, not the rule, in arbitration. They are generally used to dispose of law-based contested matters arising before the actual hearing. Because the arbitration process is not regulated by a universally applicable set of rules, arbitration motion practice may vary according to the needs and preferences of the arbitrators and practitioners in particular cases. Because the arbitration process is more informal than litigation, motions practice is informal as well. Generally, the best advice about written motions in arbitration is to strive to have none. If you must make written motions, limit them to situations where the relief you seek is fundamental to or dispositive of the case. Keep them short and simple (like this section), and responses likewise. In many arbitrations, motions are made orally by counsel and decided by the arbitrators in the preliminary hearing, as explained in more detail in section 3.5. For a comprehensive listing of arguments to support rulings on various motions and objections during arbitration proceedings, see Appendix J.

## 3.4 Drafting Position Statements

The arbitrator may request a position statement, also called a prehearing or opening brief. Such statements are usually filed simultaneously by all parties by a designated date, although arbitrators sometimes request the claimant to submit first and the respondent to submit after reviewing the claimant's pleading. When drafting your statement or brief, briefly apprise the arbitrators of the separate claims, the significant facts, the contentions, and the supporting case law. Inform the arbitrator or opposing counsel of your views on the remedies being sought, monetary and otherwise. This brief, concise document embodies the blueprint of your case; write it well and the arbitrator may refer to it during the hearing.

When an arbitrator requests a position statement, the customary format is a short (five- to ten-page) memorandum. Do not write an appellate court brief. Strive for an initial positive impression from the panel as to the merit of your positions. You will round out this initial written impression at the actual hearing by means of your oral opening statement, testimonial and documentary evidence, cross-examinations, and closing argument. The more "reader friendly" the statement or the brief, the more likely the arbitrator will begin the arbitration hearing with an accurate understanding of your case and position. An effectively written position statement gives you a "jump" on your opponent before the hearing even begins.

Because the opening statement is a persuasive document, state facts accurately and incorporate a few cases that strongly support your principal contentions. If the dispute involves interpretation of contract provisions or of a statute, quote those provisions in the fact portion of the position statement. Above all, do not allege facts in the statement that you cannot prove during the hearing.

If nonlawyers are on your panel, write in a straightforward way, without assuming they will understand legal terms. Explain Latin terms in plain English. Also, remember that if you cite cases or statutes, nonlawyers will not necessarily know how to access these documents. Provide links to, or copies of, pertinent cases and statutes. Though uncommon, when parties do not file position statements simultaneously, arbitrators occasionally permit a claimant to file a reply to respondent's position statement.

This chart sets out techniques you can use in your position statement to emphasize strong, legally significant facts and deemphasize legally significant facts that are less favorable for your client.

| FACT PERSUASION TECHNIQUES | |
|---|---|
| **EMPHASIZE FACTS** | **DEEMPHASIZE FACTS** |
| First or last | Bury in the middle |
| Group by inference | Scatter |
| Detailed | Summary |
| Short sentence | Long sentence |
| Independent clause | Dependent clause |
| Active voice | Passive voice |
| Repetition | Omit or one-shot |
| Vivid descriptions | General descriptions |
| Personalize | Depersonalize |

## 3.5 The Preliminary Hearing

A preliminary hearing, or prehearing conference, can be requested by the arbitrator or by any party. It can be conducted face-to-face, by videoconference, or by telephone. In a large case with complex issues, a preliminary hearing is indispensable. In other cases, if the arbitrator does not schedule a preliminary hearing, you will have to weigh the cost and benefits of having one. A one-hour preliminary hearing might obviate two hours of procedural arguments at the beginning of the actual hearing and may avoid the possibility that the actual hearing has to be postponed one or more times because of discovery and other prehearing squabbles. Cases that require little or no discovery and involve a few thousand dollars would probably not warrant scheduling a preliminary hearing.

A preliminary hearing provides many benefits to the parties. Employ it to discuss the exchange of documents and witness lists, technology needs, and the use of demonstrative exhibits; stipulate to uncontested facts; estimate the hearing's length; and, outside the presence of the arbitrator(s), even to explore settlement possibilities. Accomplish these goals during the preliminary hearing, and your case is likely to proceed more smoothly at the hearing; you will be able to concentrate more on the preparation and presentation of the case's substantive aspects and not worry so much about the procedural aspects.

The preliminary hearing is your first opportunity to make a favorable personal impression on the arbitrator. Be as cooperative and collaborative as possible in working out the prehearing schedule and the rules that will apply to the hearing. Do not present yourself as a nitpicker or an obstructionist, willing to argue with opposing counsel about any issue raised. If you take extreme positions not called for by the situation, the arbitrator may later rule in a way that recognizes your unnecessary petulance.

Customarily, the arbitrator commences the preliminary hearing by explaining its purpose and then moves directly into discussing the necessary preparation of the case for hearing. The first section below addresses topics you will almost always discuss in a preliminary hearing. The second section addresses topics that you may need to address.

## *3.5.1 Normally Discussed Topics*

### 3.5.1.1 Expectation of Civility and Professionalism

One of the first items on the arbitrators' agenda at the preliminary hearing will be their expectation that the advocates and the parties will treat each other with the highest standards of civility and professionalism. This statement communicates a theme of nontolerance of petty squabbling and derisive behavior on the part of the participants and sets the tone for an efficient proceeding. (See section 2.14 for a discussion of the standards of civility.)

### 3.5.1.2 Discovery

In smaller cases, any necessary informal discovery may have been completed prior to the preliminary hearing. When informal discovery has not occurred, counsel sometimes exchange documents or agree to a process for exchange of electronic documents during the preliminary hearing. In either situation, the arbitrator may hear counsel's arguments regarding relevancy, which may clarify the parties' claims and defenses in the arbitration.

In larger cases, you may have attempted more formal discovery prior to the preliminary hearing. If you and opposing counsel disagree about the range of discovery requested by one side, use the preliminary hearing to discuss the issue with the arbitrator. For example, if opposing counsel withheld documents not subject to privilege as part of an arbitration strategy, ask the arbitrator to direct your opponent to produce the withheld documents. Such oral motions obviate the time-consuming, costly practice of drafting motions to compel. The parties can present their respective arguments to the arbitrator and receive an immediate ruling on the issue.

In complex cases where there are multiple parties, voluminous electronic documents, and several witnesses to depose, arbitrators may require counsel to submit a discovery plan by a certain date. If that occurs, contact opposing counsel and negotiate a schedule for producing documents and deposing witnesses. Also, clarify at the preliminary hearing—with the arbitrator present—which discovery rules apply. The arbitrator can rule on any dispute about the discovery rules or about the nature and scope of the discovery before you waste time and money bickering over the rules of the game.

Normally, arbitrators permit the parties to depose experts prior to the hearing on the merits. Cut-off dates for these depositions are normally set during the preliminary hearing. If these experts are not deposed before the hearing, counsel engage in a "fishing expedition," wasting valuable hearing time asking preliminary and exploratory questions.

In the average case, do not waste your time and your client's money deluging the arbitrator with motions or briefs prior to the preliminary hearing. Experienced arbitrators can hear and dispose of most procedural matters presented orally at the preliminary hearing. If briefing of a matter is required, the arbitrator can set a briefing schedule and a ruling date during the preliminary hearing.

#### 3.5.1.3 Witness Lists

The arbitrator normally sets a date by which the parties must exchange a list of witnesses that they reasonably expect to call at the hearing on the merits. This list should contain the name of each witness and a short summary of anticipated testimony (when required). Also attach the curriculum vitae of any experts and copies of any pertinent expert reports. If the arbitrator does not bring up the topic of witness lists at the preliminary hearing, do so. More arbitrations are stalled or interrupted because of complaints of "surprise witnesses" than for any other reason. You need your opponent's list of witnesses at least two or three weeks before the hearing so you can prepare your cross-examinations and decide how to prepare your own witnesses. After receiving your opponent's witness list, you may want to seek leave of the arbitrator to amend your list to add or delete witnesses. You have a continuing obligation to update witness lists as soon as such information becomes available. At the time you submit your witness list, double-check the availability of your witnesses to appear at the hearing. Sometimes the arbitrator will require you to indicate on the witness list the order in which you intend to call witnesses at the hearing. Be aware that arbitrators may have to make ethics disclosures regarding the witnesses that counsel identify.

### 3.5.1.4 Hearing Exhibits

Normally, the arbitrator sets a date by which counsel must exchange exhibit lists or actual copies, hard and electronic, of premarked exhibits they plan to introduce at the hearing on the merits. By that same date, provide the arbitrator or the administering organization with a list of the exhibits or, if the arbitrator directs, a hard and electronic copy of each exhibit. Even in virtual hearings, sending the arbitrator and opposing counsel hard copies before the hearing can make referencing and referring witnesses to documents easier. Providing electronic copies can make it easier for the arbitrator to refer to and quote documents if they write an opinion with their award. In more complex cases, place the exhibits in binders and tab them by exhibit number. The term "exhibits" also includes any schedules, diagrams, charts, audiotapes, videotapes, etc. that you intend to present for the arbitrator's review and consideration in making their decision on the merits. Arbitrators often require counsel to get together before the hearing and agree on a set of joint exhibits to avoid duplicate exhibits.

### 3.5.1.5 Fact Stipulations

Arbitrators will encourage counsel to stipulate uncontested facts and will usually set a date for the stipulations to be filed. Stipulations reduce the testimony and the number of exhibits needed at the hearing on the merits. If you submit stipulations, read them aloud when the hearing on the merits commences. This procedure, of course, will vary depending on the preferences of individual arbitrators.

### 3.5.1.6 Sequestering Witnesses

At the preliminary hearing, discuss and decide whether witnesses will be permitted to be present in the hearing room when other witnesses testify. Usually, the advocates agree that the witnesses on both sides should be sequestered—that is, kept out of the hearing room at least until after they testify, and even after they testify. Sequestration prevents witnesses from conforming their testimony to each other, rather than speaking from their separate memories of the events as they occurred. If there is a dispute on the sequestration issue, decide the matter at the preliminary hearing. An entity's counsel is usually permitted to have at least one entity representative present during all the testimony, even if that person will testify as a witness at some point in the case.

If your witnesses are sequestered, suggest that they bring reading material on the hearing day to occupy themselves while they are waiting to testify. For virtual hearings, the parties should decide whether the attorney and each witness will be in the same room using the same computer or different rooms with different computers, and address how they will ensure witnesses are not viewing testimony of other witnesses.

#### 3.5.1.7 Burden and Standard of Proof

Topics commonly omitted from the agenda of a preliminary hearing are the burden and standard of proof applicable to the evidence adduced at the hearing on the merits. These topics deserve special attention, especially in multiparty cases or cases with counterclaims, crossclaims, and third-party claims. Which party has the burden of proof and the burden of going forward, and what standard of proof that each party must satisfy to prove their separate claims are matters that will impact how each advocate prepares their case for the hearing. If these matters are not discussed at the preliminary hearing, and an attorney comes to the hearing not expecting to present the evidence supporting their affirmative claims until the second or third day of the hearing, the attorney may be unprepared to go forward, not having pertinent documents with them and not having their witnesses available. Or an attorney could come to the hearing believing that the applicable standard of proof relating to their claims is preponderance of the evidence, when in fact the proper standard is clear and convincing evidence. If that standard could have been met if it had been realized in advance of the hearing, then the arbitrator will be deprived of the necessary evidence to fairly decide the case. Discuss burden and standard of proof at the preliminary hearing in conjunction with the topic of order or sequence of proof to be presented at the hearing on the merits.

#### 3.5.1.8 Designating the Place of Hearing; Arranging the Hearing Room

Use the preliminary hearing to designate where the hearing on the merits will be held. If the arbitration is administered, the hearing normally will be at the administering organization. In a multiparty case or in a nonadministered case, however, a larger hearing space may be required. The arbitrator may also desire a particular arrangement of the tables in the hearing room depending on the number of parties, counsel, and observers. Discuss and decide these matters at the preliminary hearing.

For a virtual hearing, discuss what video conferencing system will be used and where counsel, parties, and witnesses will be, and arrange breakout rooms for all involved, if necessary.

#### 3.5.1.9 Estimate of Hearing Length

The arbitrator will ask each side how much time they will need to present their case. Counsel tend to underestimate their time needs. In fact, arbitrators joke that to arrive at an accurate estimate of a hearing time, take the separate estimates of counsel for all parties, add them together, multiply by two, and then add an extra day. When you estimate the time required to present your case, take into account the time required for any preliminary matters, opening statements, direct examination of your witnesses, cross-examination of your witnesses by your opponents, redirect examinations of your witnesses, recross-examinations, arguments over evidence, extended lunch breaks (so counsel may tend to their other clients), waiting for witnesses to arrive, delays caused by taking witnesses out of order, delays caused by unanticipated evidence, rebuttal evidence, surrebuttal evidence, closing arguments, answering questions of the arbitrators, site visits, technological transitions of witnesses, and technological difficulties.

Then add an extra day.

#### 3.5.1.10 Subpoenas

In virtually all jurisdictions, arbitrators can issue subpoenas to require the parties and certain witnesses to attend the arbitration hearing and to produce documents at the hearing. If the arbitrator in your case does not raise the matter of subpoenas, you should. It is important to subpoena every witness that you intend to call to testify in the arbitration proceeding. In many situations, you will need to call the opposing party as an adverse witness and other witnesses who are employed by the opposing party or are under their control. Discuss these matters at the preliminary hearing so that opposing counsel is not surprised when the subpoenas issue. Also, let the arbitrator know you will be submitting the subpoenas far in advance of the hearing so that the witnesses can adjust their schedules accordingly. Also ensure that the arbitrator will be available to sign the subpoenas when presented.

In some jurisdictions, you may be able to compel nonparties to produce documents prior to the hearing. Having the documents in advance will aid you to prepare for hearing. Research whether your jurisdiction interprets Section 7 of the Federal Arbitration Act and Rule 45 of the Federal Rules of Civil Procedure to limit subpoenas to compelling attendance and production at a hearing. If so, decide whether to have an additional preliminary hearing at which the arbitrator can be present to secure the documents in advance of the arbitration hearing.

#### 3.5.1.11 Prohibition Against Ex Parte Communications with Arbitrators

Arbitrators invariably remind counsel that there should be no ex parte communication with them, with certain limited exceptions. In administered cases, send all pleadings to the administering organization, which in turn will send the documents to the arbitrators. In emergency situations, send pleadings directly to the arbitrator with simultaneous service on opposing counsel. Obviously, where there is no administering organization, send your pleadings directly to the arbitrator, but do not include any communication that is not also provided to opposing counsel. Where arbitrators are party appointed, they may have ex parte communication with their appointing parties and counsel to the extent permitted by applicable ethics rules or codes.

#### 3.5.1.12 Audiovisual Aids

Demonstrative exhibits and audiovisual aids are important to the effective presentation of any case, but they are particularly important in cases where proof requires the demonstration of the condition of physical objects as they were at the time of or immediately before or after a particular event. At the preliminary hearing, the arbitrator will normally inquire whether the advocates will be using audiovisual aids so that there will be no surprises about these matters on the morning the hearing is to begin.

#### 3.5.1.13 Final Oral Arguments; Post-Hearing Proposed Findings of Fact and Conclusions of Law

Although it may seem to be premature to raise at the preliminary hearing, it does no harm to discuss final oral arguments and post-hearing briefs or post-hearing findings or conclusions. This topic may directly impact the advocates' thinking about how they intend to present their cases and whether to arrange for the services of a court reporter. If the parties wish to defer these matters for discussion until near the end of the hearing on the merits, the arbitrator will move on to the next topic on the preliminary hearing agenda.

#### 3.5.1.14 Nature and Form of Award

At the preliminary hearing, the arbitrator may want to confirm the nature and form of the award that the parties desire—the customary short award without a statement of reasons or an award incorporating a reasoned opinion. Realize that an award with a reasoned opinion provides a basis to challenge the award by way of a motion for reconsideration. Such a motion may benefit you if you lose the case on the merits, but if your opponent is the losing party, such motion may extend the proceedings, cause additional costly briefing, and delay the enforcement of the award. In the rare case, the reasoned opinion may even provide the basis for a court challenge on the grounds that the arbitrators exceeded their authority or jurisdiction—whether or not there is actual merit to such challenges. Therefore, before you opt for an award with a reasoned opinion, carefully weigh the advantages and disadvantages of having one in the circumstances of your case.

### *3.5.2 Other Topics*

#### 3.5.2.1 Applicable Rules and Law Governing the Procedure in the Particular Arbitration and the Parties' Claims

Of course, it is important that the arbitrator knows what rules and what laws govern the interpretation of the arbitration clause, the arbitration procedures, and the substantive law affecting the decision and the enforcement of the award in the case. Be prepared to confirm these matters with the arbitrator at the beginning of the preliminary hearing. If counsel disagree which rules or law apply to the case, the arbitrator will likely direct that the relevant issues be argued or briefed, if necessary. The arbitrator will want to decide these issues as soon as possible.

### 3.5.2.2 Arbitrability of All Issues

The arbitrator will also want to know whether anyone disputes the arbitrability of all the issues raised in the demand, the cross-claims, and counterclaims, if any. The party opposing arbitration usually bears the burden of establishing that a particular claim, issue, or matter falls outside the scope of the arbitration agreement. Whether the arbitrator or a court must decide issues of arbitrability varies among jurisdictions, but as a general principle, if parties submit a matter to arbitration, a court will defer to the arbitrator's decision on the issue of arbitrability of a dispute if it appears that the parties intended for the arbitrator to decide the arbitrability issue(s). Courts generally do not assume, however, that parties agreed to arbitrate the issue of arbitrability unless there is clear and unmistakable evidence that they did so. Thus, if an issue of arbitrability arises, before you agree to permit the arbitrator to determine the issue of arbitrability look to the arbitration clause or submission agreement to determine whether there is clear and unmistakable evidence that the parties intended for the arbitrator to decide issues of arbitrability.[7]

Realize, also, that questions of arbitrability are not always patent. Sometimes they are latent and intricate. They can be raised with respect to various aspects of the validity of the underlying contracts containing arbitration clauses or of the clauses themselves, including fraud in the inducement, lack of mutuality, or contract termination.[8] They can involve issues of the power or authority of the arbitrator to grant certain kinds of relief or an appropriate remedy such as an injunction, specific performance, or the awarding of consequential or punitive damages. Thus, in some situations, a question may arise whether a party has waived the right to object to the arbitration on grounds of nonarbitrability if the objection was not made before or at the beginning of the hearing on the merits of the legal claims. Waivers of arbitrability issues are fact-specific and different courts can reach different outcomes; if such an issue arises in a case you are arbitrating, review carefully the applicable case law of the pertinent jurisdiction.[9]

---

7. *See* Stephen J. Ware & Ariana R. Levinson, Principles of Arbitration Law § 26(b) & (c) (2d ed. 2023). Beijing Shougang Mining Inv. Co. v. Mongolia, 11 F.4th 144, 153 (2d Cir. 2021) ("Question of whether parties have submitted particular dispute to arbitration, that is, the question of arbitrability, is an issue for judicial determination unless the parties clearly and unmistakably provide otherwise.").

8. Ware & Levinson at §§ 18, 20, 46(b)(3). Aerotek, Inc. v. Boyd, 624 S.W.3d 199, 209 (Tex. 2021) (Whether e-signature was effective for contract formation); Berman v. Freedom Fin. Network, LLC, 30 F.4th 849, 855 (9th Cir. 2022) (Lack of mutual acceptance); Vazquez v. SaniSure, Inc., 319 Cal. Rptr. 3d 878, 882 (2024) ("Cause of action that arises after contract terminates may be subject to arbitration if arbitration agreement survives termination of the remainder of the contract.").

9. Stephen J. Ware & Ariana R. Levinson, Principles of Arbitration Law § 46(b)(1) (2d ed. 2023); Harris v. B&L Delivery LLC, No. CV 5:20-29-KKC, 2023 WL 3609154, at *2 (E.D. Ky. May 23, 2023) ("[A]lthough a court is usually the proper venue for decisions about arbitrability, if the parties 'clearly and unmistakably' submit the issue to the arbitrator 'without reservation,' then the parties have waived their right to have a court make the decision."); Crossville Med. Oncology, P.C. v. Glenwood Sys., LLC, 485 F. App'x 821, 823 (6th Cir. 2012) "[A] party in arbitration who lodges no form of objection whatsoever is deemed to have acquiesced to the arbitrator's authority to determine the arbitrability of the dispute.").

Cases vary as to the appropriate action courts should take when arbitrable and nonarbitrable claims arise out of the same transaction and are intertwined legally and factually.[10] The decisions in these cases usually depend on the totality of the factual and procedural circumstances. The Supreme Court has held that a court can proceed to determine nonarbitrable claims in litigation but should not stay arbitration of a related arbitrable claim.[11] Some courts stay litigation of nonarbitrable claims until the completion of the arbitration of the arbitrable claims.[12] On the other hand, under California state law in multiparty situations, the court may litigate all claims, even the arbitrable claim.[13] When an issue of arbitrability arises, research the applicable law in your jurisdiction and be prepared to brief the issue.

#### 3.5.2.3 Amended Pleadings

It may become apparent in discussing the state of the pleadings or the amount of needed discovery that a claim, answer, or counterclaim of your opponent is not sufficiently detailed. In such instances, ask the arbitrator to direct that a pleading be amended to include more details.

#### 3.5.2.4 Addition or Joinder of Parties

It may also become apparent during the preliminary hearing that other parties need to be notified of the arbitration and of their opportunity for voluntary addition as parties. Or they need to be joined as additional parties because of the existence of multiple arbitration clauses making them named parties to the dispute.

#### 3.5.2.5 Observers and Other Attendees

In some cases, parties may wish to have persons present who are not actual parties or witnesses in the case. These attendees often have an interest in the proceeding and its outcome, or they simply want to be there to assist a party to present its case efficiently. Sometimes a spouse wants to accompany a party to provide moral support; sometimes a corporate representative wants to be present to coordinate the timing of the appearance of witnesses as the hearing progresses. It is within the arbitrator's discretion to allow observers to be present and to limit their number. If an observer will predictably disrupt a hearing, the arbitrator may rule at the preliminary hearing that the person should not be permitted to be present.

---

10. Ware & Levinson, Principles of Arbitration Law at § 28.
11. KPMG LLP v. Cocchi, 565 U.S. 18, 22 (2011) (per curium); *see also* Silverman v. DiscGenics, Inc., No. 2:22-cv-00354-JNP-DAO, 2023 U.S. Dist. LEXIS 42753, at *9 (D. Utah March 13, 2023) (compelling arbitration of certain claims and proceeding with litigation as to others).
12. *See, e.g.*, G&C Closed Circuit Events, LLC v. Castillo, No. 14 CV 2073, 2017 U.S. Dist. LEXIS 42022, at *35 (N.D. Ill. March 22, 2017) (compelling arbitration of certain third-party claims and staying litigation in entirety pending resolution of the arbitration).
13. Cal. Civ. Proc. Code § 1281.2(c).

### 3.5.2.6 Order of Evidence

In multiparty cases with counterclaims, cross-claims, etc., the arbitrator will discuss with the advocates the order in which the parties will be proceeding in the presentation of their evidence at the hearing on the merits. Often, the arbitrator sets time limits for the advocates' opening statements and even for case presentations if it is appropriate and the parties agree.

### 3.5.2.7 Position Statements or Prehearing Briefs

In most cases, an arbitrator will direct the advocates to submit prehearing position statements or prehearing briefs a few days in advance of the hearing on the merits. Position statements, also called prehearing or opening briefs, are usually filed simultaneously by all parties by a designated date, though sometimes an arbitrator may direct that they be filed sequentially. A position statement or brief is a short memorandum embodying the blueprint of each party's case. Five to ten double-spaced pages in the average case, it succinctly apprises the arbitrator of the significant facts, the separate claims, the contentions, and supporting law. It should also contain the advocate's views on the remedies being sought, monetary and otherwise. If properly prepared, the arbitrator will refer to it during the hearing to help put the parties' evidence in context.

### 3.5.2.8 Stenographer or Recording

If either party desires a recording of the arbitration hearing, resolve this at the preliminary hearing.

Many arbitrations do not need a record of the proceedings, especially given the widespread availability of audio and video recording technology. In certain circumstances, however, it may be advantageous to have a professionally created record of the proceedings. The parties may agree to hire a court reporter and share the cost for a complex case where the hearing will extend over several days or weeks. A transcript of the hearing will aid in preparing post-hearing briefs. You may also want to use a court reporter when one or more witnesses who will be testifying under oath in the arbitration proceeding are also testifying in a court case involving the same subject matter. While arbitration proceedings are considered confidential, witnesses who testify in court can be impeached by any prior statement made under oath, even if made in an arbitration proceeding.

When holding a virtual hearing, the videoconferencing platform normally has an option to record. Commercial firms can provide a service where they create and link a written transcript to the video. Even for a live hearing, an audio or video recording can be made. Sometimes the arbitrator will record the hearing for later reference when writing the award and crafting an opinion. Often in arbitration, though, no recording is needed.

#### 3.5.2.9 Interpreter

Any party desiring an interpreter at the hearing must arrange for one, and unless otherwise agreed, must assume the service's costs. If applicable, it is wise to discuss the need for an interpreter at the preliminary hearing. Lack of an interpreter on the hearing date may cause a hearing to be postponed. Do not have a family member or a fellow employee serve as an interpreter for a party or witness. Such persons may not have a good enough grasp of one of the two languages and may not be familiar with necessary figures of speech. When you need an interpreter, hire a certified interpreter, and ideally, one who provides interpreter services in court.

#### 3.5.2.10 Necessary Accommodations

At the preliminary hearing, the arbitrator will normally inquire whether anyone attending the hearing requires special accommodations. If so, discuss with the arbitrator and other advocates how to accommodate those needs.

#### 3.5.2.11 Site Inspections

In some arbitrations, you may need the arbitrator to visit a particular site or accident scene. Site inspections are most common in construction and accident cases, particularly catastrophic accidents. Arrange the site visit; in most situations the arbitrator, the advocates, the parties, and some of the testifying witnesses will attend. Occasionally, opposing counsel may request that they be permitted to take photographs and/or videos of the site during the arbitrator's site visit for use later when the hearing resumes. Unless there is a serious reason to refuse, grant those requests—your cooperation may not be reciprocated, but obstinacy certainly will. Photographs and videos not only preserve the scene as the arbitrator saw it, they are also valuable visual aids at the hearing. Used in context with other evidence, you can demonstrate a view of the site that the arbitrator did not see, or one they saw but did not appreciate the relevance of at the time.

#### 3.5.2.12 Experts

Utilize expert opinions when the matter in question is technical and only a person with specialized skills can clarify the issue for the arbitrator(s). If opposing counsel intends to call an expert witness, you will most likely need to call an expert also. Avoid calling multiple experts to testify on the same technical issue. Rarely does cumulative expert evidence provide any tactical advantage and it only prolongs the hearing. At the preliminary hearing, the arbitrator normally inquires whether the advocates intend to introduce expert testimony at the hearing. If they do, the arbitrator will designate a date by which the depositions must be taken. The timing of the exchange of experts' curriculum vitae and their written expert opinions often generates disagreement among advocates in arbitration. Discuss and decide them at the preliminary hearing.

### 3.5.2.13 Appeal Procedures

The rules of some dispute resolution organizations include provisions allowing parties to pre-elect a second panel of arbitrators to hear any appeals from the first panel's decision. This appellate procedure is normally used in cases involving huge damage claims where the stakes are so high that the parties are unwilling to risk a single arbitration panel issuing an unchallengeable binding award. If you represent a client in this type of arbitration, consider raising appeal procedures at the preliminary hearing, or consider discussing this matter with a representative of the administering organization in a separate conference outside the presence of the arbitrator.

### 3.5.2.14 Pre-Arbitration Mediation

If the parties' arbitration clause or submission agreement does not provide for pre-arbitration mediation, the arbitrator may ask the parties to consider that option at the preliminary hearing. Alternatively, the arbitrator might ask the administering organization to raise this matter with the advocates in a separate conference.

A different neutral normally conducts the mediation. A skillful mediator can resolve in a few hours many cases that would require days or even weeks of arbitration. In most situations, there is much benefit and very little risk in trying mediation first. Even if the mediation process fails to resolve the dispute, it might result in the informal disclosure of information that obviates the need for further discovery in the subsequent arbitration. Mediation might drain anger and hostility from the dispute, permitting the arbitration to proceed more efficiently and guaranteeing a less-costly arbitration.

Some situations do not benefit from mediation. The parties may need an opinion with the award to guide their future conduct, and mediations do not result in opinions, or scheduling mediation could delay the arbitration hearing in a time-sensitive situation.

### 3.5.2.15 Additional Preliminary Hearings

If any issues remain unresolved at the end of the preliminary hearing and require a later status report or briefing and oral argument by counsel, the arbitrator may schedule additional hearings.

| PRELIMINARY HEARING TOPICS | |
|---|---|
| **NORMALLY DISCUSSED** | **SOMETIMES DISCUSSED** |
| Civility and professionalism | Rules and law |
| Burden and standard of proof | Prehearing briefs |
| Discovery | Stenographer |
| Witness lists | Mediation |
| Exhibits | Arbitrability |
| Stipulations | Amended pleadings |
| Sequestration | Joinder of parties |
| Hearing date | Observers |
| Place and format of room for hearing | Interpreter |
| Hearing length | Accommodations |
| Subpoenas | Site inspections |
| Audiovisual aids | Experts |
| Final oral arguments | Additional preliminary hearings |
| Post-hearing briefs | |
| Nature and form of award | |

## 3.6 Prehearing Discovery

Historically, there has been no right to formal discovery in arbitration proceedings. Opponents of arbitration discovery argue that the discovery process is incompatible with speedy, economical resolution of disputes—which is the goal of arbitration. Proponents argue that without discovery, parties cannot uncover key information relevant to the arbitrator's decision, and this leads to unjust results. Also, without discovery, there is a high risk that surprise evidence will be offered for introduction at the hearing and that the hearing will be interrupted to permit counsel to argue the admissibility of such evidence or to allow counsel time to arrange for and introduce controverting evidence. These interruptions and delays, argue the discovery proponents, may take up more time than limited prehearing discovery.

While this argument continues, discovery decisions are often in the hands of the parties or the arbitrator. In some instances, parties have selected arbitration for reasons other than efficiency and low cost, such as to have a panel of experts or to preserve confidentiality, and are amenable to extensive discovery.

The upshot of all this is a trend toward permitting at least some limited discovery in arbitration proceedings. Most arbitrators, for example, permit counsel to depose witnesses who will not be available for the hearing. Others allow broad discovery, depending on the complexity of the case, and particularly where the parties can agree on the scope of discovery. When faced with a decision whether to ask for or resist discovery, ask yourself, "Without discovery, will the arbitration hearing simply be a series of glorified depositions, supervised by arbitrators whose time must be compensated, and consisting largely of a search for proof instead of a showing of truth?" If you answer yes to this question, it is probably in the best interests of your client to seek or accede to reasonable discovery.

Once you decide to participate in discovery, the next question is how to proceed. Like litigation, discovery in an arbitration proceeding allows counsel to gather information they will use to support their various contentions at the arbitration hearing. However, unlike court litigation where a specific set of procedural rules governs the discovery process, absent a specific statutory provision or court rule, no uniform set of rules govern arbitration discovery practice. Some administering organizations may have default discovery rules for certain types of arbitration.[14] In most circumstances, discovery procedures in arbitration are left to the discretion and agreement of counsel. When counsel cannot agree, the arbitrator will specify the discovery procedures. They may designate procedures of their own formulation or direct the parties to use all or a portion of the federal discovery rules or the discovery rules of the local jurisdiction. Discuss these matters at the preliminary hearing. Leave the preliminary hearing with a clear understanding of the specific limitations that the arbitrator has placed on various forms of discovery, including 1) depositions, 2) interrogatories, 3) requests for production of documents, and 4) requests to admit.

---

14. *See, e.g., Initial Discovery Protocols for Employment Arbitration Cases*, Am. Arb. Ass'n. (Apr. 2013), https://www.adr.org/sites/default/files/document_repository/Initial-Discovery-Protocols-for-Employment-Arbitration-Cases.pdf (last visited Jun. 2024).

# • Chapter Four •

## Preparing for the Arbitration Hearing

*The work is hard but it is worth it. Don't give up.*
*—Lin-Manuel Miranda*[1]

Preparing for the hearing, although time-consuming and tedious, is singularly important to a successful outcome in arbitration. Like preparing a case for trial, getting ready for an arbitration hearing includes preparing your client, your witnesses, and your exhibits. Paramount is refining your initial story design—enhancing the drama of your story while keeping your case theory clearly perceptible through all the dramatic details. Your goal is effective persuasion. Accomplishing this refinement precedes everything else in your arbitration preparations.

If you approach all the hearing preparation tasks described in this chapter with an attitude of thoroughness and attention to detail, your ultimate hearing presentation will weather any storm. Your experience will be much like that described in a story about a farmer's hired hand. Interviewing a potential helper, the farmer asked about his faults. "Well," the man answered, "the last fellow I worked for said I was awful hard to wake up during a bad windstorm at night." The farmer hired him, and a few weeks later a heavy windstorm hit the area. The farmer woke instantly and went to waken the hired hand so they could check on stock and equipment, but the man would not wake up. Frustrated, the farmer ventured out alone. When he got to the barn, he found the barn doors securely fastened. The haystack was tightly anchored with a heavy tarpaulin. The lumber pile had heavy stones on top. A great light dawned on the farmer. He now knew why his hired man slept soundly while the wind blew hard at night.[2]

### 4.1 Designing the Persuasive Trial Story

If you are an effective advocate, by the time you are preparing your client and your case for the arbitration hearing, you have given considerable thought to the

1. Lin-Manuel Miranda (@Lin_Manuel), Twitter (Dec. 31, 2017, 3:19 PM), https://twitter.com/Lin_Manuel/status/947562956140752897?lang=en (last visited Jun. 2024).
2. Anecdote adapted from Jacob M. Braude, New Treasury of Stories for Every Speaking and Writing Occasion, 306 (1959).

persuasive trial story you will present to the arbitrators. Let's take a moment, though, to review the techniques for designing such a story (Lore & Lubet, *MTA*).

| SIX BASIC CHARACTERISTICS OF A PERSUASIVE TRIAL STORY |
| --- |
| Explains the reasons people acted as they did |
| Accounts for all the known or undeniable facts |
| Told by credible witnesses |
| Supported by factual details |
| Accords with common sense; contains no implausible elements |
| Organized in a way that makes each succeeding fact more likely |

Your story must have two principal aspects: a theory and a theme. The theory is simply the adaptation of your story to the legal issues in the case. You should be able to communicate it in a short paragraph. A successful theory is simple, logical, credible, and addresses the legal elements of your case. In developing your theory, ask yourself three questions:

1) What happened?
2) Why did it happen?
3) Why does that mean that my client should win?

Primarily, your theory should appeal to logic. Your theme, on the other hand, should be a single sentence that appeals to moral force. It should justify the morality of your theory and appeal to a sense of justice.

A typical theme might be:

> The decedent lived the last three years of their life not knowing that the defendant was methodically draining all the assets from their estate.

or,

> The defendant invested the plaintiff's money in stocks that they thought were secure enough to risk a substantial part of their own wealth.

It may sound backward, but the best way to design a successful trial story is to plan your final argument. This technique also lays the groundwork for the structure of your opening statement. In your final arbitration preparations—before you prepare your client and witnesses and select your exhibits—think through that final argument. Ask yourself:

- What do I want to say in the final argument?
- What evidence must I introduce or elicit so I can say it?

The answers to these questions provide a broad outline of what your ideal trial story. This also provides an outline for how to prepare your case in chief for the hearing. When doing this:

- First list the legal elements of every claim or defense that you hope to establish through your story.
- List the evidence (potential testimony and documents) that you have available to support each element.
- Evaluate the strengths and weaknesses of each witness. Consider inconsistencies and gaps in each witness's testimony, the admissibility of the testimony, and the credibility of each witness.
- Select witnesses whose testimony is both necessary and sufficient to tell your story.
- Establish an order in which the witnesses will testify based on 1) your need to have arbitrators remember the details of the testimony (usually testimony at the beginning and the end of a hearing is best remembered); 2) your need for logical progression of your story; 3) your need to maximize their dramatic impact.

If you have not already done so, research the law applicable to your client's situation to enable you to list the legal elements or factors of every claim or defense. Although you are arbitrating the case, jury instructions can still assist with identifying the law that must be proved. Also include in the outline any contractual requirements you must prove or disprove. An arbitrator, unlike a jury, will not be persuaded simply by a theme—your case theory must align with the legal requirements. The law and contract are the bedrock of your case preparation.

Next, if you have not already done so, make a timeline of the legally significant facts. A timeline enables you to synthesize a chronological story for your opening statement and direct examinations and helps establish the order in which the witnesses will testify. Use a case matrix to list the evidence for each legal element or factor and evaluate the strengths and weaknesses of that evidence. Appendix C has an example of a case evaluation matrix and explains how to use it.

Next, plan your cross-examination of your opponent's witnesses. Your goal is to diminish the persuasiveness of your opponent's trial story by defeating the logic of your opponent's theory and by undermining its theme or moral force. Planning for cross-examination has four steps:

1) List every potential witness that your opponent is likely to call to testify.
2) Consider all the grounds for precluding the testimony (e.g., competence, privilege, hearsay, etc.). Do the same thing for all documentary exhibits that your opponent might attempt to introduce through each witness.
3) Consider factual weaknesses related to the testimony of the witnesses (e.g., inconsistencies in testimony, witnesses' character, impeachable prior statements, etc.).
4) Consider how the witnesses can amplify your own theme and provide information favorable to your case.

Once you design your persuasive trial story, go back and reevaluate everything to ensure that your theory and theme are sufficiently developed and fully supported by credible, noncumulative evidence, and that your planned cross-examinations will defeat your opponent's trial story and not negatively impact your own. In designing your opening statement and final argument, begin and end each one with your theme. Consider where you can invoke your theme to your advantage in each while communicating a coherent theory of your case.

We now turn to a discussion of the details of preparing your client, your witnesses, and your exhibits for the arbitration hearing.

## 4.2 Preparing the Client

### *4.2.1 Explain the Arbitration Process*

When preparing your client, first fully explain the arbitration process, how it works, how it differs from litigation, and, if the arbitration is binding, how the award becomes a final judgment when filed in court and is subject to extremely limited challenges on appeal. This last point is very important. If you lose the arbitration, you do not want your client complaining that you never informed them that the arbitrator's award was, for all practical purposes, final and binding. In fact, during client preparation, it is a very good idea to have your client sign a statement that they understand the binding nature of the arbitrator's award. The key point here is to explain the process as clearly and as simply as possible.

### *4.2.2 Make Your Client Feel at Ease*

Be especially attuned to anxious feelings your client may be experiencing. To counteract those feelings, put your client at ease and provide answers to any questions they might have about what will occur at the hearing. The more your client becomes comfortable while talking to you about the dispute, the more comfortable they will be discussing it in front of opposing counsel and the arbitrator. Share with them your strategy for winning the case. Identify the strong as well as the weak points of your case. Explain how their testimony helps to implement your overall strategy.

### 4.2.3 *Explain How to Testify*

Your client may want to know exactly what to say at the hearing and how to say it. Explain that the rules governing truthful testimony in arbitration are the same as in litigation, namely that untrue statements can constitute perjury. Advise your client also that opposing counsel will have the opportunity to cross-examine after the direct examination. Tell your client it is important not to say something that they know is not fully true on direct examination, because they will most probably be forced to admit or imply its partial falsity on cross-examination. This, you should advise, would be most damaging to their case and perhaps quite humiliating personally as well. Mark Twain learned this lesson when he was disembarking from a trip to Europe. The world-acclaimed humorist became annoyed when a customs official began rummaging through his baggage. "My good friend," he politely remarked to the official, "you don't have to mix up all my things. There are only clothes in there—nothing but clothes."

The official pulled out a full quart of bourbon, exclaiming, "You call this 'just clothes'?"

"Sure thing," Twain retorted. "That's my nightcap!"[3]

### 4.2.4 *Ask Your Client Questions as You Would on Direct Examination*

Take your client through the direct examination as you will at the arbitration hearing.[4] Ask nonleading questions. Explain that narrative responses are fine with respect to certain questions, particularly relating to their educational background, work experiences, and the background events defining the dispute. But explain that other questions require them to answer only what is asked and keep responses shorter. When your client is answering your questions in this exercise, revise your bullets of the questions to indicate where you should use closed, rather than open, questions to focus on legally significant information. Take your client through the whole case—touching on issues of both liability and damages—in this manner. Then run through your revised questions with the client to make sure the examination flows well and emphasizes key parts of your client's testimony.

### 4.2.5 *Subject Your Client to Cross-Examination*

Cross-examine your client as opposing counsel is most likely to do. Do not soft pedal. If possible, let your client experience the effects of impeachment in this exercise.

---

3. Anecdote adapted from BRAUDE, *supra* note 2, at 24.
4. *See* section 5.3.

Ask them a series of questions relating to their direct testimony. Then, if available, give them a copy of the transcript of the deposition or their notes taken some months before. Let your client squirm in the chair while searching for words to explain away seemingly contradictory statements appearing in the transcript or notes. Allow your client to recognize the limits of their memory, and instruct your client that it is all right to answer "I don't remember" to a question from opposing counsel. If you are working with an associate, the practice cross-examinations can be performed by them so the client also experiences having a different attorney perform the examination.

### 4.2.6 Encourage Your Client to Divulge to You Both Good and Bad Information Relating to the Case

Even during hearing preparation, your client may avoid giving you all the pertinent information regarding their case for fear of damaging their claims or defenses. Let them know that it is very important that they tell you everything about the events in question—both good and bad—so that you will be prepared to adequately respond to the evidence opposing counsel offers at the hearing. Impress on your client that withholding "bad" evidence may seriously jeopardize your ability to adequately represent them at the hearing. Ask probing questions. Be thorough. Your own professional reputation can be damaged if your client is impeached or is shown to be testifying falsely. If your preparatory questioning is incomplete, you may be placing yourself squarely in the jaws of an embarrassing defeat.

The importance of asking the right questions is ably illustrated by the story of the teenager who was sitting one day on a log at the edge of a beautiful lake in a southern state. They were lazily watching their fishing line bobbing in the water. A car drove past, then stopped. Several tourists looked over the fresh, inviting water of the lake, and one of them said, "Are there any snakes in this lake?"

"Nope, no snakes in this lake," replied the teen. So, the visitors peeled off their clothes and went in for a swim. For half an hour they swam and splashed in the cool water and had a good time.

When they emerged from the lake, one of them had a thought, and said to the teen, "How come there are no snakes in this lake?"

With a half grin, they replied, "Because the alligators ate them all up."[5]

### 4.2.7 Avoid Judging or Criticizing Your Client's Role in the Events Giving Rise to the Dispute

Do not give your client the impression that you are being judgmental in any way, or that you disapprove of any statements they made or actions they took with respect to

---

5. Anecdote adapted from BRAUDE, *supra* note 2, at 386.

the events that precipitated the dispute. If you do, they may skirt the important issues at the arbitration hearing and attempt to misrepresent what really happened. Keep a neutral tone during the preparatory session, and express sympathy for their situation. Most importantly, listen carefully to everything your client says during the session. Make sure you fully understand all the information they are trying to communicate to you. You may discover a new fact that is quite important to your case. An attorney we know refers to these as piñata cases—every time you poke at it, another fact falls out.

### *4.2.8 Warn Your Client to Avoid Inappropriate Body Language When Not Testifying*

Counsel the client about the negative impact of the client's nonverbal communication during the arbitration hearing at the times they are not testifying. Your client's frowns, grimaces, sneers, scowls, mocking laughter, and the like during the presentations of either side will not advance their chances of a favorable award. Counsel your client to appear interested, objective, and reasonable when the opposing side's witnesses are testifying. Even a silent face can speak a thousand words. Justice John Harlan once played golf with his friend, the Episcopal Bishop of Washington. On the third tee, the bishop missed the ball several times—but made no comment. He looked, however, a picture of disgust. Justice Harlan grinned. "Bishop," he said, "that was the most profane silence I ever witnessed."[6]

## 4.3 Preparing the Witness

You normally call witnesses in addition to your client when you present your case. Choose your witnesses carefully, only calling those with directly relevant testimony or information you cannot get from your client that is central to the case. A weak witness may hurt your case more than help it. The only way to anticipate how a witness will perform at the hearing is through preparation.[7]

The key to effective witness preparation is determining how the witness will answer your questions and those of opposing counsel. The best way to determine this is through a hearing simulation. Conducting a hearing simulation requires additional preparation but will result in a great benefit during the hearing.

### *4.3.1 Conducting a Hearing Simulation*

When conducting a hearing simulation, recreate the environment of an actual hearing. Hold the simulation in a conference room or an empty office if you will be having a live hearing—somewhere away from familiar surroundings for your

---

6. Anecdote adapted from James C. Humes, Speaker's Treasury Of Anecdotes About The Famous 59 (1978).
7. *See* sections 5.3 and 5.4.

client or witnesses—or on the virtual conference system that the hearing will use for a virtual hearing. If you are having a virtual hearing where the witness will be with you in the same room, practice that way; if you will be in separate locations, have the witness practice from the same location they will use for the hearing. Also, if you will conduct the direct examination of the witnesses, prepare that witness yourself. You lose much of the advantage of preparation if someone else prepares your witnesses. Make the connection between you and your witness, not between your associate and your witness.

### *4.3.2 Both You and the Witness Should Be Fully Aware of the Witness's Prior Testimony*

If the witness has made any written statements or has been deposed, you should both review those statements before the hearing simulation. Make sure the witness does not change any facts previously stated or change the story in any way. If the witness has already made previous inconsistent statements, find out what the witness intends to say under oath during the hearing, and prepare for opposing counsel to impeach your witness.

### *4.3.3 Put the Witness Through a Direct Examination*

Prepare your direct examination questions ahead of time and rehearse what will happen at the hearing. Make sure you:

- cover all the questions,
- listen actively to the witness, and
- ask follow-up questions to elicit any legally significant facts the witness left out.

How? Bullet your questions. Below each primary bullet, have sub-bullets of the critical facts.

Proceed through this exercise without critiquing the answers—as if the witness were actually testifying at the arbitration hearing. Critique after the exercise. If, however, an answer regarding a critical aspect of your case completely surprises you, stop and discuss it in detail so the witness can think through what they just said and clarify the precise facts. Re-ask the problem questions at the end of the exercise and evaluate the answers again. Remind the witness that you are only interested in their truthful testimony, but if answers are subject to misinterpretation by the arbitrator, you want the witness to use words that clearly and truthfully communicate what occurred.

Never tell the witness how to answer. Instead, modify your questions to elicit truthful answers that will make sense to the arbitrator(s). Once under oath at the hearing, your witness is much more likely to revert to the answer that comes to them rather than using any wording you told them to use.

### 4.3.4 *Put the Witness Through a Cross-Examination*

If your witness is not prepared for cross-examination, opposing counsel may neutralize any gains you made with the arbitrator during the direct examination. Prepare a list of questions you think opposing counsel may ask (and even some difficult ones you don't think opposing counsel will ask) and see how the witness responds. If your witness seems unsure of the answers, even though you know they are giving true testimony, practice the routine until you both become comfortable with the procedure.

Ask the questions in a tone and manner that opposing counsel is likely to use. Get a feeling for how the witness may respond to a question asked in the accusatory tone of an adversary conducting a cross-examination. Acting in the manner of the opposing attorney prepares your witness for the hearing much more effectively than simply explaining the questions that the other side may ask.

### 4.3.5 *Preparing Expert Witnesses*

Prepare each expert thoroughly, including presenting the expert with a hypothetical question or questions regarding your case. Your expert must convince the arbitrator that they are the person with the answers. Prepare your expert's testimony on qualifications, showing that their opinions on the precise topic at issue are highly valued by other experts in the same field. Stress to your expert that sound reasoning in their answers will determine whether they appear credible to the arbitrator. Warn the expert in advance that you will likely not stipulate to credentials at the hearing because you want the arbitrator to hear them firsthand. Also inform your expert that at the hearing you may offer to stipulate to the credentials of your opponent's expert to reduce any positive impact of their qualifications.

### 4.3.6 *Remind Witnesses of the Danger of Nonverbal Communication*

You warned your clients about the adverse effects of body language; similarly inform your witnesses. Body language—particularly facial expressions—may send signals that conflict with a witness's spoken words or that make them less credible. Watch for such facial expressions while preparing your witnesses and point them out, explaining the impact of the nonverbal communication in relation to their spoken words. Although there are exceptions, in most situations it is best if witnesses remain essentially expressionless when testifying. Though elementary in theory, this is not always simple in execution—even if your witness is naturally expressionless.

### 4.3.7 *Advise Witnesses as to Proper Attire*

Instruct your witnesses to dress in attire appropriate for a courtroom trial. The informal setting should not induce your client or witnesses to dress casually for a hearing of this nature. Ordinarily, your witnesses should dress in clean, neat, conservative clothes. There may be reasons for your witnesses to "dress down" depending on the location or setting of the arbitration or the impression you wish to convey to the arbitrators; obviously, give the witnesses specific instructions in such instances.

#### 4.3.8 Inform Witnesses of the Order of Testimony

If you will be calling more than one witness, make sure each witness knows when they are scheduled to testify. If witnesses are to be on call, make sure you know how to reach them to let them know when they should appear to testify. If witnesses are appearing remotely, confirm that their connection is working and that they are waiting on standby. Do not rely on the equipment test you did a week before; internet failures happen at the most inconvenient times. Have a backup plan, even if it is only a phone call, and confirm that the witness can access that backup equipment on the day they are scheduled to testify.

#### 4.3.9 Warn Nonclient Witnesses Regarding Possible Inquiry Into Witness Preparation

Advise your nonclient witnesses that they may be required to testify about what you and they discussed while preparing for the arbitration hearing.

## 4.4 Preparing the Exhibits

Before preparing your client and other witnesses, you will have selected most of the exhibits you need to present your case effectively. Premark evidentiary exhibits—documentary evidence—and place them in the sequence in which you intend to introduce them into evidence. If there are group exhibits or summaries, mark them as such. In larger cases, place the exhibits in binders and tab them. Create a set of exhibits for each arbitrator, a set for the witnesses, and, normally, a set for opposing counsel. Practice entering the documents into evidence and having your witnesses read pertinent parts when you prepare your witnesses.

If you are using a laptop or tablet with trial presentation software, it may enable you to search documents by bates stamp number, or even permit you to use an exhibit outline with bar codes to link to each document.

#### 4.4.1 Preparing Demonstrative Exhibits

Prepare demonstrative exhibits that are both eye-catching and interesting.

Good demonstrative exhibits help tell your story to the arbitrator. They not only help the arbitrator understand your case, but remember it as well. Large reproductions of original documents, in color as opposed to black and white, can be very persuasive in conveying your story, particularly if they are left exposed for reference by witnesses from time to time as the hearing proceeds. White on black slides can sometimes be more easily read than color slides, particularly if your arbitrator is red/green color blind.

Technology provides opportunities for a wide array of demonstrative exhibits. Using computer-generated graphics, an animator can recreate past events in a simulation, depict an object that rotates and increases in size, represent complex interactions, generate a timeline, or enable a witness to annotate or draw attention to a document with a callout box.

### 4.4.2 Preparing Photographs and Visual Recordings

As mentioned earlier, have a professional photographer or videographer take photographs and videos of evidence. This ensures the quality desired for an effective exhibit. Also, the photographer or videographer, an outside party from the arbitration proceedings, can authenticate the location of the scene in the photograph or video. Always take several shots of the same scene to offer different views and perspectives. When deciding on which photos or videos to use as exhibits, look at the scene from the perspective of both parties and choose the depiction that best suits your case.

### 4.4.3 Securing Physical Objects

If you will be displaying an actual object (i.e., a piece of machinery) as an exhibit, locate and secure that object as soon as possible. This will prevent the object from being altered or disappearing. Label each object before the hearing.

### 4.4.4 Anticipating Opponent's Exhibits

Try to anticipate any exhibits your opponent will use and be prepared to present your own form of that exhibit. For example, if you anticipate that your opponent will use a photograph of an accident scene as an exhibit, bring your own photo of the same scene so the arbitrator can view it from both parties' perspectives. This prevents the other side from obtaining any advantage by introducing one-sided evidence to the arbitrator.

### 4.4.5 Ensure Witnesses Have Identical Perceptions of Exhibits

Make sure your client and your witnesses are familiar with your exhibits and that they can identify and explain any objects in the exhibits. Also, as an example, if the exhibits represent a particular area, make sure the witnesses are all familiar enough with the area that they can identify what is in the picture as well as the surrounding area. Do not underestimate the risks of inconsistent testimony among witnesses caused by differing perceptions of exhibits. It is common knowledge that when looking at any object, some witnesses might observe something that is not there, and other witnesses might not observe accurately what is there. Dr. Theodor Billroth, a famous Viennese surgeon, once told his medical students that a doctor needed two abilities: freedom from nausea and the power of observation. He then dipped his finger into a bitterly foul fluid and licked it off, requesting them to do the same. They did it quite mechanically and without flinching. Grinning broadly, Dr. Billroth said to his pride-filled class, "You have passed the first test well, but not the second, for none of you noticed that I dipped my first finger in the liquid but licked the second."[8]

---

8. Anecdote adapted from HUMES, *supra* note 7, at 142.

# • Chapter Five •

## Advocacy During the Arbitration Hearing

*It has got a lot of issues as a story in terms of a film adaptation. Something that's not film friendly, so to speak . . . . It is episodic. That was a big challenge. You do tumble from one adventure to the next, not necessarily building on each other and not necessarily interconnected, either. . . . But having to take that chance as a screenwriter when you're adapting a novel, and figure it out and to make it work, it does mean you take liberties.*

—*Phillipa Boyens*[1]

*Just because you make a good plan, doesn't mean that's what's gonna happen.*

—*Taylor Swift*[2]

Designing and telling stories is an important function to the arbitration advocate, but never lose track of larger whole—the screenwriter function.[3] By this stage of arbitration, you are like a novelist: you have written the story and know how it opens, how it ends, and the chapters between. Now, you become the screenwriter, adapting the story to a dialogue format and inserting acting cues and directions. You must plot out the crossings and groupings of witnesses and the problems of sets (audiovisual equipment, etc.). You must visualize each scene; hear the words of each witness.

Screenwriters use multiple devices in their scripts for heightening effect, increasing dramatic impact, and economizing exposition. Examples of the last device might be a prologue, such as Galadriel's monologue at the beginning of *The Fellowship of the Ring*,[4] or the text scroll from the beginning of *Star Wars*,[5] telling the audience how to understand the movie as it unfolds, and an epilogue, like Red's

1. Ethan Gilsdorf, *Hobbit Week: A Conversation with Hobbit Screenwriter Philippa Boyens,* Wired (Dec. 11, 2012), https://www.wired.com/2012/12/philippa-boyens/ (last visited Jun. 2024).
2. Brian Hiatt, *Taylor Swift in Wonderland,* Rolling Stone (Oct. 25, 2012), https://www.rollingstone.com/music/music-news/taylor-swift-in-wonderland-180107/ (last visited Jun. 2024).
3. *See Generally,* David Ball & Joshua Karton, Theater For Trial (2017); Daniel P. Selmi & Rebecca A. Delfino, Principles Of Appellate Advocacy (2d. ed. 2021); Mary Beth Beazley, A Practical Guide To Appellate Advocacy (6th ed. 2022).
4. The Lord Of The Rings: The Fellowship Of The Ring (New Line Cinema, 2001).
5. Star Wars (20th Century Fox, 1977).

recap near the end of *The Shawshank Redemption*,[6] through which the audience learns the significance of what they just saw. These devices correspond quite neatly to the opening statement and the closing argument in arbitration.

After you, in screenwriter mode, complete and deliver the converted mental script, the real work begins. You must now add "director" to your roles: casting (choosing witnesses), rehearsing (preparing witnesses), costuming (ensuring witnesses are properly dressed), staging (making hearing room arrangements), and nearly all aspects of preproduction.

Unlike in a movie, however, you don't get to sit in the audience and watch your work unfold. The final step is less like a movie and more like premiering on Broadway: you must act in the show and direct it as well. Fortunately, there is very rarely singing. During the entire arbitration hearing, you must wear three artistic hats simultaneously—those of writer, director, and actor. You are continuously refining the script while the show (hearing) is in progress. As director, you bring the script to life, coordinating all elements of the courtroom production to give the presentation unity and proportion and assisting each participant—including yourself—in making their maximum contribution to the hearing.

***Online Catalog***

Throughout this chapter are references to the online catalog, which includes demonstration videos. These are available at:

https://www.nita.org/modern-trial-advocacy
Password: NITAModTriAd6

Demonstrations 1.1 and 1.2: Repetition and Duration during Cross

Demonstration 5: Refreshing Recollection

Demonstrations 7.1 and 7.2: Supportive versus Destructive Cross

Demonstration 8: Reasserting Control during Cross

Demonstration 9.1: Impeachment by Prior Inconsistent Statement

Demonstration 13: Admitting an Exhibit—Business Record

Demonstration 15: Admitting an Exhibit—Text Message

Alas, you are not the only director of this production—another screenwriter/director/actor is here with their own version of the story. And then there are the producers (the arbitrators) retaining authority over the whole production, even those aspects of the drama that you consider purely artistic. Nonetheless, you are ultimately responsible for communicating your vision to the audience—the arbitrators/producers—and molding their perception of the logical and emotional content of

6. The Shawshank Redemption (Columbia Pictures, 1994).

the production ultimately created. If you cannot adapt to their demands while maintaining your vision, you will be blamed—just ask Zack Snyder.[7]

This artistry must be accomplished within the constraints of applicable procedural rules. To this topic, we now turn.

## 5.1 Procedural Rules

The procedural rules applicable to a trial will not automatically apply in an arbitration hearing. Hearing rules may vary depending upon the content of the arbitration clause, the rules of any administering dispute resolution organization, the needs or desires of counsel, and the preferences of individual arbitrators. Therefore, before the scheduled hearing date and ideally even before the preliminary hearing, carefully read the arbitration clause and the pertinent rules of the administering dispute resolution organization.

If you note any unusual and undesirable requirements, raise these matters for discussion at the preliminary hearing. Hearing rules drafted years before into an arbitration clause—and perhaps by counsel not currently involved in the arbitration—are sometimes inappropriate for the current dispute. Work with opposing counsel and the arbitrator to modify such rules during the preliminary hearing.

The same holds true for the rules of administering organizations. On many occasions, their rules need to be clarified in relation to your dispute's idiosyncrasies, or to the parties' identity and configuration. Here are a few illustrative examples:

### *5.1.1 Application of the Federal Rules of Civil Procedure*

Your dispute resolution organization may require the arbitrators to apply the Federal Rules of Civil Procedure to any procedural question that arises in the hearing. If applying these rules will work a hardship on you or your client in arbitrating the dispute, bring specific matters to the arbitrator's attention prior to the hearing. If the rules are causing you problems, because of expense or inconvenience, then opposing counsel may be experiencing similar problems.

### *5.1.2 Testimony Not Required to Be Under Oath*

You will want all witness statements made at the hearing on the merits to be under oath. Arbitrators generally have authority to administer an oath and may do so at their own initiative, but it is safest to explicitly request that all witnesses be under oath in advance of the hearing.

---

7. Anthony Breznican, *Justice League: The Shocking, Exhilarating, Heartbreaking True Story of #TheSnyderCut* (Vanity Fair, Feb. 22, 2021), https://www.vanityfair.com/hollywood/2021/02/the-true-story-of-justice-league-snyder-cut (last visited Jun. 2024).

### 5.1.3 Evidence by Affidavit

Some organizations' rules permit the arbitrators to consider affidavits of witnesses in lieu of their appearance and testimony at the hearing. If you object to affidavit evidence, notify opposing counsel and the arbitrator of your objection before the hearing so you can either work out an agreement or have the arbitrator rule on your objection.

### 5.1.4 Authorized Representative

Ordinarily, organizations do not require parties to be represented by counsel during an arbitration hearing. Some rules permit a party to be represented by an "authorized representative" and to notify the opponent of such representation a few days before the hearing. If you receive notice of an authorized representative's identity, and it is a person you intend to subpoena and call as a witness, immediately bring this matter to the attention of the opposing party and the arbitrator, so that the representative's "independence" problem can be resolved. Once the problem is brought to their attention, the opposing party may opt to enlist another authorized representative, who can serve better in the capacity of independent advisor.

### 5.1.5 Decision and Award

Arbitration rules require arbitrators' decisions to be by a majority, unless a unanimous decision is required by the arbitration agreement or by law. If you and opposing counsel want the liability determination to be unanimous and any damage award to be by a majority, or some other such variation, raise this matter with the arbitrators before the hearing. Also, rules rarely include a provision explaining what occurs if one of three arbitrators finds it necessary to withdraw during an arbitration hearing due to ill health or a discovered conflict of interest, etc., and the remaining two arbitrators disagree on the result. If the parties are concerned this might happen, they should address it by prehearing agreement. Some rules require the arbitrators to provide no reasons for the award, and others permit arbitrators to award prejudgment interest. If you would prefer something different than what such rules allow, raise these matters in the prehearing stage and, perhaps ideally, in the preliminary hearing.

Above all, keep in mind that dispute resolution organizations' rules commonly have an automatic "waiver of rules" provision stating that any party who proceeds with an arbitration after knowing that any provision or requirement of the rules has not been complied with, and who fails to object in writing, is deemed to have waived the right to object. Thus, if you do not carefully review the arbitration rules pertinent to your case, you may find that you have wandered into a procedural quagmire from which you cannot gracefully escape. Some of these avoidable traps could affect your client's substantive, as well as procedural, rights. An ounce of prevention in these situations may, indeed, be worth a pound of cure.

## 5.2 Opening Statement

After calling the arbitration hearing to order, acknowledging their oath, and hearing any preliminary matters, the arbitrator will request that counsel proceed with the opening statements. Both claimant and respondent—or if multiple parties, all parties—are entitled to present an opening statement. The claimant usually speaks first, followed by the respondent.

The opening statement helps the arbitrator understand the evidence you are about to present. Its structure presents an oral synopsis, a prologue if you like, of the real-life human drama that is to follow. The outline identifies issues for the arbitrator while their mind is still fresh and uncluttered by volumes of evidence. It also alerts the arbitrator to questions of fact and law that the arbitrator will decide later.

The opening statement normally follows a simple format:

1) Introduction
2) Summary of facts, law, and theories
3) Presentation of facts
4) Brief statement of any applicable law, as appropriate
5) Comment on opposition's case
6) Restatement of summary of facts, law, and theories
7) Statement of any request for relief

We will explore each of these topics but will devote the most attention to the presentation of facts. We will also touch on the rule against argument, delivery technique, and objections. But first, we review some fundamental differences between an opening statement in an arbitration and an opening statement in a trial.

### *5.2.1 Basic Differences Between Arbitration and Trial Opening Statements*

You might expect that the opening statement you present in arbitration is much the same as you would give in court before a jury or judge. Not all arbitrators, however, conduct arbitration proceedings in the same way. Lawyers with trial experience who serve as arbitrators are likely to expect trial-like opening statements. But nonlawyers who become professional arbitrators may have very different expectations about the opening statement's purpose and use and about the "rules of the game" related to it. You may encounter an arbitrator or a chair of an arbitration panel who is highly judgmental, a stickler for precision of words, and one who views the arbitration process through lenses of strict compliance and hyper-technicality. On the other hand, you may experience an arbitrator who fails to take control of the proceeding, allows counsel to dictate the direction of the process at whim, and permits counsel wide latitude in the opening statement's content and length. If you have the misfortune to engage either of these types of arbitrators, be prepared for a trial by ordeal. Do not be surprised in such situations if you experience some of the following unusual opening statement procedures.

#### 5.2.1.1 Stipulations May Be Read Aloud

Be prepared for the arbitrator who requires that stipulations be read aloud at the time of the opening statement. An arbitrator may require this in more complex cases when a stenographic record is taken or an audio or video recording, which may be translated to text, and when the award will contain a reasoned opinion. Some arbitrators like to have a clear understanding up front of which facts are uncontested and which are not. Having the stipulations read at the beginning of the hearing allows the arbitrator to truncate later testimony that refers to already stipulated matters. Also, when preparing their reasoned opinion, all the stipulated facts will be consolidated conveniently in the beginning of the transcript or recording for drafting a statement of facts, and for reference, as needed. Having to unexpectedly read fact stipulations at the hearing's beginning might catch you off guard, particularly if you have prepared a condensed trial story that integrates both stipulated and contested facts. Clarify with the arbitrator at the preliminary hearing their preference for handling of stipulations.

#### 5.2.1.2 Written Opening Statements

Arbitrators who comprehend information more easily by reading than by listening may require counsel to submit written opening statements prior to the hearing in lieu of presenting oral opening statements. Also, some arbitrators believe oral opening statements are a waste of time—time that parties can better use presenting their evidence and making closing arguments. If you face such a situation and believe that an oral opening statement would better lay your client's story's groundwork, evaluate the pros and cons of requesting to present an oral opening statement. Consider the personality of the arbitrator, their proclivity to resist change, and all the surrounding circumstances. You do not want to antagonize an arbitrator by the very vehicle you intend to use to enlighten them.

#### 5.2.1.3 Claimant May Request to Make Opening Statement After Respondent

As pointed out above, in arbitration, as in a court trial, the claimant customarily makes an opening statement first, followed by the respondent. In a court trial, defense counsel sometimes waits until the beginning of their case to present an opening statement. That also occurs sometimes in arbitrations, although as a respondent's attorney it behooves you to make an opening statement before any evidence is offered to take advantage of the primacy effect and to frame the evidence in a way favorable to your client. But unlike a court trial, from time to time in arbitrations, a claimant might make a request to present an opening statement at the hearing's beginning, but after the respondent.

The parameters of the opening statement are entirely within the arbitrator's discretion. The arbitrator can limit the length and scope of opening statements, their detail or brevity, and their general manner or character. They can also entertain requests for changing the sequence of the opening statements and may, in fact, permit the claimant to present an opening statement after the respondent.

A respondent who has the burden of proof on a significant issue or has filed a counterclaim may be expected to proceed first. Or a claimant may have strategic or tactical reasons for presenting their opening statement second.

First, such a request can throw the respondent off balance. A lawyer for a respondent who has not conscientiously prepared an opening statement—waiting to hear claimant's opening statement first to formulate their response—may find themselves stumbling and at a loss for words if the arbitrator requires them to proceed first. In addition, claimant's counsel may find it advantageous to proceed second to have the last word. In the appropriate case, there might be a clear benefit to your client in addressing points covered by respondent's opening statement, outlining the claimant's position, and then quickly following that up with claimant's testimony while the pillars and framework of your trial story are still fresh in the arbitrator's mind.

A nonlawyer arbitrator or an arbitrator who lets the lawyers control the hearing might permit a claimant to proceed second. As respondent's counsel, you can of course object to such request; as claimant's counsel, you may consider making the request in the appropriate situation.

#### 5.2.1.4 Statements May Be Deemed to Constitute Admissions

Some arbitrators and hyper-technical opponents will listen carefully to your opening statement, hoping to catch you in some type of admission against your client's interest. Some arbitrators may hold you to these admissions of adverse facts—consciously or subconsciously—even though your evidence does not bear them out. Therefore, consider requesting that the arbitrator not hold against your client any inadvertent misstatement of fact that you might make in the opening statement.

#### 5.2.1.5 Omissions May Constitute Waiver of Claim or Defense

Similar to admissions against interest, though to a much lesser extent, an arbitrator may view what you omit in your opening statement to be a waiver of a claim or defense. Thus, if the arbitrator is a stickler for details, make it clear in your opening statement that your remarks are intentionally abbreviated in the interest of efficiency and economy and that, even though you do not specifically address a matter in your opening statement, you are not waiving any claim in your written demand or any defense in your written answer.

#### 5.2.1.6 Arbitrator May Permit a Reply and Surreply

Unlike a judge in a court proceeding, an arbitrator, on counsel's request, may permit a reply or a surreply to an opening statement. Although rare, this may occur in cases where there are counterclaims and/or where several arbitrations have been consolidated.

### *5.2.2 Rule Against Argument*

Opening statements in court prohibit argument, and arbitration practice generally corresponds. However, argument is a relative concept, defined in the eye of the beholder. Thus, in arbitration, as in court proceedings, certain types of remarks by counsel in the opening statement would satisfy a "bright line" test for constituting argument; others would not. Examples of remarks falling in the "obviously prohibited argument" category might include 1) urging the arbitrator to draw inferences from the facts and making certain conclusions, 2) explaining the importance of certain evidence, 3) suggesting how evidence should be weighed, 4) commenting directly on the credibility of witnesses, and 5) appealing overtly to a sense of mercy or justice. That said, you have significantly more leeway to include these arguments in your opening statement in arbitration than you would in a trial, but doing so may backfire in terms of persuasive advocacy.

As a general principle, impermissible argument occurs when an advocate seeks to tell the arbitrator how they should reach a decision. Because this broad principle is difficult to apply, other narrower tests have been developed to help make distinctions.

- The ***witness test*** questions whether a witness would be permitted to testify to the information in the opening statement; if so, it is deemed to be factual, and the opening statement would be proper. If the witness called to testify would not be permitted to testify to the information because it was deemed a conclusion—not helpful to the decision-maker—then the opening statement would be improper.
- The ***verification test*** questions whether the content of the opening statement can be verified, the point being that facts can be verified, argumentative conclusions cannot.
- Finally, under the ***"link" test***, remarks descend to the level of impermissible argument when counsel must supply a nonevidence-based explanation—a rhetorical embellishment to link independent evidence with the point they are trying to make.

An arbitrator may apply other tests related to counsel's delivery style to determine whether they have engaged in improper argument in the opening. Tone of voice can turn a simple factual statement into scornful argument. Rhetorical questions, even innocently formulated, can be piercingly argumentative and elicit anger. Finally, extreme repetition of facts can be deemed argumentative and even hostile during an opening statement.

The rule against argument does not mean that counsel can make no comments about the applicable law. In almost every opening statement, whether in court or in arbitration, there is a need to include some information about the law, if for no other reason than to let the trier of fact know what information is relevant to their determination. It is improper, however, for counsel in an opening statement to argue for a particular interpretation or construction of the law.

The essence of "argument" in the opening statement can perhaps best be summed up by the expression, "What is one person's expedient is another person's art."

There is a story told about Robert Henri, a well-known twentieth-century artist and art teacher. He was in a gallery standing before a fine Sargent painting when he noticed a brawny individual admiring the same canvas and murmuring: "They have given me a good place at last."

"You in this sort of work?" Henri inquired.

"Been in it for years," replied the man, "and this is the first time that I ever got on the line."

"Ah, indeed!" exclaimed Henri, "And where is your painting?" The man pointed to the Sargent.

"That?" asked Henri. "Why, Sargent painted that!"

The man sighed contentedly. "Yeah, I think Sargent was the bloke who painted the picture—but it was me who made the frame."[8]

### 5.2.3 Introduction and Summary

Your introduction and summary should orient the arbitrator to the disputants and the dispute. After introducing yourself and your client, immediately summarize the more detailed story that is to follow. The summary should contain a few sentences describing the dispute's factual contours, your theories of claims and defenses, and any necessary law to put the dispute in context. Often, counsel begins with a statement of theme—a single sentence that captures the moral force of the case. After that, focus on the overall theory of the case by describing the requirements of each claim or defense and answering the questions: What happened? Why did it happen? Why is my client's version correct? How can we be sure? Why does all this make sense? These questions are then answered in more detail during the next stage of the opening statement—the presentation of facts.

8. Anecdote adapted from Jacob M. Braude, New Treasury of Stories for Every Speaking and Writing Occasion 331 (1959).

## 5.2.4 *Presenting the Facts*

In your presentation of facts, state only facts that 1) you will support with evidence, 2) you believe to be true, and 3) you believe to be admissible. These three constraints protect you from discussing facts that you can only partially prove and from referring to facts for which you have no supporting evidence. They also prevent you from straying into collateral matters or from referring to topics that are not admissible. Beyond this simple formula for selecting facts, always practice the following principles when planning and delivering your opening statement (Lore & Lubet, *MTA*, section 13.3).

### 5.2.4.1 Be Brief and Keep it Interesting

Most arbitrators appreciate brevity in opening statements—particularly arbitrators who prepared for the hearing by reading the demand, answer, pleadings, and position statements. Brevity, however, is a relative concept. If you represent a claimant in a case against several respondents and you have separate theories involving different facts concerning each one, a "brief" opening statement may take forty-five minutes or more. If you represent a respondent in such a case, your opening may extend only ten to fifteen minutes. Frugally tailor the time to the task. And keep your presentation interesting. Convey to the arbitrator that your words will facilitate their decision-making.

### 5.2.4.2 Apply the Principle of Primacy

The arbitrator is more apt to remember information that they hear first in an arbitration proceeding than information buried in its succeeding stages. Start with information with the greatest impact on the arbitrator's decision and incorporate key facts that are critical, legally significant parts of your story.

### 5.2.4.3 Tie the Evidence to Legal Issues

Explain why these facts are important to the arbitrator's decision. Clearly relate selected evidence to the legal issues that the arbitrator must take into account when deciding the case.

### 5.2.4.4 Put the Puzzle Together

Tell your story in a narrative style and make it interesting. Proceed chronologically unless you are deviating from chronology to enhance your story. If combining or juxtaposing facts yields more persuasion than chronology, jettison chronology. Do not use a witness-by-witness approach. The technique, such as, "Mr. Jones will testify that . . ." and "Ms. Smith will testify that . . . " is boring and nonintegrative. If there are several witnesses, the arbitrator may get confused and start daydreaming. Once you lose the arbitrator's attention in your opening statement, you may also lose their sympathy for your client's plight—for good. Keep your story dynamic. Organize your story around a series of principal concepts supported by evidentiary details; weave in references to witnesses without making them the focal point of your narrative; connect the facts for the arbitrator; synthesize.

Do not leave the arbitrator's understanding of your message to chance. Put the factual puzzle together. If you let the arbitrator do it, important pieces may be omitted and its communicative value lost.

#### 5.2.4.5 Focus on Operative Facts

Arbitrations are won or lost on their facts, not solely on the applicable law. Focus the arbitrator's attention on the operative facts of your case. Operative facts include action and key events; the physical scene; transactions and agreements; relationship of the parties; business context, if any; and motives and motivations of the parties or key players.

#### 5.2.4.6 Emphasize Undisputed Evidence

Use your story to identify and highlight your central evidence. It should consist of the facts most essential to your case and, at the same time, the facts least likely to be disputed.

#### 5.2.4.7 Discard Tangential Facts

Eliminate "nice to know," nonessential information from your opening statement. The fact that your client, as a youth, won the national soapbox derby competition three years consecutively might be true, but it will not impress the average arbitrator. Tangential facts distract the arbitrator from your true message. They might even imply that your case is weak and you are grasping at any straw to bolster your client's chances.

#### 5.2.4.8 Deal Minimally with Bad Facts

If you are certain that opposing counsel will reveal negative information about your client or a witness during the arbitration hearing, control its affect by mentioning it in the opening statement. After introducing all the favorable information about your client or witness, disclose the negative in a brief, passing way, without dwelling on it, before moving on to the rest of your opening statement.

### *5.2.5 Brief Statement of Law*

Reserve the bulk of your legal arguments for the closing argument. But remember, an arbitration in which the arbitrator is a lawyer approximates a bench trial in court. Advocates have much more latitude in discussing legal issues than they do in a jury trial. At a minimum, the claimant should set out the requirements of each claim that the evidence will prove, and the respondent should specify which requirements the evidence will show are unmet during the initial summary of the case theory. As mentioned above, if you feel that an arbitrator must understand the law to comprehend your opening statement, then you may wish to refer sparingly to pertinent cases or statutes during the presentation of facts. When necessary, refer to applicable administrative rules, regulations, or rulings. This is still an opening statement, however; refrain from arguing the proper interpretation or construction of the law or regulations.

### 5.2.6 Comments on Opposition's Case

In planning your opening statement, determine how much attention you wish to devote to the opposition's case. This is true whether you represent a claimant or a respondent. Here are some pointers to consider.

#### 5.2.6.1 Anticipating the Respondent's Opening

In most opening statements in arbitration, there will be no reply or surreply. If you represent a claimant and respondent's counsel discusses affirmative defenses or counterclaims in their opening statement, you have no opportunity to reply.

Anticipate what the respondent will say about these topics and address them in your own opening statement. Concentrate on your own case for most of the opening statement, then address the affirmative defenses and counterclaims, if any, one by one. Be firm, unapologetic, and straightforward. Alternatively, deemphasize affirmative defenses and counterclaims by addressing them as deemphasized facts during your story.

#### 5.2.6.2 Avoid Being Personally Derisive

As claimant's counsel, you will not be certain that the respondent will actually assert the matters you anticipate. Acknowledge that you are addressing the matters because they were raised in the respondent's answer and related pleadings, and that you believe the arbitrator should be fully apprised of claimant's position with respect to them. Avoid deriding your opponent, because you can reasonably expect to receive the same back from the opponent in their opening statement.

Remember what happens when Lin-Manuel Miranda's characters diss each other—it's not pretty. Here's an example from *In the Heights*.

> **Benny**: You ain't got no skills!
>
> **Usnavi**: (Benny!)

**Benny**: Yo, lemme get a

**Usnavi**: (Milky Way)

**Benny**: Yup, and lemme also get a

**Usnavi**: (Daily News)

**Benny**: And a

**Usnavi**: (Post)

**Benny**: And the most important, my Boss's second coffee, one cream
Five sugars! I'm the number one earner

**Usnavi**: (What?!)

**Benny**: The fastest learner

**Usnavi**: (What?!)

**Benny**: My boss can't keep me on the damn back burner!

**Usnavi**: (Yes, he can)[9]

#### 5.2.6.3 Avoid Addressing Respondent's Case in Detail

Refer to respondent's case summarily; avoid going into factual details. Do not specifically refer to respondent's witnesses or to their expected testimony. Respondent's counsel may decide not to call certain witnesses, or a witness may not actually testify to facts as you predict, and the arbitrator may feel misled. You risk damaging your client's case by quoting directly from the respondent's own deposition, a letter they wrote at a critical time, or from a provision of the contract that they signed.

#### 5.2.6.4 Commenting on the Claimant's Opening

Delivering your opening statement as respondent's counsel affords the distinct advantage of knowing precisely what your opponent's case will be. Listen carefully to your opponent's opening statement. Your preparation identified in advance many of the legally significant facts they emphasize. Be flexible and modify your statement to address each of claimant's specific assertions, accusations, or claims. A blanket denial will seem mechanical, even pompous or insincere, to the arbitrator.

---

9. Lin-Manuel Miranda & "In the Heights" Original Broadway Company, *In the Heights*, *on* In the Heights: Original Broadway Cast Recording (Ghostlight 2008); *In the Heights*, "In the Heights," (Lin-Manuel Miranda and Warner Bros. 2021).

Do not simply list all the claimant's unpleasant accusations, denying each one in sequence. Sanitize the accusation and then answer it by drawing on the positive aspects of your own case. If claimant pointed to certain evidence as support for one of their important claims and you intend to introduce specific, controverting evidence, identify that evidence for the arbitrator.

When you listen to claimant's opening statement, note any evidentiary gaps in their prima facie case that they will be unable to fill. Exercise discretion, however, when deciding whether it is strategically sound to point out these omissions in your opening statement. Despite what appears to be a chance to gain some points with the arbitrator, you may just educate the claimant on what evidence they need to round out their case. Consider saving comments about those omissions until your closing argument.

Where, however, claimant's opening statement omits any comment on evidence that harms their case and cannot be explained away easily or be controverted, bring these omissions to the arbitrator's attention. Do not gloat over these evidentiary defects; just alert the arbitrator to these gaps so they will watch how the claimant deals with them in the hearing. There will be plenty of opportunity for you to argue these omissions vigorously in your closing argument.

Ordinarily, it is unwise to comment on the credibility of your opponent's witnesses in the opening statement. As pointed out previously, the witnesses may not be called to testify. If, however, claimant's counsel praises the superior credibility of their witnesses or attacks witnesses' credibility, respond in your opening statement. Do not give the arbitrator the impression that you are acquiescing in your opponent's claims about witness credibility.

### 5.2.7 *Summary and Request for Relief*

The beginning of an opening statement previews positions and supporting evidence. The concluding portion recapitulates the preview to remind the arbitrator how you want them to perceive your story. Briefly summarize the facts you will present through your evidence. Restate any facts you have admitted or to which you have stipulated. Reiterate factual issues and your factual theories. Note the standard of proof and the required burden of proof. Explain how your evidence will disprove your opponent's theories. Finally, close by discussing what the arbitrator must find for you to prevail and conclude with a statement of the damages, remedies, or relief you seek.

### 5.2.8 *Objections and Responses*

Arbitrators do not appreciate counsel objecting to their opponent's opening statement. Objections can be disruptive, distracting, rude, and antagonistic. They may give the arbitrator the impression that the speaker has struck a nerve and that the objector has something to hide. They can also draw attention to matters that the arbitrator may not have fully comprehended had the objection not been made. Thus, objections can be self-defeating, accomplishing the reverse of their intended purpose. Circumstances, however, may compel you to object to your opponent's opening statement. Some of these instances follow.

#### 5.2.8.1 Improper Argument

If your opponent's opening statement is essentially a closing argument, object. Approach with caution; arbitrators usually will not sustain an objection to a couple of sentences that seem to be argumentative. If you object to such a peccadillo, you may irritate the arbitrator. But if your opponent is making extensive legal arguments—applying specific cases and drawing legal conclusions based on evidence that has not yet been admitted—object. The arbitrator will most likely welcome it. The arbitrator would probably also sustain your objection to an opponent's misstating or misquoting the law and extended attacks on the credibility of your witnesses who have not yet testified.

#### 5.2.8.2 Personal Knowledge of Facts

Counsel is not a witness in the case. As a nonwitness, counsel should not give their personal opinion in the opening statement, tout their own credibility, or assert personal knowledge of the facts. This is irrelevant and improper. If such comments are extensive, object.

#### 5.2.8.3 Raising Issues or Matters Outside the Pleadings

If your opponent begins discussing claims or defenses not framed by the pleadings, you may properly object. If you are representing a respondent, and your opponent's objectionable comments are very brief, you may decide to address them in your own opening statement.

#### 5.2.8.4 Discussing Excluded Evidence

Your opponent's discussion of evidence ruled inadmissible by the arbitrator's prehearing ruling would clearly be a proper basis for an objection. Object immediately to avoid the impression that you are waiving your prehearing objection. In the extreme situation, your opponent's flouting of the arbitrator's ruling might serve as a basis for requesting sanctions in the form of dismissal of a claim or defense or precluding introduction of certain documents or testimony.

#### 5.2.8.5 Opponent's Comments Demeaning Your Client or Witnesses

Your opponent may disparage your client's character or motives. Use your discretion in determining when your opponent has overstepped the bounds of fair play. If your client is present during your opponent's opening statement, you may feel compelled to object immediately to demonstrate you are intent on protecting your client's interests. If you are representing a respondent, you may decide that it makes more sense to respond to the demeaning comments in your own opening statement. These same considerations apply when your opponent demeans your witnesses.

Humor can lighten the atmosphere when your opponent says something unpleasant about your client or witnesses in the opening statement, but you walk a narrow diplomatic line here.

#### 5.2.8.6 Exceeding Limits on the Opening Statement

If the arbitrator has set limits on the opening statement's scope or duration and your opponent exceeds them, you would be well within the ambit of appropriate advocacy to object.

## 5.3 Direct Examination

You have developed your story, identified your sets and props, written your script, and practiced your blocking. Now, it's show time.

Direct examination is the stage on which your case plays out. This is where you prove your story by eliciting the testimony of witnesses and introducing the exhibits that confirm that testimony. It is the time to offer the evidence available to establish the facts you need to prevail. In this section we review the goals, basic rules, and planning considerations of direct examination. We also explore proper questioning technique, how to deal with adverse and hostile witnesses, and ethical issues related to direct examination (Lore & Lubet, *MTA*, Ch. 5).

### *5.3.1 Goals of Direct Examination*

Design your direct examinations to accomplish one or more of the following basic goals.

#### 5.3.1.1 Introduce Undisputed Facts

In most arbitrations, many important facts are not in dispute. Nonetheless, such facts cannot be considered by the arbitrator, and will not be part of the record for any later challenge, until and unless they have been placed in evidence through a stipulation or through a witness's testimony. Undisputed facts often establish an element of your case. Failing to include them in direct examination could lead to an unfavorable award.

#### 5.3.1.2 Enhance the Likelihood of Disputed Facts

The most important facts in an arbitration will normally be those in dispute. Direct examination is your opportunity to put forward your client's version of the

Break each topic down into these components—it is a great exercise for judging each question you plan to ask. Does it tell what happened? Why it is important? If not, do you really need to ask it?

### *5.3.2 Basic Rules Governing Direct Examination*

Some very basic rules govern the manner and means by which testimony may be presented in an arbitration hearing.

#### 5.3.2.1 Competence of Witnesses

Every witness called to testify on direct examination must be legally competent to do so, meaning that the witness possesses personal knowledge of some matter at issue in the case, can perceive and relate information, recognizes the difference between truth and falsity, and understands the seriousness of testifying under oath or on affirmation.

#### 5.3.2.2 Nonleading Questions

You may not lead the witness. A leading question contains or suggests its own answer. Since the party calling a witness to the stand is presumed to know what the testimony will be, prohibiting leading questions ensures that the testimony will come in the witness's own words.

There are, however, numerous exceptions to the rule against leading questions on direct examination. A lawyer is generally permitted to lead a witness on preliminary matters, on issues that are not in dispute, to direct the witness's attention to a specific topic, to expedite the testimony on nonessential points, and, in some jurisdictions, to refresh a witness's recollection. In addition, it is usually permissible to lead witnesses who are very young, very old, infirm, confused, or frightened. Finally, it is always within the arbitrator's discretion to permit leading questions to make the examination effective for the ascertainment of the truth, avoid needless consumption of time, protect the witness from undue embarrassment, or as is otherwise necessary to develop the testimony.

#### 5.3.2.3 Narrative Testimony

Witnesses, other than experts, may not testify on direct examination in narrative form. The term narrative has no precise definition but usually means an answer that goes beyond responding to a single specific question. Open-ended questions that invite a lengthy or run-on reply are said to "call for a narrative answer." An example of a nonnarrative question is, "What did you do next?" The objectionable, narrative version would be, "Tell us everything that you did that day."

#### 5.3.2.4 The Nonopinion Rule

Witnesses are expected to testify as to their sensory observations. What did the witness see, hear, smell, touch, taste, or do? Witnesses, other than experts, generally may not offer opinions or characterize events or testimony. A lay witness, however, is allowed to give opinions that are "rationally based upon the perception of the witness." Thus, witnesses will usually be permitted to draw conclusions on issues such as speed, distance, volume, time, weight, temperature, and weather conditions. Similarly, lay witnesses may characterize the behavior of others as angry, drunken, affectionate, busy, or even insane.

#### 5.3.2.5 Refreshing Recollection

Although witnesses are expected to testify in their own words, they are not expected to have perfect recall. The direct examiner may refresh the witness's recollection. It is most common to rekindle a witness's memory by using a document such as their prior deposition or report. It is also permissible to use anything, whether a photograph, an object, or even a leading question. Avoid, though, appearing to feed the witness answers.

Refreshing recollection is Demonstration 5 in the *MTA* online catalog.

### *5.3.3 Planning the Direct Examination*

Three fundamental aspects govern every direct examination:

1) Content;

2) Organization; and

3) Technique.

Content and organization are discussed in this subsection; technique is addressed in the following subsection.

#### 5.3.3.1 Content

Content—what the witness has to say—is the driving force of every direct examination. Begin your planning by asking yourself the following questions:

- Why am I calling this witness?
- Which elements of my claims or defenses will the witness address?
- How can the witness controvert an element of the other side's case?
- What exhibits can be introduced through the witness?

- How can the witness bolster or detract from the credibility of others who will testify?
- How can the witness add moral strength to the presentation of the case or appeal to the arbitrator's sense of justice?

After developing this information, prioritize and prune. Here are some pointers on what you should include and exclude:

### *What to include*

List the witness's facts that are necessary to establish your theory.

- What is the single most important thing the witness has to say?
- What are the witness's collateral facts that make the central information more plausible?
- What is the next most important part of the potential testimony?
- What secondary facts make that testimony more believable?

Continue this process for every element of your case. Be sure to include those thematic facts that give your case moral appeal.

In addition to central facts and supporting details, consider the following sorts of information for your content checklist:

- Testimony explaining the witness's own actions;
- Detailed explanation where the witness's testimony is not self-explanatory;
- Testimony bolstering the witness's own credibility.

In an arbitration hearing, the witness's credibility is always in issue. Devote some part of every direct examination establishing the witness's credibility. You can enhance credibility in numerous ways. Show that the witness is neutral and disinterested. Demonstrate that the witness had an adequate opportunity to observe. Allow the witness to deny any expected charges of bias or misconduct. Elicit the witness's personal background of probity and honesty.

### *What to exclude*

Unless you have an extraordinarily compelling reason to include them, discard facts that fall into the following categories:

#### Clutter

This may be the single greatest vice in direct examination. Details are essential to corroborate important evidence; they are worse than useless virtually everywhere else. Aimless detail detracts from true corroboration. To determine whether a certain fact is clutter, ask yourself the following questions:

- What does it contribute to your story's persuasiveness?
- Does it supply a reason for the way someone acted?
- Does it make an important fact more or less likely?
- Does it affect a witness's credibility?
- Does it enhance your story's moral value?

If all the answers are negative, you're looking at clutter.

#### Unprovables

Unprovables are readily disputed facts. While not "false," vigorous and effective dispute may render them a liability.

- Is the witness the only person who claims to have observed a certain event, while many other credible witnesses swear to the precise contrary?
- Is the witness less than certain? Is the testimony contradicted by credible documentary evidence?

It is usually better to pass up a line of inquiry than to pursue it and ultimately have it rejected.

#### Implausibles

Some facts collapse under their own weight. They might be true, they might be useful, they might be free from possible contradiction, but they still just will not fly. Testimony that is simply too far-fetched, if offered, will give the trier of fact something unnecessary to worry about. It will inject a reason to doubt the other testimony.

#### Impeachables

These statements are contradicted by the witness's own prior statements. By the time of the arbitration hearing, many witnesses have given statements in the form of interviews, reports, and depositions. Many also have signed or authored documents, correspondence, and other writings. With some limitations, witnesses' previous words may be used to cast doubt upon their credibility; this is called impeachment by a prior inconsistent statement. Statements that contradict a witness's hearing testimony are dramatic and damning when revealed through cross-examination. Unless you can provide an extremely good explanation why the witness has changed, or seems to have changed, their story, omit impeachables from direct testimony.

#### Door openers

Some direct testimony "opens the door" for cross-examination that otherwise would not be allowed, because fairness requires that the cross-examiner be allowed to explore any topic deliberately introduced on direct. Before opening the door to any topic on direct, make sure you do not mind if a cross-examiner follows you inside.

### 5.3.3.2 Organization

Organization translates the witness's memory of events into a coherent and persuasive story. This requires idiom, art, and poetry. Artists do not paint everything they see. Rather, they organize shapes, colors, light, and impasto to present their own image of a landscape. In the same manner, an arbitration advocate does not simply ask a witness to "Tell everything you know," but instead choreographs the placement and sequence of the information to heighten and clarify its value.

#### *Principles of organization*

The key principles of this artistic process are primacy and recency, apposition, duration, and repetition. Primacy and recency refer to people's tendency to remember best those things that they hear first and last. Cover the important parts of a direct examination at its beginning, and again at its end. Sandwich less important—or more troublesome—information in the middle. Apposition juxtaposes important facts to emphasize their relationship. Duration refers to how long you spend on each aspect of the direct examination: dwell on the more important points, using the very length of coverage to emphasize the topic's significance. Limit the time spent on less important matters. Repetition is a corollary of duration. Repeat important points, preferably throughout the direct examination, to increase the likelihood that the arbitrator will retain and rely on them.

#### *Structural guidelines*

When applying the previous principles, realize there is no set pattern for a direct examination's structure, just as there is no correct way to paint a landscape. The following structural guidelines, however, may be helpful.

***Start strong and end strong.*** Both the overall direct examination and the sub-examinations should begin and end on strong points. Strong points possess these features:

- admissibility
- theory value
- thematic value
- dramatic impact
- undeniability

***Organize chronologically.*** Chronology is almost always the easiest organization for the arbitrator to follow. The natural progression of events builds a logical foundation and framework.

In some situations, however, topical or thematic organization works best. Even if this is the case, help the arbitrator keep track of the order of events with quick reviews of how your topic fits in the course of events. In this way, you can arrange various components of the witness's testimony to reinforce each other, you can isolate weak points, and you can develop your theory in the most persuasive manner.

Testimony happens in a single room, with a single set of questions and answers, each asked one after another. The events, however, may have occurred simultaneously, so even when organizing chronologically, there may be points in the testimony where you have followed one timeline and now must back up to question the witness about an event outside the chronological order you just pursued. As an advocate, your challenge is to arrange the storytelling so the story has maximum logical force.

***Do not interrupt the action.*** Do not disrupt the dramatic flow of your story, the description of the crucial events, to fill in minor details. Suppress the lawyerly impulse to be thorough; let the scene play out, filling the arbitrator's imagination with your story. One caution, however: derail the story if your witness ventures into details that you cannot support. Unprovables, implausibles, and even impeachables can sneak by in the excitement of the moment. The arbitrator may be caught up in your action movie, but opposing counsel is making notes.

***Give separate attention to the details.*** The details are your denouement. Details add strength and veracity to a witness's testimony. Switching metaphors, treat the details as your instant replay, drawing them out like a commentator draws the moves on the field, while explaining their importance.

***Avoid scattering circumstantial evidence.*** Circumstantial or inferential evidence is at its strongest when you combine a series of circumstances to lead to the desired conclusion. It is therefore effective to present all the related circumstantial evidence at a single point in the direct examination, rather than scatter it throughout. This will not always be possible. The logic of a witness's testimony may require you to elicit items of circumstantial evidence at different points in the testimony. Chronological organization dictates introducing the circumstances in the order that they occurred or were discovered. Even topical organization may require assigning individual circumstances to separate topics. Nonetheless, group your circumstantial evidence when possible, and use repetition and clustering to emphasize important facts.

### *Defensive direct examination*

From time to time, you will need to reveal potentially harmful or embarrassing facts on direct to blunt their impact on cross-examination. Bad information has less sting if the witness volunteers it, particularly if they can explain the circumstances leading to the harmful fact. Conversely, your opponent will bring the information out in the most damning way possible, implying that the witness tried to hide the bad facts. Any explanation given afterward just looks like a poor excuse.

#### *Affirmation before refutation*

Witnesses are often called both to offer affirmative evidence of their own and to refute others' testimony. In such cases, offer the affirmative evidence before proceeding to refutation. This accentuates the positive aspects of your case and avoids making the witness appear to be scolding.

#### *Get to the point*

A direct examination is not a treasure hunt or murder mystery, and there is seldom a reason to keep the arbitrator in suspense. The best form of organization is often to explain exactly where the testimony is headed, and then to go directly there.

#### *End with a clincher*

End every examination with a clincher, a single fact that capsulizes your theory or theme. To qualify as a clincher, a fact must be:

- absolutely admissible;
- reasonably dramatic;
- simple and memorable; and
- stated with certainty.

## *5.3.4 Questioning Technique*

Since content is the moving force behind every direct examination, your questioning technique must focus attention on the witness and the credible testimony. Here are some suggested questioning techniques to help you achieve that goal.

### 5.3.4.1 Use Short, Open Questions

Do not ask a witness, "Did you go to the bank?" The answer to that short question will probably be an even shorter "Yes." Instead, ask questions that invite the witness to describe, explain, and illuminate the events of their testimony. Your witness's own words are more memorable and believable. Short, open questions will advance that goal. Open questions generally start with the words, "who," "what," "why," "where," or "how."

#### 5.3.4.2 Use Directive and Transitional Questions

You cannot use open questions to begin an examination or to move from one area of the examination to another. To do so, you would have to start with "When were you born," and proceed to ask "What happened next" in almost endless repetition. A better approach is to use directive and transitional questions. Directive questions, quite simply, direct the witness's attention to the topic that you want to cover. For example, "after that meeting, did you meet with Jean again?"

#### 5.3.4.3 Reinitiate Primacy

The typical arbitrator will pay maximum attention to the witness at the very beginning of the testimony. Make further use of primacy by continuously "re-beginning" the examination. That is, every time you seem to start anew, you will refocus the arbitrator's attention.

Reinitiate primacy by:

- using general headline questions;
- explaining where you are going;
- using effective body movement;
- using incremental questions;
- drawing verbal images reflecting time, distance, and intensity;
- repeating important points; and
- using visual aids.

### *5.3.5 Dealing with Adverse and Hostile Witnesses*

From time to time, it may be necessary to call a witness, such as the opposing party, who will be hostile to your case. Because you cannot expect unfriendly witnesses to cooperate in preparation, most jurisdictions allow the use of leading questions for the direct examination of such witnesses. Unfriendly witnesses fall into two broad categories: adverse witnesses and hostile witnesses.

#### 5.3.5.1 Adverse Witnesses

Adverse witnesses include the opposing party and those identified with the opposing party. Examples of witnesses identified with the opposing party include employees, close relatives, business partners, and others who share a community of interest. There are limited situations in which it may be profitable to call an adverse witness. The first is where the adverse witness is the only person who can supply an essential element of your case. For the same reason, an adverse witness might also be called to authenticate a necessary document or to lay the foundation for some other critical exhibit. Finally, and most perilously, an adverse or hostile witness might be called solely for the purpose of making a bad impression on the arbitrator. Needless to say, this tactic has a strong potential to backfire. It is within the arbitrator's discretion to determine whether any witness is sufficiently identified with the opposition to allow leading questions on direct examination. Always alert the arbitrator and opposing counsel that you are calling an adverse witness, signaling your intent to ask leading questions.

#### 5.3.5.2 Hostile Witnesses

A hostile witness is one who, while not technically adverse, displays actual hostility to the direct examiner or their client. The necessary characteristic may be manifested either through expressed antagonism or evident reluctance to testify. Additionally, a witness may be treated as hostile if their testimony legitimately surprises the lawyer who called them to the stand. Whatever the circumstances, it is generally necessary to have the arbitrator declare a witness to be hostile before proceeding with leading questions.

### *5.3.6 Redirect Examination and Rehabilitation*

#### 5.3.6.1 Purpose of Redirect

Redirect allows counsel an opportunity to respond to the cross-examination. Redirect serves several purposes. The witness may be asked to explain points explored during the cross, to untangle seeming inconsistencies, to correct errors or misstatements, or to rebut new charges or inferences. In other words, the purpose of redirect is to minimize or undo the damage, if any, caused by the cross-examination. Keep redirect short—its purpose is not to rehash direct examination testimony.

#### 5.3.6.2 Basic Rules of Redirect

***Scope.*** Because redirect is allowed for counteracting or responding to the cross-examination, the material you can cover on redirect is technically limited to the scope of the cross. The interpretation of this rule varies among arbitrators; some are strict and others are lenient. Almost all arbitrators, however, forbid counsel from introducing a wholly new matter on redirect. Redirect must have some reasonable relationship to the cross-examination.

***Some leading permitted.*** Many arbitrators allow a certain amount of latitude during redirect, especially for leading questions. Even without indulgence, leading questions are always permissible to direct the witness's attention or to introduce an area of questioning. A certain amount of leading may be necessary on redirect to focus the examination on the segment of the cross-examination you wish to explain or rebut.

***Recross-examination and additional redirect.*** Redirect examination may be followed by recross, which may be followed by additional redirect, and so on into the night. Each additional examination is limited to the scope of the one immediately preceding it. Thus, recross is restricted to the scope of the redirect and a second redirect would be confined to the scope of the recross. There is no right to continue an infinite regression of successive reexaminations. Rather, the arbitrator has discretion to allow or deny a request for, say, re-recross. Most arbitrators routinely allow at least one redirect and one recross.

***Reopening direct examination.*** Reopening direct examination, as an alternative to redirect, allows you to pursue a line of questioning that is beyond the scope of the cross-examination. This is risky. The arbitrator will wonder why a topic important enough for such a request was overlooked on direct. But if circumstances demand it, swallow your pride and ask. It is strictly within the arbitrator's discretion to allow counsel to reopen a direct examination.

#### 5.3.6.3 Conduct of Redirect

Content is the most important aspect of redirect examination. The redirect should concentrate on a few significant points. These can typically include explanations or rehabilitation.

##### *Explanations*

Obtain explanations by asking for them. Do not be coy or clever. Focus the witness's attention on the pertinent area of the cross-examination and then simply ask them to give their explanation.

##### *Rehabilitation*

On redirect, rehabilitate a witness who has been impeached with a prior inconsistent statement. You can also use redirect to rehabilitate a witness with the witness's own prior consistent statements.

***Rehabilitating after impeachment.*** Conduct rehabilitation as you would any other explanation: direct the witness's attention to the supposed impeachment and request clarification. The alleged inconsistency may be easily resolved, or perhaps the earlier statement was the product of a misunderstanding or misinterpretation. Whatever the explanation, conclude the rehabilitation with the witness's affirmative statement of the witness's current testimony.

***Rehabilitating through prior consistent statements.*** You can also rehabilitate a witness by introducing a prior consistent statement. Although a witness's own previous, prior-to-arbitration account would ordinarily be hearsay, a prior consistent statement is normally admissible to rebut an express or implied charge of recent fabrication or improper influence or motive. Accordingly, once the cross-examiner suggests the witness has changed their story, the direct examiner may show that the witness's testimony is consistent with an earlier report or other statement. In some jurisdictions, a prior consistent statement is admissible only if it predates the inconsistent statement used for impeachment.

### *5.3.7 Ethics of Direct Examination*

Most of the ethical issues in direct examination involve the extent to which it is permissible to "assist" a witness to prepare or enhance their testimony and the lawyer's duty when they suspect that a client or witness may commit or has committed perjury.

#### 5.3.7.1 Preparing Witnesses

A recurring question is the extent to which lawyers may coach witnesses in preparation for their testimony. In many countries, it is considered unethical for a lawyer even to meet alone with a witness prior to the witness testifying because of the possibility of contaminating the testimony. In the United States, however, we take a far different view. Here, it is generally considered incompetent for a lawyer to fail to meet with and prepare a witness before they testify. Difficult issues arise, however, when counsel attempts to refresh a witness's recollection, to fill in gaps in their story, or to suggest alternative possibilities. Again, this practice is usually justified on the ground that it is necessary to ensure that the truth emerges fully. Witnesses can be forgetful, especially when they are unaware of the legal importance of certain facts. The guiding principle here is that counsel must, explicitly and implicitly, prepare the witness to give their own testimony and not the testimony the lawyer would favor or prefer. Most efforts to assist or empower the witness are ethical. Efforts at substitution or fabrication, no matter how well cloaked, are not. As with the client, the best way to prepare is to practice your questions with the witness and revise your questions if you are not receiving answers that would be clear for the arbitrator.

#### 5.3.7.2 Offering Inadmissible Evidence

Arbitrators often allow evidence that the rules would exclude in court. Do not, however, regard this as permission to push past the boundaries the arbitrator sets. When evidence is admissible only for a limited purpose, it is unethical to attempt to put it to further use. The obligation of zealous advocacy does not require counsel to ignore or evade the arbitrator's rulings restricting the admissibility of evidence. It is also impermissible to prepare a witness to interject clearly inadmissible evidence. Where a motion in limine has been granted, for example, counsel cannot suggest or encourage a witness to use a narrative answer to volunteer the excluded information.

#### 5.3.7.3 Perjury

The appropriate response to witness and client perjury has perplexed our profession endlessly. While no ethical lawyer would willingly be a party to perjury, questions arise how to best prevent it without damaging the principles of confidentiality and zealous advocacy. There is no doubt that a lawyer may not call a nonclient witness who is going to testify falsely, and must "take reasonable remedial measures, including, if necessary, disclosure to the tribunal" should such a witness testify falsely.[10] The thorny problem, however, is the client. An attorney must certainly take all reasonable steps to dissuade a client from presenting untrue testimony. But what if the client insists on presenting a story that the lawyer firmly believes is false? Or what if the client's perjury on the stand takes the lawyer by surprise and becomes a fait accompli before the lawyer can stop it?

The ABA Model Rules of Professional Conduct provide that counsel, in both civil and criminal cases, must take reasonable steps to remedy client perjury, even at the cost of revealing a confidential communication.[11] Although there are not any easy solutions to these dilemmas, the trend is toward diminished latitude for the client and increased disclosure by counsel.

## 5.4 Cross-Examination

If direct examination is your best opportunity to win your case, cross-examination may provide you with a chance to lose it. A poor direct can be aimless and boring, but the witnesses are generally helpful. Your worst fear on direct examination is usually that you have left something out. A poor cross-examination, on the other hand, can be truly disastrous. The witnesses can range from uncooperative to hostile, and you constantly run the risk of adding weight or sympathy to the other side's case. Moreover, the arbitrator inevitably perceives most cross-examinations as a contest between the lawyer and witness. You can seldom afford to appear to lose.

This section discusses the role of cross-examination, its basic rules, content, organization, and technique (Lore & Lubet, *MTA*, Ch. 6). Advanced aspects of cross-examination—such as impeachment and the use of character evidence—are treated separately in section 5.5.

### *5.4.1 The Role of Cross-Examination*

Cross-examination is difficult. It is frequently dramatic, often exciting, and in many ways, it defines the adversarial method of dispute resolution. It is the ultimate challenge for the arbitration advocate. It allows you to add to your case or detract from the opposition's case by extracting information from the other side's

---

10. *See* Model Rules of Prof'l Conduct, r. 3.3(a)(3), 3.3.(b), & 3.4(b) (Am. Bar Ass'n 2020).
11. *Id.*

witnesses. Furthermore, cross-examination is inherently risky. The witness may argue with you. The witness may fill in gaps that were left in the direct testimony. The witness may make you look bad. You may make yourself look bad. Whatever good you accomplish may be subject to immediate cure on redirect examination. You cannot avoid these problems entirely, but you can minimize them. Although some cross-examination is usually expected of every witness, and the temptation is difficult to resist, cross-examine carefully and briefly. You must always set realistic goals.

### 5.4.2 Basic Rules of Cross-Examination

Some rules of cross-examination vary depending on locality, but the following rules are nearly universal.

#### 5.4.2.1 Leading Questions Permitted

The most obvious distinction between direct and cross-examination is the permissible use of leading questions. Your adversary's witnesses have little incentive to cooperate with you, and you may not have been able to interview them in advance. Consequently, in arbitration, the cross-examiner is allowed to ask questions that contain their own answers. Moreover, the right to ask leading questions includes the right to insist on a responsive answer.

#### 5.4.2.2 Limitations on Scope

Since cross-examination's purpose is to allow you to inquire of your adversary's witnesses, the inquiry's scope is restricted to subjects raised during the direct examination. The definition of scope varies from arbitrator to arbitrator, and some may not limit the scope of cross-examination beyond relevance to the dispute. For example, assume that the defendant in an auto collision case testified that they had their brakes inspected just a week before the accident. A strict approach to the "scope of direct" rule might limit the cross-examination to questioning on that single inspection. A broader interpretation would allow inquiries into earlier brake inspections and other aspects of automobile maintenance. This more generous approach to the scope of cross-examination is the modern trend.

There are two general exceptions to the "scope of direct" rule. First, the witness's credibility is always in issue. You may therefore always attempt to establish the bias, motive, interest, untruthfulness, or material prior inconsistency of a witness, without regard to the matters covered on direct examination. Second, you may cross-examine beyond the scope of the direct once the witness has "opened the door" to additional matters. In other words, a witness who voluntarily injects a subject into an answer on cross-examination may thereafter be questioned as though the subject had been included in the direct.

#### 5.4.2.3 Other Restrictions

A variety of other rules, most of which involve the manner or nature of questioning, also limit cross-examinations.

***Argumentative questions.*** You may ask a witness questions. You may suggest answers. You may assert propositions. And you can ask a series of questions that make a point—an argument. But you may not argue with the witness. As you may have guessed, the definition of an argumentative question is elusive. Much depends on your demeanor; perhaps an argumentative question is one that is asked in an argumentative tone. Here is a reasonable working definition: an argumentative question insists that the witness agree with an opinion or characterization, as opposed to a statement of fact.

***Intimidating behavior.*** You are entitled to elicit information on cross-examination by asking questions of the witness and insisting upon answers. You are not allowed to loom over the witness, to shout, to make threatening gestures, or otherwise to intimidate, bully, or (yes, here it comes) badger the witness.

***Unfair characterizations.*** Your right to lead the witness does not include a right to mislead the witness. It is objectionable to attempt to mischaracterize a witness's testimony or to ask "trick" questions. If a witness has testified that it was dark outside, it would mischaracterize the testimony to begin a question, "So you admit that it was too dark to see anything?" Trick questions cannot be answered accurately. The most famous trick question is known as the "negative pregnant," as in Senator McCarthy's inquisitional, "Have you resigned from the Communist Party?"

***Assuming facts.*** A frequently heard objection is that "counsel has assumed facts not in evidence." Of course, a cross-examiner is frequently allowed to inquire about facts that are not yet in evidence. This objection should only be sustained when the question uses the nonrecord fact as a premise rather than as a separate subject of inquiry, thus denying the witness the opportunity to deny its validity. An example of a question containing an unfair assumption would be: "Since you had been drinking, you were on foot instead of in your car that morning?" That the witness was drinking is an assumed fact. The problem with this sort of bootstrapping is that it does not allow the witness a fair opportunity to deny having been drinking in the first place.

***Compound and other defective questions.*** Compound questions contain more than a single inquiry: "Are you related to the plaintiff, and were you wearing your glasses at the time of the accident?" The question is objectionable since any answer will necessarily be ambiguous. Cumulative or "asked and answered" questions are objectionable because they cover the same ground twice (or more). Vague questions are objectionable because they tend to elicit vague answers.

### 5.4.3 Content of Cross-Examination

The most frequent decision you will have to make regarding cross-examination is not whether to cross-examine, but how much. Make this evaluation at least twice: once in your prehearing preparation and again at the end of the direct examination.

Prepare for cross by considering the potential direct examination.

- What do you expect the witness to say?
- How, if at all, will you need to challenge or add to the direct?

At the arbitration hearing, you must make a further determination.

- Did the actual direct examination proceed as you expected?
- Was it more or less damaging than you anticipated?

Always reevaluate your cross-examination strategy in light of the direct testimony actually produced. This process will often lead you to omit portions of your prepared cross, because they have become unnecessary. It is considerably more dangerous to elaborate on or add to your plan, although this is occasionally unavoidable. In either situation, always remember the risk inherent in cross-examination and ask yourself, "Is this cross-examination necessary?"

#### 5.4.3.1 Consider the Purposes of Cross-Examination

Though often an invigorating exercise, undertake cross-examination only to serve some greater purpose within your theory of the case. A useful cross fulfills at least one of the following objectives:

- Repair or minimize damage.
    - Did the direct examination hurt your case?
    - If so, can the harm be rectified or minimized?
    - Can you make the witness retract or back away from certain testimony?
    - Can you elicit additional facts that will minimize the witness's impact?
- Enhance your case.
    - Can cross-examination further one of your claims or defenses?
    - Can you bring out positive facts that support or contribute to your version of events?
- Detract from their case.
    - Conversely, can cross-examination establish facts that are detrimental to your opponent's case?
    - Can it create inconsistencies among the other side's witnesses?

- Establish foundation.
    - Is the witness necessary to the proper foundation for introducing a document or other exhibit, or for the offer of evidence by another witness?
- Discredit the witness's direct testimony.
    - Can you highlight internal inconsistencies?
    - Demonstrate the witness's own lack of certainty or confidence?
    - Underscore lack of opportunity to observe?
    - Illustrate the inherent implausibility of the testimony?
    - Show that the testimony conflicts with that of other, more credible witnesses?
- Discredit the witness.
    - Can you show the witness to be biased or interested in the case's outcome?
    - Does the witness have a reason to stretch, misrepresent, or fabricate the testimony?
    - Has the witness been untruthful in the past?
    - Can you show that the witness is otherwise unworthy of belief?
- Reflect on the credibility of another.
    - Can you undermine the credibility of a different witness?
    - Can you enhance the credibility of a different witness?

The length of your cross-examination will generally depend upon how many of the previous goals you expect to fulfill. It is not necessary, and it may not be possible, to achieve them all. You stand to lose more by overreaching than you can possibly gain by seeking to cover all the bases in cross-examination. Be selective.

#### 5.4.3.2 Arrive at the "Usable Universe" of Cross-Examination

In preparing your cross-examination, first determine the entire universe of potential cross-examination and then determine your usable universe.

***The entire universe***

In preparing to cross-examine any witness, contemplate the broadest possible scope, or universe, for the potential cross-examination. Review the available materials and documents and construct a comprehensive list of the information obtainable from the witness. In keeping with the purposes of cross-examination, place each potential fact in one of the following categories:

- Does it make my case more likely?
- Does it make their case less likely?
- Is it a predicate to the admissibility of other evidence?
- Does it make some witnesses more believable?
- Does it make some witnesses less believable?

This process will give you the full universe of theoretically desirable information from which you will structure your cross-examination.

***The usable universe***

To arrive at your "usable universe," ask yourself the following questions:

- Is a friendly witness available to present the same facts?
- Can the information be obtained only on cross-examination?
- Will the facts be uniquely persuasive on cross-examination?
- How certain is it that the witness will agree with you?

Constructing the usable universe depends almost entirely on your mastery of the case. To prepare for cross-examination, you must know not only everything that the witness is liable to say, but also every other fact you might obtain from any other witness, document, or exhibit. Choose those areas that do you the most good while risking the least harm.

#### 5.4.3.3 Use a Risk-Averse Approach to Preparation

Risk-averse preparation for cross-examination begins with considering your anticipated final argument. What do you want to be able to say about this witness when you address the arbitrator at the end of the case? How much of that information do you expect to be included in the direct examination? The balance is what you need to cover on cross.

Next, write out the portion of a final argument that you would devote to discussing the facts presented by this witness. This can serve as a draft for your actual closing, so limit this text to the facts contained in the witness's testimony. You need not include the characterizations, inferences, arguments, comments, and thematic references that will also be part of your real final argument. Depending upon the importance of the witness, the length of this argument segment can range from a short paragraph to a full page or more.

Write your text using short, single-thought, strictly factual sentences. You are not creating literature. Do not worry about continuity, style, or transitions. Simply arrange the declarative sentences one after another in the most persuasive order, referring to the witness in the third person.

The risk-averse approach is useful for developing the content of your cross-examination. How you organize the examination, and the structure of your individual questions, will depend upon additional analysis.

### 5.4.4 *Organizing the Cross-Examination*

As with direct examination, organize a cross-examination based on the four principles of primacy and recency, apposition, repetition, and duration. Unlike direct examination, however, on cross-examination you will often face a recalcitrant witness. Recognize this reality and temper your plan, occasionally sacrificing maximum clarity and persuasion to avoid "telegraphing" your strategy to the uncooperative witness. These are additional organizing principles of indirection and misdirection when planning cross-examinations.

For an illustration of an attorney using repetition and duration in a cross-examination, see Demonstrations 1.1 and 1.2 in the MTA video catalog.

#### 5.4.4.1 Additional Organizing Principles

Three further principles are basic to the organization, presentation, and technique of virtually every cross-examination.

First, cross-examination is your opportunity to tell part of your client's story and argue their case in the middle of the other side's case. Your object is to focus attention away from the witness's direct testimony and onto matters that you believe are helpful. On cross-examination, you want to make a point, or a few points. To do so, you must always control the testimony and the witness.

Second, cross-examination is never the time to attempt to gather new information. Never ask a witness a question simply because you want to find out the answer. Rather, use cross-examination to establish or enhance the facts you have already discovered.

Finally, an effective cross-examination often succeeds through indirection and misdirection. It is not necessary, and it is often harmful, to ask a witness the "ultimate question." By indirection, or indirect questioning, you establish small and incontrovertible factual components of a theory, and only later address the theory itself. Final argument is your opportunity to point out the relationship between facts, make characterizations, and draw conclusions based upon the accumulation of details. Misdirection is an arch-relative of indirection, used when you think the witness is particularly deceptive or untruthful. Here, the cross-examiner not only conceals the object of the examination but attempts to take advantage of the witness's own inclination to be uncooperative. Knowing that the witness will fight the examination, the lawyer creates, and then exploits, a "misdirected" image.

### 5.4.4.2 Guidelines for Organization

There are a variety of ways in which you can employ the previous principles.

***Do not worry about starting strong.*** Lawyers dream of beginning every cross-examination with a strong, memorable question that absolutely drives home their theory and theme. Unfortunately, this will seldom be possible. You may have to begin with a shakedown period, during which you acclimate yourself to the tenor of the witness's responses and when you also attempt to put the witness in a cooperative frame of mind. Unless you can start off with a true bombshell question, take the time necessary to establish predicate facts through indirection. Start with questions about undisputable facts as part of a series of questions that make a strong, legally significant point.

***Use topical organization.*** Topical organization is essential in cross-examination. Your goal on cross-examination is not to retell the witness's story, but rather to establish a small number of additional or discrediting points. A topical format most effectively allows you to move from area to area. Moreover, with topical organization you can take maximum advantage of apposition, indirection, and misdirection. You can cluster facts in the same manner that you would on direct examination, or separate facts and avoid showing your hand to the witness.

***Get the details first.*** Witnesses are far more likely to agree with a series of small, incremental facts before the thrust of the examination becomes apparent. Once you have challenged, confronted, or closely questioned a witness, it will be extremely difficult to go back and fill in the details necessary to make the challenge stick.

***Save a zinger for the end.*** Carefully plan the very last point that you intend to make on cross-examination. Choose a guaranteed winner, the point on which you are willing to make your exit. Write this point down at the very bottom of your note pad, underlined and in bold letters. Let it stand alone, with nothing to obscure it or distract you from it. Then if your entire examination seems to fail, if the witness denies every proposition, if the arbitrator sustains every objection, if the heavens fall and doom impends, you can always skip to the bottom of the page and finish with a flourish. Satisfied that you have made this single, telling, case-sealing point, you may proudly announce, "No further questions of this witness," and sit down. Your zinger should have all the following characteristics. It should be:

1) absolutely admissible,
2) central to your theory,
3) crafted to evoke your theme,
4) undeniable, and
5) stated with conviction.

### 5.4.4.3 A Classic Format for Cross-Examination

The following classic format is designed to maximize witness cooperation. Of course, you may have a goal in mind for your cross-examination other than witness cooperation; in that case, feel free to ignore or alter this approach. As a rule of thumb, however, you can best employ principles such as indirection by seeking information in this order.

See Demonstrations 7.1 and 7.2 in the online catalog for an example of an attorney who leads a cross with friendly information as opposed to one who leads with hostile information.

***Friendly information.*** Be friendly first. Begin by asking all questions that the witness will regard as nonthreatening. These will often be background questions. A witness will be the most forthcoming when asked about aggrandizing information at the very outset of the cross-examination.

***Affirmative information.*** After exhausting the friendly information, ask questions that build up your case's value, rather than tear down the opposition's. Much of this information will fill in gaps in the direct testimony. Plan this portion of the cross by listing the information that you reasonably hope will be included in the direct, then mark out any that direct covers. Although adverse witnesses may not be enthusiastic about supplying you with helpful information, they seldom fight you over answers that might logically have been included in their own direct.

***Incontrovertible information.*** Proceed to the well-settled or documentable facts that damage the opposition's case or detract from the witness's testimony. On these questions a witness may be inclined to hedge or quibble; minimize this possibility by sticking to information that they ultimately must concede.

***Challenging information.*** At some point, of course, you will have to ask questions that the witness will recognize as challenges: "Mr. Defendant, the fact is that the first thing you did after the collision was to telephone your office?" Such questions are necessary. When used in their proper place, they will not prevent you from first exploiting the other, more cooperative testimony from the witness.

***Hostile information.*** Hostile information involves directly confronting the witness. You may extract the necessary answers to hostile questions, but you eliminate all hope of cooperation both then and thereafter.

Hostile questions involve assaults on the witness's honesty, probity, peacefulness, character, or background:

- Didn't you spend time in prison?
- You never intended to live up to the contract?
- That was a lie, wasn't it?

***Zinger.*** Always end with one.

### 5.4.5 Questioning Technique

You know what you want to cover on cross-examination, and you know the order in which you want to cover it. Next you need to know how to ask questions that will ensure your success.

The goal of cross-examination is witness control. Control can be either assertive or nonassertive. With a cooperative or tractable witness, control may mean nothing more than asking the right questions and getting the right answers. A hostile, evasive, or argumentative witness may require that you employ more assertive means. The following questioning techniques can help ensure witness control. At a minimum, however, every question on cross-examination should have the following bedrock characteristics:

***Short.*** Questions on cross-examination must be short in both execution and concept. If a question is more than ten words long, it is not short in execution. Shorten it. If a question contains more than a single fact or implication, it is not short in concept. Divide it.

***Leading.*** Make every question on cross-examination leading. Include the answers in the questions. Tell the witness exactly what to say. Cross-examination is no time to seek the witness's interpretation of the facts. It is the time for you to tell a story by obtaining the witness's assent. A nonleading question invites the witness to wander away from your story.

***Propositional.*** The best questions on cross-examination are not questions at all. Rather, they are propositions of fact that you put to the witness in interrogative form. You already know the answer—you simply need to produce it from the witness's mouth. Every question on cross-examination should contain a proposition that falls into one of these three categories:

1) you already know the answer;

2) you can otherwise document or prove the answer; or

3) any answer will be helpful.

An example of the latter sort of question would be the classic inquiry to a witness who must admit having previously given a false statement: "Were you lying then, or are you lying now?"

#### 5.4.5.1 Plan for Control

Controlling a witness on cross-examination begins with your plan and is achieved, in large measure, on your outline. In other words, a cross-examination is only as good as your outline.

***Use written questions to prepare.*** It can be useful to write out cross-examination questions in preparation for an arbitration hearing, but when it comes to the actual examination, it is easier to use an outline. For a jury, or even a bench trial, do not read questions; it fails to convey the level of knowledge about the case that using an outline does and deprives your examination of the appearance of spontaneity. Reading from a set of questions may deprive you of the control that comes from eye contact with and observation of the witness—though much of your eye contact should be on the arbitrator(s) in any event; it is they to whom you are trying to convey your points. Sometimes, issues of cost prohibit you from having the time to study, hone, rearrange, and discard your questions in favor of a topical outline; in such cases, read your questions, but strive to look up after each question, listening to the witness and engaging the arbitrator. If you do have time, preparing an outline will undoubtedly improve your cross-exam.

***Use an outline.*** Your outline should remind you of the points you intend to make on cross-examination and ensure that you do not inadvertently omit anything. Your outline is not a script but rather a set of cues or prompts, each of which introduces an area of questioning. Beneath each main prompt, list the key details that you intend to elicit from the witness. Your outline can follow the same format that you have used since high school. Principal topics are represented by Roman numerals, subtopics are denoted by capital letters, and smaller points or component details are represented by Arabic numerals. Although the form for academic outlines goes on to involve lowercase letters, small Roman numerals, and other levels ad infinitum, the outline for a cross-examination will become too complex if it extends beyond the third level.

Let's say you represent a small business as claimant in a trade secret misappropriation case. You want to cross-examine a witness to establish that the customer list was not easily ascertainable to those who would derive economic value from it. Here are questions you might write out:[12]

1) You worked at the Torneau Lakeside Lodge, correct?
2) As a fishing guide?
3) As an independent contractor, right? (Morgan's Deposition; Page 23; Lines 25–29)
4) So, you weren't an employee of the lodge? (Morgan's Deposition; Page 23; Lines 25–29)
5) The lodge guest's contact information was stored on a computer, wasn't it? (Morgan's Deposition; Page 26; Lines 15–21)

12. These questions are based on the ABA Student Division Arbitration Problem for 2018. Peter B. Knapp, *American Bar Association Law Student Division, Arbitration Competition 2018 Case File*, A.B.A., https://www.americanbar.org/content/dam/aba/ administrative/law_students/competitions /arbitration/2017-18-arbitration-problem-and-clarification.pdf (last visited Jun. 2024).

6) The computer was located behind the front desk, right? (Morgan's Deposition; Page 26; Lines 15–21)
7) To access the contact information required a username, correct? (Morgan's Deposition; Page 26; Lines 15–21)
8) And a password, didn't it? (Morgan's Deposition; Page 26; Lines 15–21)
9) The front desk workers had access to the username, didn't they?
10) And to the password, right?
11) To enable them to get the guests' contact information, right? (Morgan's Deposition; Page 26; Lines 15–21)
12) And the front desk workers were employed by the lodge, weren't they?
13) Most of the time you would ask the front desk workers to give you a guest's contact information, right? (Morgan's Deposition; Page 26; Lines 15–21)
14) When the front desk workers weren't there, you would enter the username yourself, right? (Morgan's Deposition; Page 26; Lines 15–21)
15) And the password, correct? (Morgan's Deposition; Page 26; Lines 15–21)

Then at trial your outline or bullets would look something like this:

1) worked at lodge
2) fishing guide
3) independent contractor (Morgan's Deposition; Page 23; Lines 25–29)
4) not employee (Morgan's Deposition; Page 23; Lines 25–29)
5) contact info on a computer (Morgan's Deposition; Page 26; Lines 15–21)
6) behind front desk (Morgan's Deposition; Page 26; Lines 15–21)
7) username (Morgan's Deposition; Page 26; Lines 15–21)
8) password (Morgan's Deposition; Page 26; Lines 15–21)
9) front desk workers—username
10) and password
11) get the guests' contacts (Morgan's Deposition; Page 26; Lines 15–21)
12) employed
13) most of the time ask front desk workers (Morgan's Deposition; Page 26; Lines 15–21)

14) when weren't there, you enter username (Morgan's Deposition; Page 26; Lines 15–21)

15) and password (Morgan's Deposition; Page 26; Lines 15–21)

***Reference your outline.*** Once you draft the outline for your cross-examination, reference it. Referencing allows you to refresh the recollection of forgetful witnesses, and to impeach or contradict witnesses who give you evasive, unexpected, or false answers.

Across from every important subtopic and crucial detail, record the source for the point you intend to make, referencing your notes line by line. At a minimum, reference every point you consider essential to your case, as well as those that you expect to be controverted or challenging to the witness. In addition to deposition transcripts, reference sources can come from letters, reports, memoranda, notes, and even photographs. The best sources, of course, are the witness's own prior words. Adequate secondary sources may include documents that the witness reviewed, acted upon, or affirmed by silence. In most circumstances, the testimony of a different person, though perhaps useful, will not be a reliable source for referencing a cross-examination.

### 5.4.5.2 Use Questions That Achieve Control

Having reviewed the principles for organizing and outlining the cross-examination, we are now ready to consider the precise techniques that provide maximum control over a witness's testimony.

***Use incremental questions.*** Conduct cross-examination in a series of small, steady steps. This technique allows you to do two things. First, it blocks the escape route for a witness who is inclined to argue or prevaricate. The incremental questions provide small targets for a witness's inventiveness. More importantly, it lets you know early in the sequence whether the witness is likely to disagree with you. Incremental questions allow testing the witness for cooperation, and determining whether your own factual assumptions are correct, before you reach an embarrassing point of no return.

***Use sequenced questions for impact.*** Use sequencing on cross-examination for a variety of purposes. First, as on direct, sequencing (or apposition) clarifies your story or enhances its impact upon the arbitrator. Eliciting two facts in close proximity underscores relationships, contrasts, inconsistencies, connections, or motives. The apposition of otherwise disparate facts can help develop your theme.

***Use sequenced questions for commitment.*** Using sequenced questions in combination with incremental questions, you may compel important concessions out of an unwilling witness. Arrange facts so that their progression unfolds a logic of its own. When the initial facts in a sequence are sufficiently small and innocuous, you may lead a witness to embark upon a course of concessions that will be impossible to stop.

***Create a "conceptual corral."*** As we have seen, cross-examination's purpose is often to box in a witness so that crucial facts cannot be averted or denied. Think of this process as building a conceptual corral around the witness. After building the first three sides of the corral, close the gate with your final proposition. Each side of the conceptual corral is formed by a different sort of question. One side consists of the witness's own previous admissions or actions, another is formed by undeniable facts, and the third is based upon everyday plausibility. The length of any particular side, or the extent to which you will rely on any of the three sorts of information, will differ from case to case. With almost every witness, however, you can construct the three sides of the corral to form an enclosure from which the witness cannot escape.

***Avoid the ultimate question.*** It will often be tempting to confront an adverse witness with one last conclusory question: "So you just ignored the fire truck, didn't you?" Resist this temptation. If you establish the incremental facts that lead to your conclusion, you gain little by making the question explicit. At best you repeat what has become obvious, and at worst you give the witness an opportunity to recant or amend the foundational testimony. Even worse, you may not have established the incremental facts as fully as you thought. Under these circumstances, the witness will not only disagree with your ultimate proposition, but will explain exactly why you are wrong.

***Listen to the witness and insist on an answer.*** There is more to controlling a witness on cross-examination than asking the right questions. You must also make sure that you have gotten the correct answers. This requires that you listen to the witness. Even the most painstakingly prepared question can elicit the wrong answer. The witness may not have understood you, or they may have detected an ambiguity in your inquiry. Some witnesses will argue with you for the sake of argument, some will try to deflect your examination, and some will simply answer a question different from the one you asked. In any event, always recall that it is the witness's answer that constitutes evidence. Listen carefully to ensure that the evidence is what you expected. You can often correct an incorrect answer by restating your question.

#### 5.4.5.3 Avoid Questions That Lose Control

The pitfalls of cross-examination are well known: refusals to answer; unexpected answers; and argumentative, evasive, and slippery witnesses. Significantly, virtually all these problems derive from the same basic error on the part of the cross-examiner—failure to control the testimony. Avoid this error by avoiding questions that cause you to lose control of the witness. Here are a few examples of those sorts of questions.

***Nonleading questions.*** The cardinal rule on cross-examination is to use leading questions. The cardinal sin is to abandon that tool. We have discussed at length the advantages of stating your questions in the form of leading propositions. For some reason, however, many lawyers seem impelled to drift into nonleading questions once an examination begins. This is a mistake you should avoid like the plague.

***"Why" or explanation questions.*** Never ask a witness to explain something on cross-examination. If you already know the explanation, use leading questions to tell it to the witness. If you do not already know the explanation, cross-examination surely is not the time to learn it. No matter how assiduously you have prepared, no matter how well you think you understand the witness's motives and reasons, a witness can always surprise you by explaining the unexplainable. Asking a witness to explain is the equivalent of saying, "I've grown tired of controlling this cross-examination. Why don't you take over for a while?"

***"Fishing" questions.*** Fishing questions are the ones that you ask in the hope that you might catch something. It has been said before, and it is worth repeating here: Do not ask questions to which you do not know the answers. For every answer you think will be favorable, there are a dozen answers you have not imagined, all of which suggest disaster.

***Long questions.*** Long questions have an almost limitless capacity to deprive a cross-examiner of witness control. Long questions, by their very nature, multiply a witness's opportunity to find something with which to disagree. The more words you use, the more chance there is that a witness will refuse to adopt them all. Long questions are also easily forgotten or misunderstood. The witness may insist on answering the question they thought you asked, rather than the one that you meant to ask.

***"Gap" questions.*** Gap questions constitute an especially enticing subset of explanation questions. Gaps are found in direct testimony more often than one might expect. A witness may neglect to testify about one of a series of important events or may omit testimony concerning a crucial document. Alternatively, a witness might leave out important evidence on damages, or may fail entirely to testify as to an element, such as proximate cause, of the opposition's case. How can you avoid the temptation to ask gap questions? The key is to remember that it is the opposition's burden to prove their case. Everything they leave out of their case works in your favor.

***"You testified . . ." questions.*** Another common method of surrendering control to a witness is questions that challenge the witness to recall the content of their earlier direct testimony. These can be referred to as "you testified" questions, because they inevitably contain some variant on those words. The problem with "you testified" questions is that they invite the witness to quibble over the precise wording used on direct examination. The exact language of the witness's earlier answer is seldom essential, but the "you testified" format inflates its apparent importance, often almost to the point of seeming to pick a fight.

***Characterizations and conclusions.*** Do not request that a witness agree with a characterization or conclusion. Assume that you are cross-examining the plaintiff in a personal injury case. The plaintiff testified on direct that they were struck by a vehicle at midnight on a seldom-traveled country road. Your defense is misidentification of the driver. Wishing to take advantage of the time and place of the events, you ask, "It was too dark to see very well, wasn't it?" The plaintiff, being nobody's fool, answers: "I could see just fine."

Instead, ask the plaintiff about the facts that led you to the characterization: the sun had gone down, there was no moon that night, there were no streetlamps, there were no house lights, there were no illuminated signs. Save the characterization for final argument.

#### 5.4.5.4 Reasserting Control

Notwithstanding your best efforts and preparation, some witnesses will inevitably wander beyond your control. A witness typically falls out of control in one of three ways:

1) they have refused to agree with you;
2) they have been invited to explain an answer; or
3) they are being impermissibly uncooperative.

In the first two instances the problem is your fault, and you can usually cure it with further questions. In the third case the witness is at fault, and you may need help from the arbitrator.

| REASSERTING CONTROL | |
|---|---|
| **SITUATION** | **SOLUTION** |
| The witness fails to agree | • Self-identify why the witness refused to agree<br>• Break the question into constituent questions until the disagreement is eliminated |
| The witness explains | • Self-identify why the witness explained<br>• Avoid interrupting the witness (unless the witness is about to blurt out some devastating inadmissible fact or is violating the arbitrator's prior ruling prohibiting explanations)<br>• Try a stern look, upraised hand, or sliding in a question during a pause in their testimony<br>• If those techniques do not work, simply allow the witness to finish the answer and then proceed to another question that does not invite explanation |
| The witness is impermissibly uncooperative | • Use one of the previous techniques<br>• Repeat the question<br>• Repeat the question with a preface of "yes or no," or<br>• Ask the witness to agree you asked a "yes" or "no" question and then repeat the question<br>• If still unsuccessful, seek help from the arbitrator. |

Demonstration 8 in the MTA video catalog shows an attorney using different tactics to reassert control of a witness during cross.

### 5.4.6 Ethics of Cross-Examination

While lawyers generally consider cross-examination to be an "engine" of truth-seeking, we are often criticized for using cross as a device for distortion and obfuscation. And in truth, like all powerful rhetorical tools, cross-examination can be used to mislead and deceive. Accordingly, certain ethical principles have developed that circumscribe a lawyer's use of cross-examination.

#### 5.4.6.1 Factual and Legal Basis for Questioning

To protect against the unscrupulous use of cross-examination, a lawyer may not, in trial, allude to any matter that the lawyer does not reasonably believe is relevant or that will not be supported by admissible evidence.[13] Ordinarily, in a court case subject to discovery, counsel is not free to make up assertions at trial, or even to fish for possibly incriminating material. Rather, as a predicate to any "propositional" question, counsel must ordinarily be aware of specific facts that support the allegation. In arbitration, where little or no discovery has been authorized, the good-faith basis in fact requirement is somewhat relaxed because counsel may be examining a witness for the first time at the hearing itself.

Also, in a court trial, the good-faith basis for a cross-examination question cannot be comprised solely of inadmissible evidence. Trial counsel cannot allude to any matter "that will not be supported by admissible evidence." Thus, in a court trial, a good-faith basis cannot be provided by rumors, uncorroborated hearsay, or pure speculation. In an arbitration, this rule is somewhat relaxed because hearsay is normally permitted. However, allegations based on evidence deemed inadmissible by the arbitrator may lead to a sustained objection, an admonition by the arbitrator, or even sanctions.

#### 5.4.6.2 Assertions of Personal Knowledge

In a court trial, it is unethical for counsel to "assert personal knowledge of facts in issue . . . or state a personal opinion as to the justness of a cause, the credibility of a witness, the culpability of a civil litigant or the guilt or innocence of an accused."[14] While this problem most frequently occurs during closing argument, it also arises during cross-examination. Cross-examination questions often take a "Do you know?" or "Didn't you tell me?" format. Both types of questions are improper, because they put the lawyer's own credibility in issue. "Do you know?" questions suggest the lawyer is aware of true facts which, while not appearing on the record, contradict the witness's testimony. "Didn't you tell me?" questions argue that the witness and the lawyer had a conversation, and that the lawyer's version is more believable. In either case, the questions amount to an assertion of personal

---

13. *See* Model Rules of Prof'l Conduct, r. 3.4(e) (Am. Bar Ass'n 2020).
14. *Id.*

knowledge. In the informal setting of arbitration, some arbitrators may relax the enforcement of this rule, but other arbitrators may enforce it strictly.

#### 5.4.6.3 Derogatory Questions

It is unethical to ask questions that are intended solely to harass, degrade, or humiliate a witness, or to discourage them from testifying.

#### 5.4.6.4 Discrediting a Truthful Witness

In arbitration, you cannot degrade or debase a witness simply to cast doubt on otherwise unchallenged testimony. On the other hand, true factual information may be used to undermine the credibility of a witness whose testimony is legitimately controverted.

#### 5.4.6.5 Misusing Evidence

The same rules apply on cross as on direct about misusing evidence that has been admitted for a limited purpose.[15]

## 5.5 Impeachment

While much cross-examination consists of demonstrating inaccuracies or rebutting a witness's testimony, impeachment discredits the witness as a reliable source of information. Successful impeachment renders the witness less worthy of belief, as opposed to merely unobservant, mistaken, or otherwise subject to contradiction. There are three basic categories of witness impeachment, each of which provides a reason to place less credence in a witness's testimony (Lore & Lubet, *MTA*, Ch. 7).

The most common method of impeachment is the use of a prior inconsistent statement, action, or omission. Eliciting a prior inconsistency demonstrates that the witness's current testimony is at odds with their own previous statements or actions. In essence, this examination says, "Do not believe this witness because their story has changed."

A second method of impeachment is the use of character, or "characteristic" evidence. This form of impeachment is aimed at demonstrating that the witness possesses some inherent trait or characteristic, unrelated to the case at hand, that renders the testimony less credible. Perhaps the witness is a convicted felon or suffers a memory defect. This examination says, "This witness is not trustworthy on any matter, because of who they are."

The third method, "case data" impeachment, involves establishing facts that make the witness less reliable, although only within the context of the case in

15. See section 5.3.7.2.

arbitration. The witness might have a financial interest in the outcome of the case or might be prejudiced against one of the parties. In other words, "Give less weight to the witness because of their relationship to the case."

Impeachment generally begins and ends during cross-examination. When a witness concedes the existence of the impeaching information, nothing further must be done, and the cross-examiner may go on to other matters. If, however, the witness denies the truth of the impeaching matter, the cross-examiner may be required to perfect or complete the impeachment by offering extrinsic evidence, or evidence that is adduced through the testimony of someone other than the subject of the impeachment. This can occur whether the original impeachment was based upon prior inconsistency, character, or case data.

### *5.5.1 Tactical Considerations*

Impeachment is a powerful tool. Unlike "standard" cross-examination, which may rely on unspoken premises and subtle misdirection, there can be no mistaking or hiding the intended impact of impeachment. All three kinds of impeachment are inherently confrontational. They challenge the witness's believability, perhaps even their veracity. For this reason, use the techniques of impeachment sparingly, both to preserve the method's potency and to avoid crying wolf over unimportant details.

#### 5.5.1.1 Impeach the Witness Only on Significant Matters

Avoid impeaching witnesses on irrelevant, trivial, or petty inconsistencies. The process of impeachment, particularly by prior inconsistency, is generally so confrontational that there is a great risk of creating an annoying dissonance between expectation and reward. If the "punch line" fails to justify the buildup, the result can be embarrassing or damaging to your case.

#### 5.5.1.2 Impeach the Witness Only on True Inconsistencies

The purpose of impeachment by a prior inconsistency is to show that the witness has made contradictory statements. The technique works only when the two statements cannot both be true. If the two statements can be harmonized, explained, or rationalized, the impeachment will fail.

#### 5.5.1.3 Impeach a Witness Only When Success Is Likely

Failed impeachment can be disastrous. A lawyer who begins an assault that cannot be completed will look ineffective at best and foolishly overbearing at worst.

#### 5.5.1.4 Do Not Impeach on Favorable Information

Impeachment is not like mountain climbing. It should not be undertaken simply because it is there. Impeachment's purpose is to cast doubt on the credibility of some or all of a witness's testimony. You gain nothing by casting doubt on testimony that helps your own case. Thus, even if an opposing witness has given a prior inconsistent statement, do not impeach favorable hearing testimony.

#### 5.5.1.5 Consider the "Rule of Completeness"

The Rule of Completeness provides that once a witness has been impeached from a prior inconsistent statement, opposing counsel may request the immediate reading of additional, explanatory portions of the same statement. Under the Federal Rules of Evidence, for example, the adverse party may introduce any other part of the statement "which ought in fairness to be considered contemporaneously with it." Thus, even a true gem of an impeaching statement may be immediately undercut if some other part of the impeaching document explains or negates the apparent contradiction.

#### 5.5.1.6 Consider Refreshing the Witness's Recollection

Not every gap or variation in a witness's testimony is the result of an intentional change. Witnesses often become confused or forgetful. A witness may have testified inconsistently with their prior statements quite innocently or inadvertently. In these circumstances, use the prior statement to refresh the witness's recollection, rather than to impeach their credibility. The technique for refreshing recollection is the same on cross-examination as it is on direct. Many arbitrators, however, will allow a cross-examiner to refresh a witness's recollection without first being required to establish that the witness's memory has been exhausted.

#### 5.5.1.7 Evidentiary Considerations

Prior inconsistent statements given under oath are often admissible as substantive evidence;[16] they can be used to prove the original statement's truth. Prior inconsistent statements that were not given under oath are generally admissible for the limited purpose of impeachment; they can be used only to reflect on the witness's credibility.

### *5.5.2 Prior Inconsistent Statements*

Prior inconsistent statements damage a witness's credibility because they demonstrate the witness has changed their story. Depending upon the nature and seriousness of the change, you may show the witness to be evasive, opportunistic, error-prone, or even lying. To accomplish any of these goals, of course, the prior statement must be clearly inconsistent with the current testimony, as well as directed to a subject of true significance to the case. Semi-inconsistencies concerning tangential matters will have little or no impact.

---

16. *See, e.g.*, Fed. R. Evid. 801(d)(1) & 804(b)(1); Fed. R. Civ. P. 32.

There are three steps necessary to impeach a witness with a prior inconsistent statement: 1) recommit; 2) validate; and 3) confront. The following subsections treat each of the three steps in detail. See Demonstration 9.1 in the MTA video catalog for a demonstration of impeachment by a prior inconsistent statement.

#### 5.5.2.1 Recommit the Witness

The first step in impeaching a witness with a prior inconsistent statement is to recommit the witness to their current testimony:

Question: Mr. Kaye, you testified on direct examination that the light was green for the southbound traffic, correct?

This is the traditional way to recommit the witness. The purpose of recommitting the witness is to underscore the gulf between the current testimony and the prior statement. There is no evidentiary requirement that the witness be allowed to repeat the direct testimony. On the other hand, it is difficult to imagine how the two statements could be effectively contrasted without restating the testimony that is about to be impeached.

There is an elegant alternative to the traditional approach to recommitting the witness by rephrasing the direct examination in language that is beneficial to the cross-examiner's own case. Recommitment's only purpose is to focus attention on the inconsistency between the hearing testimony and the prior statement. It is therefore possible to recommit the witness to current testimony's content without repeating it word for word. The content, in turn, can be phrased in a virtually unlimited number of ways. Consider the simple traffic light example above. The witness testified on direct examination that the light was green for the southbound traffic, but their statement to the police was just the opposite. It is your theory that the light was red for the southbound traffic. Rather than repeat the direct testimony, the cross-examiner can recommit the witness as follows:

Question: Mr. Kaye, the light was red for the southbound traffic, correct?

Answer: No, that is not true.

Question: Mr. Kaye, I would like to show you the statement that you gave to Officer Martinez.

You can now proceed to impeach the witness with their own prior statement. This format for recommittal avoids repeating the direct testimony. It also allows you to describe your own case in affirmative language: "Wasn't the light red for the southbound traffic?" Since your case rests on the proposition that the light was red for the southbound traffic, you profit from stating that affirmative fact as often as possible.

#### 5.5.2.2 Validate the Prior Statement

Once the witness has been recommitted, the next step in the impeachment is to validate the prior statement. Validation establishes that the witness actually made the impeaching statement. Depending upon the case's circumstances, you can employ further validation to accredit or demonstrate the accuracy of the earlier statement, as opposed to the witness's direct testimony.

The fact that a witness has made a prior inconsistent statement is impeaching, but it does not necessarily demonstrate that the witness's current testimony is false or inaccurate. After all, the earlier statement may have been erroneous, and the direct testimony correct. It is therefore frequently advantageous to show that the first statement was made under circumstances that make it the more accurate of the two. Since the two statements are mutually exclusive, there is a natural syllogism: If the earlier statement is true, then the current testimony must be wrong. Thus, accrediting the prior inconsistent statement further detracts from the witness's credibility. Of course, no witness is likely to admit that their pre-arbitration statement was more accurate than their sworn testimony. It is therefore usually necessary to accredit the prior statement with circumstantial evidence. Many indicia of accuracy can be attributed to the witness's earlier statement, including importance, duty, and proximity in time.

***Accreditation through importance.*** You can accredit a witness's earlier statement by showing that the witness had an important reason to be accurate when giving it.

***Accreditation through duty.*** You can also accredit the prior statement by showing that the witness was under either a legal or business duty to be accurate. The most common example of a statement given under a legal duty is prior testimony given under oath, either at trial, arbitration, or deposition.

***Accreditation through proximity in time.*** Because human memory inevitably fades, you can accredit an earlier statement because it was given closer in time to the events being described. You can employ this source of accreditation whether the impeaching material is a written statement, a deposition transcript, or a business document.

#### 5.5.2.3 Confront the Witness with the Prior Statement

The final stage of impeachment is to confront the witness with the prior statement. The purpose of this confrontation is to make the witness admit that they indeed made the earlier statement; recall that it is the fact of the prior inconsistency that is admissible as impeachment. This confrontation need not be "confrontational." It is frequently sufficient merely to require the witness to admit making the impeaching statement since most impeachment is based upon a witness's forgetfulness, confusion, or embellishment. Reserve hostility or accusation for those rare situations when you can prove the witness to be lying or acting out of some other ill motive. To be effective, accomplish the confrontation in a clear and concise manner that leaves the witness no room for evasion or argument. The classic approach is simply to read the witness's own words.

Follow two cardinal rules in confronting a witness with a prior inconsistent statement:

1) Read the statement to the witness—do not ask the witness to read the statement aloud.
2) Do not ask the witness to explain the inconsistency.

Both rules apply basic principles of cross-examination.

You can use a video deposition in lieu of a deposition transcript, which may better hold the arbitrator's attention. Commercial firms can provide a synchronized deposition—meaning you provide the video deposition which they link to a written transcript. Then by clicking on or scanning a part of the linked written transcript, you are taken directly to a specific part of the video deposition. You can also show scrolling text beneath the video so the arbitrator can both hear and read the witness's inconsistent video statement during the deposition.

When handling an arbitration for the first time, using a checklist like the one below can help you hit all the steps for a proper impeachment.

**IMPEACHMENT**

- ❑ Recommit to statement
  - Have witness deny fact you know is true based on prior testimony
  - "The light was red, correct?" "No, it was green."
- ❑ Provide prior statement to opposing counsel/witness
  - Elective
- ❑ Validate prior statement
  - Witness made prior statement
  - Accurate circumstances
    - ✓ Important reason to be accurate
    - ✓ Duty
    - ✓ Proximity in time
- ❑ Read prior statement to witness

#### 5.5.2.4 Ethical Concerns

Two primary ethical issues arise in the context of impeaching a witness using a prior inconsistent statement. The first issue is attempting to use the statement for a purpose other than that for which it was admitted.

It is unethical for a lawyer to "allude to any matter which the lawyer does not reasonably believe is . . . supported by admissible evidence."[17] Once an arbitrator has ruled that certain evidence is admissible only for a limited purpose, it is inadmissible on those issues for which it has been excluded. In light of a limiting instruction, no lawyer can reasonably believe otherwise. Thus, it is unethical to allude to a purely impeaching statement as though it had been admitted as substantive evidence.

In arbitration you need not be as concerned about unethically using an inconsistent statement for the truth of the matter rather than only for the nonhearsay purpose of impeachment. Hearsay is generally admissible.

The second ethical issue in impeachment involves the admonition not to allow a witness to explain the inconsistency. Assuming that there may be a perfectly reasonable explanation for the discrepancy between two statements, is it ethical to prevent the witness from explaining? The answer lies in the fact that it is not truly possible for a cross-examiner to prevent a witness from providing an explanation. It will always be possible for opposing counsel to ask the witness to elaborate during redirect examination. No admissible evidence can ultimately be excluded as the result of cross-examination tactics. The most the cross-examiner can accomplish will be to prevent the witness from explaining an inconsistency during cross-examination. As an advocate, it is the cross-examiner's task to present the evidence that is favorable to the client; the very purpose of redirect is to allow the other side to fill in gaps, remedy errors, and correct misperceptions. Thus, leaving potential explanations to redirect is perfectly permissible under the adversary system.

### *5.5.3 Other Prior Inconsistencies*

In addition to prior inconsistent statements, witnesses may also be impeached by prior omissions or silence or with prior inconsistent actions.

#### 5.5.3.1 Impeachment by Omission or Silence

Impeachment by omission generally follows the same theory as impeachment with a prior inconsistent statement. The witness's current testimony is rendered less credible because when they told the same story earlier it did not contain facts that they now claims are true. In essence, the impeachment is saying, "Do not believe

17. Model Rules of Prof'l Conduct, r. 3.4(e) (Am. Bar Ass'n 2020).

this witness, because they are adding facts to their story." In other words, "If those things are true, why didn't you say them before?"

To be impeaching, the witness's prior omission must be inconsistent with the current testimony. A prior omission is not impeaching if it occurred in circumstances that do not render it incompatible with the witness's testimony at the hearing. Circumstances that create the necessary discontinuity between omission and testimony include opportunity, duty, and natural inclination.

#### 5.5.3.2 Prior Inconsistent Actions

Finally, a witness may be impeached with prior inconsistent actions. The witness's current testimony is rendered less credible by pointing out that they did not act in conformity with their own story on some previous occasion: "If what you are saying now is true, why did you act inconsistently in the past?" Unlike impeachment through prior inconsistent statements or omissions, no elaborate setup is necessary to use prior inconsistent actions. It is sufficient simply to put the questions to the witness.

### *5.5.4 Character and "Characteristic" Impeachment*

"Character impeachment" refers to using some inherent trait or particular characteristic of the witness, essentially unrelated to the case at hand, to render the testimony less credible. The thrust of the impeachment is to show that the witness, for some demonstrable reason, is simply not trustworthy.

The most common forms of characteristic impeachment include:

- conviction of a crime,
- past untruthfulness and other bad acts, and
- impaired perception or recollection.

#### 5.5.4.1 Conviction of a Crime

A witness may be impeached based on their past conviction for certain crimes. While the specifics vary from state to state, under the Federal Rules of Evidence a conviction is admissible for impeachment only if the crime:

1) was a felony and the probative value of admitting the conviction is not substantially outweighed by its prejudicial effect, or
2) involved a dishonest act or false statement, regardless of whether a felony or a misdemeanor.

In addition, Fed. R. Evid. 609 provides that convictions generally may not be used if they are more than ten years old and that juvenile adjudications and convictions that have been pardoned or annulled are inadmissible under most circumstances.

#### 5.5.4.2 Past Untruthfulness and Other Bad Acts

We have discussed the rules governing impeachment based on a criminal conviction. What if a witness's untruthfulness or bad acts were not the subject of a conviction? The Federal Rules of Evidence strike a balance by allowing the impeachment of witnesses based on specific instances of past misconduct, apart from criminal convictions, only if they are probative of untruthfulness. A witness can therefore be impeached with evidence that they have lied on a specific previous occasion but not on the basis of previous violence. Moreover, an arbitrator has discretion to exclude evidence even of past untruthfulness. Finally, incidents of prior untruthfulness may not be proven by extrinsic evidence. The cross-examiner is stuck with the witness's answer. Impeachment based on past untruthfulness is therefore a very tricky matter. You must be certain that the witness will "own up" to the charge, since you will be unable to prove it otherwise.

#### 5.5.4.3 Impaired Perception or Recollection

A witness can also be impeached based on inability to perceive or recall events. Perception can be adversely affected by a wide variety of circumstances. The witness may have been distracted at the time of the events, or their vision may have been obscured. The witness may have been sleepy, frightened, or intoxicated. The witness may have poor eyesight or may suffer from some other sensory deficit. Any of these, or similar, facts can be used to impeach the credibility of a witness's testimony. As with so much else in cross-examination, this form of impeachment is usually most effective when counsel refrains from asking the ultimate question.

### *5.5.5 "Case Data" Impeachment*

Some facts are impeaching only within the circumstances of a particular case. They would be innocuous, or perhaps even helpful, in any other context. The most common forms of case data impeachment are based on the witness's personal interest, motive, and bias or prejudice.

#### 5.5.5.1 Personal Interest

A witness who is personally interested in a case's outcome may be inclined to testify with less than absolute candor. Whether consciously or subconsciously, it is a well-recognized human tendency to shape one's recollection in the direction of the desired outcome. Impeachment based on personal interest takes advantage of this phenomenon by pointing out just how the witness stands to gain or lose as a consequence of the case's resolution. The technique may be applied to both party and nonparty witnesses.

#### 5.5.5.2 Motive

A witness's testimony may be affected by a motive other than financial interest. The witness may have a professional stake in the issues being litigated or may have some other reason to prefer one outcome to another.

#### 5.5.5.3 Bias or Prejudice

Bias and prejudice generally refer to a witness's relationship to one of the parties. A witness may be well-disposed, or ill-inclined, toward either the claimant or respondent. Sadly, some witnesses harbor prejudices against entire groups of people. Bias in favor of a party is often the consequence of friendship or affinity.

## 5.6 Shaping the Process Toward a Favorable Decision

In arbitration, unlike at trial, you are not usually concerned with preserving the record for appeal. Rather, much like a sculptor, you are actively engaged in shaping the process toward a favorable decision by the arbitrator. In the words of Michelangelo, "The more the marble wastes, the more the statue grows." This process-shaping consists of several activities including:

1) introducing all pertinent evidence;
2) properly handling and using exhibits;
3) using exhibits persuasively;
4) ensuring complete and accurate transcripts;
5) making and responding to offers of proof; and
6) making and responding to objections.

### *5.6.1 Introducing All Pertinent Evidence*

No one would arbitrate a case, particularly one involving multiple documentary and other physical exhibits, without keeping a log or record of which exhibits were admitted (i.e., cleared), rejected (for insufficient foundation, irrelevancy, etc.), or offered and withdrawn. Throughout an arbitration hearing, keep an exhibit log for the exhibits that you seek to introduce into evidence and, separately, for the exhibits that the other party or parties seek to introduce. An example of an exhibit log format appears in Appendix F.

In arbitrations involving many exhibits and/or having several parties and lasting several days, you or an assistant must keep an exhibit log if for no other reason than to identify what evidence you may properly refer to in your closing argument to the arbitrator. Evidence not admitted cannot be the basis of any assertion in closing argument, and the exhibit log can give you an instant picture of the parameters governing the scope of your argument. A log of your opponent's exhibits can assist you in objecting to exhibits being argued to the arbitrator (or later in connection with post-hearing motions) that was not admitted into evidence (or was withdrawn, as the case may be). The exhibit log serves as a helpful reference when you draft any required post-hearing briefs—it is invaluable as your overview document indicating which piece of evidence was rejected, when it was rejected (pointing you to the appropriate date of transcript), and the reason the arbitrator rejected the evidence. It may also help you sift out any significant evidentiary issues to raise in a motion for reconsideration of an arbitration award. Also, exhibit logs of your and your opponents' exhibits will quickly refresh your memory of items of your evidence that were received despite your opponent's objections and why. It is also a handy exhibit index for reviewing the hearing record when you prepare a response to a motion for reconsideration of an arbitration award.

In addition to these post close-of-evidence uses, the exhibit log also benefits its users during an arbitration hearing. Arbitration advocates suffer from one horrible recurring nightmare: the one where they omit introducing into evidence the one minor, insignificant-seeming document that is critical to proving an essential element of their claim or defense. In such an instance, even small things may turn the scale. Not only can this be terribly embarrassing if it occurs; it can provide the basis for a potential legal malpractice action by the client. An exhibit log helps prevent this from happening. Review the log prior to the case's close and prior to the close of all the evidence and satisfy yourself that you have offered and admitted all critical pieces of evidence (or that there is a record of rejection). You can even indicate to the arbitrator at the conclusion of the evidence that you would like to make sure all exhibits you offered have been moved into evidence.

Review the exhibit log to ensure that all your objections to your opponent's exhibits have been clearly and comprehensively stated to the arbitrator. Sometimes additional reasons for your objecting to certain evidence will become apparent to you during the hearing's course and you may wish to have the arbitrator reconsider a previous ruling in light of your additional basis for objections. If you do not overdo it, most arbitrators will accommodate you in this regard, particularly with respect to a critical piece of evidence whose admissibility is in dispute.

Occasionally, an arbitrator reserves ruling on the admissibility of certain exhibits, pending counsel's providing additional evidence "connecting them up" and establishing their relevance. The exhibit log reminds you which exhibits require a ruling by the arbitrator. Also, arbitrators sometimes reject evidence, but, on request, permit counsel to make an offer of proof immediately or later in the proceedings. The exhibit log can remind you which exhibits need to be supported by an offer of proof prior to the close of the evidence.

In summary, an exhibit log ensures that an accurate record of the hearing evidence is properly preserved for later use, either in connection with briefing on post-hearing briefs, a motion for reconsideration of the award, or a court challenge to the award.

## *5.6.2 Proper Handling and Use of Exhibits*

### 5.6.2.1 The Role of Exhibits

Exhibits are the tangible objects, documents, photographs, video and audio recordings, and other items offered for the arbitrator's consideration. Exhibits are the only form, apart from witness testimony, in which evidence can be received. In an arbitration hearing, exhibits enhance or supplement the testimony of the witnesses. Exhibits can make information clearer, more concrete, more understandable, and more reliable. The subsections immediately following will discuss the general procedures for handling, introducing, and using exhibits (Lore & Lubet, *MTA*, section 11.3).

#### 5.6.2.2 Types of Exhibits

While the categories tend to overlap and the lines cannot be drawn with precision, it is often helpful to think of exhibits as falling into these three categories:

1) real evidence,
2) demonstrative evidence, and
3) documentary evidence.

***Real evidence.*** Real evidence refers to tangible objects that played an actual role in the events at issue in the hearing. Photographs, while obviously different from tangible objects, are so close to reality that they are also often treated as real evidence. Documents such as contracts, memoranda, letters, and other primary writings can also be considered real evidence, although the special rules that apply to out-of-court writings generally make it more convenient to treat documentary evidence as a separate category.

***Demonstrative evidence.*** These exhibits did not play an actual role in the events underlying the case, but instead illustrate or clarify a witness's testimony. Lawyers generate demonstratives, which can take the form of models, graphs, diagrams, charts, drawings, computer-generated animations, simulations, or timelines, or any other objects that explain or illustrate issues in the case.

***Documentary evidence.*** Documentary evidence refers to virtually all writings, including letters, contracts, leases, memoranda, reports, and business records, whether physical or stored electronically. Written documents, almost by definition, contain out-of-court statements, and they are typically offered because their contents are relevant to the case. Thus, most documents face hearsay hurdles in a way that real and demonstrative exhibits do not. Tangible objects are admitted into evidence because of what they are; documentary exhibits are admitted because of what they say. The value of documentary evidence cannot be overstated. Intrinsic writings can provide proof of past events in a way that mere testimony cannot.

#### 5.6.2.3 Prehearing Procedures for the Admission of Exhibits

In arbitration, the arbitrator can deal with and rule on contested exhibits in a preliminary hearing. You can file motions in limine (Latin for "at the threshold") prior to the hearing to exclude evidence or asking for a ruling declaring certain evidence admissible. The arbitrator can rule on such motions in a preliminary hearing. Stipulations and requests to admit can also be worked out in the same hearing.

#### 5.6.2.4 Offering Exhibits During the Hearing

Whether they consist of real, demonstrative, or documentary evidence, there is one basic protocol for offering exhibits at an arbitration hearing. Although the details vary somewhat from one arbitration setting to another, the following steps form a nearly universal procedure.

##### *Mark the exhibit for identification*

Mark every exhibit for identification before you offer it into evidence, or even refer to it during a hearing. Marking the exhibit identifies it for the record so it will be uniquely recognizable to anyone who later reads a transcript of the proceedings. References to "this letter" or "the first broken fastener" may be understood in the hearing room, but they will be meaningless to someone reading the transcript. "Respondent's exhibit three," on the other hand, can mean only one thing, assuming that the exhibit was appropriately marked and identified.

Exhibits are generally marked sequentially and further identified according to the designation of the party who has first offered them. Thus, the exhibits in a two-party arbitration will be called Claimant's Exhibit 1, Claimant's Exhibit 2, Respondent's Exhibit 1, Respondent's Exhibit 2, and so forth. In multiparty hearings, identify each exhibit by the name, and not merely the designation, of the party who offers it. Accordingly, you will see references to claimant Bennett Exhibit 1, or Juarez Exhibit 2. In some arbitrations, claimants may be expected to use sequential numbers for their exhibits, while respondents are requested to use letters—Claimant's Exhibit 1 and Respondent's Exhibit A. The details of the marking system are unimportant, so long as it clearly indicates which exhibit is which.

The mark itself usually takes the form of a sticker placed directly on the object or document. Stickers are available in a variety of forms. Many attorneys use color-coded sets with a space left blank for the number assigned to each exhibit. You should premark exhibits, either at a prehearing conference or in your office. The term "marked for identification" means the exhibit has been marked, and can be referred to in arbitration, but has not yet been admitted into evidence. Exhibits that have been marked for identification may be shown to witnesses and may be the subject of limited examinations for the purpose of establishing a foundation. Many arbitrators shun the "for identification" notation as redundant. All exhibits need to be marked, and the record will show which have been allowed into evidence even in the absence of a special inscription.

##### *Identify the exhibit for opposing counsel*

Identify exhibits for opposing counsel before showing them to the witness. Do this by referring to the exhibit number or by indicating its designation in the prehearing order if one has been prepared. Most arbitrators will expect you to hand or display the exhibit to opposing counsel before proceeding.

### *Examine the witness on the exhibit's foundation*

Having identified the exhibit, you may now proceed to lay the foundation for its admission.

***Show the exhibit to the witness.*** The first step is to show the exhibit to the witness. This is typically done by handing it to the witness, directing the witness to the exhibit number in the binder, or screensharing the exhibit. If the exhibit is something as large as a life-sized model or an enlarged photograph, you may point to it and direct the witness's attention. In either case, announce for the record what you are doing, using a shorthand description of the exhibit and its identification number:

Counsel: Ms. Bowman, I am handing you Respondent's Exhibit 11, which is a letter dated July 26.

The description ensures clarity and must be scrupulously neutral. While you are allowed to ask a leading question on preliminary matters, you are not allowed to begin arguing your case under the pretext of laying a foundation. Thus, you cannot say:

Counsel: Ms. Bowman, I am handing you Respondent's Exhibit 11, which is the letter in which the claimant agreed to provide repair service at no additional cost.

***Identify the exhibit.*** Next, have the witness identify the exhibit. The witness should state the basis for their familiarity with the exhibit, and then describe it in some detail:

Question: Have you ever seen Claimant's Exhibit 7 before?

Answer: Yes, I have seen it many times.

Question: What is Claimant's Exhibit 7?

Answer: It is a piece of the stationery that I received when my order was delivered from Quickset Printing.

Question: How is it that you recognize it?

Answer: I remember how it looked when I took it out of the box.

***Complete the foundation.*** In some situations, particularly those involving real evidence, identifying the exhibit provides a sufficient foundation for admission. In other circumstances, the foundation will be much more elaborate, perhaps calling for chain of custody or the establishment of a hearsay exception. These and other foundations for the introduction of real, demonstrative, and documentary evidence are discussed in Chapter 6.

***Offer the exhibit into evidence***

Once you have completed the foundation, offer the exhibit into evidence. Jurisdictions vary in the formality with which this must be done. In the simplest version:

Counsel: Ms. Arbitrator, we offer Claimant's Exhibit 3.

In any case, show the exhibit to the arbitrator, who will then ask opposing counsel if there are any objections to its admission. If there are no objections, the arbitrator will receive the exhibit into evidence.

***Use the exhibit***

Once an exhibit has been admitted into evidence, a witness can testify about its contents, and you can use it to illustrate or amplify a witness's testimony. Tangible objects can be used in demonstrations. For suggestions on ways to use exhibits persuasively in arbitration, see section 5.8.2.

When handling your first arbitration, the following checklist can help you hit all the steps to introduce documents into evidence.

**ADMITTING EXHIBITS**

- ❑ Mark for identification
- ❑ Identify/provide to opposing counsel
- ❑ Identify/provide to arbitrator
- ❑ Identify/provide to witness
- ❑ Ask witness to identify
- ❑ Lay foundation
  - ✓ what is it
  - ✓ is that your signature
  - ✓ how are you familiar with it
  - ✓ is it what it purports to be
- ❑ Move to admit
- ❑ Ask if any objections
- ❑ Arbitrator admits
- ❑ Check off as admitted
- ❑ Publish
  - ✓ Your witness reads
  - ✓ You read

Demonstrations 12 and 15 in the MTA video catalog show attorneys admitting a documentary exhibit.

## 5.7 Final Argument

### *5.7.1 The Role and Function of the Final Argument*

#### 5.7.1.1 The Whole Story

Final argument in arbitration is the advocate's only opportunity to tell the case's story in its entirety, without interruption, free from most constraining formalities (Lore & Lubet, *MTA*, Ch. 14). Unlike witness examinations, counsel delivers the final argument in their own words, and without the need to intermittently cede the stage to the opposition. Unlike the opening statement, it is not bound by rules governing proper and improper content. In other words, final argument is the moment for pure advocacy, when your organizational, analytic, interpretive, and forensic skills are brought to bear on the task of persuading the arbitrator. The final argument cannot be fully successful unless the preceding stages of the arbitration hearing were also successful. The opening statement's mental image will not stay with the arbitrator unless it is sustained by evidence from the witness stand. More to the point, the final argument cannot paint a picture that is contrary to, or unsupported by, the evidence. While final argument can and should be the capstone of a well-tried case, it is unlikely to be the saving grace of a poor one. Many arbitrators may already have reached a tentative, but relatively solid, decision before hearing final argument.

#### 5.7.1.2 Use of Theory and Theme

***Theory***

If nothing else, the final argument must communicate the advocate's theory of the case. Some witnesses can be disregarded, some details omitted, but the theory of the case is crucial. Your final argument must, therefore, illuminate your theory. Tell the arbitrator why your client is entitled to an award. Simply reciting facts is not sufficient. Rather, use the argument to coalesce and synthesize information from the various witnesses and exhibits in a way that creates only one result. To be successful, the theory you present in a final argument must be logical, believable, and legally sufficient.

***Logical.*** Your case theory, and consequently final argument, must be logical, the component facts leading to the desired conclusions. Reason, therefore, backward: start with the conclusion and then provide supportive facts.

***Believable.*** The most logical theory in the world will not win a case if the arbitrator doesn't believe it. For a theory to be sound, you must base it on facts that are likely to be accepted. The most believable information is often produced by the other side—admissions. Although not quite so powerful as admissions, undisputed facts provide a sturdy cornerstone for case theory and final argument; marshal them to cast light on disputed evidence. When key events or occurrences are in dispute, make your perception of events believable by arguing from common sense and experience. Finally, establish believability by relying upon the witnesses' credibility.

***Legally sufficient.*** The final component of a solid theory is legal sufficiency. The logic and believability of a final argument must lead to the desired legal result. In other words, a final argument must address the law as well as the facts.

#### Theme

While utilizing an explicit, one sentence theme is less important in arbitration than at trial, knowing and conveying your theme can enhance believability. Make your theme a constant presence throughout the final argument. Unlike opening statement and witness examinations, where you can only use a theme intermittently, you can organize the entire final argument to emphasize your theme. Begin with a statement of the theme and constantly return to it in each segment of the argument.

### 5.7.1.3 What Makes It Argument

Recall the cardinal rule of opening statements that you may not argue. In final argument, on the other hand, you may, should, and must argue if you are serious about winning your case. The gloves are off and the limitations are removed, but what precisely distinguishes argument from mere presentation of the facts? The following are some of the most useful elements of argument.

***Application of law.*** Apply the law to the case's facts. Discussing the law is limited during the opening statement and all but forbidden during witness examinations, but it is a staple of the final argument.

***Conclusions.*** Draw and urge conclusions based upon the evidence. Spell out the result, consequence, or repercussion that follows from the evidence in the case. It is not sufficient for a final argument to draw, or even urge, conclusions. The argument must go on to explain why the desired conclusions are the correct ones.

***Inferences.*** While a final argument can and should include broad conclusions, it may also include the sort of narrow conclusions commonly known as inferences. An inference is a deduction drawn from the existence of a known fact. In other words, you need not prove the inferred fact so long as it is a commonsense consequence of some established fact. An inference will be accepted only if it is well grounded in common understanding, so explain the basis of all but the most obvious inferences. For example, everyone will be willing to infer a child's age from knowledge of their grade in school. There is no need to explain that third graders are typically eight or nine years old. Other inferences, however, may be more complicated.

A classic example appears in the movie *My Cousin Vinny.* On cross-examination of the witness to the alleged burglary by the defendant youths, Vinny asks what the witness ate for breakfast. The type of breakfast appears to have little relation to whether the youths committed the crime until the inferences are made explicit. The argument is one of mistaken identity. The youths did not commit the crime because someone else did during the time the witness was preparing breakfast. There was enough time for someone else to come into the store and commit the robbery because the witness was having grits for breakfast. Grits take twenty minutes to prepare, which is sufficient time for one set of youths to leave and another to arrive.[18]

***Details and circumstantial evidence.*** Final argument is your only opportunity to explain the relevance and consequences of circumstantial evidence. Much of the art of direct and cross-examination consists of accumulating details that lead to a certain conclusion or result. The facts brought out through different witnesses, not to mention trial strategy and luck, may result in the scattering of such details throughout the arbitration. Final argument allows you to reassemble the details so they lead to the desired result.

***Credibility and motive.*** Now is the time to comment on, and compare, witnesses' motive and credibility. Arbitrations involve competing renditions of past events, which the arbitrator must resolve to reach a decision. Final argument is the only time when you may directly confront witness character and explain why the arbitrator should believe some witnesses and discount others. Witness examinations can bring out impeaching facts, and the opening statement can use apposition to contrast the credibility of different witnesses. But only in final argument can you make direct comparisons. Finally, you can argue motive on the basis either of proven facts or logical inferences. You may tell the arbitrator why a witness would exaggerate, waffle, conceal information, quibble, or lie. The suggested reasons need not be based on outright admissions, so long as they follow rationally from the testimony in the case.

***Weight of the evidence.*** Opening statement limited you to a recitation of the expected evidence; final argument lets you assert the weight of the evidence.

- Why is one version preferable to another?
- Why should some facts be accepted, and others rejected?
- Why is one case stronger than the other?

***Demeanor.*** It is fair game in final argument to comment on a witness's demeanor. Demeanor arguments are usually negative in nature, since it is easier to

18. My Cousin Vinny (20th Century Studios 1992) (transcript available at https://www.americanrhetoric.com/MovieSpeeches/moviespeechmycousinvinny3.html) (last visited Jun. 2024).

characterize untrustworthy conduct. An argument that your own witness "looked like they were telling the truth" seems insincere or overprotective. Negative comments, on the other hand, can be effective so long as they are adequately based on observable fact. One caveat: demeanor argument is based strictly on perception, and there is little way to ensure that your perception of the witness will be the same as the arbitrator's. Conduct you see as evidence of deception an arbitrator may regard as a reasonable response to unfair questioning. Be careful. Use demeanor arguments only when the witness's behavior has been blatant and unambiguous.

***Refutation.*** Refute opposing positions. Opening statements and witness examinations may recite and elicit facts that are contrary to the opposition case, but final argument can contest it directly by pointing out errors, inconsistencies, implausibilities, and contradictions.

***Moral appeal.*** Elaborate on the case's moral theme. Recall that a theme states, usually in a single sentence, a compelling moral basis for a verdict in your client's favor. Your theme invokes shared values, civic virtues, or common motivations. You stated the theme during the opening statement and alluded to it in witness examinations; now hammer it home in the final argument.

#### 5.7.1.4 Analogies, Allusions, and Stories

***Analogies.*** An analogy explains human conduct through reference to everyday human behavior. Strengthen or diminish a witness's testimony by comparing their version of events to some widely understood experience or activity. While analogies can be very powerful, there is always the danger that the other side can invert and exploit them. If opposing counsel has yet to argue, ensure that any analogies are "airtight." For the same reason, claimant's counsel often reserves analogies until rebuttal, when the respondent will no longer be able to reply.

***Allusions.*** An allusion is a literary or similar reference that adds persuasive force to an argument. In earlier days, before the internet, lawyers' allusions were mostly drawn from Shakespeare or the Bible, or Justice Learned Hand. Today, references are just as likely to be taken from motion pictures, streaming shows, song lyrics, fairy tales, or even advertisements. Test your allusions on a broad audience—the latest TikTok craze may not speak to your arbitrator.

***Stories.*** Stories, in the form of either hypotheticals or anecdotes, can be used effectively in final argument. You can illustrate an argument with a hypothetical story, provided the story is based on facts that are in evidence.

### *5.7.2 Format*

In most arbitrations, the parties' final arguments are divided into three distinct segments, presented in the following order: claimant's argument in chief, respondent's argument in chief, and claimant's rebuttal. Some arbitrations allow claimant to opt to argue second; in those instances, there are only two components: respondent's argument and claimant's rebuttal.

### 5.7.2.1 Claimant's Argument in Chief

A successful argument in chief defines the issues and lays out the case's entire theory. The claimant's argument in chief will fail unless it provides the arbitrator with compelling reasons to find for the claimant on every necessary issue. Claimant's initial argument in arbitration must be comprehensive. In arbitration, the standard of proof is usually a preponderance of the evidence; claimant must establish all the elements of their cause of action. Failing to address an element can be fatal. In contrast, the respondent prevails simply by disproving a single element of the claimant. To counterbalance this advantage, a claimant's attorney will often use the final argument to issue a series of challenges to the respondent, drawing the respondent's counsel into a discussion of issues that they might prefer to leave alone.

### 5.7.2.2 Respondent's Argument in Chief

The respondent enjoys substantially more latitude than the claimant in determining the content of the argument in chief. While the claimant must address every element, the respondent is usually free to "cherry pick," selecting only those elements or issues in which counsel has the most confidence. The defense theory, of course, must be comprehensive in the sense that it explains all the relevant evidence, but its legal thrust may be significantly more pointed than the claimant's. The defining characteristic of the defendant's argument in chief is that it is sandwiched between the claimant's two arguments. Respondent's counsel must respond to the claimant's argument in chief but will not be able to respond to rebuttal.

***Responding to the claimant's argument in chief.*** Reply directly to the claimant's argument in chief. After listening to the claimant's prolonged excoriation of the respondent, the arbitrator will immediately want to know what you have to say in return. This does not mean you should adopt the claimant's organization or respond point by point, but your argument cannot be entirely divorced from the structure that the claimant creates. At a minimum, deny the specific charges leveled in the claimant's argument. It is a natural human response to deny unfair or untrue accusations. The arbitrator will expect as much from a wrongly blamed respondent. Unless there is a good reason for doing otherwise, state the denial early in your argument.

The watchword for the respondent's argument in chief is flexibility. While the claimant has the luxury of composing their entire final argument, the respondent must always be alert to new issues and nuances raised once the arguments have begun. Arrive at the hearing with the majority of your final argument prepared, and then modify your argument to address any unanticipated facts or points opposing counsel makes in opening statement, or on cross-examination. Discard your well-rehearsed argument in favor of an effective one that rebuts the claimant's case as presented at the end of the hearing. Be prepared to modify your final argument once again after hearing the claimant's final argument.

***Anticipating rebuttal.*** The greatest difficulty is knowing that, ordinarily, you cannot speak again following the claimant's rebuttal. The claimant may comment on, criticize, or even ridicule your argument, but you may not reply; your perfectly good answers for everything that the claimant says on rebuttal do not matter. You can request permission to give a surrebuttal argument, but arbitrators do not always grant such requests. You must, therefore, do whatever you can to blunt the rebuttal in advance by anticipating and replying specifically to the claimant's possible rebuttal arguments.

### 5.7.2.3 Claimant's Rebuttal

Effective use of rebuttal can be elusive. While the claimant's argument in chief can be completely planned in advance and the respondent's argument in chief can be mostly planned, rebuttal must generally be delivered extemporaneously. Preparing for rebuttal typically takes place while claimant's counsel listens to the respondent's argument in chief. Nonetheless, you can apply certain principles to make rebuttal more forceful and compelling. The most important is to organize it according to the claimant's own theory of the case.

***Structure response around claimant's issues.*** A common approach to rebuttal is simply to make notes of the respondent's arguments and then to reply to the most important of them in the order in which they were delivered. This technique is easy to use and minimizes the potential for overlooking arguments. Its vice, however, is that it organizes the rebuttal according to the respondent's agenda, rather than the claimant's. It also tends to promote a boring delivery if the rebuttal falls into a repetitive cadence of short paragraphs, each one beginning, "The respondent also argued . . . ."

A more effective technique matches your arguments to the major propositions in your case. To do this, prepare a truncated outline of the three or four most important, or hotly contested, issues in the case, leaving a blank half-page or so under each heading. In this manner, you can spread four major arguments over two sheets of paper and arrange them in the order most advantageous to your case. Then, as respondent's counsel argues, write notes under the appropriate heading. When it comes time to deliver rebuttal, you have automatically organized your notes of the respondent's remarks according to your own structure. You can then deliver the rebuttal topically, disregarding the order of argument the respondent used.

***Present claimant's case affirmatively.*** Even when it is well organized, rebuttal is weakened if it becomes nothing more than a series of retorts. Effective argument presents the positive side of your own case; this is particularly important when you represent the burdened party. Consequently, even in rebuttal, frame every position as a constructive statement of the claimant's own theory, and refute the defense by explaining further or elaborating on your case.

***Avoid sandbagging an argument.*** It is inherently risky for the claimant to sandbag by completely omitting a subject from the argument in chief and then trying to argue it in rebuttal. If the respondent does not touch on the same or related topic in their argument, the arbitrator may not permit claimant to raise the topic for the first time in rebuttal. It usually is not risky, however, to withhold an analogy or story until rebuttal, thereby preventing the respondent from reversing it.

#### 5.7.2.4 Variations

It is always within the arbitrator's discretion to alter the usual order of argument to reflect the actual burden of proof in the particular case. In cases involving counterclaims or affirmative defenses, the respondent may be allowed to present the first and last arguments or may be given a surrebuttal to follow the claimant's rebuttal. In multiparty cases, the arbitrator will determine the order in which the various claimants and respondents will proceed. It is also the arbitrator's prerogative to apportion the time for argument, although the arbitrator may not effectively deny a party the opportunity to argue its case. Finally, some arbitrators do not provide automatically for rebuttal but rather require the claimant to affirmatively reserve time from the argument in chief.

### *5.7.3 Structure*

Develop your final argument's structure for maximum persuasive weight. The central thrust of the final argument must always be to provide reasons—legal, moral, emotional, logical—for an award in your client's favor. Make every aspect of the final argument contribute in some way to the completion of the sentence "My client wins because . . . ." In the broadest sense, of course, the desired conclusion should simply follow from the case's law and facts. Few cases, however, will go to arbitration unless the facts are capable of multiple interpretations. Effective argument therefore places a premium on arrangement and explanation. Topical organization is the guiding principle in the structure of final arguments. The following section discusses the various methods of employing topical organization and the drawbacks and advantages of alternative structures.

#### 5.7.3.1 Topical Organization

The importance of topical organization in final argument cannot be overemphasized. Seemingly natural methods of organization, such as chronology and witness listing, will not present the evidence in its most persuasive form. Topical organization, on the other hand, allows you to determine the best way to address the case's issues. Topical organization can use, or combine, any of the following strategies.

***Elements.*** Every legal cause or defense is composed of various discrete elements. A claim of negligence, for instance, must be supported by proof of duty, breach of duty, cause in fact, proximate cause, and damages. A claimant can therefore develop their final argument by discussing the evidence as it supports each of the distinct elements of their cause of action. A respondent, who needs to challenge only a single element to win, can use the same form of organization, but can truncate it by focusing only on those elements that are likely to be negated.

***Turning points.*** Modern cognitive theory tells us that factfinders regard a case as a series of turning points or problems. Rather than resolving the truth or falsity of every distinct fact, they focus on a limited number of contested issues. Once an arbitrator decides those issues, they will be inclined to fit the individual facts into a picture that fits that view of reality. Persuade an arbitrator, therefore, by identifying the key turning points in the hearing and explaining them in a way that comports with the legal requirements and the arbitrator's life experience and sense of reality.

***Issues.*** One of the simplest forms of organization is to divide the case into a series of discrete factual or legal issues. Large issues, such as liability and damages, are obvious, but so broad that they provide little help in ordering an argument. It is more useful to think of issues as narrower propositions of fact or law.

### 5.7.3.2 Alternative Structures

***Chronological organization.*** Chronology is the most obvious alternative structure for a final argument. Since the case's events manifestly occurred in a chronological order, it seems obvious to replay them in the same progression during final argument. While chronology certainly plays an important role in final argument, events are unlikely to have occurred in the most persuasive possible sequence. Early events can frequently be illuminated by their subsequent consequences.

***Witness listing.*** Some lawyers persist in presenting final argument as a series of witness descriptions and accounts, essentially repeating each witness's testimony. This approach diminishes the argument's logical coherence and force. Where topical organization focuses on the importance of issues and chronological organization focuses on the real-life sequence of events, witness listing depends on nothing more than the serendipity of which witness said what. It is a lazy, and usually ineffective, method of organization. While it will often be necessary to compare witness accounts during a final argument, this should not be the primary focus of the argument.

### 5.7.3.3 Other Organizing Tools

***Start strong and end strong.*** The principles of primacy and recency apply with full force to the final argument. Your final argument is a limited window in which to shape the arbitrator's imagination of the acts, events, and circumstances at issue in the case. Eliminate anything that distracts the arbitrator from the task at hand and devote prime time—the very beginning and the very end of the argument—to the case's most important considerations.

***Claimant—advance affirmative case first.*** Most final arguments consist of two distinct components: developing the affirmative case and debunking the opposing party's claims and/or defenses. Build up your own case first, deemphasizing respondent's facts and points by integrating them, and then debunk any opposition points not already addressed. Resist the temptation to begin by criticizing the respondent's case. No matter how weak or ridiculous the defenses, begin with the strong points of your own case. You bear the burden of proof, after all, and cannot win without establishing all the elements of an affirmative case. You gain little by refuting the defense if you cannot prove your own case first. Moreover, launching immediately into an assault on the respondent's case may be seen as confessing a lack of confidence in your own position. And if the arbitrator does not jump immediately to that conclusion, you can be sure that respondent's counsel will argue that precise inference: "If claimant's case is so strong, why did counsel begin by attacking the defense; they must be worried."

The respondent has more latitude. Having just heard the claimant's argument, an arbitrator is unlikely to draw any adverse inference should respondent's counsel begin by refuting the claimant's case. Indeed, most arbitrators will be waiting to hear the respondent's denial.

***Cluster circumstantial evidence and accumulate details.*** We have seen that details can give texture and support to a case's theory, and that circumstantial evidence can establish major propositions. These small, constituent facts are often presented at different times during the trial's testimonial phase. One witness may testify to several details, the importance of which will become apparent only in light of other evidence supplied by other witnesses. Final argument is the time to gather these details and harmonize them to create a symphony of persuasive thought.

***Bury your concessions.*** Every argument will need to concede certain of the opposition's claims or facts, if only to minimize or discount them. As a corollary to the "start and end strong" rule, bury such concessions in the middle of your argument.

***Weave in witness credibility.*** We noted above that witness listing is an ineffective format for final argument. Witness credibility, on the other hand, is often a subject you must address. The solution is to weave discussion of the witnesses, and their relative credibility, into the story's fabric.

***Carefully consider how to approach damages.*** In arbitration, when issues of both liability and damages are present, claimant's counsel should argue liability first and then damages. If you are respondent's counsel, you may want to address damages briefly but spend most of your argument picking apart the claimant's case on liability.

### 5.7.4 Content

The specific content of any final argument will obviously be determined by the case's facts and issues. However, you should consider certain sorts of information for inclusion in every final argument.

#### 5.7.4.1 Tell a Persuasive Story

Virtually every final argument should contain all the elements of a persuasive story. The argument should detail the evidentiary support for your case theory. A persuasive story has four basic elements, each of which answers an important question:

***What happened?*** A persuasive story accounts for all the known facts. It is not premised on incomplete information, nor does it glide over or ignore inconvenient occurrences. This is not to say that a final argument must mention every minor detail in the case, but it should accommodate the established facts. The final argument must cover the central facts of your case, taking care to support all the legally necessary elements. It must also consider the evidence produced by the opposing party.

***Why did it happen?*** Explain the reasons for the actions of the parties and other witnesses. It is not enough to state that an individual did something; reveal why those activities were consistent with that individual's self-interest, announced intentions, past behavior, lifestyle, or other understandable motivations. Articulating reasons gives logical weight to the argument and can transform it from an attorney's assertion into an acceptable statement of fact.

***How can we be sure?*** As we have seen throughout, persuasion often rests on the accumulation of supportive details. An essential aspect of final argument is the marshaling of details that give weight to your argument. The inclusion or exclusion of details is a tricky problem. While the right details at the right time can add an airtight quality to your case, too many details (or their use in supporting unimportant propositions) can drag a final argument into the depths of boredom and despair. There is no single key to making judgments in this area; we suggest the following guidelines:

- *Use details when important facts are in dispute.* Whenever there is a disagreement as to an occurrence or incident, details can effectively support your client's version of events.
- *Use details when motivations are in issue.* The presence (or absence) of motive can frequently be established with constituent facts. Explain why a party would want to act in a certain way. Look at the details that show the benefits of the actions' consequences.

- *Use details to support an interpretation of the evidence.* The meaning of certain evidence is often contested even when the underlying facts are not in dispute. Use an interpretation of the details that best supports your theory.
- *Do not use details for unimportant reasons.* The arbitrator will have a limited tolerance for details. Every time you use one detail, you diminish the effectiveness of those you will use later. So, reserve details for truly important situations. For example, do not use details, even if they are available, to attack the credibility of a witness whose testimony was not damaging to your case.

***Is it plausible?*** The ultimate test of every final argument is plausibility. Even if an argument accounts for the known facts, gives reasons for every action, is supported by credible witnesses, and might be replete with convincing details, it still will not be accepted if it does not make sense to the arbitrator. Almost every other failing can be overcome or forgiven. You cannot, however, win with an implausible argument. It is essential, therefore, that every final argument address the subject of common sense. Explain why your theory is realistic, using examples and analogies from everyday life. You can also use commonsense arguments to belittle or even ridicule the opposition's case. Every lawyer dreams of the arbitrator who adjourns the hearing and immediately concludes that the opposition's case just doesn't stack up.

#### 5.7.4.2 Tie Up Cross-Examinations

Final argument is the time to tie up the issues that you intentionally left unaddressed during cross-examination. Recall the forbidden questions. Never ask a witness to explain; never ask a witness to fill in a gap; never ask a witness to agree with a characterization or conclusion. These questions, and others like them, all risk losing control of the witness.

You refrained from asking the ultimate question; now make the point during your final argument. If your cross-examinations were artful and effective, spend some portion of the final argument drawing the previously unspoken conclusions. Use the same approach for explanations and characterizations. You did not ask a witness why something happened; now tell the arbitrator why it happened. You did not ask a witness to agree with a conclusion or characterization; draw the conclusion yourself.

#### 5.7.4.3 Comment on Promises

Attorneys on both sides of a case make various promises and commitments to the arbitrator during the hearing's course. These promises may be overt, as is often the case during opening statements: "We will produce a series of documents and work records that prove that the respondent was nowhere near the scene of the accident." Or the commitments may be implicit in the case's theory—when a claimant seeks damages for personal injury, there is an implied promise of certain proof. Whatever the case, final argument is the time to comment on promises made, kept, or broken. Point out the ways in which you fulfilled your commitments. Perhaps more importantly, and certainly more dramatically, underscore the ways in which the opposition failed to live up to their own promises.

#### 5.7.4.4 Resolve Problems and Weaknesses

Use final argument to solve problems and confront weaknesses. No matter how well the evidentiary phase of the hearing proceeded, you are sure to be left with difficult or troublesome issues. Address and resolve these issues during final argument. There are several schools of thought as to the best timing for addressing weaknesses or problems. Some authorities believe that weaknesses should never be addressed unless the opposing side raises them first. Others believe you should deal with at least certain weaknesses defensively, on the theory that you can preempt the sting by discussing the issue first. The decision is not always simple. Claimants' attorneys have the choice of dealing with weaknesses during either argument in chief or rebuttal—they can either initiate the discussion, or they can wait to see whether the defense brings up the issue during its argument in chief. Respondents, on the other hand, must be more wary. Even if the claimant omits a problem area from the argument in chief, counsel can still exploit it mercilessly on rebuttal.

#### 5.7.4.5 Discuss Damages

An arbitration consists of liability and damages. Although liability is the threshold issue, it is a mistake to underestimate the importance of damages.

***Claimant.*** Unless the hearing has been bifurcated, devote a significant portion of the final argument to the development of damages. Think of damages as comprising a "second persuasive story" in the case. Once liability has been established, you can address damages using all the persuasive story elements that we have discussed earlier. Account for the known facts that bear on damages, give the reasons for the actions of the people involved, address the credibility of the specific witnesses, delineate the crucial details, and explain why the requested damage award accords with common sense.

There are two significant aspects involved in most arguments for damages: method and amount. Explain to the arbitrator precisely how damages have been (or should be) calculated. It is also usually important to request a specific amount, rather than leaving the award to the arbitrator's guesswork.

***Respondent.*** Some defense attorneys prefer to avoid or minimize the issue of damages, reasoning that any discussion may be seen as an implicit admission of liability. Many lawyers, however, choose not to "roll the dice" on liability, concluding that a reduced damage award is the next best thing to winning the case outright.

When discussing damages as a respondent's lawyer, you have a choice. You may simply rebut the claimant's damage claim, or you may present a competing estimate of your own. The decision will rest upon the case's circumstances. Note, however, presenting a competing damage estimate does run a greater risk of seeming to concede liability.

#### 5.7.4.6 Thanks

It is only common courtesy to thank the arbitrator for serving as the decision-maker in the case. Do not overdo it or you will sound phony. A simple statement of thanks, on behalf of yourself and your client, is usually sufficient.

### *5.7.5 Ethics and Objections*

The rules of ethics, evidence, and procedure combine to place some very real, though manageable, limits on what you can say during final argument.

#### 5.7.5.1 Impermissible Argument

***Statements of personal belief.*** It is improper and unethical to "assert personal knowledge of facts in issue . . . or state a personal opinion as to the justness of a cause, the credibility of a witness, the culpability of a civil litigant."[19] This rule's purpose is twofold. First, it prevents lawyers from putting their own credibility at issue in a case. The decision-maker is required to decide a case based on the law and evidence, not on their affinity for or faith in a particular lawyer. While every advocate strives to be trusted and believed, it subverts the adversary system to make an overt, personal pitch. Moreover, a statement of personal belief inevitably suggests that the lawyer has access to off-the-record information, and therefore invites the decision-maker to decide the case based on nonrecord evidence. Banish the words "I" and "we" from the vocabulary you use during an arbitration hearing.

***Appeals to prejudice or bigotry.*** It is unethical to attempt to persuade a decision-maker through appeals to racial, religious, ethnic, gender, or other forms of prejudice. People—including arbitrators—can be swayed by their own biases, but lawyers cannot and should not seek to take advantage of this unfortunate phenomenon. An appeal to prejudice asks the decision-maker to disregard the evidence and to substitute an unreasonable stereotype or preconception. Such arguments violate the rule against alluding to "any matter the lawyer does not reasonably believe is relevant or that will not be supported by admissible evidence."[20] Mentioning race, gender, or ethnicity is not always improper. It may, for example, be permissible to refer to a party's race if it is relevant to identification by an eyewitness. On the

---

19. Model Rules of Prof'l Conduct, r. 3.4(e) (Am. Bar Ass'n 2020).
20. *Id.*

other hand, it is unethical to make racial or similar appeals implicitly or using code words. An argument based on bigotry cannot be saved through subtle language.

***Misstating the evidence.*** While it is permissible to draw inferences and conclusions, it is improper intentionally to misstate or mischaracterize evidence during final argument. Arbitrators are usually reluctant to resolve questions raised by the rule, but even so, two lessons accompany the "misstatement" rule. First, do not take the arbitrators' general reluctance to resolve questions raised by the rule as license to ignore the rule. Second, do not use the "misstatement" rule as an excuse to make spurious objections, to interrupt opposing counsel's argument, or to quibble over the meaning of the evidence. Make objections only when opposing counsel has seriously and prejudicially departed from the record.

***Misstating the law.*** Attorneys must use final argument to explain the relevant law and to apply the law to the facts of the case. You may not, however, misstate the law.

***Misusing evidence.*** When evidence has been admitted only for a limited or restricted use, it is improper to attempt to use it for any other purpose.

***Exceeding the scope of rebuttal.*** It is objectionable to attempt to argue new matters on rebuttal.

### 5.7.5.2 The Protocol of Objections

***Making objections.*** Objections during final argument follow the same general pattern as objections during witness examinations. State succinctly the ground for the objection. Present no argument unless requested by the arbitrator. Most attorneys try to avoid objecting during opposing counsel's final argument. It is common courtesy to allow opposing counsel to speak uninterrupted. Moreover, the overuse of objections may result in the interruption of one's own final argument. This does not mean, of course, that you should tolerate seriously improper arguments. It is unethical to make spurious objections simply for the purpose of interfering with opposing counsel's argument.

***Responding to objections.*** The best response to an objection is often no response. An objection disrupts the flow of final argument, and an extended colloquy with the arbitrator will only prolong the interruption. A dignified silence will usually be sufficient to allow the arbitrator to rule. Once the arbitrator rules, whether favorably, unfavorably, or inscrutably, proceed, adapting the argument to the arbitrator's ruling.

## 5.8 Persuasive Techniques

This section reviews some of the persuasive delivery and examination techniques you can use to advantage in arbitration when making your opening statements and final arguments and when using exhibits (Lore & Lubet, *MTA*, sections 13.3.3–13.3.5, 14.1.3.6).

## 5.8.1 Opening Statement and Final Argument

### 5.8.1.1 Do Not Read

Arbitration should be less costly than a trial, so if you do not have time to prepare bullets of your points, it is fine to read your opening statement or final argument. If you do have time, prepare bullets rather than reading your opening statement or final argument from a prepared text. Only the most skilled professional actors can deliver a scripted speech and still appear spontaneous and sincere. Everyone else seems stilted or labored. Your goal during your presentation should be to communicate directly to the arbitrators, not to lecture to them from a manuscript. You want to make eye contact, pick up on the arbitrator's reactions, and respond to objections and rulings by the arbitrator. Respondent's counsel, moreover, will want to reply to challenges, weaknesses, and omissions in the claimant's presentation. A written presentation prevents you from doing any of these things effectively.

The same can be said for memorizing your presentation. While exceptional memorization is better than reading, you risk forgetting a line (or more), losing your place, or being thrown off track by an objection. Very experienced lawyers may be able to deliver their presentations from memory. Novices should be wary of trying.

The best approach is to make your presentation from an outline, which could be on index cards or, if the arbitrator permits, your phone. List your major points, as well as the most important supporting details, on one or two sheets of paper. An outline allows you to organize the material and ensure that you don't leave anything out, while avoiding the perils of reading or memorization. The key, of course, is for your notes to be unobtrusive. Hence, the outline as opposed to the text.

### 5.8.1.2 Use Simple, Straightforward Language

Make your presentation straightforward and direct. In your opening statement, allow your facts to speak for themselves; it is not a time for emotional pleas or impassioned argument. In any event, in the opening statement you will not be allowed to make elaborate use of metaphors, literary allusions, biblical quotations, or any of the other rhetorical devices that can be so helpful during final argument.

Never talk down to an arbitrator.

Simple language is generally the best. In final arguments, apply simple, active language in argumentative form. Avoid the temptation during final argument to use judgmental or conclusory terms such as heinous, brutal, deceptive, unfair, virtuous, and naive. Though such language is allowed on final argument, remember that conclusory adjectives and adverbs are less persuasive than active nouns and verbs. It is one thing to assert that an accident was heinous, and quite another to describe its awful, vivid details.

#### 5.8.1.3 Verbal Pacing

The speed, tone, inflection, and volume of your speech are important persuasive tools. Change speed, tone, inflection and volume to signal transitions and to maintain the arbitrator's attention. Avoid speaking too quickly or too loudly. Pace your speech to convey perceptions of time, distance, and intensity. If you describe an event rapidly, it seems to have taken place very quickly. If you describe it at a more leisurely pace, the time frame expands. In similar fashion, rapid speech magnifies intensity and reduces distance. Slower delivery reduces intensity and increases distance.

#### 5.8.1.4 Movement for Emphasis and Transition

In some arbitrations, the hearing room's size dictates how much movement you may engage in during your presentations. In most arbitrations, counsel present their opening statements and final arguments while seated. However, if space allows and the arbitrator permits you to present while standing, the following suggestions may be beneficial. A certain amount of body and hand movement will enliven your final argument and increase the arbitrator's attentiveness. Use gestures to emphasize important points or to accent differences between your case and the opposition's. Use body movement for emphasis or transition—pausing and taking a step or two will alert the arbitrator that you are changing subjects. Moving toward the arbitrator underscores the importance of what you are about to say. Moving away from the arbitrator signals the conclusion of a line of argument.

Body movement is effective only if you avoid aimless pacing. Constant movement not only distracts the arbitrator; it deprives you of the ability to use movements purposefully. Use a lectern if you need it.

#### 5.8.1.5 Visuals and Exhibits

You need not confine your opening statement and final argument to your words alone. Visual aids and exhibits can enormously enhance the value of your presentations.

***Exhibits.*** Since your presentation's purpose is to explain what the evidence will show or has shown, you are entitled to read from or display documents and other exhibits that you expect to be admitted into evidence or which are already in evidence. If the case involves a contract, quote from the central clause. If there is a key letter in evidence, enlarge and show it to the arbitrator during your opening statement, and use the same exhibit in your final argument. Use a pointer so that the arbitrator can read along as you recite the opposing party's damning admission. During your presentations, show the arbitrator photographs, models, maps, and charts, as well as other tangible exhibits such as weapons, machinery, or even prosthetics.

***Visual aids.*** In addition to displaying actual exhibits, you may also use visual aids during your presentations. The general rule is that any visual aid must be likely to help the arbitrator understand the hearing evidence. Lawyers routinely use visual aids in arbitration to show timelines, or to draw free-hand diagrams that are not offered or received into evidence. There are limitations, of course. The visual aids must fairly summarize the evidence; in the opening statement, they cannot be misleading, and they cannot be argumentative. You could not, for example, produce in opening statement a chart captioned "Three Reasons Not to Believe the Claimant." Use of such a chart, however, would be quite permissible in final argument. Avoid disruptive objections by showing visual aids to opposing counsel before your presentation begins. It is advisable also to show visuals to the arbitrator and to obtain advance permission for their use.

***Other evidence.*** Not all exhibits are visual. It is permissible to play recordings during presentations—such as legally taped telephone conversations or 911 emergency calls—if they will later be offered or have been accepted in evidence.

#### 5.8.1.6 Using Emotion in Final Argument

There are different schools of thought regarding the use of emotion in final argument. Many lawyers believe emotion has little place at any point during an arbitration, while others believe emotion can communicate as effectively as logic or reason. There is a strong consensus, however, that false emotion will backfire. Insincerity shows through, and there is little that is less persuasive than an insincere attorney.

Save emotion for your case's moral dimension. There is no reason to wax passionate over the date on which a contract was signed. It is understandable, however, to show outrage or resentment toward a party who intentionally breached a contract, knowing that it would cause great harm to another. The absence of emotion may be taken as a lack of belief in your case's righteousness. What reasonable person would be unmoved when discussing crippling injuries to a child or perjury by the opposing party? There will be points in many arbitrations that cry out for a display of feeling, and a flat presentation may be regarded as an absence of conviction.

### *5.8.2 Persuasive Use of Exhibits*

It seems obvious to say that it is important to present and use exhibits as persuasively as possible in arbitration. Yet, time and again lawyers have entered exhibits into evidence only to forget them. The smoking gun only matters if you convince the arbitrator of its importance.

#### 5.8.2.1 Persuasive Foundations

You can use two approaches to enhance the persuasiveness of foundations. Your choice will depend on the circumstances.

***Minimalism.*** Whenever possible, use stipulations to avoid developing foundations in the arbitration hearing. If you must present foundational testimony, keep it as short as possible. Use leading questions, permissible on preliminary matters, to move the testimony along.

***Maximalism.*** Foundations are not always rote technicalities. Particularly where the exhibit's authenticity is in issue, the thoroughness of the foundation can play an important role in persuasion. In such circumstances, take time to develop the foundation fully.

#### 5.8.2.2 Creative Exhibits

The most valuable exhibits in any case seldom step forward and present themselves. Rather, you must seek, search out, and discover them. Often, they must be developed and created. Even those exhibits that are simply handed to counsel by the client can be presented in an enhanced form. Here are some creative means of finding, developing, and presenting exhibits.

***Looking for exhibits.*** It is essential to ensure your complete access to all real and documentary exhibits. While you will rarely want to introduce everything that you find, you cannot adequately represent your client until you have examined every potential item of evidence. No competent attorney would go to an arbitration hearing without having learned the identity of every witness, and exhibits are essentially silent witnesses. You must find them all—both documentary exhibits and real evidence.

***Developing exhibits.*** All exhibits fall into two categories: those that predate the arbitration and those attorneys create. You must take the pre-arbitration, or integral, exhibits as they are found, but you have wide latitude in shaping and developing other exhibits for use at the hearing. Some of the more common sorts of lawyer-generated exhibits are:

1) enlargement of a key section of the deposition transcript of an adverse witness's testimony;
2) photographs and videos;
3) models;
4) diagrams and maps;
5) explanatory graphs and charts.

The creation of these, and similar, exhibits should be considered in virtually every case.

***Presenting exhibits.*** The presentation of an exhibit can be as important as its composition or foundation. No matter how well thought out, no matter how solidly admissible, an exhibit will not accomplish its purpose if it is not understood and accepted by the arbitrator. In addition to selecting key integral documents for enhanced presentation, effective arbitration preparation also involves designing lawyer-generated exhibits. Particularly when it comes to diagrams and graphs, an ounce of professional preparation is usually worth several pounds of hearing room drawing. Decide whether a chart, graph, or diagram can improve a witness's testimony. If so, develop the desired exhibit in advance of the hearing. While witnesses can draw on blackboards or poster boards while testifying, you should usually avoid this approach. Freehand drawing is unreliable under the best circumstances, and witnesses are notoriously prone to making embarrassing mistakes when called upon to draw before the arbitrator. Whiteboards, in particular, seldom lead to a satisfying result.

- *Size.* Exhibits must be seen to be appreciated. When creating an exhibit, create a big one. When displaying an exhibit on a screen during a video conference, make sure it fills the screen or that you have sent an enlarged copy to the arbitrator and opposing counsel in advance of the hearing. When using integral exhibits, such as preexisting documents, make enlargements.
    - Physical—It might seem old-fashioned, but physical enlargements of exhibits have the advantage of immediacy. Witnesses, lawyers, and the arbitrator can all touch them. There is no reason for a lawyer-produced exhibit to be visually inaccessible. Make charts, graphs, and diagrams on oversized pieces of stiff poster board. Thin tagboard is unacceptable, since even a masterpiece will be useless if it will not stand up. Ensure that a display easel will be available in the hearing room. Photographs, whether preexisting or taken at counsel's direction, should also be enlarged.
    - Electronic—Rare is the conference room that lacks a screen, a projector, and the technology to display from your computer, and you can confirm the availability of this equipment during the initial hearing. Do not limit yourself to simply displaying documents and graphs on a big screen. Computer-generated graphics can include animations, enhancements, 3-D models, and graphs that can be changed on the fly if an arbitrator proposes a hypothetical, to name just a few possibilities. Graphics professionals can work with you to create demonstrative exhibits that pop. A word of warning, however: computer graphics may have the greatest visual and persuasive impact, but they are still prone to frustrating technical glitches. If you intend to use computer displays or models, be certain to have a contingency plan. More than one old-fashioned attorney has strutted away from an arbitration, smug that they just beat the computer whiz with only a sheet of poster board and a Sharpie.
    - Hybrid—Put the best of both worlds to work for you. Imagine an injury case where you continued to display a picture of the claimant's

injuries on the easel in the room while reviewing documents on the computer screen.

- *Copies.* Someday we will achieve a paperless world, but that day has not arrived in the law. Enter the hearing room with enough copies of every exhibit. At a minimum, this should include an original, additional copies for the witness and the arbitrator, and copies for each opposing attorney. Distributing copies at the appropriate time during the examination will prevent delays and can forestall objections. There is nothing more awkward and distracting than a lawyer leaning over a witness's shoulder while they attempt to share an exhibit. When enlargements are impractical or unavailable, make enough copies of the exhibits, whether documents or photographs, to distribute to the arbitrators. You can also assemble documents into a bound or loose-leaf exhibit book and provide copies to the arbitrators and to witnesses as necessary. For a virtual hearing, distribute exhibits in advance. Determine with opposing counsel whether you will provide the exhibits in electronic form for them to print if they desire and who will mail hard copies to the arbitrator. If possible, stipulate to all the exhibits so that you can provide hard copies of the joint exhibits in the order they will be introduced to the arbitrator in advance of the videoconference.

## 5.9 Summary of the Elements of Persuasion

### *5.9.1 The Five Objectives of Persuasive Messages*

Persuasion moves human beings to action. Persuasion creates a relationship between you and others—connecting people who were previously unconnected. More importantly, persuasion shows people the connections that already existed. Accomplish this task by mastering the five objectives of persuasive messages. Persuasive messages:

1) command the attention of the receiver;
2) are understood by the receiver as intended by the sender;
3) warrant the receiver's belief that the information presented is credible or accurate;
4) present information that conforms to the receiver's values of what is right and wrong; and
5) motivate the receiver to act.

Persuasive messages influence how receivers choose or decide which information to process. Thus, as an advocate in arbitration, you must analyze your audience—the arbitrator or arbitrators—and apply those analyses when determining how best to convey the five objectives of the persuasive message.

### 5.9.2 The Three Artistic Means of Persuasion

Aristotle identified and labeled three "artistic means of persuasion:" *ethos* (character of speaker), *pathos* (emotions aroused in audience), and *logos* (logic—true or probable argument). In other words, the arbitrator must trust you, sympathize with your position, and believe that your version of events makes sense. These three means of persuasion bear a striking resemblance to the three dimensions of attitude in modern-day psychology: behavioral (*ethos*), affective (*pathos*), and cognitive (*logos*).

*Ethos* encompasses the personal characteristics of the speaker and how perceptions of wisdom, decency, and personal goodness influence a listener's motivation to act or think in consonance with the speaker's urging. According to Aristotle, the speaker's trustworthy character was the test of the truth of what was being said. *Ethos* was the "controlling factor" in persuasion. He identified two aspects of *ethos*: 1) personal qualities of the speaker; and 2) the stereotypes by which the audience may judge the character of the speaker. Thus, in an arbitration, you must be continually conscious of your own personal qualities that project trustworthiness and the stereotypes that detract from your trustworthiness and that you should therefore avoid, as well as the stereotypes that enhance your trustworthiness and that you should therefore exhibit.

As an arbitration advocate, you also need an intimate understanding of the affective component of persuasion, *pathos*. Simply defined, pathos is the art of putting the audience in a desired frame of mind by appealing to their emotions, personal involvement, or needs reduction or satisfaction. At its foundation, *pathos* is an appeal to how one feels about concepts, values, conduct, and situations generally. There is an art to balancing an appeal to the arbitrator's emotions without coming across as smarmy or manipulative. Watch for body language that telegraphs skepticism and be ready to pull back on an emotional appeal that might backfire.

Finally, know, understand, and apply *logos* in the arbitration setting. Compared to a jury or even a bench trial, *logos* is of paramount importance because arbitrators are normally experts familiar with the applicable law, contract provisions, and variations of factual situations. *Logos*, the cognitive component of persuasion, refers to how the listener thinks, and is probably best described as an appeal to an audience's sense of reason through structured argument and evidentiary proof that favors logical consistency. This is your concrete evidence, your exhibits, your witness testimony. If your case is not backed up by the facts, *ethos* and *pathos* cannot save the day.

By knowing your audience in arbitration, you can adjust the amount of each method, *ethos*, *pathos*, and *logos*, in conveying a persuasive message to accomplish your goal in a particular interchange. If there is no opportunity to analyze your audience, or if you are unable to accurately classify it, use a balanced approach, and incorporate all three means, always realizing that *ethos* will be the controlling factor in the persuasiveness of your message.

# • Chapter Six •

## Advocacy During a More Formal Arbitration Hearing

*The courts of this country should not be the places where resolution of disputes begins. They should be the places where the disputes end after alternative methods of resolving disputes have been considered and tried.*
—*Sandra Day O'Connor*[1]

If a dispute has not been resolved through negotiation or mediation, then as Justice O'Connor recognizes, it may be reasonable to pursue litigation and a court trial. Alternatively, draft your contracts to avoid court litigation altogether, even in complex disputes, by providing for a binding decision after a formal arbitration hearing. This chapter addresses evidentiary rules that must be followed when the rules of evidence apply to an arbitration hearing; knowing these rules can improve your advocacy even when they do not apply or apply only loosely. This chapter also explains how to offer expert testimony when you will call an expert witness rather than simply stipulating to admission of expert reports. Finally, it provides tips to ensure the accuracy and completeness of a transcript when a case is complex or serious enough to warrant a court reporter.

### 6.1 Evidentiary Rules

The procedural rules that govern an arbitration hearing are those to which the parties have agreed. The same is true of the rules of evidence. In arbitration, rarely do parties agree to observe formal evidentiary rules such as the Federal Rules of Evidence. The time-consuming evidence arguments spawned by applying such rules are antithetical to the goal of efficient dispute resolution. Also, many arbitrations are like a bench trial. In most bench trials, the rules of evidence are more relaxed than in a jury trial, the belief being that judges are better able than jurors to sort reliable evidence from the unreliable. Thus, in arbitration, the criteria for precluding evidence are quite narrow, usually limited to privilege, irrelevancy, or

1. Justice Sandra Day O'Connor, Address at the Consumer Dispute Resolution Conference: Exploring the Alternatives (Jan. 21, 1983).

cumulative evidence. Only occasionally do arbitrators consult formal rules of evidence for guidance, and those are normally unique situations where a party asserts extreme prejudice to their case if the evidence is admitted. But, of course, even in those situations, the arbitrators will have to know what the evidence is to determine whether to exclude it. This fact renders a claim of prejudice questionable as a basis for objecting to evidence, because the objector may have to bring to the arbitrator's attention exactly the evidence that is arguably inadmissible.

Most arbitrators conduct arbitrations with a commonsense notion of what is important to resolve a case. They apply a low threshold for admitting evidence, and they weigh the reliability and importance of the evidence as the hearing continues and issues evolve. Some arbitrators view the arbitration process as an opportunity for the parties to vent pent-up anger and frustration as well as an arena to do legal combat. Also, many arbitrators liberally admit evidence to obviate a later court challenge to their awards based on allegations of unfair preclusion of critical evidence.

Freedom from the rules of evidence creates an opportunity for you to use your ingenuity to convince an arbitrator of your case's merits. You enjoy expanded latitude in presenting your case without constantly worrying about the technical requirements concerning evidence foundations and hearsay. However, use discretion here. Arbitrators quickly become skeptical of the merit of a party's case where counsel consistently supports their position with unreliable evidence. The best rule of thumb is to take a conservative approach with evidence supporting critical elements of your claims or defenses, and a less conservative approach with evidence relating to background or peripheral matters. Thus, in relation to required elements of proof of claims or defenses, lay proper foundations for your testimonial and documentary evidence and endeavor to comply with the rule against hearsay evidence. In relation to evidence less central to your legal claims, you can be less concerned with the technical requirements of foundations and of hearsay evidence.

On the flip side, be aware that if you seek to take at least some advantage of the relaxed evidence rules, your opponent will most assuredly be doing so to an equal or even greater degree. Thus, be on guard to detect your opponent's abuses of formal rules of evidence. When a rule violation means that unreliable evidence on a key issue will be admitted, object and use the opportunity to call to the arbitrator's attention that the evidence is unreliable and deserves little weight. Also, 1) ensure that you respond to objectionable evidence by later presenting your own controverting or rehabilitating evidence; and/or 2) remind the arbitrator in your final argument that the objectionable evidence would not be admissible in a court of law, is unreliable, and therefore should be given little or no weight in the arbitration proceeding. Use objections sparingly and to make a point.

How do you ensure that your critical evidence conforms to the formal evidentiary requirements and identify for the arbitrator portions of your opponent's critical evidence that do not comply with them and which are therefore unreliable? Know and understand the generally accepted evidence requirements.[2] Sections 6.2 through 6.4 review some of the approved techniques for introducing testimonial and documentary evidence. Sections 6.5 and 6.6 discuss how to make objections and respond to them, including offers of proof and preserving the record.

## 6.2 Foundations for Evidence

Before any evidence can be considered in a court trial, there must be some basis for believing it to be relevant and admissible. This basis is called the foundation for the evidence. In an arbitration hearing in which the parties have agreed that rules of evidence do not apply, the requirement for foundations is relaxed. But even in some of those hearings, when a piece of evidence is critical to the case, the arbitrator will require counsel to lay a proper foundation. Where the arbitration agreement or the rules of a court's mandatory arbitration program apply the rules of evidence, you must of course comply with them and lay appropriate foundations for the evidence you wish to introduce. Moreover, many foundations, whether or not required by the arbitrator, enhance the reliability or credibility of your evidence. This section will prepare you for those situations where foundations are necessary or well-advised (Lore & Lubet, *MTA*, Ch. 11).

### *6.2.1 Components of Foundation*

There are three aspects to virtually all evidentiary foundations. To be received, evidence must be shown to be: 1) relevant, 2) authentic, and 3) admissible under the applicable laws of evidence. While the discrete elements of foundation differ according to the evidence's nature and the purpose for which it is offered, these three considerations must always apply.

- ***Relevance.*** Relevance defines the relationship between the proffered evidence and some fact that is at issue in the case. Evidence will not be admitted simply because it is interesting or imaginative. Rather, it must be shown to be probative in the sense that it makes some disputed fact either more or less likely. The relevance of most evidence is generally made apparent from the case's context, but occasionally it must be demonstrated by the establishment of foundational facts.

2. *See* Stephen J. Ware & Alan Scott Rau, Arbitration 385 (4th ed., West 2020) ("When lawyers object in arbitration to the introduction of what, in litigation, would be inadmissible evidence, they often do this less in a futile attempt to keep the evidence out, and more to emphasize its unreliability, and thus perhaps to reduce the weight it might have for the arbitrator."). *See generally*, Anthony Bocchino & David Sonenshein, A Practical Guide to Federal Evidence: Objections, Responses, and Litigation Tactics For Trial Success (16th ed., NITA 2023).

- ***Authenticity.*** Authenticity refers to the requirement of proof that the evidence actually is what the proponent claims it to be. In other words, evidence is not to be admitted until there has been a threshold showing that it is "the real thing." The arbitrator decides whether an item of evidence has been sufficiently authenticated, and the criteria vary according to the nature of the evidence involved. The requirement of authenticity is not limited to tangible objects. It also applies to certain testimonial evidence. For example, a witness generally may not testify to a telephone conversation without first establishing the basis for recognizing the voice of the person on the other end of the line. That is, the identity of the other speaker must be authenticated.
- ***Admissibility.*** Evidence can be relevant and authentic and still fail to meet the threshold for consideration by the factfinder. Prepare to overcome objections to evidence such as hearsay, privilege, misleading, and other factors.

Foundation requirements apply equally during cross- and direct examinations. You must lay testimonial foundations on cross-examination for personal knowledge, voice identification, hearsay exceptions, and in every other circumstance where a foundation would be necessary on direct examination. In addition, there are special foundations for certain cross-examination techniques such as impeachment by past omission or prior inconsistent statement. It is also often necessary to use cross-examination to lay the foundation for the admission of exhibits. Respondent's counsel in particular can avoid the need to call adverse witnesses by attempting to establish foundations for their own exhibits while cross-examining a claimant's witness.

## 6.2.2 Foundations for Testimonial Evidence

### 6.2.2.1 Personal Knowledge

Witnesses are expected to testify from personal knowledge. The most common sort of personal knowledge is direct sensory perception: information gained through sight, hearing, touch, taste, and smell. Witnesses may also have personal knowledge of more subjective information, such as their own intentions or emotions, or the reputation of another person.

### 6.2.2.2 Special Foundations for Certain Testimonial Evidence

While most testimony requires a showing of personal knowledge, certain testimony calls for the establishment of additional foundational facts.

***Conversations.*** Witnesses are often called upon to testify to conversations between two or more parties. To authenticate the conversation, and thereby allow opposing counsel to conduct a meaningful cross-examination, testimony concerning a conversation generally must be supported by a foundation establishing the date, time, and place of the conversation, as well as the persons present at the time.

***Telephone conversations and voice identification.*** The foundation for a telephone conversation includes the additional element of voice identification, or of a reasonable circumstantial substitute. In the absence of a basis for voice identification, you can use circumstantial evidence as the foundation for a telephone conversation. You can authenticate a telephone call placed by the witness by showing that the call was made to a known number. You can use numerous other circumstances to authenticate telephone conversations. Subsequent verifying events can form the foundation for telephone calls either placed or received by the witness.

***Prior identification.*** Under Fed. R. Evid. 801(d)(1)(C), a witness may testify to their previous, out-of-court identification of an individual. This rule applies to both criminal and civil matters. The foundation for this testimony is that the witness made the out-of-court identification after perceiving the person identified.

***Specific admissibility.*** While evidence will generally be received if it is relevant and authentic, the law of evidence contains a host of specific provisions that govern the admissibility of various sorts of proof. In many cases, you can admit evidence only following the establishment of foundational facts. Most exceptions to the hearsay rule, for example, require such a preliminary showing. Similarly, you must lay a foundation for admitting evidence of habit or routine practice, or for admitting evidence of subsequent remedial measures.

#### 6.2.2.3 Establishing Foundations

***Single or multiple witnesses.*** The most common approach to establishing a foundation is simply to call a witness who can provide the necessary facts, and then to offer the evidence after that testimony has been elicited. Some foundations cannot be laid by a single witness. In such cases, establish separate parts of the foundation from each of several witnesses before offering the evidence.

***Conditional admissibility.*** It is not always possible to complete a foundation during the testimony of a single witness. However, a witness who is responsible for part of the foundation will in many cases have other important information concerning the exhibit. Fed. R. Evid. 104(b) allows the temporary or conditional admission of the evidence based upon counsel's representation that the foundation will be completed through the testimony of a subsequent witness.

***Using adverse witnesses.*** You can often simplify potentially complex foundations using adverse examination. In a case where executed contracts have been exchanged through the mail, for example, it may be extremely difficult for one party to authenticate the other party's signature. You can completely alleviate this problem, however, simply by calling the opposing party as an adverse witness.

***Habit and routine.*** To lay the foundation for evidence of habit or routine practice, you must call a witness with personal knowledge of the regular conduct of the person or organization involved. Furthermore, you must establish that the asserted conduct was, in fact, of a consistently repeated nature. Accomplish this through proof of either extended observation or of the existence of a formal policy or procedure.

***Individual habit.*** The most common foundation for an individual's habit is through evidence of a pattern of conduct repeated over a substantial period. The alleged habit must be clearly differentiated from independent or distinct activities.

***Business practice.*** Establish the routine practice of a business or organization either through direct observation or through evidence of an existing policy or practice.

#### 6.2.2.4 Foundations for Hearsay Statements

The rule against hearsay excludes evidence of out-of-court statements if offered to prove the truth of the matter asserted.[3] Numerous exceptions to the hearsay rule allow for admitting out-of-court statements, provided you establish the necessary foundation. The foundations for those exceptions that apply primarily to testimonial evidence are discussed below. A later section discusses foundations for hearsay exceptions that typically apply to documentary evidence. The following subsections are an abbreviated outline of the foundations for the various hearsay exceptions for those arbitrations in which the hearsay rule applies.

***Opposing Party Statement.*** Out-of-court statements made by the opposing party are generally admissible to prove the truth of the matter asserted. In brief, the opposing party's previous statements are admissible if:

1) the witness can authenticate the statement, and
2) the statement was made by the party against whom it is offered.

The opposing party's statement exception also applies to statements made by the agent or employee of a party.[4] In such situations there are two additional elements to the foundation:

1) the declarant was an agent or employee of the opposing party at the time that the statement was made, and
2) the statement concerned a matter that was within the scope of the agency or employment.

Much evidence is admissible under this rule, and it is arguably the most important hearsay exception. One good example of the power of this exception is from

3. Fed. R. Evid. 801.
4. Fed. R. Evid. 801(d)(2)(D).

*Zootopia*. The bunny, Judy Hopps, needs the fox, Nick Wilde, to help her locate a missing animal. To pressure him to help she must outfox him. She gets him to admit to tax fraud, and he retorts "it's my word against yours." She corrects him that "it's your word, against yours" after playing him the recording of his statement, which would, of course, be fully admissible against him in a tax fraud prosecution.[5]

> **Judy Hopps**: Nicholas Wilde, you are under arrest!
>
> **Nick Wilde**: *[scoffs, amused]* For what? *[mockingly]* Hurting your feewings?
>
> **Judy Hopps**: *[smiles slyly]* Felony tax evasion. *[Nick's smile drops, flabbergasted, and his eyes widen as Judy writes.]* Yeeaah . . . two hundred dollars a day, three hundred and sixty-five days a year since you were twelve, that's two decades, so times twenty which is . . . one million four hundred sixty thousand—I *think*. I mean, *[chuckles]* I *am* just a dumb bunny, but we *are* good at multiplying. Anyway, according to your tax forms, you reported, let me see here, *zero*! *[Nick's face freezes in fear]* Unfortunately, lying on a federal form is a punishable offense. Five years jail time.
>
> **Nick Wilde**: Well, it's my word against yours.
>
> *[Judy pulls out her carrot pen and plays back Nick's confession.]*
>
> **Nick Wilde's voice**: *[Through carrot pen] . . . two hundred bucks a* day, *Fluff. Three hundred and sixty-five days a year since I was* twelve.
>
> **Judy Hopps**: Actually, it's *your* word against yours. And if you want this pen, you're going to help me find this poor missing otter, or the only place you'll be selling pawpsicles is the prison cafeteria. *[grins]* It's called a hustle, sweetheart. *[Nick shows a stunned look.]*[6]

***Present sense impression.*** The present sense impression exception allows the admission of out-of-court statements "describing or explaining an event or condition made while the declarant was perceiving the event or condition, or immediately thereafter."[7] The foundation for the exception is that:

1) the declarant perceived an event,
2) the declarant described the event, and
3) the description was given while the event occurred or immediately afterwards.

---

5. Zootopia (Disney 2016) (transcript available at https://zootopia.fandom.com/wiki/Zootopia/Transcript#Scene_15:_Judy's_Hustle) (last visited Jun. 2024).
6. *Id.*
7. Fed. R. Evid. 803(1).

The declarant cannot describe inferences and conclusions—only the facts of the event. A witness may testify as to their own present-sense impression statement or that of another. It is generally necessary for the statement to have been made in the witness's presence, to satisfy the foundational requirement of personal knowledge.

***Excited utterance.*** The excited utterance exception is similar to the present sense impression rule. It allows for the admission of hearsay when the statement relates "to a startling event or condition made while the declarant was under the stress of excitement caused by the event or condition."[8] The foundation for an excited utterance is that:

1) the declarant perceived a startling event or experienced a stressful condition,
2) the declarant made a statement concerning the event or condition, and
3) the statement was made while the declarant was under the stress of the event or condition.

Unlike a present sense impression, an excited utterance can contain inferences and conclusions. As with present sense impressions, a witness may testify to their own excited utterance or to that of another.

***State of mind.*** "State of mind" provides one of the broadest exceptions to the hearsay rule. It allows the admission of statements concerning the declarant's "then existing state of mind, emotion, sensation, or physical condition (such as intent, plan, motive, design, mental feeling, pain, and bodily health)."[9] The foundation for this exception is that the statement actually be probative of the declarant's mental, emotional, or physical condition. You can best demonstrate this by the statement's content. Apart from the statement's content, there is no special foundation for the state of mind exception. However, the witness still must establish the statement's authenticity by testifying to:

1) when the statement was made,
2) where it was made,
3) who was present, and
4) what was said.

Note also that the statement must have been made during the existence of the mental, emotional, or physical condition that it describes.

---

8. Fed. R. Evid. 803(2).
9. Fed. R. Evid. 803(3).

***Statement made for medical treatment.*** The foundation for this exception is that the declarant made a statement for the purpose of obtaining medical care or diagnosis. The statement may be made to a physician, medical worker, or other person, so long as its purpose was to obtain or facilitate treatment or diagnosis. The statement may include medical history or past symptoms.[10]

***Dying declaration.*** The hearsay exception for dying declarations requires the following foundation:

1) the declarant made a statement while believing that their death was imminent,
2) concerning what they believed to be the cause of death.[11]

## 6.3 Foundations for Documents

In addition to the usual issues of relevance and authenticity, the foundation for a document usually includes two other elements. Because documents invariably contain out-of-court statements, they must be brought within an exception or exclusion to the hearsay rule. Historically, at trial the proffer needed to comply with the "best evidence" or "original writing" rule but today, you will likely focus more on authenticating electronic records.

### *6.3.1 Authentication*

Authenticating documents typically requires proof of authorship or origin and, depending on the issues in the case, may also call for proof of transmission or receipt.

***Handwriting and signature.*** You can authenticate the signature or other handwriting on a document through a variety of means. A witness may recognize a signature based on past observation or may authenticate it based on circumstantial evidence. Other possibilities include expert testimony and in-arbitration comparison by the arbitrator. A witness may always authenticate their own handwriting or signature. A witness may also authenticate the handwriting of another if sufficient familiarity can be shown.

***Circumstantial evidence of authorship or origin.*** Many documents are printed or typewritten and do not contain signatures or other handwriting. Unless such a document is somehow uniquely marked, you will need to authenticate it via circumstantial evidence. Such evidence can be in the form of a letterhead, seal, or stamp, or it can be provided by the context of the case.

---

10. Fed. R. Evid. 803(4).
11. Fed. R. Evid. 804(b)(2).

***Mailing or transmission.*** A document's admissibility will often depend upon its receipt by, or at least transmission to, another party. This is an authenticity issue since the document is made admissible only by its status as one that was actually or constructively received. In other words, proof of mailing authenticates the document as truly having been sent to the other party. Mailing can be proven either directly or through evidence of a routine business practice. Direct proof of mailing can be given in a single sentence: "I placed the document in an envelope, with the correct address, and I deposited it in the United States mail with sufficient postage."

***Emails.*** To show that an email was actually sent to the intended recipient, you must establish that the email address to which it was sent was in fact the recipient's email address. You can do so through an organizational directory or circumstantial evidence, such as prior correspondence with the intended recipient at that email address. Sometimes you may have to prove a routing chain with the help of a computer expert.

***Websites and posts.*** Generally, a party can submit its own website and posts as business records. When you offer a website that isn't your client's, you must prove that it was the party's website or post. Perhaps the webpage has a logo, or the post is initialed. You may also have to prove the version of the website you are offering is as it was on the date in question. You can use a screenshot from the date in question or witness testimony to do so.

***The original writing (best evidence) rule.*** The so-called "best evidence" rule was once a formidable obstacle to admitting documentary evidence. In its harshest form, the rule excluded all but the original of any writing, unless certain conditions could be met. Today, the rule has been softened considerably, and now allows for the easy admissibility of most copies.[12] The rule constitutes an authenticity requirement, but its terms are sufficiently unique to call for separate treatment. The essence of the "original writing" rule is that a document's content can be proved only by producing the original, or an acceptable duplicate, unless the original is lost, destroyed, or unavailable. Because under most circumstances a duplicate is admissible on the same terms as the original, the rule now operates primarily to exclude testimonial summaries or paraphrases of a document. Note also that the original writing rule applies only to proof of a document's content, not its signing, acknowledgment, or delivery.

### 6.3.2 Foundations for Hearsay Exceptions

The offer of a document inevitably sets the hearsay bell ringing in opposing counsel's mind. While writings may be admissible for nonhearsay purposes, such as proof of notice or acceptance, they are frequently submitted precisely to prove that their contents are true. Various exceptions allow the use of such documents, each

12. Fed. R. Evid. 1002.

requiring its own foundation. The following section discusses the more common exceptions.

***Business records.*** Business records can include ledgers, accounts, calendar entries, memoranda, notices, reports, statements, and similar writings. All these documents constitute hearsay if they are offered to prove that their contents are true. Under the Federal Rules, the records of any regularly conducted activity are admissible if they:

1) were made at or near the time of a transaction or event;
2) were made by, or based on information transmitted from, a person with knowledge;
3) were kept in the course of a regularly conducted business activity; and
4) were made as a part of the regular practice of that business activity.[13]

***Computer Records.*** Computer-generated records have become a common form of business record. The Federal Rules of Evidence specifically recognize "data compilations" as an acceptable form of business record. Thus, the foundation for a computer record is basically the same as that for any other business record.

***Summaries.*** Many business records or other sets of data are so lengthy and ponderous that they cannot be conveniently produced in an arbitration hearing. Even if you could produce them, they may be so extensive and technical as to be impenetrable. In these circumstances it is permissible to substitute a "chart, summary, or calculation" that fairly presents the relevant information in a usable or understandable form.[14] The foundation for such a summary includes these elements:

1) the original documents are so voluminous that they cannot be conveniently examined in the arbitration hearing;
2) the witness has examined the original data;
3) the witness is qualified to produce a summary of the information; and
4) the exhibit is a fair and accurate summary of the underlying information.

***Recorded recollection.*** A witness's written notes, or other recorded recollection, may be admitted into evidence only if the witness, at the time of trial, "has insufficient recollection to enable them to testify fully and accurately."[15] The foundation for this exception to the hearsay rule comprises these elements:

---

13. Fed. R. Evid. 803(6).
14. Fed. R. Evid. 1006.
15. Fed. R. Evid. 803(5).

1) the witness once had personal knowledge of the relevant facts or events;
2) the witness cannot currently recall the events fully and accurately;
3) the witness previously made an accurate memorandum or record of the facts; and
4) the witness made the accurate memorandum or record at a time when the events were fresh in the witness's memory.

***Public records.*** There are several hearsay exceptions that allow for the admissibility of public records, statistics, and reports. Such records are generally admissible if they were made by a public office or agency and they set forth:

1) the activities of the office or agency;
2) matters observed pursuant to a duty imposed by law;
3) in limited circumstances, certain investigative findings; or
4) officially required records of vital statistics.[16]

Because most government records are "self-authenticating," it is not usually necessary to call a witness to testify to their authenticity.[17]

***Absence of public record.*** You can also use public records to show the nonoccurrence of events. The foundation for this evidence is:

1) that such events, occurrences, or matters were regularly recorded in some form;
2) by a public office or agency; and
3) that a diligent search has failed to disclose a record of a particular fact or event.

This evidence may be offered by certification from the appropriate official, in which case no witness needs to be called. The evidence may also be offered via testimony.

***Previous testimony.*** The transcript of a person's previous testimony may be admitted into evidence if:

1) the declarant is currently "unavailable" to testify;
2) the testimony was given under oath in court or at a deposition;

16. Fed. R. Evid. 803(8) & 803(9).
17. Fed. R. Evid. 902.

3) the party against whom the testimony is being offered, or their predecessor in interest, had a fair opportunity to examine the witness when the testimony was originally given.[18]

Note that this exception allows the admission of the earlier statement as a substitute for current testimony. Unlike the use of prior testimony for impeachment, there is no requirement that the previous testimony be inconsistent with the declarant's current position. Under the federal rules, a witness can be deemed "unavailable" for a variety of reasons, including:

1) the valid assertion of a privilege;
2) persistent refusal to testify;
3) inability to attend the hearing due to illness;
4) death;
5) failure of memory; or
6) absence from the hearing notwithstanding the efforts of the proponent of the testimony to procure attendance.

***Opposing Party Statement.*** The opposing party exception applies to documents as well as to oral statements. A party statement can be contained in a letter, report, memorandum, journal, progress chart, email, blog post, or virtually any other form of writing. Once the exhibit has been authenticated, the only remaining foundation is that it was made or adopted by a party against whom it is being offered, or by an agent, servant, or employee of such a party.

## 6.4 Foundations for Real and Demonstrative Evidence

### *6.4.1 Real Evidence/Tangible Objects*

You must show real evidence to be relevant and authentic. The relevance of real evidence is typically established by the case's context, and often requires no additional attention when it comes to laying the foundation. Authenticity, on the other hand, must always be carefully established, as it is the fact of authenticity that qualifies the exhibit as real evidence. In many cases you can show the authenticity of real evidence by a witness's recognition of the exhibit. Other cases require a more detailed and complex foundation, usually referred to as chain of custody.

***Recognition of the exhibit.*** You can establish the authenticity of real evidence through the testimony of a witness who recognizes the item in question. Many objects can be identified by virtue of their unique features. Others may have been

18. Fed. R. Evid. 804(b)(1).

given some identifying mark in anticipation of litigation. In either case, the witness must testify that 1) they were familiar with the object at the time of the underlying events, and 2) they are able to recognize the exhibit in the arbitration hearing as that very same object.

***Chain of custody.*** A chain of custody establishes the location, handling, and care of an object between the time of its recovery and the time of the hearing. A chain of custody must be shown whenever 1) the exhibit is not uniquely recognizable and has not been marked, or 2) the exhibit's physical properties are in issue.

### 6.4.2 Photography and Other Recording Devices

Photographs and other recordings bridge the gap between real and demonstrative evidence. While a visual or audio recording of any sort is, strictly speaking, an illustration of a past event, its capacity to portray a scene with accuracy is so great that many arbitrators treat photographs and other recordings as tantamount to real evidence.

***Still photographs.*** The foundation for admitting a still photograph is that it "fairly and accurately" portrays the scene shown. In all but a few situations, it is not necessary to call the photographer to testify. It is generally possible to introduce a photograph through the testimony of any witness who is familiar with the scene as it appeared at a relevant time.

***Video.*** As with photographs, a video may be authenticated by any witness who is familiar with the scene or scenes portrayed. It is necessary to call the operator of the camera only if special features were employed, or if the date of the filming is in issue. A more difficult problem arises in the case of remote recording, when no person observed the events as they were recorded. In these circumstances, the foundation must include additional information on operating procedures as well as the equipment's condition.

***Audio Recordings.*** The foundation for an audio recording depends upon the purpose for which it is offered. A recording that is submitted merely as a voice exemplar, for example, may be authenticated by any witness who is able to recognize the voices of the various speakers. The same holds true for recorded music, as might be offered in a copyright dispute. Any witness who is familiar with the material recorded can lay the foundation.

***X-rays and similar images.*** X-rays and other images produced by means such as computerized axial tomography (CT scan) and magnetic resonance imaging (MRI) are essentially photographs of the body's internal composition. To lay a foundation, a physician or other qualified person must testify that an X-ray, CT scan, or MRI is a fair representation of the internal structure of a given patient's body. The identifying marks on the film (which allow the physician to recognize which X-ray belongs to which patient) are usually considered to be business records of the hospital or clinic.

### 6.4.3 Demonstrative Evidence

Demonstrative evidence illustrates, clarifies, or explains testimony or real evidence. When such an exhibit is sufficiently accurate or probative, it may be admitted into evidence.

***Admissible demonstrative evidence.*** The foundation for a map, chart, blueprint, or other diagram is essentially the same as that for a photograph. The witness must be familiar with the scene, location, or structure as it appeared at a relevant time, and must testify that the exhibit constitutes a fair representation. Additional foundation is necessary if the exhibit is drawn to scale.

***Models and reproductions.*** The foundation for a model or reproduction is similar to that for a photograph. The witness must be familiar with the real location or object and must testify to the model's accuracy. Issues regarding scale are identical to those concerning maps and diagrams.

***Illustrative aids.*** Exhibits that are insufficiently accurate to be allowed into evidence may often still be used for illustrative purposes. The foundation includes a witness's testimony that the exhibit will assist in explaining their testimony, as well as a general explanation or description of the inaccuracy.

***Animations and simulations.*** To establish the foundation for a computer animation, you need to show that it is a fair and accurate depiction of the events described by the witness and will help the arbitrator understand the testimony. Simulations create a visualization by applying technical principles to data. They normally require the testimony of an expert witness to explain the reliability of the process used to create the simulation.

## 6.5 Making and Responding to Objections

Objections raise and resolve evidentiary disputes (Lore & Lubet, *MTA*, Ch. 10). You may object to an attorney's questions, to a witness's testimony, to the introduction or use of exhibits, to a lawyer's demeanor or behavior, and even to the arbitrator's conduct. In many arbitrations, particularly those that are not recorded by a court reporter, very few objections are made. In some high-stakes arbitrations with a court reporter present, however, and/or where the parties have agreed that rules of evidence will apply, objections are made as if proceeding in court. Because objections are really the exception and not the rule in most arbitrations, this subsection is intentionally abbreviated, consisting of only a short list of common objections and some ethical considerations related to objections.

### 6.5.1 Form of Question Objections

The following list and descriptions of some common objections (and responses) is intended only as a reference or guide, not as a substitute for a thorough knowledge of evidence and procedure.

***Leading question.*** A leading question suggests or contains its own answer. Leading questions are objectionable on direct examination. They are permitted on cross-examination. *See* Fed. R. Evid. 611.

> *Responses.* The question is preliminary, foundational, directing the witness's attention, or refreshing the witness's recollection. The witness is very old, very young, infirm, adverse, or hostile. Leading questions can most often be rephrased in nonleading form.

***Compound question.*** A compound question contains two separate inquiries that are not necessarily susceptible to a single answer. For example, "Wasn't the fire engine driving in the left lane and flashing its lights?"

> *Responses.* Dual inquiries are permissible if the question seeks to establish a relationship between two facts or events. For example, "Didn't they move forward and then reach into their pocket?" Other than to establish a relationship, compound questions are objectionable and should be rephrased.

***Vague question.*** A question is vague if it is incomprehensible, or incomplete, or if any answer will necessarily be ambiguous. For example, the question "When do you leave your house in the morning?" is vague, since it does not specify the day of the week to which it refers.

> *Responses.* A question is not vague if the arbitrator understands it. Many arbitrators will ask the witness whether they understand the question. Unless the precise wording is important, it is often easiest to rephrase a vague question.

***Argumentative question.*** An argumentative question asks the witness to accept the examiner's summary, inference, or conclusion, rather than to agree with the existence (or nonexistence) of a fact. Questions can be made more or less argumentative depending upon the examiner's tone of voice.

> *Responses.* Treat the objection as a relevance issue, and explain its probative value to the arbitrator: "Ms. Arbitrator, it goes to prove . . . ." It will not be persuasive to say, "Mr. Arbitrator, I am not arguing." It might be persuasive to explain the nonargumentative point that you are trying to make. Alternatively, make no response, but wait to see if the arbitrator thinks that the question is argumentative. If so, rephrase the question.

***Narratives.*** Witnesses are required to testify in the form of question and answer. This requirement ensures that opposing counsel will have the opportunity to frame objections to questions before the answer is given. A narrative answer instead proceeds at some length in the absence of questions. An answer that is more than a few paragraphs long can usually be classified as a narrative. A narrative question is one that calls for a narrative answer, such as, "Tell us everything that you did on July 14." Objections can be made both to narrative questions and narrative answers.

*Responses.* The best response is usually to ask another question that breaks up the narrative. Note that expert witnesses are often allowed to testify in narrative fashion, since technical explanations cannot be given easily in question-and-answer format. Even then, however, it is usually more persuasive to interject questions to break up big answers.

***Asked and answered.*** An attorney is not entitled to repeat questions and answers. Once an inquiry has been "asked and answered," further repetition is objectionable.

*Responses.* If the question has not been asked and answered, point out to the arbitrator the way it differs from the earlier testimony. Otherwise, it is best to rephrase the question to vary the exact information sought.

***Assuming facts not in evidence.*** A question, usually on cross-examination, is objectionable if it includes as a predicate a statement of fact that has not been proven. The reason for this objection is that the question is unfair; it cannot be answered without conceding the unproven assumption.

*Responses.* A question assumes facts not in evidence only when it uses an introductory predicate as the basis for another inquiry. Simple, one-part cross-examination questions do not need to be based upon facts that are already in evidence. For example, it would be proper to ask a witness, "Didn't you leave home late that morning?" absent evidence of the time the witness departed. As a consequence of misunderstanding this distinction, "facts not in evidence" objections are often erroneously made to perfectly good cross-examination questions. If the objection is well taken, most questions can easily be divided in two.

***Nonresponsive answers.*** Opposing counsel can object if all, or some part, of an answer is unresponsive to the question, because counsel is entitled to insist that the examination proceed in question-and-answer format.

*Responses.* Ask another question.

### 6.5.2 Substantive Objections

***Hearsay objections.*** Depending upon the agreed procedures, hearsay may or may not be admissible in arbitrations. The Federal Rules of Evidence define hearsay as, "[A] statement, other than one made by the declarant while testifying at the trial or hearing, offered in evidence to prove the truth of the matter asserted."[19] Thus, any out-of-arbitration statement, including the witness's own previous statement, is potentially hearsay. Whenever a witness testifies, or is asked to testify, about what they or someone else said in the past, the statement should be subjected to hearsay

19. Fed. R. Evid. 801(c).

analysis. Statements are not hearsay if they are offered for a purpose other than to "prove the truth of the matter asserted." For example, consider the statement, "I warned them that their brakes needed work." This statement would be hearsay if offered to prove that the brakes were indeed defective. On the other hand, it would not be hearsay if offered to prove that the driver had notice of the condition of the brakes and was therefore negligent in not having them repaired. There are also numerous exceptions to the hearsay rule.

> *Responses.* Out-of-arbitration statements are admissible if they are not hearsay, or if they fall within one of the exceptions to the hearsay rule. In addition to statements that are not offered for their truth, the Federal Rules of Evidence define two other types of statements as nonhearsay. The witness's own previous statement is not hearsay if 1) it was given under oath at a proceeding and it is inconsistent with the current testimony; 2) it is consistent with the current testimony and it is offered to rebut a charge of recent fabrication or improper motive; or 3) it is a statement of past identification. *See* Fed. R. Evid. 801(d)(1). In addition, a statement of an opposing party is defined as nonhearsay if offered against that party. Fed. R. Evid. 801(D)(2).

Some of the more frequently encountered exceptions to the hearsay rule are as follows:

- *Present sense impression.* A statement describing an event made while, or immediately after, the declarant observes the event. For example, "Look, there goes the president." Fed. R. Evid. 803(1).
- *Excited utterance.* A statement relating to a startling event made while under the stress of excitement caused by the event. For example, "A piece of plaster fell from the roof, and it just missed me." Fed. R. Evid. 803(2).
- *State of mind.* A statement of the declarant's mental state or condition. For example, "I was so mad I couldn't see straight." Fed. R. Evid. 803(3).
- *Past recollection recorded.* A memorandum or record of a matter about which the witness once had knowledge, but which they have since forgotten. The record must have been made by the witness when the events were fresh in the witness's mind and must be shown to have been accurate when made. Fed. R. Evid. 803(5).
- *Business records.* The business records exception applies to the records of any regularly conducted activity. To qualify as an exception to the hearsay rule, the record must have been made at or near the time of the transaction, by a person with knowledge or transmitted from a person with knowledge. It must have been made and kept in the ordinary course of business. The foundation for a business record must be laid by the custodian of the record, by some other qualified witness, or by certification. Fed. R. Evid. 803(6).

- *Reputation as to character.* Evidence of a person's reputation for truth and veracity is an exception to the hearsay rule. Note that there are restrictions other than hearsay on the admissibility of character evidence. Fed. R. Evid. 803(21). *See also* Fed. R. Evid. 404–405.
- *Prior testimony.* Testimony given at a different proceeding, or in deposition, qualifies for this exception if 1) the testimony was given under oath; 2) the adverse party, or a predecessor in interest, had an opportunity to cross-examine; and 3) the witness is currently unavailable. Fed. R. Evid. 804(b)(1).
- *Dying declaration.* A statement by a dying person of the cause or circumstances of what they believed to be impending death. Fed. R. Evid. 804(b)(2).
- *Statement against interest.* A statement so contrary to the declarant's pecuniary, proprietary, or penal interest, that no reasonable person would have made it unless it were true. The declarant must be unavailable. Fed. R. Evid. 804(b)(3).
- *Catch-all exception.* Other hearsay statements may be admitted if they contain sufficient circumstantial guarantees of trustworthiness. The declarant must be unavailable, and advance notice must be given to the adverse party. Fed. R. Evid. 807.

***Irrelevant.*** Evidence is irrelevant if it does not make any fact of consequence to the case more or less probable. Evidence can be irrelevant if it proves nothing, or if it tends to prove something that does not matter. Fed. R. Evid. 401, 402.

> *Response.* Explain the relevance of the testimony.

***Unfair prejudice.*** Relevant evidence may also be excluded if its probative value is substantially outweighed by confusion of issues, misleading the factfinder, or considerations of undue delay, waste of time, or needless presentation of cumulative evidence. Fed. R. Evid. 403.

> *Responses.* Most arbitrators are hesitant to exclude evidence on this basis. A measured explanation of the probative value of the testimony is the best response.

***Improper character evidence, generally.*** Character evidence is generally not admissible to prove that a person acted in conformity with their character. For example, a driver's past accidents cannot be offered as proof of current negligence. Fed. R. Evid. 404(a).

> *Responses.* Past crimes and bad acts may be offered for nonconformity purposes, such as to prove motive, opportunity, intent, preparation, plan, knowledge, identity, or absence of mistake. Fed. R. Evid. 404(b).

***Improper character evidence, conviction of crime.*** As noted previously, the commission, and even the conviction, of past crimes is not admissible to prove current guilt. The credibility of a witness who takes the stand and testifies, however, may be impeached based on a prior criminal conviction, but only if the following requirements are satisfied: the crime must have been either a felony or one which involved dishonesty or false statement, regardless of punishment. With certain exceptions, the evidence is not admissible unless it occurred within the last ten years. Juvenile adjudications and crimes that have been pardoned or annulled are generally not admissible. Fed. R. Evid. 609.

> *Responses.* If the crime was not a felony, the conviction may still be admissible if it involved dishonesty. If the conviction is more than ten years old, it may still be admissible if the arbitrator determines that its probative value, supported by specific facts and circumstances, substantially outweighs its prejudicial effect. Fed. R. Evid. 609.

***Improper character evidence.*** As noted above, the past bad acts of a person may not be offered as proof that they committed similar acts. Specific instances of conduct are admissible for the limited purpose of attacking or supporting credibility. A witness may therefore be cross-examined concerning past bad acts if they reflect upon truthfulness or untruthfulness. Note, however, that such bad acts (other than conviction of a crime) may not be proved by extrinsic evidence. The cross-examiner is stuck with the witness's answer. Fed. R. Evid. 608(b).

> *Responses.* Explain how the witness's past bad acts are probative of untruthfulness.

***Improper character evidence, reputation.*** Reputation evidence is admissible only regarding an individual's character for truthfulness or untruthfulness (or in cases where character is at issue or when instances of sexual assault are involved). Moreover, evidence of a truthful character is admissible only after the witness's character has been attacked. Fed. R. Evid. 608(a).

> *Responses.* Explain how the reputation evidence is probative of truthfulness or untruthfulness.

***Lack of personal knowledge.*** Witnesses (other than experts) must testify from personal knowledge, which is more or less defined as sensory perception. A witness's lack of personal knowledge may be obvious from the questioning, may be inherent in the testimony, or may be developed by questioning on *voir dire*. Fed. R. Evid. 602.

> *Responses.* Ask further questions that establish the witness's personal knowledge.

***Improper lay opinion.*** Lay witnesses (nonexperts) are generally precluded from testifying as to opinions, conclusions, or inferences. Fed. R. Evid. 701.

*Responses.* Lay witnesses may testify to opinions or inferences if they are rationally based upon the perception of the witness. Common lay opinions include estimates of speed, distance, value, height, time, duration, and temperature. Lay witnesses are also commonly allowed to testify as to the mood, sanity, demeanor, sobriety, or tone of voice of another person.

***Speculation or conjecture.*** Witnesses may not be asked to speculate or guess. Such questions are often phrased as hypotheticals, such as, "What would have happened if . . . ?"

*Responses.* Witnesses are permitted to make reasonable estimates rationally based upon perception.

***Authenticity.*** You must authenticate exhibits before they may be admitted. Authenticity refers to adequate proof that the exhibit actually is what it seems or purports to be. Virtually all documents and tangible objects must be authenticated. Since exhibits are authenticated by laying a foundation, objections may be raised on the ground of either authenticity or foundation.

*Responses.* Ask additional questions that establish authenticity.

***Lack of foundation.*** Nearly all evidence, other than a witness's direct observation of events, requires some sort of predicate foundation for admissibility. An objection to lack of foundation requires the arbitrator to make a preliminary ruling as to the admissibility of the evidence. Fed. R. Evid. 104. The evidentiary foundations vary widely.[20]

***Best evidence.*** The "best evidence" or "original document" rule refers to the common law requirement that copies or secondary evidence of writings could not be admitted into evidence unless the absence of the original could be explained. Under modern practice, most jurisdictions have significantly expanded upon the circumstances in which duplicates and other secondary evidence may be admitted. Fed. R. Evid. 1001–1003.

*Responses.* Ask additional questions demonstrating either that the item offered is a duplicate, or that the original is unavailable.

***Privilege.*** Numerous privileges may operate to exclude otherwise admissible evidence. Among the most common are attorney-client, physician-patient, marital, clergy, mediator, psychotherapist-patient, and a number of others that exist either by statute or at common law. Each privilege has its own foundation and its own set of exceptions. Fed. R. Evid. 501 did not change the common law privileges but note that state statutory privileges may not pertain in arbitrations governed by federal rules.

---

20. See section 6.4.

> *Responses.* Virtually all privileges are subject to some exceptions, which vary from jurisdiction to jurisdiction.

***Subsequent remedial measures.*** Evidence of subsequent repair or other remedial measures is not admissible to prove negligence or other culpable conduct. Fed. R. Evid. 407. The primary rationale for this rule is that parties should not be discouraged from remedying dangerous conditions and should not have to choose between undertaking repairs and creating proof of their own liability.

> *Responses.* Subsequent remedial measures may be offered to prove ownership, control, or feasibility of precautionary measures, if controverted. Fed. R. Evid. 407.

***Settlement offers.*** Offers of compromise or settlement are not admissible to prove or disprove liability. Statements made during settlement negotiations are also inadmissible. Fed. R. Evid. 408.

> *Responses.* Offers and statements made during settlement discussions may be admissible for another purpose, such as to prove bias or prejudice of a witness or to negate a contention of undue delay, but not to impeach by a prior inconsistent statement. Fed. R. Evid. 408.

### 6.5.3 Ethics and Objections

Ethical issues frequently arise in the context of making and meeting objections. Because the objecting process is one of the most confrontational aspects of the arbitration, it often tests counsel's reserves of goodwill, civility, restraint, and sense of fair play. The three most common problems are discussed below.

***Asking objectionable questions.*** It is unethical to attempt to use the information contained in questions as a substitute for testimony that cannot be obtained. Some lawyers apparently believe that the idea of zealous advocacy allows them to slip information before an arbitrator by asserting it in a question, knowing full well that the witness will not be allowed to answer. The usual scenario is something as follows:

> Lawyer: Isn't it true that you were once fired from a job for being drunk?
>
> Objection: Objection, relevance.
>
> Lawyer: I withdraw the question. (Sotto voce: Who cares about the ruling? I never expected to get it in, but now the arbitrator knows that the witness is a drunk.)

This conduct, even if the information is true, is absolutely unethical. Testimony is to come from witnesses, with admissibility ruled upon by the arbitrator. It subverts the very purpose of an adversary hearing when lawyers abuse their right to question witnesses in order to slip inadmissible evidence before the arbitrator.

***Making questionable objections.*** The same general analysis applies to the use of objections as it does to the offer of evidence. Counsel need not be positive that an objection will be sustained but must only believe that there is a reasonable basis for making it. Again, in arbitration it is up to the arbitrator to decide whether to admit the evidence.

***Making "tactical" objections.*** Many lawyers, and more than a few trial advocacy texts, tout the use of so-called "tactical" objections. Since an objection is the only means by which one lawyer can interrupt the examination of another, it is suggested that objections should occasionally be made to break up the flow of a successful examination. An objection can throw the opposing lawyer off stride, or give the witness a rest, or distract the arbitrator from the testimony's content. This advice is usually tempered with the admonition that there must always be some evidentiary basis for the objection, but the real message is that you can use an objection for any purpose whatsoever, so long as you can make it with a straight face. This view is unfortunate. It amounts to nothing more than the sneaky use of objections for a wholly improper purpose. No arbitrator would allow a lawyer to object on the ground that the opposition's examination is going too well. The fact that disruption can be accomplished *sub silentio* does not justify it. The same is true of other tactical uses of objections, such as suggesting testimony to a witness. That said, you should object sparingly and to unreliable evidence offered in support of a key issue to alert the arbitrator to its unreliability.

## 6.6 Making and Responding to Offers of Proof

An offer of proof consists of actual evidence (testimonial or documentary) or of a statement of counsel (oral or written) demonstrating what evidence counsel would be seeking to introduce into evidence if the arbitrator had not sustained opposing counsel's objection. You should make an offer of proof only after the arbitrator has sustained an objection to a question propounded to a witness or to a proffered exhibit. Its primary purpose is to preserve the record so that if judicial review becomes necessary, the reviewing court will have a basis for determining whether or not the arbitrator properly excluded the evidence. A secondary purpose of an offer of proof is to serve as a basis for having the arbitrator reconsider the ruling excluding the evidence.

You may make an offer of proof in one of two forms: formally, through tendering the actual evidence (testimony or exhibits); or informally, through statement of counsel on the record. A formal offer of proof is generally preferred. Usually, testimonial offers of proof occur during your direct examination of a witness. Make clear on the record which portion of the offer of proof is being submitted.

In responding to an offer of proof, state your objections clearly and succinctly on the record. This will generally be effective in dissuading the arbitrator from reversing the original ruling sustaining your objection to the area of questioning or exhibit(s), as the case may be. Also seek to cross-examine the witness who is the vehicle for a testimonial offer of proof to further buttress your position that the arbitrator has properly excluded the evidence. State all grounds for your opposition to the proposed evidence when the offer of proof is made, or the grounds not stated may be deemed waived on later court review.

## 6.7 Standards for Expert Testimony

### *6.7.1 Areas of Expertise*

Fed. R. Evid. 702 provides that expert opinions are admissible where the expert's "scientific, technical, or other specialized knowledge will assist the trier of fact to understand the evidence or to determine a fact in issue."

Thus, there are two threshold questions:

- Does the witness possess sufficient scientific, technical, or other specialized knowledge?
- Will that knowledge be helpful to the arbitrator?

### *6.7.2 Scope of Opinion*

Fed. R. Evid. 704 provides that expert testimony, if otherwise admissible, "is not objectionable because it embraces an ultimate issue to be decided by the trier of fact." Arbitrators vary on their interpretations of the "ultimate issue" rule. Some arbitrators will allow experts to opine on virtually any issue, including such case-breakers as whether the claimant in a personal injury case was contributorily negligent or whether the respondent in a securities case violated exchange rules. Many arbitrators would also allow an expert in a medical malpractice case to testify that the failure to order the tests fell below the standard of care generally exercised by practitioners in the relevant community. Most arbitrators, though not all, would balk at permitting the expert to testify that the defendant's conduct constituted malpractice, on the theory that malpractice is a legal conclusion that is not within a medical expert's specialized knowledge.

### *6.7.3 Basis for Opinion*

Under Fed R. Evid. 705, an expert can testify to their opinion with or without explaining the facts or data on which the opinion is based. In theory, then, an expert, once qualified, could simply state their opinion on direct examination, leaving the cross-examiner to search for its basis. In practice, of course, this approach is rarely followed because the expert's opinion can hardly be persuasive until its foundation is explained. The rule's practical effect is to allow the witness to state their opinion at the examination's beginning, followed by explication, rather than having to set forth all the data at the outset.

### 6.7.4 The Expert's Overview

Just as a lawyer cannot succeed without developing a comprehensive case theory, neither will an expert be effective without a viable, articulated theory. An expert's theory is an overview or summary of the expert's entire position. The theory must not only state a conclusion, but must also explain, in commonsense terms, why the expert is correct.

- Why did they settle upon a certain methodology?
- Why did they review particular data?
- Why is their approach reliable?
- Why is the opposing expert wrong?

In other words, the expert witness must tell a coherent story that provides the arbitrator with reasons for accepting and, it is hoped, internalizing the expert's point of view.

The need for a theory is especially true in cases involving "dueling experts." It is common that if one party in arbitration retains an expert, the other will as well. The arbitrator is then faced with the task of sorting through the opinion testimony and choosing which witness to believe. It is likely that both experts will be amply qualified, and it is unlikely that either will make a glaring error in their analysis or commit an unpardonable faux pas in testimony. The arbitrator will therefore be inclined to credit the expert whose theory is most believable.

The importance of theory extends to all types of expert testimony. It is necessary, but not sufficient, for your expert to be thorough, exacting, highly regarded, incisive, honorable, and well prepared. Their testimony will suffer if they cannot support their opinion with commonsense reasons.

### 6.7.5 Offering Expert Testimony

There is a certain logic to most experts' direct examinations. While the particulars and details will vary, there are a limited number of possible patterns for organizing the testimony. It is absolutely necessary, for example, to qualify the expert before proceeding to their opinion. The following is a broad outline that can accommodate the specifics of most expert testimony.

#### 6.7.5.1 Introduction and Foreshadowing

Introduce the expert and explain their involvement in the case. Since expert testimony is qualitatively different from lay testimony, it is a good idea to clarify its purposes for the arbitrator so that they will understand what they are about to hear. Ask the witness how they came to be retained and why they are present at the arbitration hearing. Be aware that the technical requirements of presenting expert testimony often result in a considerable time gap between the witness's introduction and the substantive high points of their testimony. Thus, it is generally desirable to foreshadow the expert's opinion at the very outset of the examination.

#### 6.7.5.2 Qualification

To testify as an expert, a witness must be qualified by reason of knowledge, skill, experience, training, or education.[21] This is a threshold question for the arbitrator, who must determine whether the witness is qualified before permitting the opinion testimony. The qualification of the witness, then, is a necessary predicate for the testimony that follows. Take care to qualify the expert in a manner that is both technically adequate and persuasive.

***Technical requirements.*** The technical requirements for qualifying an expert witness are straightforward. It is usually adequate to show that the witness possesses some specialized skill or knowledge, acquired through appropriate experience or education, and that the witness can apply that skill or knowledge in a manner relevant to the case's issues.

There are, of course, many other areas of basic qualification beyond education and experience. Examples include:

- specialized training
- teaching and lecturing positions
- publications
- professional memberships
- continuing education courses
- licenses and certifications
- consulting experience
- awards and other professional honors

Establishing basic qualifications, however, should not be your entire objective. It is equally, if not more, important to go on to qualify the witness as persuasively as possible.

***Persuasive qualification.*** The technical qualification of an expert merely allows the witness to testify in the form of an opinion. Your ultimate goal is to ensure that the arbitrator accepts the opinion. Persuasive qualification is particularly important in cases involving competing experts because their relative qualifications may be one basis on which the arbitrator decides which expert to believe. It is a mistake, however, to think that more qualifications are necessarily more persuasive. An endless repetition of degrees, publications, awards, and appointments may easily overload any arbitrator's ability, not to mention desire, to pay careful attention to the witness. It is often better to introduce the witness's detailed résumé or

21. Fed. R. Evid. 702.

curriculum vitae and to use the qualification portion of the actual examination to focus in on several salient points. Experience is often more impressive than academic background. So, for example, a medical expert may be more impressive if they have actually practiced in the applicable specialty, as opposed to possessing knowledge that is strictly theoretical. When presenting such a witness, then, dwell on their experience, pointing out details such as the number of procedures the expert has performed, the hospitals where the expert is on staff, and the numbers of other physicians who have consulted them. Finally, emphasize areas of qualification where you know the opposing expert to be lacking. If your expert has a superior academic background, use the direct examination to point out why academic training is important. If your expert holds a certification that the opposing expert lacks, have them explain how difficult it is to become certified.

***Tender the witness.*** It is customary with some arbitrators that, once qualifications have been concluded, the attorney must tender the witness as an expert in a specified field. The purpose of the tender is to inform the arbitrator that qualification has been completed and to give opposing counsel an opportunity either to conduct a *voir dire* of the witness or to object to the tender. Opposing counsel may use *voir dire* examination to attempt to develop deficiencies in the witness's qualifications. This is done during the direct examination for two reasons. First, if it can be shown that the witness truly is not qualified, there will be no reason to continue the direct examination. Second, objections raised during *voir dire* can often be cured through additional direct examination. Note that *voir dire* on qualifications, as with all *voir dire* examinations, should be limited to the eventual admissibility of the expert testimony and should not be used as a substitute for cross-examination regarding weight or credibility.

#### 6.7.5.3 Opinion and Theory

***Statement of opinion.*** Under Fed. R. Evid. 705, once the witness has been qualified and accepted as an expert, they may express their opinion without additional foundation. In other words, the expert may state their conclusions without first detailing the nature or extent of their background work or investigation. Take advantage of this "opinion first" provision. Expert testimony tends to be long, arcane, and boring. The intricate details of an expert's preparation are unlikely to be interesting or even particularly understandable. They will be even less captivating if they are offered in a void, without any advance notice of where the details are leading or why they are being explained. A clear statement of the expert's conclusion can provide the context for the balance of the explanatory testimony.

***Statement of theory.*** Once the expert has stated their opinion, the expert should immediately provide the underlying theory. The theory should furnish the nexus between the expert's conclusion and the data used to support the conclusion. The examination should follow this pattern:

1) here is my opinion;

2) here are the principles that support my opinion; and

3) here is what I did to reach my final conclusion.

#### 6.7.5.4 Explanation and Support

Having stated and supported their theory choice, the expert can now detail their investigation and calculations. The arbitrator cannot be expected to take the expert at their word, so they must establish the validity and accuracy of their data and assumptions.

***Data.*** Ask the expert how they chose and obtained their data. Have them explain why their information is reliable. Ask the expert to describe any tests or computations performed. The treatment of underlying data is one of the trickiest aspects of expert testimony. Many experts will be in love with their data, and they will be anxious to lay them out in excruciating detail. Unfortunately, most arbitrators have little tolerance for lengthy descriptions of enigmatic scientific or technical processes. Strike a balance, eliciting a sufficiently detailed treatment of the data to persuade the arbitrator of its reliability but stopping well short of the point where the arbitrator's attention span is exhausted. It is not sufficient for the expert simply to relate the data's nature. Rather, the expert should go on to explain how and why the data supports their conclusions.

***Assumptions.*** Most experts rely upon assumptions. It is not necessary for your expert to explain or outline every hypothesis they used, but they should note and support the more important assumptions.

#### 6.7.5.5 Theory Differentiation

In cases involving dueling experts, there will also be competing theories. Properly prepared and presented, each expert will attempt to persuade the arbitrator to accept their theory. It can be particularly effective, therefore, to ask your expert to comment on the opposing expert's work. This technique can be called theory differentiation because it is most convincing when your expert discusses the shortcomings of the opposition theory. The timing of theory differentiation can be important. As the claimant's counsel, you will generally want to establish your expert's theory first, before proceeding to criticize the respondent's expert. Depending upon the case's circumstances, you might even want to forgo theory differentiation entirely during your case in chief, and to recall your expert for that purpose on rebuttal. The respondent, on the other hand, should address the claimant's expert's theory at some point during the direct examination of the respondent's own expert. This can be done early in the examination (to rebut the claimant's expert immediately and forcefully), or it can be done toward the end of the testimony to allow the respondent's expert to build up the positive aspects of their own theory before turning their attention to the opposition.

***Conclusion.*** An expert's direct examination should conclude with a powerful restatement of their most important conclusions.

## 6.7.6 Persuasive Expert Examination Techniques

You can use most of the direct examination methods discussed in section 5.3 with expert witnesses. In addition, you can apply the following techniques to expert testimony.

### 6.7.6.1 Humanize the Expert Witness

Many experts from scientific, technical, or financial backgrounds may appear aloof, intimidating, or even arrogant to those who do not share their special expertise. It is therefore important to humanize these witnesses as much as possible during the direct examination. If the arbitrator permits, bring out personal and family background information, and allow the witness to talk about more than strictly professional matters.

### 6.7.6.2 Keep the Testimony Accessible

***Use plain language.*** Virtually every field of expertise creates its own technical and shorthand terms, and expert witnesses will be inclined to use arcane and jargon-laden speech without even thinking about it. Guide the witness away from jargon and into the realm of everyday speech if the arbitrator is not also an expert in the field. There are three basic means to accomplish this task. First, thoroughly prepare the witness to avoid complex, professional terms. Spend sufficient time with the witness before the hearing so that they understand the importance of plain, simple language. Second, ask for an explanation when your witness lapses into their native tongue, whether it is finance-talk, engineer-ese, or medical-speak. Do this gently and without reprimand or condescension. Finally, and possibly most importantly, avoid the temptation to adopt the expert's word choices. Too many lawyers, perhaps out of a desire to appear erudite or knowledgeable, examine expert witnesses using the expert's own jargon. Such examinations come across as private, and completely inaccessible, conversations between the lawyer and the witness. It is bad enough when lawyers use legalese; it is worse when they embrace the private speech of another profession.

***Avoid narrative.*** Most arbitrators will allow expert witnesses considerable freedom to testify in narrative fashion. Many lawyers believe they should take advantage of this leeway, and they therefore encourage their experts to present their testimony in long, uninterrupted segments. This is a mistake. Long narratives are hard to follow and hard to digest. Anyone who ever sat through a long lecture or speech should understand how difficult it is to pay attention to a speaker for an extended period. This is particularly true of expert testimony, which often concentrates on complex or intricate details. Allowing an expert to testify in a long, unbroken stretch invites arbitrator inattention.

***Use examples and analogies.*** Many complex ideas can be explained with examples, analogies, or metaphors. Encourage expert witnesses to clarify their testimony using such imagery. Do not take the witness by surprise with a request for an example or metaphor. The time to consider using these explanatory tools is during preparation, not on the spur of the moment in the midst of direct examination.

***Use visual aids.*** Visual aids enhance the direct examination of almost every expert. Since expert testimony may be hard to follow, it can be particularly effective to portray the expert's concepts with charts, graphs, drawings, or models. A physician, for example, can bring testimony to life with an anatomical model or a series of colored overlays. Financial experts should illustrate their testimony with graphs or tables. An architectural or engineering expert should use diagrams or scale models. The possibilities for visual aids are practically infinite, limited only by counsel's (and the expert's) imagination.

***Use internal summaries.*** Because of the potential length and complexity of expert testimony, use internal summaries to highlight significant points. Ask the expert to point out the relevance of the most critical steps in the analysis. Request that they summarize the implications of their findings. Think of the expert's testimony as containing a series of steps or elements. At the conclusion of each step, have the expert explain how they got there, why it is important, and where they are going next.

***Use the concept of consensus.*** Almost every field of expertise contains several contending schools of thought. Opposing experts often arrive at different opinions because they approach the issues from distinct perspectives. For example, a strict Freudian psychologist is likely to evaluate a patient's mental state quite differently from a Gestalt therapist. Your expert's testimony is more persuasive if you can show that they have presented the mainstream view, as opposed to a novel or untested theory. Do this by stressing such credentials as university affiliation, professional certification, or other indicia of widespread acceptance.

#### 6.7.6.3 Use Leading Questions When Called For

Two recurrent problems in expert testimony are boredom and pomposity. Many experts are inclined to drone on at length over unimportant details. Others present themselves with an air of excessive self-importance, especially while presenting their credentials. Cut through a welter of details by using a leading question to direct the witness to the heart of the matter. You can also use leading questions to make the witness seem less haughty or pretentious.

#### 6.7.6.4 Encourage Powerful Language

There is a tradition in many technical fields of hedging or qualifying the language in which conclusions are expressed. This makes great sense when discussing research, since one's results are always subject to further inquiry. Thus, professionals commonly use terms such as "to the best of my knowledge . . ." or "according to current indications . . ." or "as far as we can tell. . . ." While this language is meant to convey open-mindedness as opposed to uncertainty, it can be fatal to a witness's testimony in an arbitration. To prevent inadvertent miscommunication, prepare your expert witnesses to testify in straightforward, unequivocal terms. Caution experts to avoid language that unintentionally qualifies or hedges their results, using instead wording that emphasizes accuracy and certainty.

#### 6.7.6.5 Use Enumeration

Audiences most often pay closer attention to information presented in numbered lists. Therefore, encourage expert witnesses to introduce concepts in terms of factors or considerations, rather than launching into extended explanations.

#### 6.7.6.6 Consider Inoculation

Expert witnesses may be open to several distinct lines of cross-examination. Consider, therefore, conducting a certain amount of explanatory or defensive direct examination to inoculate the witness against cross-examination on such matters as the payment of fees, the use of presumptions, reliance on secondary sources, and the like.

#### 6.7.6.7 Do Not Stretch the Witness's Expertise

It may be tempting to try to stretch a witness's expertise, either as a cost-saving measure or to enlarge the scope of their testimony. Both undertakings are misguided. It is risky, bordering upon unethical, to seek to have an expert testify outside of their legitimate field.

### *6.7.7 Cross-Examining Expert Witnesses*

You can adapt most of the basic approaches to cross-examination discussed in section 5.4 to expert testimony. In addition, there are certain tools you can use primarily or most effectively with expert witnesses.

Research, as much as technique, lies at the heart of expert witness cross-examination. You cannot conduct an adequate cross-examination without first thoroughly investigating all the technical aspects of the expected testimony. It is often said that you cannot cross-examine an expert without first becoming an expert yourself. Extend your research beyond the expert's subject matter area and into the witness's own professional background. Read everything the witness has ever published and attempt to obtain transcripts of prior trial and/or deposition testimony. There is nothing so effective as impeaching an expert with their own prior assertions. Other fruitful areas of investigation may include the expert's professional affiliations, past clients, governmental positions, and the like. Don't view such research as an effort to dig up dirt (although once in a lifetime you might stumble across something juicy), but rather as an attempt to obtain a rounded picture of the expert's professional status. Many experts have become closely associated with certain positions over the course of their careers, and this knowledge can be very helpful in shaping a cross-examination.

The research necessary to cross-examine an expert witness varies considerably from case to case. The balance of this section is therefore limited to techniques that can be applied to expert witnesses in general.

### 6.7.7.1 Challenge the Witness's Credentials

An expert witness's credentials are subject to challenge either on *voir dire* or during cross-examination. You can use *voir dire* to object to the legal sufficiency of the expert's qualifications, while cross-examination is the time to attack their weight.

#### Voir dire *on credentials*

Once the proponent of an expert has concluded the qualification segment of the direct examination, opposing counsel is entitled to conduct a *voir dire* of the witness. A *voir dire* examination suspends the direct so that the opponent of the proffered evidence can inquire as to its evidentiary sufficiency. Regarding the qualification of experts, this means that opposing counsel can interrupt the direct examination to conduct a mini-cross limited to the witness's credentials. It is frequently an uphill battle to persuade an arbitrator that a proffered witness should not be allowed to testify as an expert. Arbitrators often respond to such objections by ruling that they go only to the weight, and not the admissibility, of the expert testimony. Nonetheless, it is possible to disqualify an expert using *voir dire*. You can disqualify purported experts by establishing the remoteness of their credentials, the inapplicability of their specialties, the lack of general acceptance of their purported expertise, or the unreliability of their data.

#### *Cross-examination on credentials*

The arbitrator's ruling that a witness may testify as an expert means only that the witness possesses sufficient credentials to pass the evidentiary threshold. It still may be possible to diminish the weight of the witness's qualifications during cross-examination. There are three basic methods for discrediting the value of a witness's credentials.

***Limit the scope of the witness's expertise.*** Although a witness may be well qualified in a certain area or subspecialty, it may be possible to recast the case's issues in such a way as to place them beyond the witness's competence.

***Stress missing credentials.*** An expert witness may be minimally qualified to testify, but still lack certain important certifications, degrees, or licenses.

***Contrast your expert's credentials.*** It is most effective to contrast an adverse witness's missing credentials with your own expert's superior qualifications. You can contrast experts' credentials based on certification and other matters. It is fair game, for example, to point out your own witness's greater or more specific experience, your witness's teaching or publication record, or any other disparity that will enhance your expert and diminish the opposition. Note, however, that the rules of basic cross-examination apply here as well. You must be satisfied to elicit the fact of the contrasting qualifications. It will do you little good to argue with the opposing witness, or to try to extract a concession that their credentials are inadequate.

#### 6.7.7.2 Obtain Favorable Information

You can often obtain favorable concessions from the opposing party's expert witness. As with all cross-examination, it is usually wisest to attempt to extract such information near the examination's beginning. Be positive of the answers before launching into this sort of cross-examination. In general, the helpful material available from opposing experts will fall into the following categories.

***Affirm your own expert.*** Even experts who ultimately disagree may have many shared understandings. You may therefore contribute to your own expert's accreditation by asking the opposing expert to acknowledge the reliability of your expert's data, the validity of your expert's assumptions, or the caliber of your expert's credentials.

***Elicit areas of agreement.*** In addition, it may be possible to elicit concessions from the opposing expert that go to the case's merits. The adverse expert may, for example, be willing to agree with several of your major premises, even while disagreeing with your ultimate conclusion.

***Criticize the opposing party's conduct.*** Finally, it may be possible to draw from an opposing expert significant criticism of their own party's conduct. Though the expert reached a final conclusion favorable to the party, they may be unwilling to approve of all of their underlying actions.

#### 6.7.7.3 Use Learned Treatises

One form of cross-examination unique to expert witnesses is impeachment with a learned treatise. Under Fed. R. Evid. 803(18), you can confront an expert witness with statements contained in "published treatises, periodicals, or pamphlets on a subject of history, medicine, or other science or art," so long as they are established as reliable authority. Contrary to the belief of many lawyers, judges, and arbitrators, it is not necessary to establish that the witness has relied on the particular treatise, or even that the witness acknowledges it as authoritative. Under the Federal Rules of Evidence, the reliability of a learned treatise may be established by admission of the witness, by other expert testimony, or by judicial notice. Once the reliability of the treatise is confirmed, the impeachment may proceed in one of two ways. You may read a passage from the treatise into evidence without asking the expert any questions about it; the Rules require only that the passage be called to the witness's attention. The more traditional approach is to ask the witness whether they agree with the quotation. At that point the witness must either accede or disagree. If they accept the statement, your job is done. If they disagree, you may argue later that they are out of step with recognized authority. Finally, note that this rule allows an excerpt from a learned treatise to be read into evidence, but that the treatise itself may not be received as an exhibit.

#### 6.7.7.4 Challenge the Witness's Impartiality

Expert witnesses are supposed to be independent analysts, not advocates. The worst thing you can say about an expert witness is that they have altered their opinion to fit a party's needs. Accordingly, it can be very effective to cross-examine an expert on the issue of bias, if the material is there to be exploited. Cross-examination on bias falls into three basic categories.

***Fees.*** In arbitration, it is generally productive to cross-examine an expert concerning their fee only in limited circumstances. For example, it may demonstrate bias if the fee is extraordinarily large. Similarly, it may be evidence of something less than objectivity if the witness has a large unpaid fee outstanding at the time that they testify.

***Relationship with party or counsel.*** An expert's relationship with a party or with counsel may also indicate a lack of impartiality. Some witnesses seem to work hand in glove with certain law firms, testifying to similar conclusions in case after case. While such an ongoing relationship is not proof of bias, it does suggest that the association may have been sustained for a reason. It can become questionable when a firm has engaged the same expert on a dozen or more occasions. While there may be a perfectly innocent explanation for this constancy, it is certainly reasonable to bring it out on cross-examination. The same analysis pertains to witnesses who have testified repeatedly for the same party, although retained by different law firms. Finally, some cases may involve testimony by in-house experts, perhaps a company's own accountant or engineer. In most cases, such experts are susceptible to no more suggestion of bias than would be any other employee. In some situations, however, the in-house expert's own judgment will be at issue in the case. An accountant, for example, may have failed to see that a debt was under-collateralized; an engineer may not have foreseen the need for more exacting tolerances. In these circumstances, the cross-examination must bring out the witness's personal stake in the arbitration's outcome.

***Positional bias.*** With or without regard to past retention, some experts seem wedded to certain professional, scientific, or intellectual positions. Experts frequently come to testify only for plaintiffs and claimants or only for defendants and respondents. Others reach only one of a range of conclusions. For example, perhaps a civil engineer has never found a construction defect led to water damage.

Where they exist, these rigidly held positional biases can be exploited effectively on cross-examination.

***Preparing for cross-examination on bias.*** Prepare diligently before cross-examining an expert witness on bias. Partiality is a serious accusation to make against an expert witness; do not level it without a good-faith basis for the claim. Cross-examination is not the time to make random inquiries, much less baseless charges, that an expert lacks objectivity or independence.

#### 6.7.7.5 Point Out Omissions

An expert may be vulnerable on cross-examination if they have failed to conduct essential tests or procedures or neglected to consider all significant factors. The question of neglected tests or experiments will depend upon each case's unique factors. Other sorts of omissions are more commonplace. Witnesses are frequently asked to evaluate the validity or accuracy of other experts' work. A consulting pathologist, for example, might be asked to reevaluate the protocol of an autopsy conducted by the local medical examiner. No matter how prominent, a "second opinion" witness can almost always be undermined by the fact that they did not conduct the primary investigation.

#### 6.7.7.6 Substitute Information

***Change assumptions.*** As we have seen, almost all experts use assumptions of one sort or another when formulating their opinions. An expert's assumptions, however, might be unrealistic, unreliable, or unreasonably favorable to the retaining party. It can be extremely effective, therefore, to ask the witness to alter an assumption, substituting one that you believe to be more in keeping with the case's evidence.

***Vary the facts.*** A related technique is to vary the facts upon which the expert has relied, or to suggest additional facts.

***Degree of certainty.*** It is also possible to challenge an expert's degree of certainty by suggesting alternative scenarios or explanations.

***Dependence on other testimony.*** An expert witness's opinion often depends upon facts to be established by other witnesses. Thus, the expert's testimony may be undermined, not by anything you ask the expert directly, but rather by challenging its factual underpinnings during the cross-examination of the fact witnesses. It is necessary only to obtain the expert's concession that the other witness's facts are essential to their opinion.

#### 6.7.7.7 Challenge Technique or Theory

The most difficult, though frequently the most tempting, form of expert cross-examination is to challenge the witness's method, theory, or logic. It is possible, but extremely unlikely, that an expert will agree that they made a mistake or that their reasoning is faulty. In most cases you have little to gain by confronting an expert with any but the most glaring flaws, since that will only afford them an opportunity to explain. It is usually far more effective to use your own expert to point out the opposition's errors, and then to draw your own conclusions during closing argument.

### 6.7.8 Ethics of Expert Examination

***Fees.*** Unlike other witnesses who can be reimbursed only for expenses, an expert may be paid a fee for preparing and testifying in an arbitration.[22] There is authority that an expert's fee must be "reasonable," but that limit has never been well defined. In any event, an unreasonably large fee would render the witness extremely vulnerable on cross-examination. A more salient restriction is the rule against paying contingent fees to expert witnesses, which is found in virtually every jurisdiction. Contingent fees are prohibited because they provide the expert with an unacceptable incentive to tailor their opinion to the interests of the party retaining them.

***Influencing testimony.*** Lawyers typically retain experts for one reason only: to help win the case. Given the expense involved, there may be a temptation to view the expert as simply another team member you can enlist to provide whatever advocacy is necessary. It is therefore not unknown for attorneys to attempt to persuade experts to alter the content of their opinions. This is wrong. It is no more acceptable to attempt to persuade an expert to change their opinion than it would be to try to convince a percipient witness to change their account of the facts. The entire system of expert testimony rests upon the assumption that experts are independent of the retaining attorneys. Counsel must take care not to attempt or appear to use the fee relationship to corrupt the expert's autonomy.[23] As with other witnesses, it is not unethical to help an expert prepare for trial. You may inform the witness of the questions you will ask on direct examination and may alert the witness to potential cross-examination. You can advise an expert to use powerful language, to avoid jargon, to use analogies, to refrain from long narratives, or to use other means that will help them convey their opinion accurately. A boundary is crossed, however, when counsel's preparation leaves the realm of presenting the testimony and enters the sphere of changing it.

***Disclosure and discovery.*** In arbitration, where discovery is usually the exception and not the rule, testifying experts are generally subject to discovery. Purely consulting experts are usually exempt from discovery, other than in extreme circumstances. The question that arises is whether it is ethical to attempt to interview an opposing party's consulting witness, from whom formal discovery is not

---

22. Model Rules of Prof'l Conduct, r. 3.4(b) cmt. 3 (Am. Bar Ass'n 2020).
23. Model Rules of Prof'l Conduct, r. 3.4(b) (Am. Bar Ass'n 2020).

available. Needless to say, you must take care to determine the relevant jurisdiction's law on this issue—or better yet, obtain the arbitrator's permission—before attempting to interview the opposition's nontestifying expert.

## 6.8 Ensure Completeness and Accuracy of Transcripts

If a court reporter is transcribing the hearing, being courteous to your court reporter will be a small investment that will reap huge returns. The court reporter is part of the team consisting of yourself, opposing counsel, and the arbitrator whose goal is to produce a complete and accurate record of events as they occur in the hearing. You as a team member must help the court reporter achieve that end.

### *6.8.1 Ensure Completeness of Transcripts*

To help the court reporter make a complete record, you should:

- Avoid speaking when the court reporter is changing paper, marking exhibits, etc. Important statements may be unintentionally excluded.
- Avoid speaking simultaneously with other lawyers or the arbitrator, or—worse yet—speaking before the witness is finished answering your questions. Even the most competent court reporters are sometimes unable to completely unscramble simultaneous oral statements and may omit important information from the subsequently prepared transcript.
- When appropriate, describe off-the-record trial events on the record, and invite other counsel and the arbitrator to clarify your characterization as they perceived the events or discussion.
- Orally (and accurately) describe witnesses' gestures if it is in your client's interest to do so. For example, if a witness for the opposing party uses body language or gestures indicating an evasive, untruthful, disrespectful attitude, you might want to describe this conduct, diplomatically, for the record.
- Be aware that witnesses are not usually experienced at telling their stories in anything other than everyday language. Sometimes witnesses omit details because they assume they are communicating only with people in the hearing room. You must carefully fill in the omitted details through additional questioning. For example, a witness's description of the distance between themselves and the point of impact of two automobiles as the distance between the witness and the rear wall of the hearing room would have little meaning to a reader of the transcript who was not present in the hearing room.
- Clearly indicate when you wish to go off the record and when you wish to resume on the record.

### 6.8.2 Ensure Accuracy of Transcripts

Aside from ensuring there will be no unintentional omissions in the testimony, colloquies, or oral descriptions on the record, you must ensure that the printed words ultimately appearing in the transcript will be accurate. Ways in which you can help the court reporter produce an accurate transcript include the following:

- Take reasonable measures to acquaint the court reporter with the nature of the case. Provide the court reporter with a pleading or order which contains an accurate case caption and the names of counsel. If the pleading briefly encapsulates the nature of the case and stage of the proceedings, all the better. Physically identify the counsel and other persons (parties, interpreters, paralegals, etc.) present at the hearing.
- If the proceedings involve complicated terminology and spellings (medical malpractice case, environmental case, etc.), provide the court reporter with a glossary of terms in advance of the proceeding. Also, it is helpful to provide the court reporter with passages from text of complicated material or list of case citations you will be referring to in an oral argument before the arbitrator.
- Avoid blocking the court reporter's view of the witness when questioning the witness in the hearing room.
- If a witness uses a figure of speech or metaphor ("the claimant appeared to be 'knee high to a grasshopper' next to the towering respondent"), make sure through questioning that the record is clarified regarding the height of the claimant in relation to the respondent.
- Make sure the spellings of persons' names, street names, etc., are accurate. Ask the witness to spell them if they are the least bit unusual. Be certain, however, that the witness knows how to spell them. It can be embarrassing for the witness and you if they boggle the spelling. If you know the witness may be unprepared or unable to spell the word, ask for a stipulation of the correct spelling of the word.
- Ensure that dates and times are accurately stated and that there is no ambiguity about which date or time the witness is testifying.
- Be careful how a witness uses pronouns (he, she, they, etc.). Sometimes, when testifying about several individuals, it is necessary that the witness minimize the use of pronouns, and attribute conduct to named persons.
- Always refer to documents by exhibit number (and page).
- Markings made by witnesses on a photograph or large demonstrative exhibit should be designated by the witness's initials or designated number or letter.

# • CHAPTER SEVEN •

## POST-HEARING ADVOCACY

*To get over the past, you first have to accept that the past is over. . . . No matter how many times you revisit it, analyze it, regret it, or sweat it . . . it's over. It can hurt you no more.*

—*Mandy Hale*[1]

This chapter traces the possible activities of the arbitration advocate from the completion of the arbitration hearing through an appeal. An overriding theme governs this chapter: The law and courts discourage all post-hearing activity beyond enforcement of the arbitrator's award. Because arbitration's primary purpose is to avoid the cost and time of traditional in-court dispute resolution, courts frown upon the judicial challenge of any arbitration award, whether at the trial or appeal level. The bases upon which a losing party may challenge the arbitrator's award are, by federal and state statutes, extremely limited. Coupled with a strong judicial preference toward enforcement, that legislative policy allows very few opportunities for a losing party to complain about an arbitrator's award. For all practical purposes, if the parties have agreed to binding arbitration, the award is final, and the parties must live with it.

There are, however, a few exceptions to the rigid no-court-challenge rule, and these are discussed in sections 7.5 and 7.6. Because these exceptions will rarely apply to an arbitration in which you are involved, your efforts are better expended convincing the arbitrator of your position's merit before issuance of the award—in your post-hearing briefs, if they are requested; or, if necessary, after the issuance of the award—in a motion for reconsideration of the award or for rehearing. These post-hearing and post-award briefing situations will put your storytelling skills to the ultimate test. It is in these situations that something as simple as a sentence's meaning can be our most helpful ally or our most ruthless enemy. To these post-hearing advocate activities—most of which rely on the power of the pen—we now turn.

1. MANDY HALE, THE SINGLE WOMAN: LIFE, LOVE, AND A DASH OF SASS, 49–50 (2013).

## 7.1 Drafting Post-Hearing Briefs

Occasionally, an arbitrator will request counsel to file post-hearing briefs in lieu of closing arguments or in addition to them. If the arbitrator requests such briefs, take the request very seriously and ask the arbitrator what format and content they prefer. Usually, arbitrators request these briefs in complex factual cases where it is not completely clear, even from the counsel's oral arguments, whether there is sufficient evidence to sustain elements of the claims or defenses. However, there may be other reasons for requesting briefs. For example, the arbitrator may face difficult legal questions and require citations to the cases supporting the parties' respective positions. In other situations, arbitrators may need the parties' respective views on how scientific or highly technical testimony of expert witnesses supports their legal positions. Do not assume you understand why the arbitrator is requesting the post-hearing brief—you may end up like the man whose friend comes upon him searching the ground for his keys; when asked why he's searching in the middle of the street instead of by the bush where he dropped them, the man said, "The light's better here." Before leaving the hearing room for the last time, ask the arbitrator whether they want you to focus on any particular topics covered by the evidence submitted and the arguments heard.

If the arbitrator does not request that post-hearing briefs be filed, consider requesting permission to file a brief. Occasionally, there are evidence situations so delicate, so intricate, or so fraught with the potential for misunderstanding, that the only way to handle them effectively is through a meticulous review and marshaling of the evidence. There may be other reasons why you conclude that post-hearing briefs are necessary. In a high-stakes case, where defeat would mean substantial monetary loss to your client, you might request permission to file briefs. If you do not, and your client loses big, you may always wonder whether a brief might have made a difference. Briefing will, of course, cost your client further expense and will most likely delay the award's issuance. Advise your client of these facts when you discuss your reasons for seeking to file a brief.

If you are directed or are permitted to file a post-hearing brief, draft it with the same care you would take in drafting a good appellate brief. Write with brevity, clarity, and succinctness, bearing in mind that the more there is to read, the more time it will take the arbitrator to read it. Follow all the arbitrator's rules and requests. Never exceed any page limitation. Make thorough reference and citation to the hearing transcript, if there is one, and to any pertinent exhibits introduced during the hearing. Avoid superfluous arguments and minimize alternative arguments. If an arbitrator has asked the parties to address a specific point for the sake of clarity, address only that point. Additional ramblings about what you think is important will not endear you or your client to the arbitrator.

When you draft a post-hearing brief, think like the arbitrator. That is, put yourself in the arbitrator's shoes and think about what you want to know about the case to render a fair and just decision. Craft the facts to capitalize on the persuasive trial story you created through your hearing evidence. Concentrate on the important legal and factual issues—the ones that the arbitrator may have asked questions about at the hearing. Realize that the arbitrator might be as swayed by the situation's equities as by the legal technicalities. This is a particularly important consideration if your arbitrator is a nonlawyer. Sometimes, the mechanical application of law can yield results that defy common sense. As you write the brief, continuously ask yourself, "What seems fair?" and "What would be the commonsense approach to this situation?" Don't harp on hyper-technicalities in your brief. Instead, be sure your story both addresses the law and is compelling. If you completely disregard the human element, do not be surprised if you receive an unfavorable decision from the arbitrator.

Make your brief reader-friendly, well organized, and divided by headings and subheadings where appropriate. Keep your writing style simple and direct. Using unnecessary words and legalese, archaic, or intellectual language is always inappropriate, and more so when the arbitrator is a nonlawyer. Choose words carefully, and heed appropriate conventions of style, grammar, construction, and punctuation. Do not repeat yourself. Avoid bluster and a self-important style with a passion. A post-hearing brief that successfully builds rapport with the arbitrator's sense of justice and fairness will, more often than not, precipitate a decision in your favor.

## 7.2 Requisites of an Award

An arbitrator fashions an award based upon their evaluation of the applicable law and the case's facts. The arbitrator may grant any just and equitable relief within the scope of their authority. The parties may, however, limit the scope of the allowable remedies or relief available to the arbitrator, and by agreement may exclude specific remedies. This can be done either in the submission agreement or in the arbitration clause included in the original contract.

The arbitrator's award should always be in writing, signed by the arbitrator, and dated. If required by rules or the parties' agreement, the award should also be notarized and witnessed. It should be clear and concise. Often, the award does not include a written opinion explaining the arbitrator's reasoning, but it must contain a ruling on all claims (principal claims, counterclaims, third-party claims, etc.) and damage requests (compensatory, consequential, punitive, etc.) in issue. It must name the winning party on each claim, and the party against whom the award is rendered. The precise dollar amount of the award on each claim must also be specified. The award is the arbitrator's last act in the discharge of their duties. As such, in addition to making liability and damage determinations, it also apportions all administrative fees and expenses for the hearing and assesses the arbitrator's fees and attorney's fees, if appropriate.

A written opinion is often not required in arbitration because it slows down the process and encourages appeals by losing parties who wish to challenge the arbitrator's reasoning. Court challenges to reasoning in an arbitrator's opinion are usually unsuccessful, even if the arbitrator completely misconstrues the applicable law.

An award may be either binding or nonbinding, depending on the parties' pre-arbitration agreement. Binding awards are enforceable under the Federal Arbitration Act, which covers commercial arbitration, including construction and securities arbitration, consumer arbitration, and employment arbitration. In instances when the FAA is not applicable, such as some family law or real estate disputes, then state arbitration and contract law render the awards enforceable. In most jurisdictions, a binding arbitration award, if properly filed and confirmed in court, has the same effect as a court judgment, except that it is subject to appeal on much narrower grounds.

A nonbinding award has no legal effect, but the parties can, of course, still agree to accept it. Even if the parties do not accept the nonbinding award, they can still use it to facilitate settlement. In some jurisdictions, a party who rejects the result of a court-annexed arbitration may in certain circumstances be liable for the opponent's costs and attorney's fees.

Normally, the parties will set the time period in which the arbitrator must render the award. They may do this through the pre-arbitration agreement or in the arbitration clause in the original contract. This period may also be fixed by dispute resolution organization rules, local court rules, a judge's guidelines, or statute. Dispute resolution organizations commonly have rules allowing thirty days for an arbitrator to issue an award. An experienced arbitrator with knowledge of the subject matter should, however, be able to render an award almost immediately after an arbitration hearing.

## 7.3 Motion to Reopen Hearing or to Modify or Correct Award

After closing the hearing, the arbitrator may reopen it on their own motion or on the motion of any party. Reasons for an arbitrator's reopening of a hearing might include apparent insufficient evidence on an aspect of the case, doubt as to applicable law, or the need for additional information. Customarily, if the hearing's reopening would delay issuance of the award beyond the time limitation specified in the arbitration agreement, the arbitrator may not reopen the hearing without the parties' consent. Usually, a hearing may not be reopened after the award is issued.

If a party moves to reopen the hearing, the party must demonstrate good cause. Satisfactory "good cause" would normally include newly discovered evidence that could not have been known or presented at the time of the hearing. The moving party must show that the evidence was unavailable at the time of the hearing or that there is a reasonable explanation for its nonproduction. The movant must also demonstrate that the reopening will not seriously affect a substantial right of the other party.

More common than the motion to reopen proceedings is the motion to modify or correct the award. The latter is akin to a motion for reconsideration, but normally the reconsideration does not permit any material modification of the award. A motion to modify or correct an award is made where:

- There is an evident material mistake in the figures referred to in the award.
- There is an evident material mistake in the description of any person, thing, or property referred to in the award.
- The arbitrators have issued an award concerning a matter not submitted to them.
- The form of the award is incorrect.
- Information needs to be added or deleted to effect the intent of the award.
- Clarification is needed to promote justice between the parties.

A motion for modification or clarification must demonstrate indefiniteness or confusion in the interpretation of the award. A sufficient basis for such a motion would be a movant's assertion of no reasonable certainty as to how to comply with the award.

## 7.4 Enforcing the Award

The procedure for enforcing arbitration awards is summary in nature. The filing in court of a petition to confirm an award and to enter judgment (with a proposed order and judgment) is the usual method of enforcement provided by most state statutes. Typically, the state court statutory period for filing the petition is one year from the date of the award. The Uniform Arbitration Act permits objections or a counterclaim to vacate the award within ninety days of filing the petition to confirm.[2]

The procedure is similar in the federal court system under the Federal Arbitration Act (9 U.S.C.§ 9). One party files a complaint or petition and a motion to confirm an award; a disagreeing opponent may file a counterclaim or petition and move to vacate it. Where there are no genuine issues of material fact, the confirmation order is granted and summary judgment is entered. To enter summary judgment, the court normally requires the following documents to be on file:

- the arbitration agreement;
- papers dealing with the selection or appointment, if any, of an additional umpire;

2. Available on the website of the Uniform Law Commission at https://www.uniformlaws.org/viewdocument/final-act-2?CommunityKey=a0ad71d6-085f-4648-857a-e9e893ae2736&tab=librarydocuments (last visited Jun. 2024).

- any written extension of time within which to make the award;
- the award; and
- each notice, affidavit, or other paper used upon an application to confirm the award, and a copy of each court order upon such application.

A judgment confirming an arbitration award is docketed as in any other action and has the same force and effect as any other judgment.

## 7.5 Challenging the Award

There are only a few grounds for challenging arbitration awards in court, and even those are very narrowly construed. Usually only statutory exceptions apply.[3] These exceptions do not include mistakes of fact, errors of law, poor reasoning on the part of the arbitrator, or arbitrary and unjustified determinations. In fact, to secure judicial inquiry, a challenging party must demonstrate extraordinary circumstances that indicate an arbitrator's abuse of power or use of power beyond their jurisdiction. The challenging party also carries the burden of proof.

In almost every instance, when a court is considering statutory exceptions to enforcement, it does so with a very strong pro-enforcement bias. There are, however, several grounds upon which an arbitration award might be vacated. These include:

### *Contract*

- No written agreement to arbitrate.
- Party breached part of agreement to arbitrate.
- Arbitration agreement is invalid.
- Arbitration was demanded after contract or statutory limitation.

### *Hearing*

- Arbitrator conducted hearing contrary to the arbitration statute or rules.
- Party committed fraud in the arbitration.
- Arbitrator refused to consider material facts.
- Parties agreed to reopen the hearing because of the discovery of new evidence, but the arbitrator refused.

---

3. *See* Stephen J. Ware & Ariana R. Levinson, Principles of Arbitration Law §§ 41 & 42 (2d ed. 2023).

### *Arbitrator*

- Arbitrator displayed bias and partiality.
- Arbitrator failed to disclose a serious conflict of interest.
- Arbitrator was corrupt.
- Arbitrator refused to postpone hearing when good cause was shown.
- Arbitrator exceeded authority.

### *Award*

- Arbitrator decided nonarbitrable matters.
- Arbitrators failed to make a mutual, final, and definite award.
- Award was procured by corruption, fraud, or undue means.
- Award was not timely rendered, despite party's protest.
- Evident material miscalculation of figures in the award.
- Evident material mistake in the description of a person, thing, or property referred to in the award.
- Award is contrary to public policy.

Nonarbitrability of a dispute is a threshold matter of enforceability which can generally be resolved at the outset of the arbitration hearing and, if necessary, ruled upon by a court at that time. Some courts will hold that this issue is waived if it is not brought up at the appropriate time. Arbitrability may also be challenged on the ground that the arbitration clause is invalid under the laws governing the original contract entered into by the parties. This type of challenge is rare because the mere existence of an arbitration clause in a valid contract is difficult to rebut.

If an arbitrator makes a decision regarding a matter not included within the arbitration's scope, a party may challenge the award. This challenge is construed as narrowly as any other challenge, however, and the burden of proof is just as high. Courts are normally unwilling to second-guess an arbitrator's interpretation of the parties' agreement.

Evident partiality or corruption are also grounds upon which you may challenge an award. However, standards of conduct for arbitrators differ depending on who appointed them. An arbitrator appointed by a party, as opposed to one appointed as a neutral, often will not be held to the same requirement of impartiality. Courts have ruled that an arbitrator will not be held to the same standards of impartiality as a judge. There are also circumstances under which parties may not have the defense of bias available to them. These include prior knowledge of facts suggesting the arbitrator's partiality and waiver based on lack of objections to partiality at the time that knowledge was gained.

Improperly refusing a postponement or refusing to hear evidence may constitute a procedural, due process ground upon which an award may be challenged. However, as in all other cases of award challenges, the threshold of proof is very high. The challenger must demonstrate not only disregard of due process, but the actual harm resulting from such disregard. Inability to fully cross-examine a witness and inability to reschedule a hearing because of a witness's prior speaking engagement have both been found to not violate a party's procedural due process rights.

Rulings contrary to law are also difficult to establish as a basis for challenging an arbitrator's award. The challenging party must demonstrate that an arbitrator appreciated the existence of a clearly governing standard but decided to ignore it. In some jurisdictions, in order to be judicially vacated, the arbitrator's finding must be completely irrational. Courts will find a foundation for any award so long as in some logical way the award is derivable from the original contract's wording.

Challenges based on awards being contrary to public policy have rarely been successful. This is generally because courts view the public policy favoring arbitration to override any dissatisfaction with an award based on its violation of some lesser public policy consideration.

The standard of proof required to establish corruption, fraud, or undue means is clear and convincing evidence. A party must demonstrate that it could not have discovered the fraud with the exercise of due diligence prior to the arbitration. The challenger must also demonstrate that the fraud was materially related to an issue in contest in the arbitration. Proof of perjury can be a successful challenge if it meets the clear and convincing standard. So might a failure to disclose fees paid by one party to the arbitrator. In any case, for a challenge based on fraud, corruption, or undue means to be successful, that fraud, corruption, or undue means must stem from the arbitrator's behavior.

Because the grounds for challenging an arbitration award are very narrow, agreed-to challenges may be a subject that parties wish to explore, negotiate, and specify in an arbitration agreement. Some state courts will honor contractually agreed standards of review if a claim is brought under a state arbitration statute. The Supreme Court has interpreted the grounds for vacatur under the FAA as exclusive and does not permit parties to contract for additional grounds of review.[4] As an alternative, in appropriate situations counsel may wish to design the arbitration process initially to provide for a pre-designated appellate arbitration tribunal, should the losing party in the arbitration wish to appeal.

4. Hall St. Assocs., L.L.C. v. Mattel, Inc., 552 U.S. 576 (2008); Strickland v. Foulke Management Corp., 475 N.J. Sup. 27, 30 (2023) ("we conclude that when the FAA controls an arbitration agreement, its vacatur terms are exclusive and cannot be modified by contract.").

## 7.6 Appeal

If an arbitration award is challenged in court and a final judgment is entered, the judgment, as in any other case, is appealable to the appellate court. On appeal, the appellate court can confirm, vacate, recommit, modify, clarify, or correct an award. Rarely, if ever, would an appellate court reverse an award on the merits, even if there were a transcript of the arbitration proceedings. Instead, the appellate court might vacate an award, requiring the arbitration process to begin anew.

Most appellate courts reviewing appeals from judgments entered on arbitration awards abide by these presumptions:

- The award is presumed to be valid.
- There is no review for errors or misinterpretations of fact or law.
- The arbitration proceedings will not be invalidated for failure to meet rules of evidence or other procedural requirements applicable to trials.
- The arbitrator does not have to give reasons for the award.

The Federal Arbitration Act (9 U.S.C. §§ 16, *et seq.*) specifies district court orders related to arbitration proceedings that are appealable and those that are not appealable.

The appealable orders and decisions are as follows:

- order refusing to stay litigation;
- order refusing to compel arbitration;
- order confirming an arbitrator's award or partial award;
- order denying confirmation of an arbitrator's award or partial award;
- order modifying an arbitrator's award;
- order correcting an arbitrator's award;
- order vacating an arbitrator's award;
- interlocutory order granting, continuing, or modifying an injunction against an arbitration; and
- a final decision with respect to an arbitration.

The nonappealable interlocutory orders and decisions are:

- order staying litigation which allows arbitration to proceed;
- order compelling or directing arbitration to proceed;
- order refusing to modify or correct an award;

- order refusing to grant, continue, or modify an injunction against an arbitration subject to the act; and
- order which is interim and nonfinal.

From the above listings, it is evident that the Federal Arbitration Act contains an intended legislative bias in favor of honoring parties' agreements to arbitrate their disputes to conclusion without judicial interference.

# • Chapter Eight •

## Hybrid Processes

*I tell them there's no problem. Only solutions.*

—*John Lennon*[1]

Pure mediation or pure arbitration may not be the most appropriate alternative means for resolving a particular dispute. In these situations, you need to exercise creativity in selecting or designing an appropriate hybrid process to satisfy your client's specific needs. Med-arb, discussed in section 1.1, is just one of many available hybrids. In binding mediation (which on its face seems to be an oxymoron), if mediation is unsuccessful, the mediator makes a binding decision at a figure within the mediated bracket.

As the opening quote suggests, you must simply examine the alternatives and use your best judgment to select or design the appropriate solution to your client's situation. To do this effectively, you must have a clear understanding of the principal hybrid processes already in standard use. Some of the principal hybrid ADR processes are described below.[2]

### 8.1 High-Low Arbitration

A form of arbitration used in personal injury and other types of disputes is high-low arbitration, also called bracketed arbitration. It is commonly used where liability is not an issue, though that condition is not a prerequisite. In this process, the parties negotiate to impasse, and then proceed to arbitration. Plaintiff's last settlement demand and defendant's last offer establish a bracket defining the limits of the arbitrator's award in the case. The arbitrator conducts the arbitration without knowledge of the endpoints of the bracket. The parties are free to make any evidence-based arguments they wish regarding damages, and the arbitrator decides on damages (or liability and damages, if any) as if it were ordinary arbitration.

---

1. John Lennon, *Watching the Wheels*, on Double Fantasy (Geffen Rec. 1980).
2. *See generally*, Jay Folberg, et al, Resolving Disputes: Theory, Practice, and Law, ch. 2 & 25 (2022).

When the arbitrator renders an award, neither party will be liable for a figure outside the agreed-to bracket.

For example, assume that in a particular case the claimant's last demand was $100,000 and the respondent's last offer was $50,000. The parties then proceed to an arbitration hearing at which the plaintiff argues entitlement to damages in the amount of $150,000 and the defendant argues that plaintiff is entitled to $25,000, at most. If the arbitrator renders an award of $125,000, the defendant will pay no more than $100,000. If the arbitrator renders an award of $35,000, the plaintiff will receive no less than $50,000. If the arbitrator renders an award of $75,000, the plaintiff will receive $75,000 because that figure falls within the pre-agreed bracket.

There are several advantages to high-low arbitration. First, it reduces the risk of allowing a third party to decide your fate. Going into arbitration, both parties know the lower and upper limits on the award. Second, it encourages vigorous bargaining because the claimant wants to establish the highest minimum award possible and the respondent seeks to fix the lowest maximum award possible. This situation usually forces the parties to find a reasonable settlement range, and at the same time, a reasonably narrow bracket. If the bracket is too large, say, $25,000 and $1,000,000, when the parties proceed to arbitration, there is very little advantage of high-low arbitration over ordinary arbitration—unless, of course, one side or the other has thoroughly misjudged the case's value. Finally, high-low arbitration is more economical than going to trial after an unsuccessful mediation. Typically, a skillful mediator helps the parties arrive at a reasonable settlement range, which can serve as the bracket in a subsequent high-low arbitration conducted by another neutral.

## 8.2 Baseball Arbitration

Baseball arbitration is a type of final offer arbitration in which the disputing parties agree in writing to negotiate to only one position—their last and best offer—and then submit the dispute to arbitration. In baseball arbitration, the arbitrator must choose the final offer of one of the parties and may not find a different result in any circumstance.

This type of final offer arbitration had its origin in player salary negotiations in major league baseball but now is an ADR method adaptable to practically any type of dispute involving a monetary solution. A quick decision is a valuable feature of the classic version of baseball arbitration. The arbitrator must pick one figure or the other and is encouraged to render their decision within twenty-four hours. The decision is binding, and there can be no compromise. Also, the arbitrator may give no explanation for the decision.

The rigidity of final offer arbitration is its main selling point. It is also its own deterrent. Labor experts believe that the risk involved in having your offer rejected and the other side's offer selected promotes good faith bargaining, encourages a narrow, negotiated settlement bracket, and in practice provides an incentive for parties to resolve differences without an arbitration hearing.

## 8.3 Factfinding

Factfinding is a dispute resolution process that provides a more efficient, speedy, and sensitive resolution of claims. It is particularly helpful in resolving claims for which the traditional adversarial resolution process cannot meet all participants' needs—sexual harassment claims, for example.

In a factfinding intervention, the court normally appoints a factfinder or team of factfinders to investigate the complaint and issue a written report of findings. Because factfinders are generally used in cases involving sensitive issues, confidentiality is a paramount requirement. A factfinder must be sensitive to others' concerns, a good judge of credibility using little information, able to keep absolute strict confidentiality, and a skillful interviewer. Whenever possible, factfinders should have expertise in the field that they are investigating.

A factfinder must also have unlimited access to relevant information, witnesses, and documentation. Parties who agree to the factfinding process will gain little by not cooperating. The factfinder interviews the pertinent parties and any other persons who have relevant information. Where at all possible, this is done outside the presence of the parties' lawyers with the knowledge and permission of the parties and their lawyers.

The factfinder's report states what the factfinder believes happened and identifies any issues about which the factfinder is unable to draw conclusions. Since the factfinder is neutral and uninvolved, this report serves as a basis for resolving the conflict. The report does not reach any legal conclusions. For example, in a sexual harassment case, the report does not say whether sexual harassment has occurred. Unless the parties have previously agreed otherwise, the report does not recommend remedies. It does, however, assess the credibility of all those interviewed.

The factfinder's report is submitted to the court and to each party. The court usually gives the parties a reasonable period to resolve the dispute on their own before it takes its next step—which may be to commence the litigation process or to move on to a mediation or arbitration process. Generally, it is not a good idea to have the factfinder go on to serve as either a mediator or arbitrator following the investigation. Depending on the specific circumstances and the agreements of the parties, the court may provide the factfinder's report to the mediator or arbitrator. At this stage, the parties are usually represented by counsel.

In some sexual harassment claim situations, the court appoints two factfinders, typically one to match the gender of each party. This team approach allows the process to avoid the insensitivity of the usual adversary process to both the plaintiff and the defendant. The more sensitive, specialized environment provided by factfinding greatly increases the likelihood that the parties will reach mutually acceptable results on their own and avoid litigation that would be costly, both financially and emotionally, to all involved.

## 8.4 Co-Med-Arb

The ADR process called co-med-arb arose as an antidote to many of the ills which plague the process of med-arb, described in section 1.1. As you recall, med-arb is a combination of the mediation and arbitration processes in which a neutral serves in the role of mediator initially and attempts to settle the dispute. If mediation is unsuccessful, the same neutral serves in the role of arbitrator, hears evidence presented by the parties, and then renders an arbitral award. Med-arb "has been praised for its efficiency gains and condemned for resulting in a 'confusion of roles' that jeopardizes both the effectiveness of mediation and the integrity of arbitral decision making."[3]

The basic concept of co-med-arb is to use two neutrals, one in the role of mediator and one as arbitrator, but to have them work as closely as possible together to maximize their efficiency while avoiding confusion of roles. Even though co-med-arb employs two neutrals, the design of the process seeks to avoid duplicative expenses by saving time needed to bring the arbitrator "up to speed" should the mediation prove unsuccessful.

The parties select both the mediator and the arbitrator prior to the dispute or after the dispute arises. The two neutrals jointly tend to procedural matters such as conducting a prehearing conference, setting dates for meetings, and scheduling the filing of briefs. The mediator and arbitrator review all submitted documents prior to the hearing. At the initial session of the hearing, they sit as a panel to hear the parties' opening statements in what is called the open phase. During this open phase, the arbitrator presides and both the arbitrator and mediator may ask clarifying questions of counsel, but the mediator withholds asking "sensitive" questions regarding the parties' needs and interests until the second, or confidential, phase of the process. After the open phase closes, the rules preclude the mediator from discussing the substance of the dispute with the arbitrator, though the two neutrals may usually confer on procedural matters.

In the confidential phase, the mediator attempts to mediate the dispute to resolution. If the parties reach an impasse, they proceed to the third phase of the process and present their evidence to the arbitrator. When this occurs, the mediator is usually "on call" in the event that the parties desire to resume mediation at one or

---

3. Christian Bühring-Uhle, *Co-Med-Arb Technique Holds Promise for Getting Best of Both Worlds*, World Arb. & Mediation Rep., Jan. 1992, at 21. *See also* Bette J. Roth et al., The Alternative Dispute Resolution Practice Guide § 37:12 (2022).

more points during the arbitration. If the parties resume mediation, the mediator sets strict time limits on the mediation conference.

Although mediation efforts may not initially succeed in resolving the entire dispute, they can lead to a variety of possible beneficial results including streamlining the arbitration, achieving a stipulation of facts or agreed limitation of issues, and resolving several of the contested issues. The mediator may also be helpful after the arbitration hearing concludes. If the parties desire, the arbitrator may withhold the award until after the parties have a limited-duration final session with the mediator to attempt to work out a mutually satisfactory settlement. If the mediation is successful, the parties agree that the award should not issue, and they enter into a settlement agreement. If the mediation is unsuccessful, the arbitrator issues the award, and if the parties desire, they can request that the mediator conduct a post-award settlement conference.

Although the co-med-arb process is generally more expensive than pure mediation or pure arbitration, the process can prove to be a very wise investment. In complex, high-stakes disputes, the value of co-med-arb's collateral benefits may outweigh its cost in dollars. Because of the continuous availability of mediation, there is opportunity for a settlement early in the co-med-arb process, or at any number of points during the process. Moreover, the process may avoid damaging any continuing relationships that your client needs to maintain with one or more of the parties. In short, choosing the two-neutral, co-med-arb tandem process may allow you to extract the best of both the mediation and the arbitration processes while minimizing the disadvantages associated with using one or the other or with using their sequenced amalgam, med-arb.

## 8.5 Summary Jury Trial

In 1980, Federal District Judge Thomas D. Lambros created the summary jury trial method of alternative dispute resolution as a case management option, because he found himself with a massive docket of toxic tort cases, primarily asbestos cases. Each of these cases had reached a point where the parties considered them unsettleable. In conceiving the summary jury trial, Judge Lambros had three objectives. First, he wished to facilitate settlements by allowing parties who have failed to settle in traditional pretrial settlement conferencing the opportunity, at very low cost, to see the reactions of actual jurors to their case, within the courtroom environment. Second, he wished to give parties the opportunity to define their issues and learn how the presiding judge would rule on their arguments. Third, he sought to give parties the opportunity to debrief jurors following a proceeding in order to give the lawyers and parties an idea of how a jury would react to and understand their arguments.

A summary jury trial is an actual, nonbinding trial that can usually be completed in less than one day. It is designed to facilitate a settlement. A party may entirely disregard the findings of the summary trial jury, but when cases that have been argued in summary proceedings go to full trial, it is quite likely that the full trial jury will find in the same way.

To ensure that a trial with the potential to last for weeks can be completed in one day, the lawyers and the judge must work together to strip from the summary trial all unnecessary tasks. To accomplish this, the lawyers present all the evidence in a narrative fashion, based on affidavits and depositions gathered throughout discovery, which usually has already been completed. Evidentiary objections are not made at the summary trial, rather they are resolved at a comprehensive pre-summary trial conference.

At the final pre-summary trial conference, the judge rules on all pending motions and sets a date for the summary trial. Since no witnesses will be called, lengthy notice periods can be avoided, allowing a summary trial to commence within a week of the decision to have one. The judge normally directs each party, a few days prior to the summary trial, to submit a short trial brief, arguing only the issues pertinent to the summary trial. These briefs also contain proposed jury instructions. The judge normally requires the parties (or their representatives) to accompany their attorneys to the summary trial so they see firsthand how jurors react to their arguments. The judge also sets time limits on counsels' presentations. Usually, each side is given roughly fifteen minutes for an opening statement, one hour for its case-in-chief, one-half hour to rebut, and the opportunity to carve out time in reserve for a closing statement, at the party's option.

This final pre-summary trial conference serves more than just laying the hearing's ground rules. It is an opportunity to provide momentum for the case to settle. Roughly one third of all summary jury cases settle between the final pre-summary trial conference and the summary trial. This happens for several reasons. Parties see how the judge is likely to rule on motions in limine and evidentiary objections in a full trial. For this reason, it is necessary for the judge to use the same evidentiary standards at the summary trial that they would at a full trial and to try to rule in a similar way. Also, attorneys see the risk of having their claims defeated, which makes settlement more attractive. Plus, a party who loses a summary jury trial, whether they intended to go to full trial or not, has greatly diminished their bargaining power.

It is vitally important that the summary jury trial mirror an actual trial. A jury is empaneled through a *voir dire* process, just as in a full trial. The major differences are that the jury in summary jury proceedings is usually six persons rather than ten or twelve, and that the judge conducts the *voir dire*. The judge may ask jurors to fill out profiles before the date of the summary trial. Furthermore, the judge must be careful to empanel a jury that would be just like a jury at a full trial for the litigants to gain the full effect of the summary trial jury's input. For this reason, the judge may allow each party's attorney two peremptory challenges.

Once the jury is empaneled and sworn, the trial proceeds in much the same order as a full trial would, with the attorneys presenting evidence in narrative form. Some judges permit videotapes of expert witnesses and critical occurrence witnesses to be played. The attorneys may use any physical evidence, exhibits, or other devices that they would be permitted to use in a full trial. Unless the summary jury trial proceeds as a full trial would proceed, litigants will not have as much confidence in the jury's findings as they normally would and will have less incentive to settle.

Following the verdict, the jurors are debriefed by the judge and the lawyers, and sometimes by the litigants themselves. The debriefing is quite instructive, making the parties aware of the specific reasons supporting the jury's evaluation of the case.

Immediately following the debriefing, post-summary trial settlement conferencing begins. This conferencing may last for several weeks, as needed. If a reasonable time elapses without a settlement being reached, the court may set the case for full trial. Most cases that go through the summary jury trial process settle. But even in those that do not, the summary trial allows a streamlined full trial, usually shorter and usually with stronger arguments from both sides.

## 8.6 Mini-Trial

The mini-trial, as apparent from its name, is an abbreviated trial or hearing. The parties conduct an abbreviated trial, with witnesses and evidence, to a three-person panel consisting of a business executive from each party and a neutral, after which that panel meets to negotiate a settlement. This method of dispute resolution has two major advantages: first, mini-trials curtail much of the discovery process; and second, mini-trials involve high-level businesspersons early in the dispute resolution process. Because discovery is limited, and because the hearing itself is in fact a miniature hearing, this method of dispute resolution can be dramatically less expensive than traditional litigation. However, compared to other methods of dispute resolution, the mini-trial is relatively more expensive.

The mini-trial method is best suited to large disputes and complex litigation, such as cases involving breaches of complex contracts, particularly if there are intricate technical issues; patent cases; antitrust cases; major construction cases; and product liability cases. This is because the panel asked to decide the case will include business experts in the field—a high-level management executive of each party. The parties initiate a mini-trial by negotiating a mini-trial agreement.

Mini-trials are most successful when each party makes a genuine effort to limit discovery to only those documents and depositions absolutely necessary to resolve the particular issue or issues at hand. The mini-trial agreement usually prohibits mass exchange of documents and limits the number and length of depositions. In some instances, depending on how much discovery has already taken place when the decision for a mini-trial is made, discovery may not be necessary at all. If the decision for a mini-trial is made early in the litigation process and discovery is necessary, the mini-trial agreement should always establish a discovery time limit. Sixty days is standard. When possible, the mini-trial agreement lists the deponents and fixes a time limit, perhaps two hours, for each deposition. If the mini-trial agreement does not appropriately limit discovery, the cost-saving purpose of the mini-trial may be defeated.

When discovery is complete, the parties to the mini-trial exchange brief position summaries, including document and witness lists to be used at the hearing. The summaries help avoid surprises and advise the panel members of each party's position before the hearing. The number of witnesses and trial exhibits designated in the summaries is kept to a minimum. The parties make a concerted effort to use a simplified process for the dispute's resolution. Without such an effort, the mini-trial is ineffective.

The mini-trial agreement also specifies who will make up the panel for the mini-trial, normally a business executive from each side and a third-party neutral. The third-party neutral is instrumental in keeping the resolution process on course. For example, a party may be over-inclusive when designating documents and witnesses in its summary. The third-party neutral ensures that only relevant witnesses and documents are listed and used. The neutral is usually an attorney with expertise in the dispute's subject matter.

The business executives appointed to the panel by the parties must have the full authority to negotiate a settlement. Without that power, the hearing may be for naught. An executive deeply involved with the case should not be designated as a panel member. No panel member should be asked to pass judgment on a superior or a person who reports directly to them in the ordinary course of the party's business. The selected panel members should also be provided with a technical advisor from their respective companies, if complex issues demand it. This will, of course, increase the hearing's cost, but will provide the panel members with necessary assistance regarding difficult technical issues.

At the hearing's close, negotiation commences. The success of the entire process rests on this period of negotiation. To ensure its success, the mini-trial agreement sets up its parameters in a way most conducive to achieving settlement. The negotiation normally extends into several sessions. Ideally, the two business executives are the only people present. The third-party neutral may be consulted for advice or clarification but should not be an active participant. This is a time for the parties to resolve their dispute. Normally, the lawyers for the parties do not participate. If negotiations break down completely, the mini-trial agreement normally provides for a mandatory time to elapse before the decision is made to resume the original litigation. A "cool-down" period often allows the parties an opportunity to rethink their reasons for entering mini-trial negotiations in the first place and often generates new settlement ideas.

Mini-trials result in settlements a high percentage of the time. They can quickly turn complex business disputes into mutual-gain settlements. As a result, the mini-trial stands as a highly effective tool for cost cutting.

## 8.7 Simulated Juries

Any party may employ a simulated or mock jury to evaluate a case for trial or settlement. A simulated jury is very much like a "dress rehearsal." In most situations, it is a one-party endeavor. Its singular advantage as an ADR method is that the party employing it has complete control over the process. You may decide to use a mock jury simply to rehearse your case. Or you may use it to choose one of two or more case theory options.

The simulated jury experience allows you to observe how a panel of people, assembled purposefully to "mirror" potential jury makeup, will evaluate each aspect of a case. It is a useful tool in pointing out the case's weaknesses and strengths. You may also use it to demonstrate for a client a reaction to certain trial strategies about which you and the client disagree. Watching the jury deliberate after hearing your presentation of the case, or of both sides of the case, can provide valuable insight into the hearts and minds of an average jury panel. The experience may convince you and your client to settle the case.

For these reasons, you must take great care to ensure that a simulated jury resembles, as closely as possible, an actual potential jury. If your client can afford it, you may hire a consulting firm to research and assemble a simulated jury. This is helpful, but expensive, and by no means a necessity. As an alternative, you or a paralegal can assemble a jury at minimal cost through telephone solicitation or posting with local employment agencies or college campuses.

Many attorneys assume this process is too expensive. However, if used as a tool to facilitate settlement, the expense can be a cost saver when considering the time and energy you avoid expending by settling prior to trial. If used as a tool to fine-tune a case during trial preparation, it may also provide a more favorable trial result.

## 8.8 Special Masters

Fed. R. Civ. P. 53 creates the special master. Special masters are judicial adjuncts who provide judges specialized assistance in managing their dockets and facilitating settlement. In the past, special masters were viewed primarily as factfinders with respect to discrete issues in complex cases. However, courts have expanded the special master's role to include case management in preparation for trial. This can include overseeing certain aspects of the discovery process or overseeing the entire pretrial stage of the litigation. Special masters also have become more active as settlement facilitators, mediating the resolution of specified issues and conducting settlement conferences, particularly in complex cases.

Generally, the intervention of a special master occurs pursuant to the parties' agreement. The court may, however, appoint a special master without such agreement, in limited circumstances. The goal in either case is usually cost reduction. Special masters may even choose to incorporate other forms of mediation or arbitration, such as early neutral evaluation or mini-trials. These forms of dispute resolution are particularly useful since they, as well as special master intervention, are well suited for cases involving technical subject matter with complex issues that could benefit from the experience of a seasoned intervenor. Usually, the special master is an attorney with many years of experience in litigation and settlement negotiation. Magistrates or retired judges are also commonly appointed to serve as special masters.

A judge may appoint a special master solely to develop a case management plan expressly for settlement. Typically, a judge selects a special master, directs the parties to attend a status hearing, and defines the special master's objectives in the presence of both parties and their counsel. The judge may set a deadline by which the special master must submit a plan that will include schedules of limited discovery and a deposition schedule, both pared to include only what is needed for the purposes of settlement. The special master works with the parties to help them eliminate issues on which there is essential agreement. The schedules help streamline the process and keep the case moving toward settlement.

Once the special master has submitted the case management plan for settlement, depending on the parties' desires or the court's orders, the special master's duties may end. Alternatively, they may continue in the capacity of mediator. Some judges and special masters believe it is not appropriate to have the same person who developed the case management plan act as the settlement mediator. Some judges and masters prefer that the settlement special master ("settlement master") not have the authority to rule on discovery disputes. Each of these determinations must be made at the initial status conference with the parties, their counsel, and the special master present. Other details may also need to be discussed there, such as whether ex parte communication will be allowed and how much the special master will communicate, and for what purpose, with the judge.

The settlement master hosts and conducts settlement conferences, mediating actual disputes between parties, or at least identifying them, and eliminating areas of essential agreement. Often the parties prefer to have ex parte meetings with the settlement master, although this is not generally done without each party's consent. Through such caucuses, the settlement master very often can shepherd the case to a successful settlement.

## 8.9 Early Neutral Evaluation

In 1985, the U.S. District Court for the Northern District of California began a judicial experiment in alternative dispute resolution now known as early neutral evaluation. A committee examined how the court could reduce the cost of litigation for the client. The committee determined that the greatest wasted expense was in the pretrial stage of litigation. Pretrial posturing by attorneys, vague pleadings that did not allow the opposition to understand the claims against it, and poor pretrial communication all contributed to inflated expense.

The committee created the early neutral evaluation system as a response to these problems. In this ADR process, a neutral evaluator conducts a short, usually two-hour, case evaluation conference early in the litigation process. The evaluator is normally a highly respected private attorney chosen by the court. The evaluators have no judicial power and enter no binding orders.

The court usually requires the parties themselves to attend the evaluation conference with their counsel. At the evaluation conference, each party presents its position within a fifteen- to thirty-minute time period. The evaluator then identifies areas of agreement or near agreement to allow trial counsel to limit the dispute's scope. Stipulations are encouraged. The evaluator discourages alternative arguments, arguments with multiple themes, or boilerplate arguments. This phase of the conference helps limit discovery to actual, rather than perceived, disputes. The evaluator recommends a discovery plan that will help keep the case moving toward settlement. This may save the court and both parties considerable time, energy, and money.

In the next phase of the evaluation conference, the evaluator assesses for each party the relative strengths and weaknesses of their case, and, if possible, their opponent's case. The evaluator also estimates, within a certain range, each party's chance for liability and the amount of damages. In doing this, the evaluator draws upon considerable trial and settlement experience; to do this effectively, the evaluator must be credible and respected. The evaluator also comments on the likely cost of full discovery without settlement.

At this point the evaluator may offer to explore settlement possibilities with the parties or, if the parties wish, the process may end here. If the parties choose to explore further settlement talks, the evaluator relies on their experience to help the parties develop a plan to approach settlement. If the parties choose to explore settlement, the evaluator develops a discovery plan and shares it with the parties. The discovery plan is geared to putting the case in the best possible posture for settlement. The evaluator may also suggest a motion plan or a deposition schedule. The evaluator must be consistent in their effort to separate information that will be necessary for settlement negotiations and that which may be necessary at full trial. Preparation for settlement, not trial, is the goal.

When early neutral evaluation works as intended, it helps parties lower their litigation costs, improve pretrial communication with their opponents, and analyze their cases realistically while considering the input of a highly respected attorney in the field. Parties also avoid unnecessary discovery and, normally, increase their chances for early settlement.

## 8.10 Expert Panels

A court may appoint a panel of experts to help it in any number of ways, but the most typical use of an expert panel is to instruct and educate a court on complex scientific evidence in order for the court to determine the admissibility of such evidence. More and more, however, parties are using expert panels to facilitate settlements. Generally, a court issues an order that functions much like a pre-arbitration agreement, defining each aspect that the panel of experts will be expected to cover. As an alternative, the parties may accomplish this by agreement.

Included in the order or agreement are the panel's composition or the selection method; the subject matter of the area of inquiry; any specific duties of the panel, such as conducting physical examination of evidence; time limits for accomplishing these duties; whether a report will be filed and what is to be included in that report; how the panel members will function throughout the rest of the discovery process and trial; and how much the panel is to be compensated and by whom.

Courts can employ expert panels to manage and control discovery in cases where a judge may be wholly unqualified to do so. Scientific expert panels, therefore, can be most helpful in large-scale cases involving difficult scientific issues. These cases include asbestos litigation, pharmaceutical products liability cases, and tobacco industry litigation. Experts in these cases can help parties strip their cases of superfluous arguments, identify important issues of actual and significant disagreement, and guide parties in meaningful settlement negotiation. A judge may ask experts to serve as a conduit for either the parties or the judge to convey scientific issues to the court, or legal issues to the parties, respectively. A judge may accomplish this by scheduling frequent status meetings with the parties and the experts.

When serving in a settlement mode, a court-appointed expert normally confers with both parties together and each party individually. This approach promotes candor and enables the expert or experts to freely discuss settlement in light of the party's overall case. The court-appointed experts can also consult with the judge outside the parties' presence regarding the panel's investigation and findings. This process works most effectively when the judge appointing the experts for settlement purposes is not the judge who will serve as the trial judge in the case. The experts typically have access to all relevant documents, deposition transcripts, and witnesses, including the parties' experts. Fully informed about the litigation's subject matter, expert panels can conduct their own investigation, draw their own conclusions, and draft a report that will be used to facilitate settlement.

For this reason, the parties must agree on an expert or experts. The parties must be confident in these individuals' abilities and must respect their ability to draw intelligent conclusions from the information they gather. The court must take great care to ensure the experts have no ties to any party. Impartiality is vital. A court selects credible, impartial experts by submitting a list of ten or twenty experts to the parties. Each party has unlimited peremptory challenges to any potential panelist.

The list then is pared down to only those experts who the parties believe are impartial and credible. Experts must remove themselves from consideration for conflicts of interest.

The process of information gathering by the experts may take a few months to complete, but when considered in the light of litigation that has the potential to last five or ten years, the investment of a few months of earnest effort toward a mutually agreeable settlement may well be worth it. The expert panel provides its findings to the court and to all parties. Based on this report, the parties begin settlement conferencing facilitated by the experts. By the time the settlement conferencing begins, the panel of experts may have already ascertained what each party would require in a mutually satisfactory settlement. The court, without conducting a settlement conference, may use the panel's information and conclusions to fashion a settlement proposal on its own. It has knowledge of the parties' requirements for a settlement and may forgo further negotiations if it thinks a settlement can be accomplished solely based on the work of the expert panel.

## 8.11 Co-Mediation

An ADR hybrid that has gained increased use over the past few years is co-mediation. Simply defined, co-mediation is a process in which more than one person serves as a mediator. It involves the concepts of team mediation and interdisciplinary problem solving, and it can be tailored to the needs of a particular dispute. Depending on the ethnic, cultural, gender, or age characteristics of the disputants, two or more mediators having characteristics matching those of the adverse parties may be able to facilitate rapport-building and communication more easily than a single mediator with whom the disputants have difficulty identifying. Multiple mediators are commonly used in complex disputes where there are multiple parties, sometimes on each side of the case, and an intricate configuration of claims, crossclaims, and counterclaims. Such complex cases routinely exist in the fields of construction, tort, and environmental law. In such situations, the mediators may be assigned specific functions, or they may be assigned to specific disputants or specific aspects of the dispute. One mediator is designated as the lead mediator. That person is the chief strategist, coordinating the mediation activities of the other mediators and serving as an advisor and clearinghouse of information for them.

The most widespread application of co-mediation is in the field of family law, particularly in divorce mediation. Divorce cases especially lend themselves to resolution by interdisciplinary problem solving. Usually, the co-mediators in a divorce case are a lawyer and a nonlawyer, though in some situations two nonlawyers may share the mediator role. The nonlawyers are usually from disciplines other than law, for example, counseling, psychotherapy, financial or estate planning, or accounting. In a combined neutral arrangement, the lawyer usually serves as the process expert and the nonlawyer as the technical expert to provide independent opinions on particular issues (value of a business enterprise or an investment portfolio, for example) or to help develop alternative solutions that could be part of a negotiated settlement.

## 8.12 Arb-Med

In arb-med, a process free of the impediments of med-arb (see section 1.1) and binding mediation (see section 8.13 below), the parties first proceed to arbitration before an arbitrator who will render a binding decision. When the arbitrator reaches a decision and drafts the award, it is not shown to the parties. Rather the arbitrator places the award in a sealed envelope or locked electronic file. Thereafter, the parties can negotiate a resolution on their own, or they can involve the arbitrator as a mediator to help mediate a resolution. The arbitrator's decision, having already been made, will not be influenced by any confidential information of the parties. If the negotiations or mediation are unsuccessful, the parties open the sealed envelope or receive the password to the electronic file, read the award, and, by pre-agreement, are bound by it. Parties negotiating in the shadow of the sealed award tend to reach a joint decision for themselves rather than to entrust their fate to an imposed solution of unknown value.

## 8.13 Binding Mediation

Med-arb is often confused with a different form of ADR—"binding mediation." Insurance companies and plaintiffs' lawyers in search of finality in smaller-damage personal injury cases are turning to binding mediation routinely to avoid the disadvantages of arbitral or court adjudication—namely, the substantial delay and costs associated with discovery, trial preparation, trial, and possibly appeal. The concept of binding mediation is simple: if the parties and their counsel spend two hours in a mediation with an experienced mediator or former judge, why should the parties not have that neutral determine what the fair settlement value of the case is and pre-agree to be bound by that determination? Med-arb and binding mediation have distinctive and significant differences in their respective results. The result of a med-arb is an award—a decision on the merits of the parties' claims and defenses, based on evidence—which can be filed and enforced in a court of law. The result of a binding mediation is a neutral evaluation of the fair settlement value of a case—which may in fact have little relation to the ultimate merits of the case. Rather, fair settlement value is based on the risks of going forward to proof and the probabilities of success measured at the present stage of the litigation, sometimes without the benefit of expert evidence. This is definitely a process of speculation and "best guess" evaluation by a mediator, and the parties and counsel using it should be so informed. Binding mediation, which has no separate evidentiary phase, has been criticized for this "best guess" feature and for its susceptibility to being abused by unscrupulous counsel who exaggerate the strength of their potential evidence in caucuses. Neutrals who conduct binding mediations must be careful to detect such exaggerations and evaluate them accordingly. Counsel who participate in binding mediations must be careful to limit their risk of an unfair outcome by requiring the other side to pre-agree to a reasonable high-low bracket of which the mediator is unaware. This bracket safeguards each party to the binding mediation against the possibility of a "runaway" or biased evaluation. Alternatively, counsel may consider using other mediation hybrids, including arb-med and co-med-arb.

## 8.14 Hybrid ADR Process Selection

This section presents a tool to assist neutrals, parties, and their counsel in designing the appropriate hybrid ADR process for a particular dispute. The chart takes into account the hybrid mediation processes and also the other hybrid processes discussed above in this chapter. The chart identifies special needs of a client or situation and simultaneously describes the hybrid process having features satisfying those special needs. An assumption underlying the use of this chart is that the general needs of the client are: 1) to accelerate resolution of the dispute as compared to the time required for resolution by traditional court adjudication and 2) to lessen or minimize the costs of resolution.

**HYBRID ADR SELECTION CHART**

| Hybrid Process | Special Need(s) of Client or Situation | Process Feature Satisfying Special Need(s) of Client or Situation |
|---|---|---|
| **High-Low Arbitration** | Desires binding result | Binding award |
| | Wants to minimize risk of aberrant adverse binding award | Parties pre-agree to maximum/minimum award bracket |
| | Does not want arbitrator(s) to be influenced by final negotiated offers and demands | Parties pre-agree not to disclose bracket to arbitrator(s) |
| **Baseball Arbitration** | Wants to limit potential losses to a known tolerable level and to maximize potential gain | Parties pre-agree to limit the arbitrator's function to choosing either the high or the low end of the parties' negotiated bracket |

| | | |
|---|---|---|
| | Desires to maximize effectiveness of the negotiation process | Arbitrator's limited function influences parties to negotiate to a narrow bracket and cases often settle without need of arbitration |
| **Med-Arb and Co-Med-Arb** | Wants to go through evidentiary hearing only if absolutely necessary | Evidentiary arbitration hearing conducted only if mediation unsuccessful |
| | Wants to preserve relationship with other side, if at all possible | Mediation can help heal and preserve relationships |
| | Desires to first attempt to find a creative solution | Mediation can result in creative solutions |
| | Desires to use threat of arbitration to enhance opportunity for mediated result | Expense or inconvenience of arbitration can influence parties to work hard to settle case in mediation |
| | Desires finality | Arbitration yields a final, enforceable award if mediation is unsuccessful |
| | Situation appropriate for use of two neutrals | One neutral serves as mediator, the other, as arbitrator |
| | Wants to preserve option for mediated result throughout arbitration process | Dual neutrals preserve opportunity for settlement |
| **Arb-Med** | Does not want mediation process to taint evidentiary hearing in arbitration | Arbitration award withheld pending post-hearing mediation |
| | Wants an arbitrated result only as absolutely final alternative | Arbitration award revealed only in instance where mediated result is not possible |

| | | |
|---|---|---|
| **Binding Mediation** | Does not want an evidentiary hearing (e.g., case not fully discovered; unfavorable evidence, etc.) | Mediator attempts to settle dispute by facilitative caucusing; if unsuccessful, makes binding evaluation |
| | Wants to settle case without neutral's evaluation, if possible | Mediator attempts to settle dispute, first |
| | Desires neutral to evaluate case based on information disclosed in mediation | Mediator gives opinion of case value if mediation is unsuccessful |
| | Desires finality | Binding case evaluation |
| **Co-Mediation** | Wants input of expert or person with special expertise or having ethnic, cultural, or gender characteristics matching those of parties | Mediator teams up with psychologist, technical expert, accountant, etc. |
| | Wants to facilitate rapport-building and communication | Mediation team relates to needs and interests of parties |
| **Mini-Trial** | Capitalize on executives' expertise in making effective business decisions | Corporate executives are on panel that hears the abbreviated case presentations |
| | Enhance opportunities for collaboration by executives | A disinterested neutral facilitates negotiation between executives after case presentations |
| | Executives need to see evidence on both or all sides | Presentations made to panel by the attorneys on both (or all) sides |
| | Executives need to separate themselves from dispute to get objective view of case | Objectivity is achieved by putting executives in a temporary "neutral" role |
| | Parties need to limit risk of adverse result | Process is nonbinding |

| | | |
|---|---|---|
| **Simulated Jury** | Party needs private rehearsal to learn strengths and weaknesses of its strategies/tactics | Case is presented in an abbreviated manner to preselected jury |
| | Need for impartial evaluation by people closely mirroring potential jury | Jurors deliberate and reach a verdict |
| | Party needs opportunity for feedback from one or more juries | Party and counsel debrief jurors |
| | Party needs to determine whether case should be settled | Jurors' verdict(s) and comments often lead to decision to settle |
| **Special Master** | Need for individualized case management<br><br>Need for overseeing certain aspects of discovery process<br><br>Need for issue-framing, issue-shaping, issue reduction<br><br>Need for specialized settlement skills or experience<br><br>Need for neutral to help parties and counsel design a case-appropriate dispute resolution process or case-management plan<br><br>Court needs neutral to read pleadings, hear evidence and oral argument, and report and recommend an appropriate disposition | Court-appointed attorney or former judge can provide individualized case management and serve the other needs described in the adjacent column |

| | | |
|---|---|---|
| **Early Neutral Evaluation** | Need to minimize pretrial posturing by attorneys early in the life of the cases<br>Need to clarify vague pleading<br>Need to improve pretrial communication among counsel<br>Need for early evaluation of strengths and weaknesses of claims and defenses<br>Need to limit case to actual rather than merely perceived disputes | Highly respected, court-appointed panel conducts evaluation conference early in case, minimizes pretrial posturing, and serves the other needs described in the adjacent column |
| **Factfinding** | Facts needed before decision made on approach to resolution | Factfinder or team appointed to investigate and issue report |
| | High degree of confidentiality required | Factfinder/team maintains strict confidentiality |
| | Sensitivity to parties' feelings/reputation is paramount | Factfinder is sensitive to others' concerns and is skillful interviewer |
| **Expert Panel** | Judge or private neutral needs to be educated on one or more areas of complex scientific evidence | Experts can examine complex information and translate it into simple-to-understand concepts |
| | Scientific specialist needed to manage or control discovery | Technical experts are able to communicate on counsel's and parties' level |
| | Parties need to explore settlement options in technically complex case | Experts' report can be used as a tool by parties to settle case |

| | | |
|---|---|---|
| **Summary Jury Trial** | Need to see jury reaction to facts in an accelerated judicial proceeding in a courtroom environment | Six jurors selected by profiles; brief videotapes of expert and critical witness testimony |
| | Need to define critical legal issues and to learn how judge would rule on them | Comprehensive pretrial conference; evidentiary objections and jury instructions ruled on by judge |
| | Need to know why jury ruled a certain way | Through jury debriefing, parties learn specific reasons for jury's evaluation of case |

# • CHAPTER NINE •

## Online Arbitration and Dispute Resolution

> *The outbreak of COVID-19 has caused numerous changes to business almost across all the industries, and the legal and dispute resolution sector has not been immune. In times of social distancing, technology has become our lifesaver in maintaining stable operations when physical meetings and hearings are not an option. Amongst others, online dispute resolution (ODR) has undergone rapid development globally during such trying times. While the new normal settles upon us, there is no going back . . . .*
>
> —*Teresa Cheng*[1]
>
> *(Secretary for Justice of Hong Kong, 2018–2022)*

Before 2020, technologies like Zoom and other videoconferencing platforms offered remote solutions to legal processes, but many businesses and lawyers were slow to accept or adopt these technologies. Then COVID-19 arrived, changing the landscape worldwide. In the United States, the pandemic caused a significant expansion of the use of videoconferencing and online dispute resolution, and many arbitration hearings are now held by videoconference.

What does this mean for the twenty-first century advocate who wants to represent clients effectively not only in traditional business and personal transaction and dispute settings but also in cyberspace? It means, quite simply, that advocates must adapt to electronic methods of communication and ever-changing technology so that they can best represent their clients in a dynamic and ever-expanding world of high-velocity information exchange. The enormous quantity of personal interactions and commercial transactions occurring on the internet generates millions of disagreements and much thinking, on lawyers' parts, about how to resolve the resulting disagreements efficiently. Advocates may have to discard some traditional legal concepts and old ways of doing things in favor of more cyber-apropos methods. Newer and faster ways of conducting commerce via the internet, the development of artificial intelligence, and the use of blockchain will continue to present a

1. Teresa Cheng, Secretary for Justice of Hong Kong, Final Announcements of 18th Willem C. Vis (East) International Commercial Arbitration Moot (Mar. 21, 2021), https://www.doj.gov.hk/en/community_engagement/speeches/pdf/sj20210321e1.pdf.

wide variety of risks and exposures for companies and consumers alike. Advocates and their clients will need to focus on some of the new legal issues that continue to arise. They also need to consider new ways of incorporating technology in resolving disputes that arise both in "real world" traditional ways and in cyberspace itself.[2] Advocates, more and more, represent clients involved in disputes, commercial and otherwise, of an international character.[3] In doing so, advocates need to become proficient in online dispute resolution, which includes online mediation and arbitration. It is the purpose of this chapter to introduce you to online dispute resolution and online arbitration.

## 9.1 Types of Online Alternative Dispute Resolution Services—Generally

Most dispute resolution organizations provide mediation, arbitration, or other innovative dispute resolution services over the internet.[4] The purpose of this section is to make you aware of the variety of types of online dispute resolution (ODR) services available, generally.

### *9.1.1 Examples of Primary ODR Services*

#### 9.1.1.1 Online Arbitration

Many arbitration hearings and prehearing conferences are held by videoconference. Online arbitration reduces the need for travel and the costs involved. For instance, AAA provides for arbitration via Zoom and issued a *Model Order and Procedures for a Virtual Hearing in Videoconference*.[5] JAMS provides Zoom at no cost to the parties and issued assorted videoconference guides.[6] Other forms of online

---

2. *See generally* Ethan Katsh & Janet Rifkin, Online Dispute Resolution: Resolving Conflicts in Cyberspace (2001); Ethan Katsh, *Online Dispute Resolution: Some Lessons from the E-Commerce Revolution*, 28 N. Ky. L. Rev. 810 (2001).
3. *See generally* Robert C. Bordone, *Electronic Dispute Resolution: A Systems Approach—Potential, Problems, and a Proposal*, 3 Harv. Negot. L. Rev. 175 (1998); Alan Wiener, *Regulations and Standards for Online Dispute Resolution: A Primer for Policymakers and Stakeholders (Part 1)* Mediate.com (Feb. 15, 2001), https://mediate.com/regulations-and-standards-for-online-dispute-resolution-a-primer-for-policymakers-and-stakeholders-part-1/ (last visited Jun. 2024).
4. *See generally*, Alan Wiener, *Opportunities and Initiatives in Online Dispute Resolution*, SPIDR News (Summer 2000), at 17, https://mediate.com/opportunities-and-initiatives-in-online-dispute-resolution/ (last visited Jun. 2024).
5. AAA-ICDR, *Model Order and Procedures for a Virtual Hearing via Videoconference* Am. Arb. Ass'n, https://go.adr.org/rs/294-SFS-516/images/AAA270_AAA-ICDR%20Model%20Order%20and%20Procedures%20for%20a%20Virtual%20Hearing%20via%20Videoconference.pdf (last visited Jun. 2024).
6. *See Resolve Your Dispute at JAMS via Videoconference or Conference Call*, JAMS (Feb. 2023), https://www.jamsadr.com/files/uploads/documents/jams-videoconference-guide.pdf; *Virtual ADR–Frequently Asked Questions [FAQ]*, JAMS, https://www.jamsadr.com/faq-virtual-adr (last visited Jun. 2024); *Tips and Techniques for a Successful Videoconference*, JAMS, https://www.jamsadr.com/files/uploads/documents/jams-virtual-adr-tips.pdf (last visited Jun. 2024); *See also* Amy J. Schmitz

arbitration do not involve videoconference and rely instead on written communication. Typically, parties complete and submit online an agreement to arbitrate. The service provider then issues a schedule for stating and answering positions on various disputed issues. When that part of the process is completed, the provider schedules a five-day email hearing. The parties select the arbitrator, and they open the hearing. Each party presents their case online. The online arbitrator may pose questions online to the parties as the hearing progresses. On the last day of the hearing, the parties submit final arguments to the arbitrator by email. The online arbitrator then closes the hearing, reviews and considers the evidence, and renders a decision by United States mail within twenty days. Some service providers limit their services to particular types of disputes (for example, e-Resolution, which deals with internet domain name disputes).[7]

#### 9.1.1.2 Online Mediation

Both online and traditional dispute resolution service providers offer online mediation services, also sometimes called cyber-mediation. Much mediation is online mediation because the mediator meets with the parties pre-session and for the mediation session via videoconferencing platform, such as Zoom, Teams, or Google Meet. AAA offers virtual hearing managed services for mediation, and JAMS offers updated videoconferencing technology at resolution centers available for virtual mediation sessions.[8]

In the pure form of online mediation, one party initiates the process by completing a confidential form on the service provider's internet site. The form requires a party to identify the disputants, the nature of the dispute, and the desired outcome. The service provider contacts the other named parties, advises them of the submission, explains the online mediation process, and invites their participation. If the parties desire to participate, they typically sign an agreement to abide by the online mediation ground rules, protocols, and procedures. The parties mutually agree to use a cyber-mediator from a list provided by the service provider. The selected cyber-mediator conducts email communication with the parties, jointly or in caucuses as appropriate, and attempts to facilitate a mutually agreeable solution. If an agreement is reached, it is commonly reduced to writing.

---

& Claire Mendes, *Online Arbitration Protocols* (University of Missouri School of Law Legal Studies Research Paper No. 2021-13), SSRN (July 28, 2021), https://ssrn.com/abstract=3894707 (last visited Jun. 2024) (documenting different online arbitration protocols).

7. *See generally* Joseph W. Goodman, *The Pros and Cons of Online Dispute Resolution: An Assessment of Cyber-Mediation Websites*, 2003 Duke L. & Tech. Rev. 4 (2003).

8. *What We Do: Virtual Hearing Managed Services*, Am. Arb. Ass'n, https://www.adr.org/virtual-hearing-managed-services (last visited Jun. 2024); *Virtual Mediation, Arbitration and ADR Services*, JAMS, https://www.jamsadr.com/online?tab=overview (last visited Jun. 2023).

### 9.1.1.3 Online Negotiation

Many attorneys continue to use the telephone and email for negotiations, while some use videoconferencing. Some evidence suggests people can more easily identify the other person's emotions over the phone than via videoconference, so perhaps this is one reason negotiating by phone continues to often be used.

In other instances, parties use an exclusively online system to negotiate. One type of online system, called "automated negotiation" or "blind negotiation," is a popular online method of resolving monetary disputes. In this process, parties confidentially submit, normally by email, monetary offers and demands in "rounds" to the service provider. If the offer and demand of negotiating parties match, fall within a defined range, or overlap, the parties, by pre-agreement, settle the case for the matching amount, the average of the offer or demand if within a defined range, or the demand in the event of an overlap. In most systems, parties can keep the negotiation open and confidentially email their respective offers and demands at will. This allows parties to continue to engage in blind negotiation even as discovery ensues. If there is a settlement, the service provider immediately notifies the parties by email.

## 9.2 *Cost or Financing of Service*

Fees for use of ODR services are generally of three types: bilateral or multilateral, unilateral, or external source.[9] In the bilateral or multilateral model, each party pays its proportional share of the user fee. This seems fair on its face, but one problem with this model is that the cost for the consumer may be disproportionate compared to the amount at stake.

In the unilateral user fee model, the business (merchant or insurance company) pays the entire fee for the ODR service. The payment can be in the form of an annual membership fee (e.g., a trustmark fee) or a fee per case. The problem with this model is the inevitable appearance of bias. It might appear to the nonbusiness user, for example, that the business payor of the user fee is being favored in the process. The appearance of bias can be lessened by the ODR provider's implementation of strict procedural rules, ensuring the availability of an adequate selection of independent neutrals, publishing clear policies of neutrality and impartiality, and establishing an independent supervisory or auditing body.

In the external source fee model, a third party—university or a governmental or nongovernmental organization (such as a consumer association) pays the entire fee for the ODR service. In general, this model provides the highest guarantee of independence and impartiality.

---

9. *See* Thomas Schultz et al, *Online Dispute Resolution: The State of the Art and the Issues* 74–77 (E-Com Research Project of the University of Geneva, Dec. 2001), SSRN (May 2, 2006), https://papers.ssrn.com/sol3/papers.cfm?abstract_id=899079 (last visited Jun. 2024).

On the question of independence, advocates selecting ODR provider organizations may want to take into account the provider's organizational structure and outside financial support. Some ODR providers are nonprofits while others are for-profit organizations.

## 9.3 Cyberspace Netiquette

Communication on the internet involves different dynamics and rules than does communication through other media.[10] When you are communicating messages or conducting an arbitration online, consider the benefits and limitations of this medium in order to capitalize on the experience. Compare three common forms of quick communication, for example, email, verbal communication, and text messaging. Email has an advantage over verbal communication in that you have the opportunity to compose, read, reflect, and modify the content of your message before you send or convey it. You can catch errors, unintentional misstatements of facts, or undiplomatic phrasings before you communicate them—a hastily-written response can be edited before sending, whereas a hastily-made remark cannot be taken back. On the other hand, text robs you of this advantage, and you must take care to carefully and tactfully craft your message as your fingers fly—a careless verbal statement fades into memory, but an insensitive text lingers on the screen.

When you are arbitrating online, you may find this set of communication guidelines—or "netiquette"—helpful. In the discussion that follows, no communications are ex parte; that is, no counsel or party is communicating with the arbitrator without simultaneously copying the opposing party, and the arbitrator is sending emails to the parties simultaneously.

### *9.3.1 Communicate Only With Permission*

You must take special precautions to ensure that you know who is "in the loop" for communicating online. Clarify with other counsel whether they prefer to have your email sent solely to them or whether they want copies sent to their clients also. Specify whether you want your client to receive participants' email. In some situations, you may want your client to receive the arbitrator's email, but not the email of other lawyers. There may be other people outside of the circle of actual participants in the online arbitration who need to be kept abreast of various happenings during the arbitration. Make sure you know who you are and are not authorized to contact. Sending an email message to a person not authorized to receive it could doom an arbitration.

10. *See generally* Jeffrey G. Kichaven, *Virtual Mediation*, Bus. L. Today, May/June 1996, at 7–8.

### 9.3.2 Be Conscious of Time Zones

You may be communicating with people who live and work in various parts of the United States and even in various countries in the world who are in different time zones. Some of these people may even be traveling through various time zones during an extended online arbitration. If you are in New York and you send an email in the early morning to someone in San Francisco, don't expect even the earliest response to be before noon. You must factor in not only the time zone differential, but also the time it will take the party to communicate with others before the party can respond to you. Be mindful of these delaying factors and avoid setting unrealistic reply deadlines for your online arbitration participants.

### 9.3.3 Respect People's Space

Avoid overwhelming the arbitrator, the parties, and their counsel with email messages. It is disconcerting for someone to open their mailbox to find a whole list of emails from the same person. Take the time to review the emails you have received and respond to them cumulatively, if appropriate. Compose your emails as you would a letter, rather than dashing them off as you would a text message or chat. Otherwise, your unrelenting email bombardment may unnecessarily increase the costs for all parties in the case, including your own client. Realize that every email you send not only documents time you've spent on the case, but also takes up time of the arbitrator and of other counsel who must communicate with their clients and get back to you and the arbitrator. Fees can mount quickly, with little to show for the time spent.

### 9.3.4 Request and Provide Confirmations

Breakdown in communication may occur simply because the arbitrator and other counsel never received your email communication. This may occur because of an address error, misdirection, or even an inadvertent failure to send the prepared message. If you are dispatching an important email message, request the addressees to acknowledge receipt of the message even before they review and consider its content—make this request in the subject line so that the recipient will see it even if they delay opening the email. If you do not receive confirmation from each addressee, you can investigate right away to determine whether you need to resend the message or relay it to them via another mode of communication. Similarly, if the arbitrator or other counsel request that you acknowledge receipt of an email, confirm receipt immediately and respond to the substance of the message later.

### 9.3.5 Check and Answer Email Regularly

This seems obvious, in this day and age, but experience tells us it must be said. As an advocate in an online arbitration, you will need to check and answer email periodically during each day. Because email is not as intrusive as telephone contact, you will find that counsel, parties, or the arbitrator may send you emails on the weekend. The policy you adopt for handling email communication on the weekends will conform to your individual preferences or lifestyle. Some online arbitration participants prefer not to respond to such communications until the next business day; others prefer to sustain the momentum of dialogue or to keep their mailboxes cleared out.

### 9.3.6 Give Notice of Extended Absences

Let the participants in your online arbitration know when you are going to be unavailable for email communication for a day or more. They will appreciate your courtesy, and by mutual agreement you and they might arrange some alternate mode of communication to substitute for email in case of an emergency.

### 9.3.7 Forward Emails with an Explanation

When forwarding messages, insert a short explanatory note prior to the body of the forwarded message so that the receiving party will understand why you are sending it and whether they need to respond to you in some way. You may think the reason is self-explanatory, but the recipient will appreciate context.

### 9.3.8 Attach Only Necessary Documents

Respect people's time. Before you attach a document to an email, review your list of addressees and segregate those out who do not need to receive it. Then send a separate email to those people without the document attached.

### 9.3.9 Police Hostile or Hurtful Language

Email and text messages can quickly degenerate into an abusive exchange. It can create a faceless "bunker" mentality among opposing counsel that is regrettably conducive to sniping and taking insulting pot-shots at others. Whether sent privately or in a group email, such exchanges can quickly escalate. As a professional matter, halt even the slightest signs of hostile or hurtful language. Left unattended, such offensive remarks can disrupt the online arbitration at the very least, and at worst they can cause the process to disintegrate.

Model the written communication that you expect the others to use in an online arbitration. If you use polite, respectful, and diplomatic language, the other participants will do likewise.

### 9.3.10 Keep Communications Crisp, Pithy, and Relevant

Most of us have experienced online communication where a participant goes well outside the relevant topic and writes interminably about matters that fail to move the discussion to a common goal. In an online arbitration, counsel may engage in such communication to divert the process from an issue where their position is weak to issues where they can speak from a position of strength. This kind of communication may be counsel's attempt to control the agenda. Normally, the arbitrator will nip this behavior in the bud and encourage the participants to keep communications crisp, pithy, and relevant. But if the arbitrator does not control this conduct, you may want to email the arbitrator (with a copy sent to other counsel) and suggest that the arbitrator set length limits on the email communications.

### *9.3.11 Mind Your Grammar, Spelling, and Punctuation*

Write emails to outside counsel, the arbitrator, and other participants with the same attention to grammar, spelling, and punctuation as you would a physical letter. In some cases, email is the only formal communication you will exchange with these parties; keep it professional. Save emojis and abbreviations for personal or interoffice email.

### *9.3.12 Pick Up the Telephone*

When arbitrating online, sometimes there is no substitute for picking up the telephone and talking directly to someone, such as opposing counsel. Some people communicate better verbally than in writing—voice conveys subtleties of meaning and emotion more effectively than the written word. In a spoken exchange, you can give support, provide detailed explanations, and answer questions more quickly and sensitively. Informal negotiations can proceed with more candor absent a written record. While written online communication can be very effective in arbitration, a phone call will also be quite useful from time to time.

### *9.3.13 Save Your Email Correspondence*

Save (and digitally back up) all your email correspondence relating to a particular arbitration, at least until the arbitration has concluded, and sometimes well beyond the conclusion. By this we do not mean that you simply do not delete the email from your inbox. Save emails to the case file or folder, where they can be located like all other case documents. Whether you save them digitally or in print, select the final email in an exchange and save it with all the related emails in the chain so that the entire conversation is preserved. You will find it helpful to refer back to certain email communications from time to time—especially near the end of the arbitration when you are drafting your final briefs or preparing your closing argument. The email correspondence may also help you long after the arbitration if an issue arises as to whether a party is in compliance with the arbitrator's award. Exactly how long you retain your email correspondence after the conclusion of the arbitration will be dictated by your firm's own retention policies or, perhaps, the rules of your jurisdiction.

# • CHAPTER TEN •

## EFFECTIVE ADVOCACY IN ONLINE ARBITRATION

*We must keep a very firm eye . . . on the types of dispute that will actually arise in the future, for surely they will not be the kind of disputes that arose in the past. They will be digitally based—disputes concerning on-chain transactions, purchases made on Apple and Amazon platforms, and disputes arising from digital rather than paper documentation.*

*—Sir Geoffrey Vos*[1]

*(Master of the Rolls and Head of Civil Justice in England and Wales, 2021–present)*

This chapter will prepare you to represent clients effectively through the process of online arbitration—which, as the opening quotation suggests, will continue to arise in the future. Chapters 2–8 have already provided much of what you need to succeed in online arbitration today. The process still starts with a claimant filing a demand, although it may be received electronically rather than through the mail, or the parties entering into a submission agreement, although that may involve text and email exchanges rather than telephone and letters or faxes.[2] The methods of selecting an arbitrator remain the same, although the dispute resolution service may provide the arbitrator list online or by email rather than mail. A virtual hearing, held on a videoconferencing platform like Zoom, still proceeds with opening statements, witness examinations, and closing arguments, while a solely written online process involves the same writing and emphasis techniques used in any position paper, whether a demand or prehearing brief. This chapter addresses some specifics

1. Sir Geoffrey Vos, Master of the Rolls and Head of Civil Justice in England and Wales, Keynote Address at the London International Disputes Week 2021 (May 10, 2021), https://www.judiciary.uk/wp-content/uploads/2021/05/MR-to-LIDW-10-May-2021.pdf (last visited Jun. 2024).

2. Short for facsimile machine, a method of sending documents electronically, traditionally over a telephone line, where the recipient's fax machine would receive the telephonic signal that transmitted a document that the machine would print out. Facsimile machines are still used by some government agencies and doctor's offices, meaning that this archaic technology is not yet dead and you might encounter it, though most faxes are now received by computer programs and converted to PDF files.

of online arbitration that may differ from an arbitration process culminating in a live hearing.

## 10.1 Comparison of Live Face-to-Face, Videoconference, Telephone, and Written Communication in Arbitration

The twenty-first century advocate who represents a client in arbitration is constantly confronted with the question of what mode of communication they should be using at various stages of the arbitration process. The reason for this is that the advocate in arbitration has many modes of communication from which to choose, including in person face-to-face, videoconferencing, telephone, letter, email, fax, or combinations of these modes. In this section we will review the relative advantages and disadvantages of the three primary modes of communication: in person face-to-face, videoconference, telephonic, and written. It is hoped that the information here will assist you in choosing the appropriate mode of communication as the arbitration progresses.[3]

### *10.1.1 Face-to-Face Communication in Arbitration*

When people communicate with one another, 93 percent of the meaning of their messages is contained in their facial and vocal cues, rather than in the content of the messages. This is why the most communicatively efficient mode of arbitration is in person, face to face.

In some situations, videoconferencing serves as a near-equivalent substitute for a live face-to-face meeting. In-person arbitration may be simply impossible because of geographical distance between or among the parties and their counsel. Even when not impossible, eliminating travel reduces cost and minimizes the disruption of lost time, logistical considerations, and the possibility of travel delays. Videoconferencing does require pre-planning to avoid technological SNAFUs, and some research suggests the time lag involved may impact turn-taking and contribute to fatigue.[4] Even so, consider videoconferencing as a solid substitute for a live arbitration hearing.

There may also be situations where the disputing parties are so emotionally hostile toward one another that a face-to-face arbitration, or videoconference, would

---

3. *See generally* Charles B. Craver, Effective Legal Negotiation and Settlement 228–34 (9th ed. 2020); Edward Brunet et al., Alternative Dispute Resolution: The Advocate's Perspective 186–94 (5th ed. 2016); Ethan Katsh et al., *E-Commerce, E-Disputes, and E-Dispute Resolution: In the Shadow of "eBay Law,"* 15 Ohio St. J. on Disp. Resol. 705 (2000); Janice Nadler, *Electronically-Mediated Dispute Resolution and E-Commerce,* 17 Negot. J. 333 (2001); Michael Morris et al, *Schmooze or Lose: Social Friction and Lubrication in E-mail Negotiations,* 6 Group Dynamics: Theory Res. & Prac. 89 (2002).
4. Julie E. Boland et al., *Zoom Disrupts the Rhythm of Conversation,* 151 J. Experimental Psychol: Gen. 1272, 1280 (2022).

do more harm than good. A face-to-face meeting might also be counter-indicated if there is no continuing relationship to be preserved. In other arbitration situations, while a face-to-face meeting may be helpful during a portion of the process, an advocate might conclude for strategic, tactical, or other reasons that another mode of communication might fit other phases of the process.

Keep in mind, however, that behavioral research has demonstrated that it can take four times as long for a three-person group to make a decision in a real-time videoconference than in a face-to-face conference. It can take ten times as long for a four-person group, having no time restrictions, to come to a joint decision. These research results have implications for arbitrators in decision making, as well as for advocates who try to jointly decide how to plan a discovery schedule.

### 10.1.2 Telephonic Communication in Arbitration

For some people, the telephone offers a more effective and efficient way to arbitrate than arbitrating in person. Some advocates, for example, are better skilled at sensing audible cues suggesting true meaning of a participant's telephone statement than they are at discerning nonverbal aspects of messages in a face-to-face meeting. These audible cues consist of, among others, pitch, pace, tone, volume, inflection, sighs, and pauses. Nonverbal, visual cues to meaning can be distracting and overwhelming to some people in an in-person situation. One study suggests that listeners can better glean emotions from voice-only rather than face-to-face communication, including videoconferences.[5]

There are some major disadvantages to arbitrating over the telephone. It is often difficult to discern the identity of the speakers if several participants, including the arbitrator and several disputing parties, are engaged in the teleconference. Furthermore, in a document-rich case, discussing documents over the telephone can be a cumbersome task if the documents are not quickly identifiable by volume and page number. Teleconferences can also become rambling, directionless conversations without strong supervision by the arbitrator. Teleconferences are usually less personal than face-to-face conversations. Such faceless verbal exchanges sometimes facilitate competitive or even deliberately deceptive tactics.

### 10.1.3 Written Communication in Arbitration

Written communication in arbitration permits the transmission of detailed information to the arbitrator and/or the other parties. The writer has the luxury of their written communication not being interrupted. Written communication also serves as a permanent record of an opposing counsel's evidence and arguments.

5. Jyoti Madhusoodanan & Michael W. Kraus, *Listeners Glean Emotions Better from Voice-Only Communications*, Yale Insights (Oct. 10, 2017), https://insights.som.yale.edu/insights/listeners-glean-emotions-better-from-voice-only-communications (last visited Jun. 2024).

Avoid misunderstandings by taking the time to be careful and accurate in your written communications to the arbitrator, opposing parties, and co-counsel. Written communication allows you as much time as necessary to review proposals and obtain input from your client, your partners, or co-counsel. Complete, rather than excerpted, written affidavits or deposition transcripts can sometimes enable the arbitrator to make credibility decisions better than hearing a live witness who is purposefully or inadvertently giving nonverbal miscues.[6]

Email enables efficient written communication. You can instantaneously communicate your pleadings to the arbitrator and opposing counsel. Amending and correcting pleadings is also facilitated. Advocates can prepare and transmit their pleadings from any place in the world; likewise, arbitrators can issue their rulings from any location. Another advantage of email arbitration is that no split-second tactical decisions need to be made. Advocates and their clients can take time to consider and respond to positions or pleadings. Studies have also shown that the absence of social status cues can influence people to respond openly and less hesitatingly than in a face-to-face setting.

Email communication in arbitration, however, is not without its shortcomings. The instantaneous nature of email can lead to an informality that is easily misunderstood or misinterpreted. When people treat email as an informal conversation rather than a formal exchange of information, an emotive aspect can enter the content of the message. Consider the email statement, "You consistently have all the right answers." It is not clear whether the writer is exhibiting deference or sarcasm. More problematically, insults take on permanence. Hostile exchanges can escalate rapidly when there is no cooling-off period between receiving a message and replying. Innocuous language can be perceived as deliberately inflammatory and reinforce prior impressions of recipients, compounding misinterpretations to a crisis point.

Unless you exercise special care, you can also easily compromise the confidentiality of the arbitration process. The split-second sending of an email to an unintended addressee can be disastrous.

Mail or delivery might in some instances be used in addition to email, such as providing hard copies of exhibits to the arbitrator and opposing counsel. While letters and faxes are no longer often relied on, they are also options for delivering written information.

---

6. Olin Guy Wellborn, *Demeanor*, 76 Cornell L. Rev. 1075, 1091 (1991) ("Transcripts are probably superior to live testimony as a basis for credibility judgments because they eliminate distracting, misleading, and unreliable nonverbal data and enhance the most reliable data, verbal content.").

| ARBITRATING USING WRITTEN RATHER THAN FACE-TO-FACE COMMUNICATION | |
|---|---|
| **ADVANTAGES** | **DISADVANTAGES** |
| Transmit detailed information | Messages can be misunderstood and/or misinterpreted |
| No interruptions | Insults take on permanence; hostile exchanges can escalate rapidly |
| Permanent record of opponent's positions, pleadings, evidence, and correspondence | Delays: takes up to four times longer for a group to reach consensus or a joint decision |
| Misunderstandings more easily avoided | Unless care is exercised, confidentiality can be easily compromised |
| You have time to review proposals and get input | |
| Messages instantaneously communicated | |
| Advocates can prepare and transmit pleadings and arbitrators can issue rulings from anywhere in the world | |
| Amendments or corrections to pleadings can be distributed immediately and simultaneously | |
| Messages can be broadcasted to any number of people simultaneously | |
| Absence of social status cues can influence people to respond openly and less hesitatingly than in a face-to-face setting | |
| Split second tactical decisions do not normally have to be made | |

## 10.2 Benefits and Limitations of Online Arbitration

There are both benefits and limitations associated with the use of online arbitration.[7] These are discussed generally in section 10.2.1. Two topics that deserve

7. *See generally* Paul Schiff Berman, *The Globalization of Jurisdiction*, 151 U. Pa. L. Rev. 311 (2002); Karen Stewart & Joseph Matthews, *Online Arbitration of Cross-Border, Business to Consumer Disputes*, 56 U. Miami L. Rev. 1111 (2002); Lucille M. Ponte, *Throwing Bad Money after Bad: Can Online*

special analysis under this heading are confidentiality and cost of service. These topics are discussed in sections 10.2.3 and 10.3, respectively.

### *10.2.1 Benefits*

Some of the benefits of online arbitration are as follows.

#### 10.2.1.1 Availability

Participants can be located anywhere in the world. Participants may communicate asynchronously—they choose when they want to respond, day or night.

#### 10.2.1.2 Cost

One of the obvious advantages of online arbitration over live arbitration is reduced cost. Either a videoconference hearing or written synchronous or asynchronous arbitration should be less expensive than travel costs for several people. Expense of travel and accommodations is often prohibitive in small-dispute situations. Other cost considerations are discussed in section 10.5.2.1.

#### 10.2.1.3 Speed

Instantaneous transmission of information by electronic means accelerates the resolution process in most cases. Videoconference may also be more efficient than a live hearing because it is easier to schedule a time when all involved can be online rather than a time when all are available to be at a single location. And once the arbitrators reach consensus, their computer-transcribed written discussions, along with the digital findings and conclusions submitted by the advocates, often allow them to quickly formalize, draft, and issue their award and, if appropriate, supporting opinion.

#### 10.2.1.4 Arbitrator Expertise

A worldwide pool of arbitrators with special expertise can enhance the quality of the arbitration process.

---

*Resolution (ODR) Really Deliver the Goods for the Unhappy Internet Shopper?* 3 Tul. J. Tech. & Intell. Prop. 55 (2001); William Krause, *Do You Want to Step Outside? An Overview of Online Alternative Dispute Resolution* 19 John Marshall J. Computer & Info. L. 457 (2001); Richard Michael Victorio, *Internet Dispute Resolution (IDR): Bringing ADR into the 21st Century*, 1 Pepp. Disp. Resol. L. J. 279 (2001); Elizabeth G. Thornburg, *Going Private: Technology, Due Process, and Internet Dispute Resolution*, 34 U.C. Davis L. Rev. 151 (2000); Paul D. Carrington, *Virtual Arbitration*, 15 Ohio St. J. on Disp. Resol. 669 (2000); Tiffany J. Lanier, *Where on Earth Does Cyber-Arbitration Occur? International Review of Arbitral Awards Rendered Online*, 7 ILSA J Int'l & Comp. L. 1 (2000); Frank A. Cona, *Application of Online Systems in Alternative Dispute Resolution*, 45 Buff. L. Rev. 975 (1997).

#### 10.2.1.5 Less Confrontational

In asynchronous online arbitration, the parties can choose when they want to respond or participate in the process as it proceeds through its various stages. This allows time for parties to reflect on the materials they receive from opposing parties and co-parties, get initial legal advice, strategize with counsel or co-parties, carefully craft what they want to say, and even get final input from counsel or co-parties before they finally commit to a response or argument that their counsel will communicate to the arbitrator and to the other side. The online nature of the process eliminates the pressure to respond immediately to a received communication. Online arbitration minimizes the effects of confrontational dynamics.

#### 10.2.1.6 Cyberspace Ensures a Neutral Forum

Cyberspace itself provides a neutral forum akin to an arbitrator's office or conference room. A dominant party is not able to exploit "home court advantage."

### *10.2.2 Limitations*

#### 10.2.2.1 Enforcement of Arbitral Awards

Determining what law governs the initial commercial contract and the terms of any award may be challenging. The parties can circumvent these problem areas by carefully crafting an arbitration agreement to include terms defining jurisdiction, applicable laws, and enforcement and review procedures. Self-executing award mechanisms, trustmark withdrawal, and escrow accounts are a few of the measures that can be used to ensure the enforcement of arbitral awards.

#### 10.2.2.2 Uncertainty Regarding Confidentiality, Privacy, Anonymity, and Authenticity

As discussed more thoroughly in section 10.2.3, maintaining confidentiality of communications in cyberspace can be a difficult task. The witnesses' fear of information leaks and invasion of privacy can create barriers to unfettered communication. Also, because of the faceless interaction in cyberspace, the identity of communicators and the authenticity of communications can sometimes be difficult to guarantee.

#### 10.2.2.3 Absence of Human Factors

Written online communication often lacks the spontaneity and vigor of face-to-face interaction and oral discussion. Studies have shown that parties proceeding online are more likely to distrust and suspect lying or deceit on the part of other participants, and they are more likely to "flame" and reach an impasse in negotiating fact stipulations or resolving discovery matters.

### 10.2.2.4 Computer Accessibility and Literacy

Varying degrees of computer accessibility and literacy may affect the quality of online communication between counsel and client. Occasionally, online technology can create a power imbalance among the parties or counsel. This imbalance may result from varying quality of computer equipment or software, the relative competence of the online arbitration participants to use the internet, or the unequal experience with using the services of an online arbitrator. If you are representing an unsophisticated client with little or no computer experience, you can still use online arbitration with some extra effort on your part: bring your client into your office for online sessions or consider loaning a laptop to the client if equipment quality is the problem. While Zoom and other videoconferencing applications can be used with a cell phone, such a connection should be a last resort and only used in an emergency.

### 10.2.2.5 Unsuitability of Disputes for Online Arbitration

Some disputes are comfortably amenable to resolution by online arbitration. These includes disputes originating in cyberspace—intellectual property disputes, e-commerce disputes, and disputes that are fundamentally economic such as insurance claims and construction defects. Certain types of disputes may not be as appropriate for online arbitration. Personal injury cases where claimants need to demonstrate the nature of their injuries, scars, etc. may be more appropriate for traditional arbitration or videoconferenced arbitration than written arbitration. Similarly, a patent or product liability case, where it is helpful to a resolution for the arbitration participants to see the configuration or operation of a particular piece of equipment, may be a candidate for a traditional arbitration.

The above-described benefits and limitations of online arbitration and others are outlined in the following chart.

| BENEFITS AND LIMITATIONS OF ONLINE ARBITRATION | |
|---|---|
| **BENEFITS** | **LIMITATIONS** |
| Reduced cost in comparison with live face-to-face arbitration | Enforcement of arbitral awards may be a problem |
| Accelerated proceedings | Determining what law governs the initial commercial contract and the terms of any award may be challenging |
| Participants can be located anywhere in the world | Varying degrees of computer accessibility and literacy may exist among counsel and their clients |
| Participants may communicate asynchronously—they choose when they want to respond, day or night | Power imbalance may be created by unequal online expertise/experience/equipment of parties or counsel |
| Arbitrators with special expertise may be hired worldwide | Online communication lacks the spontaneity and vigor of face-to-face interaction and oral discussion |
| Online arbitration minimizes the effects of confrontational dynamics | Parties are more likely to distrust and suspect lying or deceit on the part of other participants |
| Cyberspace itself provides a neutral forum in an arbitrator's office or conference room | Parties may have uncertainty regarding confidentiality, privacy, anonymity, and authenticity |
| Parties can craft communications in an emotion-free setting | Some disputes may not be suitable for resolution by means of online arbitration |
| Advocates have easy access to legal and expert sources to help them give realistic advice to clients at particular points in the arbitration proceedings | Viewing an injury or real evidence is difficult |
| Often, after the arbitrators reach consensus, using their generated written discussions, they can quickly formalize, draft, and issue their award and supporting opinion, as appropriate | |

### *10.2.3 Confidentiality*

Confidentiality is often an important aspect of the arbitration process. The participants' agreement to maintain the confidentiality of the arbitration proceedings is usually sufficient in live face-to-face arbitrations to guarantee nondisclosure of sensitive information. Each participant in offline or online arbitrations is responsible not to mistakenly disclose information by email or other means. ODR, however, introduces a new threat to arbitration confidentiality.[8] Regardless of the participants' agreement to maintain confidentiality of online arbitration proceedings, security breaches can originate externally from nonparticipants who intentionally invade, acquire, and perhaps even alter information the participants want to preserve as confidential and unchanged. All parties to an arbitration must comply with security protocols that provide protection for both the transmission and the storage of confidential arbitration information. These two aspects require different means of protection. The risks to be protected against are the risk that unauthorized third parties will gain access to the information (i.e., risk of compromising the confidentiality of the message) and the risk that such third parties will alter it (i.e., the risk of compromising the integrity of the message). You will need to understand and protect against well-known risks—such as sending unencrypted email—and whatever is the latest risk to security to arise, such as AI recording a videoconference arbitration without anyone involved being aware of it. Using a dispute resolution organization that employs specialists in cybersecurity is one way to effectively manage these risks.[9]

## 10.3 Ethics of Advocacy in Online Arbitration

The state codes of professional conduct for lawyers, most of which incorporate the American Bar Association's Model Rules of Professional Conduct, guide an advocate's conduct in representing clients in online arbitration.[10] (See section 2.7.) The ABA and others have instituted protocols for virtual arbitrations that address ethical concerns, such as cybersecurity and online etiquette.[11]

One critical ethical duty of advocates in online dispute resolution is maintaining client confidences. Online communication presents a minefield of opportunities for inadvertent and harmful disclosures of client information by incautious and unwary advocates.[12] Following the guidance presented below will help you avoid making those instant and unintentional harmful disclosures.

---

8. *See generally* Thomas Schultz et al, *Online Dispute Resolution: The State of the Art and the Issues*, 44–50 (E-Com Research Project of the University of Geneva, Dec. 2001), SSRN (May 2, 2006), https://papers.ssrn.com/sol3/papers.cfm?abstract_id=899079 (last visited Jun. 2024).
9. *See, e.g.*, *What We Do: Virtual Hearing Managed Services*, Am. Arb. Ass'n, https://www.adr.org/virtual-hearing-managed-services (last visited Jun. 2024).
10. *See generally* Louise Ellen Teitz, *Providing Legal Services for the Middle Class in Cyberspace: The Promise and Challenge of On-line Dispute Resolution*, 70 Fordham L. Rev. 985, 991 (2001).
11. P. Jean Baker, *During the Pandemic, Virtual Arbitration Offers a Promising Alternative—Provided You Know What You Are Doing*, 74 Disp. Resol. J. 157 (2020); *See also* Amy J. Schmitz & Claire Mendes, *Online Arbitration Protocols* (University of Missouri School of Law Legal Studies Research Paper No. 2021-13), SSRN (July 28, 2021), https://ssrn.com/abstract=3894707 (last visited Jun. 2024) (documenting different online arbitration protocols).
12. M. Ethan Katsh, *Dispute Resolution in Cyberspace*, 28 Conn. L. Rev. 953, 971–74 (1996).

### 10.3.1 Carefully Manage the Power of the "CC"

When communicating by email, check that all the addressees actually need to receive or would even want to receive the information you are sending. There are times when, on behalf of your client, you will want to communicate with all participants in the arbitration, but there will be other times when the information sent will be merely ministerial and applicable to only one or two participants or co-parties. Do not bother participants with a message that has no relevance to them only because it is convenient for you to click only once without thinking, sorting, and deciding. Also, while the "cc" option is a powerful email tool, it is also a horrible accident waiting to happen. Critical, highly confidential information can be disclosed in a split second and can compromise an arbitration and perhaps put a lawyer's career in jeopardy. Before commencing an online arbitration, arbitrators normally take great pains to advise parties and counsel about the dangers of unintentional disclosures of client confidences and to discuss procedures for preventing it from happening. This advice should be explicitly heeded.

### 10.3.2 Take Security Precautions Vis-à-Vis Other Web Users

If you are engaged in the arbitration of a high-profile case online, do not be too surprised if you have interlopers—related to the dispute or not—trying to acquire information on the arbitration's progress. If you use chat rooms or videoconferencing platforms, make sure they are secure and keep an eye out for new entrants whose identity you do not know.

### 10.3.3 Maintain Appropriate Confidentiality Within Your Groups

It was pointed out above that the "cc" feature of email is a powerful and useful tool, but that it can cause disastrous disclosures of information. Before you send any email messages, ensure that the principal addressees and the "cc" addressees are appropriate. If you are simultaneously involved in several online dispute resolution processes, it is vital for you to keep the email addresses of participants in the various cases segregated from each other so that you don't inadvertently send an email to a participant in a separate dispute.

## 10.4 Online Arbitration Protocols

Several ODR service providers publish protocols on their websites. These protocols establish the ground rules governing the participants' conduct in the particular ODR process selected. Protocols may address subjects such as technology and platform, accessibility, cybersecurity, online etiquette, and testimonial and documentary evidence.[13] The AAA and JAMS, for example, each have virtual arbitration protocols.[14]

## 10.5 Considerations in Selecting an Online Arbitration Service and Arbitrator

### *10.5.1 The Online Arbitration Process*

Before selecting an ODR service provider and an online arbitrator or a panel of arbitrators, decide what kind of online arbitration process you, your client, and the opposing side desire. One of the first questions to ask yourself is whether you want to be limited in your choice of arbitrators by an ODR provider's "mandatory" list of neutrals. If you and opposing counsel have in mind a particular arbitrator to hire, consider eliminating from consideration those providers that limit your choice of arbitrators to their list or panel.

All ODR providers do not provide the same type of arbitration process. The nature of the arbitration process provided by each ODR provider depends on the type of technology available on the website. For example, some provider guidelines only allow for email communication and disable all chats or private chats. You may also want a provider that offers mediation as a tandem process option as you proceed through the arbitration. In still other situations, you may desire a provider that provides only a technology platform for arbitration, which the parties can use along with their independently selected arbitrator(s). In many respects, choosing the appropriate provider of online arbitration is often much more challenging than selecting an offline arbitration service provider.

---

13. Schmitz, *supra* note 11.

14. *AAA-ICDR® Model Order and Procedures for a Virtual Hearing via Videoconference* Am. Arb. Ass'n, https://go.adr.org/rs/294-SFS-516/images/AAA270_AAA-ICDR%20Model%20Order%20and%20Procedures%20for%20a%20Virtual%20Hearing%20via%20Videoconference.pdf (last visited Jun. 2024); *AAA-ICDR Virtual Hearing Guide for Arbitrators and Parties Utilizing ZOOM*, Am. Arb. Ass'n (May 9, 2020), https://go.adr.org/rs/294-SFS-516/images/AAA269_AAA%20Virtual%20Hearing%20Guide%20for%20Arbitrators%20and%20 Parties%20Utilizing%20Zoom.pdf (last visited Jun. 2024); *AAA-ICDR® Virtual Hearing Guide for Arbitrators and Parties*, Am. Arb. Ass'n (May 9, 2020), https://go.adr.org/rs/294-SFS-516/images/AAA268_AAA%20Virtual%20Hearing%20Guide%20for%20Arbitrators%20and%20Parties.pdf (last visited Jun. 2024); *Resolve Your Dispute at JAMS via Videoconference or Conference Call*, JAMS (Feb. 2023), https://www.jamsadr.com/files/uploads/documents/jams-videoconference-guide.pdf (last visited Jun. 2024); *Virtual ADR–Frequently Asked Questions [FAQ]*, JAMS, https://www.jamsadr.com/faq-virtual-adr (last visited Jun. 2024); *Tips and Techniques for a Successful Videoconference*, JAMS, https://www.jamsadr.com/files/uploads/documents/jams-virtual-adr-tips.pdf (last visited Jun. 2024).

## 10.5.2 Selecting an Online Arbitration Service

### 10.5.2.1 Initial Considerations

Online dispute resolution eliminates location as a factor in choosing an arbitration service. Parties can choose any ODR service provider worldwide based on, among other criteria, reputation for high-quality service, reputation for high-quality justice, website confidentiality features, specialty in processing specific types of disputes, competence and impartiality of neutrals, availability of binding and nonbinding process alternatives, speed of resolution process, satisfaction of foreign language needs, and effective enforcement mechanisms.

When discussing the selection of an online arbitration service with your client, address whether binding online arbitration is the only appropriate process to resolve their dispute. Nonbinding, online arbitration may be a better choice, or an online negotiation or online mediation service might adequately satisfy their needs and cost less than proceeding directly to the more formal and time-consuming binding online arbitration process. Alternatively, you might really need online arbitration, but want to preserve the option of a consensual dispute resolution process. Such situations call for selecting a service provider that offers adjudication (online arbitration) and consensual dispute resolution (online mediation or online facilitated negotiation).[15]

We suggest the following criteria for selecting an arbitration ODR service. The provider should, at a minimum:

1) provide an adequate means for parties and their counsel to select a neutral third party;
2) allow parties to be represented by counsel;
3) provide parties an opportunity to receive notice and a statement of reasons giving rise to the dispute, and an opportunity to respond;
4) make the ADR process as accessible and convenient as possible for the parties, at a reasonable cost;
5) ensure that ODR communications are confidentially maintained;
6) provide adequate expertise or instruction to assist the parties, technologically, in the use of the online dispute resolution services;
7) ensure that neutrals permit the parties and counsel to voice their views and needs fully;
8) ensure that neutrals accord standing to the parties and counsel by treating them with politeness, dignity, and respect;

---

15. *See generally* Teitz, *supra* note 10; Ponte, *supra* note 7.

9) ensure that neutrals act in an unbiased and impartial manner and with a concern for achieving an accurate understanding of the facts and other relevant information;
10) ensure that the ODR process is reasonably speedy and that the ODR organization has clear operational policies and provides full disclosure of statistics and financial support and links;
11) allow the parties the opportunity to present evidence, including witnesses (via affidavit, deposition transcript, or live testimony), in support of their positions;
12) ensure the parties' right to know opposing evidence;
13) provide the right to cross-examine opposing witnesses when a party requests;
14) keep a record of the evidence presented;
15) render a decision based on and limited to the evidence in the record and the applicable law.

#### 10.5.2.2 ODR Service Providers and Principal Services Offered

The chart in Appendix I identifies organizations that provide online arbitration services as of June 2024.[16] It also states the principal type or types of disputes serviced, the web address, and other descriptive information. Organizations without a secure website are not included.[17]

### *10.5.3 Selecting an Online Arbitrator*

The criteria discussed in section 2.6.3 will help you choose an online arbitration service provider; from there, you will select the individual arbitrator. Two obvious attributes to look for are a candidate's degree of computer literacy and their training or experience in resolving disputes online. Do not be afraid to interview candidates and ask them direct questions about their online dispute resolution experience. Also talk to other counsel that you know who have participated in one or more online arbitrations and obtain their recommendations of effective arbitrators.

---

16. Much of the initial information compiled in Appendix I was derived from Amy J. Schmitz & Janet Martinez, *ODR and Innovation in the United States, in* Online Dispute Resolution: Theory and Practice: A Treatise on Technology and Dispute Resolution, 611 (Mohamed S. Abdel Wahab et al. eds., 2d ed. 2021).
17. For a list that includes unsecure as well as secure websites, see *id.*

# • Chapter Eleven •

## Online Arbitration Walk-Through

This chapter simulates preparing and planning for an online arbitration in a four-party dispute scenario.[1] To take full advantage of this walk-through experience, put yourself in the role of counsel for each of these parties immediately before and during the preliminary hearing and think through the design and planning of the appropriate online arbitration process and communication format procedures. As in traditional arbitration, the preliminary hearing is a critical stage of the online arbitration process; critical decisions are reached by the parties or imposed by the arbitrator concerning the conduct of the evidentiary part of the proceeding. In actuality, the results of the preliminary hearing—particularly in online arbitration—can make or break a party's chances of prevailing on the merits in an online hearing. The advocate's ability to negotiate the appropriate evidentiary and communication procedures or to prevail in their arguments with respect to them significantly impacts the ultimate results in the online arbitration proceeding.

### 11.1 Online Arbitration Walk-Through Scenario

The dispute concerns the construction of a new medical office building in Nita City, Nita, that tenant doctors complain has a faulty air-conditioning system. The building was completed in the last week of August, and the doctors moved in during the first week of September. The owner of the building is withholding a final $1,000,000 payment to the general contractor until the problem is corrected. The four parties to the dispute are the general contractor, Best Contracting Co. ("Best"), a national company headquartered in New York, with local office in Nita City; the heating and cooling subcontractor, PerfecTemp Co. ("PerfecTemp"), located in Milwaukee, Wisconsin, with outside counsel in Milwaukee; the project engineer, Imagineering, Inc. ("Imagineering"), a national engineering firm headquartered in San Diego, California; and Aircon Fabricators Ltd. ("Aircon"), the cooling system manufacturer, a company in Frankfurt, Germany, with international counsel in London, England. PerfecTemp purchased the cooling system from Aircon through a business-to-business internet transaction.

1. This scenario is a timeframe modified version of the one that appears in John W. Cooley, Mediation Advocacy 275–82 (2d ed. 2002).

Because of the importance of solving the problem within a few months' time, the relatively modest dollar amount of the corrective measures that might need to be taken, the geographic distances separating the parties and even counsel to parties, and the prohibitive costs of a live face-to-face meeting, the parties and their lawyers have agreed to engage in online arbitration to avoid extremely costly and time-consuming live arbitration or litigation. Aircon refused online mediation, feeling it needed an arbitrator's decision to defend against claims in the future that it manufactures faulty products. Counsel for the parties have secured the services of an online arbitrator on the panel of CyberSolutions, a full service ODR provider located in Sydney, Australia. The chart below identifies the participants in the online arbitration and their geographic locations. The parties have chosen, as their neutral, the world-famous construction dispute mediator and arbitrator Rodrigo Fairman, who lives in Melbourne, Australia.

### 11.1.1 Online Arbitration Participants and Their Locations

| PARTY | PARTY'S REP. | LOCATION OF PARTY'S REP. | PARTY'S COUNSEL | LOCATION OF PARTY'S COUNSEL |
|---|---|---|---|---|
| BEST | District manager of general contractor | Nita City, Nita | Best's in-house general counsel | New York, New York |
| PERFECTEMP | CEO of heating and cooling installation subcontractor | Milwaukee, Wisconsin | Outside litigation counsel | Milwaukee, Wisconsin |
| IMAGINEERING | President of engineering firm | San Diego, California | Retained local litigation counsel | Nita City, Nita |
| AIRCON | Technical supervisor and sales manager of air-conditioner manufacturer; bilingual | Frankfurt, Germany | International bilingual counsel; mega law firm | London, England |

### 11.1.2 General Information Concerning Construction Dispute

Best completed construction of a two-story (98,000 square feet) medical office building in the Nita City area during the last week of August. The tenants—who are all doctors practicing in various medical specialties—moved in during the first week in September. The first two weeks in September were unusually hot in Nita City. The doctors complained to the building's owner that the building's air-conditioning system was not operating properly. Four doctors reported having to send their office staff home early on four occasions because their office temperatures approached 90 degrees. These four doctors wrote letters to the owner documenting their complaints. The temperature fortunately cooled down during the third week of September and so did the tempers of the doctors. During the next few months, the air conditioning will not be an issue. But the air-conditioning matter must be resolved prior to April, when cooling of the building will be necessary.

After emailing the four letters of complaint to Best's district manager in Nita City in the third week of September, the owner called the district manager and told them to get the air conditioning corrected. The owner told Best that the medical building's director of maintenance had carefully followed the procedures detailed in Aircon's air-conditioner manual in an effort to correct the problem, but to no avail. Best's director of maintenance emailed Aircon's technical supervisor and sales manager in Frankfurt, Germany who informed the director of maintenance that the procedures they followed were correct and that the problem was "definitely not with the air-conditioning equipment." Aircon suggested that the problem was with the ductwork, and that if anyone was at fault, it was either the heating and cooling subcontractor (PerfecTemp), or the project engineer (Imagineering). The director of maintenance emailed each of these companies, and they both denied responsibility, claiming the problem was caused by the other or by the air-conditioner manufacturer, Aircon.

Best's district manager emailed their company's in-house general counsel in New York, who contacted the lawyers for the other three parties to discuss the possibility of online mediation. Because of Aircon's objection to that process, the parties finally agreed to use the online arbitration process. After email back and forth for a few days in the first week of October, they all agreed to use CyberSolutions in Australia as the ODR provider and, specifically, Rodrigo Fairman, a broadly experienced and highly skilled construction online arbitrator and cyber-mediator.

### 11.1.3 Confidential Information for Best, the General Contractor

You are Best's in-house general counsel in New York. You have interviewed Best's Nita City district manager by telephone. The district manager said that when the owner called, they were irate. Many doctors had called the owner, "raising Cain" about the air-conditioning problem. The owner said they wanted the situation corrected immediately. The doctors were demanding 50 percent discounts on their monthly rent payments, and the owner told your district manager that they would have to recoup the value of such discounts from Best. The owner further told your district manager that they were withholding the final $1,000,000 payment owed to Best on the project "until the doctors are happy as larks" with the temperatures of their offices. The owner said they wanted to stay out of it—they didn't want any more expense, like hiring a lawyer or paying for mediation or arbitration. They said it was Best's responsibility to "straighten out this mess."

Best's Nita City district manager further told you that, after they talked to the owner, they immediately telephoned PerfecTemp's CEO and advised them of the situation. The Nita City district manager also reminded PerfecTemp's CEO that, under their contract with Best, they were subject to liquidated damages in the amount of $5,000 a day if their installation of the cooling system was determined faulty. PerfecTemp's CEO got angry. They vigorously asserted that their crews installed the equipment and ductwork according to Imagineering's and Aircon's specifications. They further said that any problems with the air conditioning were not their fault. They said either Imagineering or Aircon or both were to blame.

Best's Nita City district manager told you that they had no idea whether the equipment, the installation, or the engineering was to blame, but they were convinced that this problem had to be solved quickly to minimize any costs to Best.

Finally, Best tells you that it still owes Aircon $480,500 for the medical building cooling system and that it has initiated the purchase of ten other cooling systems for buildings it is constructing around the United States. Also, Best still owes PerfecTemp $200,000 for the installation work on the medical building complex. The cash flow of the Nita City District Office is currently in dire straits pending receipt of final payment from the owner of the Nita City medical building and due to other substantial unpaid receivables.

### 11.1.4 Confidential Information for PerfecTemp, the Installer

You are PerfecTemp's outside litigation counsel in Milwaukee, Wisconsin. You have interviewed the CEO of PerfecTemp in person. Since the CEO's office is in Milwaukee, you see them quite often and know them well. In the interview, they told you the general information appearing above and the following information.

The CEO said that Best's district manager told them in a phone call that, under PerfecTemp's contract with Best, PerfecTemp is subject to liquidated damages in the amount of $5,000 per day if PerfecTemp is found to be responsible for the faulty cooling condition of the building. PerfecTemp's CEO further told you that they vigorously asserted in the phone conversation that PerfecTemp was not at fault here, but that either Imagineering or Aircon were to blame.

PerfecTemp's president also admitted to you that despite what they told Best's district manager on the phone, they in fact did not know whether PerfecTemp may be responsible or partially responsible here. They said that when the building was completed, they tested and balanced the air-conditioning system. It was a relatively cool day—about 70 degrees. They said that they noted in their internal report that even under those mild temperatures, the building took an inordinate amount of time to cool down and that the temperatures fluctuated from floor to floor. In examining some of the exposed ductwork, they noticed that several sections had much smaller dimensions than Imagineering's specifications in the engineering drawings. At the time, they believed this to be inconsequential, and so they did nothing about it. The CEO, however, took pictures of the undersized ductwork.

Finally, PerfecTemp's president told you that Best still owes PerfecTemp $200,000 for the installation work on the medical building complex.

### 11.1.5 Confidential Information for Imagineering, Project Engineer

You are Imagineering's locally retained litigation counsel in Nita City, Nita. Imagineering is headquartered in San Diego, California. You have done some minor litigation work for Imagineering in Nita City in the past, but you have never worked with the president of the company directly. You have interviewed Imagineering's president by telephone recently. In the interview, they told you the general information appearing above and the following information.

Imagineering's president told you that they are taking this complaint very seriously because their company is in the process of doing engineering drawings for approximately ten similar medical buildings around the United States. They also have several engineering contracts in process and about to be executed. They did not want any bad publicity over this Nita City medical building because it might adversely affect their relationships with their present clients and the development of relationships with new clients. They were very happy that this dispute was being kept out of court through online arbitration conducted by someone in Australia. They preferred to use online mediation, but they will accede to using online arbitration to minimize any adverse publicity.

Imagineering's president further told you that the Imagineering engineer that worked on the project originally had since left the company. They said that when they first got word about the air-conditioning problem in the Nita City medical building, they pulled the file on the project and reviewed it.

They said that they noticed something startling. They said that because of a typographical error in an early analysis of the project, an error was made in specifying the appropriate tonnage of the cooling system for the project. This error was carried through to all documents and specifications related to the project. The final specifications called for a 250-ton cooling system, whereas the tonnage specification based on the building size and floor area should have been 280 tons. Luckily, the error was smaller than it could have been, but it certainly does carry with it some professional malpractice implications.

Finally, they told you that luckily, all the other specifications, including the size of the ductwork, were appropriate for the higher tonnage (280-ton) cooling system.

Now we are ready to analyze how this dispute might be processed in an online arbitration. Apart from the advocacy suggestions presented below in the next four sections, you are encouraged to imagine other ways you might handle each situation as counsel for one of the four parties. By agreement of the participants, the manager of CyberSolutions has emailed the contact information to all participants, including email addresses, regular addresses, telephone numbers, fax numbers, and company web addresses.

## 11.2 Designing the Online Arbitration Procedures Through the Vehicle of the Preliminary Hearing

The preliminary hearing is a critical stage of the arbitration process, including for the online arbitration process. While some of the issues covered in a normal preliminary hearing can be addressed in the arbitration agreement itself (either pre- or post-dispute) the relevant procedural issues typically do not fully crystallize until the parties and their counsel have failed to negotiate an early resolution of the dispute. Before that occurs, parties usually do not want to incur substantial legal expense to plan for an arbitration that may become moot through a negotiated settlement.

Use the time immediately before a preliminary hearing and during the preliminary hearing itself as opportunities to design an arbitration process that is efficient, economical, and just. The following matrix shows the configuration of claims that exist as the parties in the walk-through scenario proceed to a preliminary hearing.

### *11.2.1 Claims Matrix*

| COMPLAINANT | RESPONDENT | NATURE OF CLAIMS | REMEDIES SOUGHT |
|---|---|---|---|
| Best | Aircon | Breach of Contract Breach of Warranty | Damages; Substitution of Equipment |
| Best | Imagineering | Professional Negligence<br>Breach of Contract | Damages |
| Best | PerfecTemp | Breach of Contract | Compensatory Damages; Liquidated Damages |

| | | | |
|---|---|---|---|
| Aircon | Best | Breach of Contract | Payment of Amounts Owed $480,500; Consequential Damages |
| PerfecTemp | Best | Breach of Contract | Payment of Amounts Owed $200,000; Consequential Damages |

In the analysis that follows in this section, assume that, by agreement of the parties, you are an approved observer witnessing a preliminary hearing in progress, conducted in a teleconference set up by CyberSolutions in late October. CyberSolutions has voice-to-text software, and the teleconference discussion will be preserved as part of the record in both digital and hard copy form. Some of the parties are watching the discussions of counsel and the arbitrator as nonparticipating observers. Other parties opted not to be on the videoconference because they could review the full text of the discussions later.

In the two weeks prior to the preliminary hearing, the parties have communicated by email, chat rooms, and instant messaging in an effort to lay the ground rules for the online arbitration proceedings. There was no pre-dispute arbitration agreement. They have entered into a bare bones post-dispute agreement to arbitrate and have signed a strict confidentiality agreement. In their recent email discussions, counsel have agreed on some procedural issues and not others. Further negotiations regarding procedures will occur during the preliminary hearing itself, with input from the online arbitrator. Counsel for Best volunteered to consolidate, from counsel's prior online discussions, a summary of the points of agreement and contested points and respective arguments relating to preliminary hearing topics. They emailed this summary to each of the other counsel for approval. After receiving approval from counsel, they emailed a copy of the summary to the arbitrator (with copies to counsel) to be used by the arbitrator and counsel in the preliminary hearing. The summary was prepared in order to minimize time spent in the preliminary hearing sorting the agreed points from the contested ones and arguing respective positions.

Counsel and their clients understand that if counsel cannot agree to certain procedures, the arbitrator will decide the pertinent procedural issues. As you witness the unfolding of this design process, put yourself in the role of each counsel for the parties and of the arbitrator. Consider how you would handle these procedural issues if you were in the shoes of each counsel, and how you would decide these issues—or foster agreement—on them, if you were the arbitrator. Be creative. You may think of much better solutions to the procedural issues than all the counsel and the arbitrator in the case! Good luck.

## *11.2.2 Stages of the Arbitration Process and Communication Formats and Technology*

### 11.2.2.1 All Counsel

CyberSolutions, the ODR provider jointly selected by counsel, has few procedural rules, most of which are protocols relating to confidentiality, privacy, and security of information. This is because CyberSolutions's business philosophy is that the parties, working with counsel, can tailor-make the procedures to fit the dispute. In online discussions, counsel examined the various technologies and communication formats available to them in constructing the appropriate process. Ironically, the variety of communication tools available through CyberSolutions made their task more difficult. The list of communication tools and formats include regular mail, email, telephone, chat rooms, threaded discussions, instant messaging, teleconferencing, and videoconferencing. CyberSolutions also has hybrid forms of these tools, depending on the parties' needs. It is this availability of numerous communication options that makes the preliminary hearing in online arbitration more challenging and lengthier than one held in a traditional, in-person, face-to-face arbitration. The numerous options must each be addressed, and counsel must agree on which to use to resolve the dispute. Finally, counsel agreed that a copy of all pleadings and documents (digital or hard copy, as the arbitrator might direct), would as a matter of course be provided to CyberSolutions's administrator. They have agreed to assume the responsibility to maintain the official record in the case. The following chart shows, in order of increasing expense, the available communication modes, the best situation(s) for use, and some of their respective advantages and disadvantages. The in-person communication mode, which is normally the optimal, but most expensive, mode does not appear in the chart.

### 11.2.2.2 Communication Modes

| COMMUNICATION MODES | | | |
|---|---|---|---|
| **MODE** | **BEST USE** | **ADVANTAGES** | **DISADVANTAGES** |
| Email | For sequential, leisurely written communication where quick reply is not normally needed or expected. | Messages can be broadcast to any number of people simultaneously. | Confidentiality can be easily compromised. |

| | | | |
|---|---|---|---|
| Threaded Discussions | For sequential, leisurely communication in which all the written dialogue of several participants remains on the screen. | By scrolling up, participants can view all dialogue occurring previously on a particular topic. It produces a record of the conversation. | A couple participants may dominate dialogue on minor points while other participants are trying to get them involved in discussing topics more important to the group. |
| Instant Messaging | Provides a private space for real-time written conversation with another individual. | System can alert the two users that they are simultaneously online so they can engage in conversation. | Is there a disadvantage to IMs? Perhaps the difficulty transmitting that information with the other parties? |
| Texting | Provides a way for two or more people to engage in real-time written conversation. | Many people have the function readily available on their smartphones. | The record of a text conversation must be transferred from the smartphone to the electronic case file. |
| Chat Rooms | Provide a private space where several persons may engage in real-time written conversation. | Persons can schedule a chat room meeting at mutually convenient times, accommodating time zones and locations of participants. | Conversations can become sarcastic and hostile, depending on the topic being discussed. Note that this is something that could happen in any format. |

| | | | |
|---|---|---|---|
| Regular Mail or Traceable Carrier | Provides an alternative to digitally sent written materials, where addressees do not have the necessary or adequate equipment to send or receive the material by electronic means. | Addressees are more likely to receive accurate duplicates of original hard-copy pages. Objects may be sent by mail, which is not possible using the internet. | Mail may be delayed in arriving at its destination, or it may get lost. International mailing takes extra time. There may be customs problems. Cost of mailing may be prohibitive. |
| Teleconference | For use when it is more efficient for people to talk orally with one another. | It allows full exploration of topics by a limited number of participants in a relatively short period of time when they are prepared by reading pre-conference material. It facilitates and accelerates decision-making. | It is often difficult to know who the speaker is during the conversation. The number of participants in a teleconference is limited by practical considerations of complexity of interactions, time, and expense. |
| Videoconference | For use when it is important that several participants at different sites interact electronically with each other visually and auditorily; useful for meetings and for depositions where seeing and hearing the testifying witness is important. | The videoconference most closely imitates face-to-face communication between any number of participants. | Internet connection problems can disrupt videoconferences. |

### 11.2.3 Civility and Professionalism

In their email discussions prior to the preliminary hearing, Best's counsel wrote first and suggested that all counsel and parties deal with one another civilly and professionally. They cautioned against allowing email conversations or chat room or telephone discussions to careen out of control into fields of hostility and personal attack. They said that they had been involved in several other online arbitrations in which this occurred, and it led to continuing animosity, distrust, and an unnecessarily extended process. They suggested that counsel, up front in the preliminary hearing, jointly tell the online arbitrator, Rodrigo Fairman, that they intended to proceed with an attitude of mutual professional respect and consideration. They thought that would get them off to a good start before the arbitrator. The other counsel agreed to communicate similar intentions to Fairman at the beginning of the preliminary hearing, which they did.

### 11.2.4 Applicable Rules and Law Governing the Procedure in the Arbitration; Law Applicable to Claims

Counsel could not agree on this topic, except to agree that their respective positions would be argued to the online arbitrator in the preliminary hearing and that the rules of any jurisdiction would not apply strictly. Hearsay would be admissible in the online arbitration proceedings, subject to counsel's arguments of nonrelevance, substantial unreliability, and/or substantial prejudice. Since there was no pre-dispute arbitration agreement, the issues of the applicable procedural and evidentiary rules (for guidance) and the law governing the procedure and the award are wide open.

#### 11.2.4.1 As Counsel for Best

In the teleconference at the preliminary hearing, Best argues that Nita's rules and laws relating to arbitration procedure, evidence (for guidance), the parties' claims, and the award should govern the online arbitration proceedings. They premise their argument on the facts that the building and the allegedly defective product is in that state, practically all the significant events are clustered there, and if Best filed a lawsuit against these parties, it would naturally file it in the Circuit Court of Darrow County, in Nita.

#### 11.2.4.2 As Counsel for Aircon

Aircon sees the applicable rules and law issues quite differently. Aircon argues at the preliminary hearing that this is not a simple, interstate dispute. It is an international dispute and, accordingly, international rules and law should apply. They point out that they could easily file an action for declaratory judgment in the court in Frankfurt, Germany, where Aircon is headquartered. They assert that the rules of an international arbitration firm, such as the Chartered Institute of Arbitrators or the American Arbitration Association, should govern the procedural rules and that the laws of Germany should govern issues related to the claims between Best and Aircon and the award. If they were allowed to prevail on these issues, they would agree to using the Federal Rules of Evidence guidance, if necessary, on evidentiary questions.

#### 11.2.4.3 As Counsel for Imagineering

A primary concern of Imagineering is the integrity and security of the arbitration process. It wants to avoid any possibility of information leaks that could damage its professional reputation in the business world. California, where Imagineering is located, has very strict rules relating to confidentiality of the arbitration process and competence of arbitrators, so Imagineering argues in favor of having California arbitration rules apply. It would agree to applying Nita law to issues relating to the claims and the award. It would not object to having the Federal Rules of Evidence be used for guidance if significant evidentiary questions arise.

#### 11.2.4.4 As Counsel for PerfecTemp

In the view of PerfecTemp, Best's position makes the most sense. Besides, PerfecTemp wants more business from Best in the future, so they don't want to aggravate Best over an issue that is inconsequential. They have compared Nita and Wisconsin law and those states' respective arbitration rules and have not detected any material differences.

#### 11.2.4.5 Arbitrator Fairman

After reading their pre-filed summary and hearing counsel's arguments during the preliminary hearing, Fairman rules as follows:

> The AAA International Arbitration Rules shall apply, as modified by the agreement of the parties or the rulings of the arbitrator where no clear guidance is contained in those rules. Furthermore, the Federal Rules of Evidence shall be used as guidance, when necessary, on evidentiary questions, and the law of the State of Nita shall govern all issues related to the parties' claims and to the entry and/or enforcement of the award. For purposes of the award, the State of Nita is the site of the arbitration.

### *11.2.5 Ability to Arbitrate All Issues*

Counsel agreed in their email discussions that all issues related to the present factual circumstances involving all four parties would be arbitrable. Counsel for

PerfecTemp wanted to arbitrate, in the present arbitration, an outstanding bill that Best had refused to pay from another building project. Best agreed in email correspondence to mediate that matter separately after the present arbitration is completed and after the time for objecting to or appealing the award has expired. PerfecTemp acquiesced in Best's suggestion for a later mediation of the other dispute.

## *11.2.6 Discovery*

### 11.2.6.1 All Counsel

In their email discussions, counsel had very different ideas about the quantity and the type of discovery that should be undertaken, and the communication mode(s) that should be used. The only item that they could agree to was that the question of experts and expert testimony would be discussed separately from document and fact witness depositions.

### 11.2.6.2 As Counsel for Best

At the preliminary hearing, Best takes the position that document requests should be exchanged by November 7 and that documents should be produced or email objections sent to CyberSolutions by November 21. Best thinks that documents could be sent by traceable carrier in hard copy form with two-day delivery directions. Best wants to depose PerfecTemp's CEO (who inspected the ductwork), Imagineering's president (who reviewed and approved the cooling system specifications), and Aircon's chief design engineer (who was very familiar with all aspects of the cooling system in question). Best thinks that these depositions could be in the form of written interrogatories, with the deponents providing written responses under oath. Best further thinks that this should be accomplished in a hard-copy format by overnight mail sent through a traceable carrier. Best suggests that the questions be served on the deponents and counsel by November 14 and the responses should be received by Best by November 28.

### 11.2.6.3 As Counsel for Aircon

Counsel for Aircon points out that arbitration "discovery" does not exist in Germany, where Aircon is headquartered. In Germany, applications can be made to a court before or during a pending arbitration for the court to undertake a judicial inspection, question witnesses, or take expert evidence. Aircon's counsel acknowledges that such procedure would not be appropriate here. Instead, they argue that relevant documents should be produced by all counsel immediately in digital form. Documents not in digital form should be scanned and produced in digital form. Confidentially, Aircon believes it has nothing to hide. Complaints from customers in Brazil and Italy have not been fully resolved, but they should be resolved within the next couple of weeks. Besides, Aircon has letters from purchasers of the cooling system from all over the world praising the functioning of the system. Aircon strongly believes that its cooling system is not defective, and it wants to prove that fact as soon as possible. It has numerous purchase orders for the cooling system pending worldwide (ten have been ordered by Best alone). Aircon further argues that no depositions of fact witnesses are necessary. It strongly opposes any request by a party to depose Aircon's chief design engineer. They speak German only and securing their testimony (indeed their cooperation) would be very difficult. They are very proud of their products and a deposition would be viewed as an insult.

#### 11.2.6.4 As Counsel for Imagineering

The president of Imagineering wants to get this arbitration over quickly. Imagineering believes that no formal discovery requests need to be made, and it says so at the preliminary hearing. Counsel for the parties, it argues, should cooperate and turn over the relevant documents. Imagineering privately believes that the documents containing the typographical error, buried in the mound of plans and drawings, might be overlooked by the other counsel, or "lost in the shuffle." At the preliminary hearing, Imagineering takes the position that no depositions should be taken. It does this in part to shield its president from being deposed and having to admit to errors in tonnage specifications.

#### 11.2.6.5 As Counsel for PerfecTemp

PerfecTemp insists that discovery be limited to document exchange in hard-copy form, through a traceable carrier guaranteeing two-day delivery. PerfecTemp could live with Best's proposed document production schedule. PerfecTemp believes that no depositions need to be taken. In its view, they are a waste of time and money because the parties would have to live through the testimony a second time when they went before the online arbitrator at the hearing. PerfecTemp wants to keep the costs of the online arbitration as low as possible. In comparison to the other parties, PerfecTemp is a very small company with limited cash flow. It could not justify spending much money on this case, considering that it only had a $200,000 claim.

#### 11.2.6.6 Arbitrator Fairman

After reviewing counsel's arguments in the summary and hearing the points they made in the teleconference, Fairman states that it is their goal to rule as fairly as possible on these discovery issues, while taking into account the economical, technological, and efficiency concerns of the parties. They say that they have to balance the parties' desire to obtain a speedy resolution of this dispute with realistic predictions of time and work required for them to accomplish the quantity and quality of discovery to enable them to adequately present their cases. They then rule as follows:

1) Counsel will email (with copies to all) their document requests by November 7.

2) Counsel will respond to the document requests, by either producing responsive documents or submitting objections to the requests (with reasons) by November 21. Any responses to the objections will be emailed to all by December 1. Documents will be produced in electronic form via a secure file share system maintained by the dispute resolution organization. Every document produced will have an identifying number stamped on each page. Technology, such as Adobe, quickly and easily Bates stamps electronic documents.

3) The arbitrator will rule on all document objections by December 8.

4) A maximum of four fact witness depositions will be taken in this case. Each of the four parties in this dispute has the option to depose one fact witness. By December 8, counsel shall advise each other of their desire to take a deposition, and the identity of the person to be deposed. If one or more counsel decide not to take a deposition, their deposition opportunity will pass to the remaining counsel who have opted to take a deposition. If three counsel opt to take a deposition and one does not, the three counsel shall determine whether any of them want to take an additional deposition. If two or three of them do want to take another deposition, they will determine, by lot, who will have the right to choose a second fact witness deponent. If two counsel opt to take a deposition, and two counsel do not, each of the two counsel opting to take depositions will have the option to take an additional deposition. If one those two deposing counsel does not want to take an additional deposition, the other deposing counsel has an option to take a third deposition.

5) All depositions will be taken by videoconference set up by CyberSolutions. Each deposition will be limited to two hours. The counsel who seeks to depose the fact witness will be limited to one hour of questioning. Counsel may reserve part of their one-hour limit to question the witness after the other three counsel have their opportunity to examine the witness. Each of the other three counsel will be entitled to question the witness for twenty minutes.

6) CyberSolutions will record the videoconferences and provide the arbitrator with a copy of the videorecording as soon as possible after each deposition. Deponents will testify under oath during the videoconferences, and their testimony there will serve as their testimony at the hearing on the merits of this matter.

7) All depositions will be noticed and taken by January 15 of next year. Any counsel who, without good cause, fails to notice and take a deposition by that date will forfeit the right to take the deposition.
8) If necessary, the arbitrator may schedule a chat room session or a teleconference with counsel and a fact witness or witnesses so that the arbitrator can ask them additional questions.

### *11.2.7 Prehearing Motions, Pleading Amendments, and Briefing Schedules*

In their email discussions prior to the preliminary hearing, counsel agreed that there would be no formal prehearing written motions, related briefing, or amendments to pleadings. All prehearing requests would be made in the preliminary hearing teleconference.

### *11.2.8 Addition or Joinder of Parties*

In their prehearing discussion, the parties agreed that all the necessary parties were participating in the online arbitration.

### *11.2.9 Witness Lists; Experts; Expert Reports; Subpoenas*

#### 11.2.9.1 All Counsel

In their email discussions, counsel agreed that, except for Aircon's chief design engineer, all fact witnesses will cooperate and make themselves available to testify, rendering subpoenas unnecessary. If the chief design engineer is noticed for deposition and they object, the noticing counsel will move for a ruling of the arbitrator and the issuance of a subpoena. Counsel also agreed that their combined witness list would be composed of the person(s) who were deposed in prehearing discovery. They disagreed, however, on several matters relating to experts.

#### 11.2.9.2 As Counsel for Best

Counsel for Best wants to call two experts of their choice—experts that they have used in other construction-related cases. One is an expert in the technical aspects of manufacturing cooling systems; the other is an expert in the installation of cooling systems. Both reside and work in Nita City. They are willing to produce their reports a week before their depositions. They prefer that the depositions be taken in a chat room session.

#### 11.2.9.3 As Counsel for Aircon

Counsel for Aircon wants to call one expert of their choice—an English-speaking German professor of engineering reputed to be the foremost expert in the world in the technical aspects of cooling systems. They had used this expert in several cases around the world in the last two years. Aircon thinks that the deposition of this expert should be taken by videoconference. Counsel for Aircon would produce the expert's report three days before this deposition.

#### 11.2.9.4 As Counsel for PerfecTemp

Focusing on the additional costs of having experts testify and noting that counsel would have to be present for several depositions of experts, PerfecTemp takes the position that no expert testimony is necessary in the case. PerfecTemp believes that this case can be decided based on the documents and any fact witness testimony presented by counsel for the parties.

#### 11.2.9.5 As Counsel for Imagineering

Counsel for Imagineering also takes the position that no expert is needed in this case. Confidentially, it is paranoid that an expert going through the documents may notice the typographical errors in the tonnage requirements.

#### 11.2.9.6 Arbitrator Fairman

Making it clear that they are trying to minimize the costs of the arbitration and referring to Article 22 of the AAA International Arbitration Rules, Fairman rules that they will appoint an independent expert to report in writing to the arbitrator. Fairman will distribute the report to counsel by email attachment. CyberSolutions will provide counsel with a list of five experts (together with their curriculum vitae), located geographically near Nita City, each of whom are combined experts in cooling system technology, specifications, and installation. Counsel will have seven days to strike any expert or experts from the list. If no expert on the list survives this process of elimination, CyberSolutions will provide counsel with another list, until counsel can agree on one expert. Counsel will provide the selected expert with pertinent documentation. CyberSolutions will also instruct the expert to visit the site prior to their deposition. CyberSolutions will schedule a videoconference deposition of the expert at a time convenient to all counsel during the period January 15 to January 30 of next year. The deposition will be limited to two hours and counsel will each have thirty minutes to ask the expert questions. CyberSolutions will record the videoconference and provide the recording to the arbitrator as soon as possible after the deposition. If necessary, the arbitrator may schedule a chat room session or teleconference with counsel and the expert so that the arbitrator can ask additional questions of the expert.

### 11.2.10 Observers and Other Attendees

In their email sessions, counsel for Best said that the owner of the building expressed an interest in being present for some of the chat room, teleconference, or videoconference sessions. Counsel agreed that they would email each other with the names and relationship to the dispute subject of any persons they are requesting to be present at such sessions. They stipulated that approved observers would have to sign a confidentiality agreement.

### 11.2.11 Hearing Exhibits and Fact Stipulations

In their email session, counsel agreed that the hearing exhibits would consist of all the documents produced in discovery, with their pages appropriately stamped with identifying numbers. They also agreed that they could come up with an agreed statement of the background facts before any formal hearing or arguments before the arbitrator.

### 11.2.12 Order of Presenting Evidence

In their email session, counsel agreed to the following order of the presentation of evidence or of their final arguments to the arbitrator. Best will present first, with Aircon, PerfecTemp, and Imagineering following in sequence. Best will have an opportunity to reply to all three presentations in a combined presentation. They agreed that an email closing argument with a subsequent teleconference session with the arbitrator might be the best format. If documents are referenced in the email closing argument, they will be identified by stamped page numbers. This gives counsel leeway to emphasize certain aspects of their closing and allows the arbitrator to ask questions of counsel.

### 11.2.13 Sequestration of Witnesses

In their email session, counsel agreed that all nonparty witnesses would not participate in any chat room sessions, teleconferences, or videoconference, except those in which they were testifying. Party witnesses, of course, could be present in the cyberspace sessions at any time.

### 11.2.14 Burden and Standard of Proof

In their email discussions, counsel agreed that the complainant or the counterclaimant would have the burden of proof, and the applicable standard of proof would be "preponderance of the evidence." Imagineering had requested the more stringent "clear and convincing" standard of proof for the professional negligence claim but had no legal support for requesting it. Eventually, Imagineering acquiesced to a preponderance of evidence standard for all claims.

### 11.2.15 Position Statements or Prehearing Briefs

In their email discussions and subject to the arbitrator's approval, counsel would present closing arguments only in writing by email attachments.

Those closing arguments would contain references to documents and pages of documents by stamped page number. The testimony of witnesses would be referenced by identifying the page or pages of the digital recording made from the videoconference. As a practical matter, the arbitrator would review the closing arguments and related evidence prior to their final teleconference, when counsel would be available to answer the arbitrator's questions.

### 11.2.16 Stenographer and Interpreter

In their email discussions, counsel agreed that no stenographer or interpreter was necessary. The only exception concerning an interpreter would be if Aircon's chief design engineer were to be deposed.

### 11.2.17 Interpreters and Accommodations

In their email discussions, counsel for Best pointed out that their client was deaf in one ear. That, they said, should be taken into account if they were to be deposed orally in the online arbitration proceedings. No other counsel had issues that would require interpreters or accommodations.

### 11.2.18 Scheduling of Hearing; Length of Proceedings

In their email and chat room discussions, counsel agreed that the final hearing in the matter (the closing arguments) should occur in the last week of February of next year. This would allow time for all the depositions—fact witnesses and the expert—to be viewed by the arbitrator; it would also allow counsel enough time to prepare their email closing arguments.

### 11.2.19. Final Oral Arguments; Post-Hearing Proposed Findings and Conclusions

In their email and chat room discussions, counsel agreed that their final oral arguments would be preceded by email attachments, properly citing the record, sent to the arbitrator and to each other. There would be no post-hearing proposed findings and conclusions. They also agreed that their final oral argument would be by teleconference, and each counsel would be allotted twenty minutes, with the arbitrator being allotted whatever time necessary to ask questions of counsel.

## *11.2.20 Nature and Form of Award*

### 11.2.20.1 As Counsel for Best

Counsel for Best wants an award with a reasoned opinion so that there will be no question as to which party or parties are liable and why.

### 11.2.20.2 As Counsel for Aircon

Counsel for Aircon wants an award and a reasoned opinion because they want an opportunity, if necessary, to ask the arbitrator to reconsider their conclusions.

### 11.2.20.3 As Counsel for Imagineering

Counsel for Imagineering wants no reasoned opinion. The less the better, if the company is found to be negligent.

### 11.2.20.4 As Counsel for PerfecTemp

PerfecTemp wants no reasoned opinion because that would mean that PerfecTemp would have more expenses—the arbitrator's additional fees.

### 11.2.20.5 Arbitrator Fairman

The arbitrator rules that a brief supporting opinion will accompany the award.

## *11.2.21 Appeal Procedures and Enforcement of the Award*

In their email and chat room discussions, counsel agreed that the arbitrator's decision would be final, and that there would be no pre-planned appeal process.

Of course, in the unlikely event a party had grounds, it could challenge the award as the law allowed in the jurisdiction which the arbitrator designated to be the site of the arbitration for purposes of the award. They also agreed in writing to abide by the arbitrator's award and to subject themselves to the laws of the State of Nita regarding the enforcement of judgments entered on arbitration awards.

## *11.2.22 Pre-Arbitration Mediation*

Because one of the parties objected to pre-arbitration mediation, counsel agreed that none would take place.

## *11.2.23 Additional Preliminary Hearings*

In their email and chat room discussions, counsel agreed that there would be no additional preliminary hearings, except on motion by counsel.

### *11.2.24 Prohibition Against Ex Parte Communication with Arbitrator*

In their email and chat room discussions, counsel agreed not to engage in ex parte communication with the arbitrator.

At the conclusion of the telephonic preliminary hearing, counsel for Best volunteered to draft a ruling incorporating counsel's agreements and the arbitrator's rulings on the preliminary hearing topics. They agreed to email the draft ruling to counsel for their suggestions and approval prior to emailing it to the arbitrator for signing and issuance.

# EPILOGUE

You have learned the skills to represent a client in arbitration from start to finish. You are ready to handle at least a relatively straightforward dispute, and perhaps a complex one, depending on the depth of your already-existing skills in litigation, trial, and administrative processes and hearings. Whatever level you are at, you now have more arbitration advocacy skills than most entry-level, and many other, attorneys.

# Appendices

# CONTENTS

# • APPENDIX A •

## ARBITRATION FORUM AND PANEL SELECTION CHECKLIST

1) Choosing the appropriate arbitration forum
   - — Court-annexed arbitration programs
   - — State or local government arbitration programs
   - — Bar association arbitration programs
   - — Nonprofit ADR organizations
   - — Private for-profit ADR organizations

2) Deciding on the number of arbitrators
   - — Single arbitrator
   - — Three arbitrators
   - — Other

3) Choosing individuals to serve as arbitrators
   - — What is the nature of the dispute?
     - — Area of law requiring special arbitrator knowledge or experience
     - — Technical or scientific subject requiring special arbitrator knowledge or experience
     - — Mostly factual issues
     - — Mostly legal issues
     - — Mixed factual and legal issues
   - — Considering the type of dispute and the nature of the parties, what status of arbitrator would be appropriate?
     - — Former judge

    — Attorney
    — Nonattorney
    — Academic
    — Business expert
    — Technical expert
    — Financial expert
    — Scientific expert
    — Other

— Does the arbitrator you are considering possess the most important basic qualities of a good arbitrator?

    — Honesty, integrity, ethical standards
    — Impartiality, neutrality, confidentiality
    — Patience
    — Flexibility
    — Open-mindedness
    — Ability to control proceedings
    — Good listening and communication skills
    — Appropriate sense of humor
    — Respect for lawyers and clients
    — Good judgment

— Does the arbitrator possess the necessary training and experience to decide this dispute?

    — Training in arbitration
    — Certified as an arbitrator by a court system or dispute resolution organization
    — Conducts training in arbitration
    — Substantial arbitration experience appropriate to the present dispute
    — Candidate has been appointed by the court as an arbitrator or special master in the past
    — Sufficient litigation experience, if required

- — Candidate will provide lawyer references from prior arbitrations they have conducted
- — Is listed on the panels of one or more dispute resolution organizations
- — Has a reputation for professional excellence among dispute resolution practitioners
- — Member or officer in local or national professional associations

— Can the arbitrator satisfy the practical needs of the parties?

- — Affordable fees: hourly, daily, by sessions
- — Policy on fees if hearing is canceled or postponed
- — Willing to conduct preliminary hearings if parties believe it necessary
- — Willing to travel to provide arbitration services
- — Fees charged for travel time
- — Types of expenses
- — Provide, schedule, or suggest facilities where the arbitration can be held
- — Available to serve as arbitrator for the number of sessions and at the times the parties and their counsel are available

# • APPENDIX B •

## DRAFTING THE PLEADING; PRELIMINARY HEARING CHECKLIST

1) Drafting Arbitration Demands

- — Timing
    - — Time period specified in the arbitration clause
    - — Statute of limitations applying to any claims
    - — Court rule time limit
- — Requirements of arbitration clause
    - — Does the nature of the dispute fall within the arbitration clause?
    - — Does the arbitration clause provide for a specific arbitrator or arbitration association?
- — Claims
    - — Names of all parties involved
    - — Chronological statement of the facts
    - — Arbitration clause quoted directly, or a copy of the clause attached
    - — Specific statement of the dispute
    - — Detailed synopsis of the relief sought
    - — Signed by claimant or counsel
- — Filing
    - — What do the dispute resolution organization's rules require?
    - — Service by certified or registered mail
    - — Filing fee or administrative fee included

2) Drafting the Response to the Demand

— Drafting the answer

— Include a general denial of the claim

— Include a protest of the relief sought

— Describe the facts of your side of the matter, and support any legal conclusions with proper authority

— If desired, include general, unspecific affirmative defenses

— If desired, request a specific place for the hearing

— Sign the answer

— Drafting counterclaims

— File at the same time as the response

— Include the same elements required in a demand

— Pay the appropriate fee requirements (same as a demand)

— Serve the counterclaim in the same manner as you would a demand

— Drafting motions and responses

— Always present a dispositive motion or a motion seeking fundamental relief in writing

— Give the factual background of the request for relief

— Specify the relief requested in simple terms

— Give the legal basis for the relief requested (rules, statutes, case law)

— State why your client needs the specific relief

— Evaluate your strategy before filing any motion or response to make sure it won't do more harm than good

— Send a copy of your motion to opposing counsel

3) Drafting Position Statements

*Claimant*:

— A caption containing the names of the claimant(s), respondent(s), and the case number, if applicable

— The date of the cause of action

— A brief summary of the facts of the case

— A statement of the issues presented for arbitration

— An argument stating your position supported by a few important citations to case law and any applicable statutes

— Your name, address, and telephone number

*Respondent*:

— A caption containing the names of the claimant(s), respondent(s), and the case number, if applicable

— A restatement of the facts if your knowledge of the facts is different from claimant's

— If responding to claimant's position statement, a direct reply to each of claimant's arguments, supported by case law and applicable statutes. This part of your brief should distinguish claimant's cases and cite cases favorable to your position.

— Your name, address, and telephone number

4) Preliminary Hearing

— Cover all pertinent topics with parties and counsel

— Expectation of civility and professionalism

— Applicable rules and governing law

— Arbitrability of all issues

— Discovery

— Prehearing motions and briefing schedules

— Amended pleadings

— Addition or joinder of parties

— Witness lists

— Observers and other attendees

— Hearing exhibits

— Fact stipulations

— Order of evidence

— Sequestration of witnesses

— Burden and standard of proof

— Position statements or prehearing briefs
— Stenographer
— Interpreters for people who speak different languages, including sign language
— Accommodations for attendees who may need them
— Hearing date
— Place of hearing; arrangement of hearing room
— Length of hearing
— Subpoenas
— Prohibition against ex parte communications
— Site inspections
— Audiovisual aids
— Experts
— Need for final oral arguments; post-hearing briefs
— Nature and form of award
— Any appeal procedures
— Pre-arbitration mediation
— Additional preliminary hearings

— Considering procedural alternatives

— Videotaped or telephone testimony
— Bifurcation
— Consolidation of claims
— Phasing the arbitration
— Class action procedure

# • Appendix C •

## Case Evaluation Matrix

| Claim or Defense #1: ____________ | | | |
|---|---|---|---|
| **Essential Elements or Factors** | **Evidentiary Facts** | **Source** | **Probative Value** |
| | | | |
| | | | |
| | | | |
| | | | |
| | | | |
| | | | |

| Claim or Defense #2: ____________ | | | |
|---|---|---|---|
| **Essential Elements or Factors** | **Evidentiary Facts** | **Source** | **Probative Value** |
| | | | |
| | | | |
| | | | |
| | | | |
| | | | |
| | | | |

To use the matrix, begin by listing each claim or defense that you will need to prove or disprove as a separate chart with four columns. In the first column, Essential Elements or Factors, list every element or factor that you or the opposing attorney must prove. Place each element or factor in a separate row. These requirements may be found in the substantive law or the applicable contract.

If you must prove the claim or defense, then identify for each element or factor listed in the column Evidentiary Facts, in the row next to each element or factor, the precise evidence from a witness, document, or real evidence you will use to prove each element or factor. You should list multiple pieces of evidence whenever available. If you must disprove only one element or prove only some factors (generally as a respondent demonstrating claimant failed to meet their burden of proof), for every element or factor you have evidence to address, identify the evidence in the column Evidentiary Facts in the same row as the element or factor it addresses.

For each piece of evidence you list, list in the same row in the third column, Source, the source of the evidence. The source should be the particular witness, document, or other evidence that will testify to or that contains the evidentiary fact.

Finally, in the fourth column, Probative Value, assess the relative weight of each evidentiary fact. Is it direct testimony but the witness is not very credible? Or is it circumstantial evidence but all parties agree and will stipulate to the document's authenticity?

# • APPENDIX D •

## CLIENT, WITNESS, AND EXHIBIT PREPARATION CHECKLIST

1) Client Preparation Checklist

   __ Explain the arbitration process

   __ Make your client feel at ease

   __ Explain how to testify

   __ Take client through a direct examination

   __ Subject client to realistic cross-examination

   __ Encourage client to divulge both good and bad information

   __ Avoid being critical about client's role in the events giving rise to dispute

   __ Ensure client(s) (and witnesses) have identical perceptions of exhibits

   __ Warn client to avoid inappropriate body language

   __ Advise client as to proper attire for hearing

   __ Advise client of the date, time, and place of hearing

2) Witness Preparation Checklist

   — Cover same points with witness as with client. In addition

      — Ensure you are aware of any prior relevant testimony or written statements of witness

      — Warn nonclient witnesses regarding possible inquiry into witness preparation

3) The Dos and Don'ts of Testifying

   — The dos of testifying

  - — Do tell the truth
  - — Do listen carefully to each question
  - — Do ask for clarification if you don't understand a question
  - — Do take your time when answering questions
  - — Do allow the questioner to finish the question before answering
  - — Do testify politely—refrain from being hostile, defensive, or humorous
  - — Do speak clearly, distinctly, and confidently when answering questions
  - — Do look the questioner squarely in the eye when responding
  - — Do be cautious of friendly cross-examiners
  - — Do keep your answers brief

- — The don'ts of testifying
  - — Don't answer a question on cross-examination until the arbitrator rules on your counsel's objection to it
  - — Don't let the other side "bully" you into giving answers that you don't believe are true
  - — Don't give memorized answers or read answers from notes—this will look rehearsed and will not have as much credibility as natural, spontaneous answers
  - — Don't be afraid to clarify any statements you make or correct any mistakes in your testimony
  - — Don't volunteer any information on cross-examination—don't elaborate
  - — Don't be afraid to answer "I don't know" or "I don't remember" if you don't know the answer to a question
  - — Don't try to impress the arbitrator or opposing counsel with a large vocabulary
  - — Don't limit your later memory of events. Don't say "That's all that happened" or "No one said anything more"
  - — Don't be inconsistent. During cross-examination, don't try to improve on the story you told on direct examination
  - — Don't testify about what you heard from someone else or about information which you cannot personally verify

4) Exhibit Preparation Checklist

— Demonstrative exhibits

— Photographs

— Physical exhibits

— Anticipate opponent's exhibits

# • APPENDIX E •

## ARBITRATION HEARING CHECKLIST

1) Procedural Rules
   - — Rules to apply to proceeding
   - — Are statements to be taken under oath?
   - — Is evidence by affidavit admissible?
   - — Rules regarding decision and award

2) Opening Statement
   - — Oral/written
   - — Introduction and summary
   - — Presentation of facts
     - — Be brief
     - — Apply principles of primacy and recency
     - — Tie evidence to legal issues
     - — Put puzzle together
     - — Focus on operative facts
     - — Emphasize undisputed evidence
     - — Discard tangential facts
     - — Deal with bad facts minimally
   - — Brief statement of law
   - — Comments on opposition's case
     - — Anticipate the respondent's opening, if you're the claimant
     - — Comment on claimant's opening if you're the respondent

    — Avoid being personally derisive
    — Avoid addressing opponent's case in detail
- — Summary and request for relief
- — Objections and responses during the opening statement
- — Improper argument
- — Personal knowledge of facts
- — Raising issues or matters outside the pleadings
- — Discussing excluded evidence
- — Comments demeaning client or witnesses

3) Direct Examination

- — Goals
    - — Introduce undisputed facts
    - — Enhance likelihood of disputed facts
    - — Lay foundations for introduction of exhibits
    - — Reflect upon the credibility of witnesses
    - — Hold attention of the arbitrator
- — Basic rules governing direct examination
    - — Witnesses must be legally competent
    - — Use nonleading questions
    - — Avoid questions eliciting narrative testimony
    - — Avoid opinion testimony from lay witnesses, with narrow exceptions
    - — Recollection may be refreshed by document or a leading question
- — Questioning technique
    - — Use short, open questions
    - — Use directive and transitional questions
    - — Reinitiate primacy

4) Cross-Examination

- — Basic rules governing cross-examination

- — Leading questions permitted
- — Limit to scope of direct examination
- — Avoid argumentative questions
- — Avoid intimidating behavior
- — Avoid unfair characterizations
- — Do not assume facts not in evidence
- — Avoid asking compound or other defective questions

— Purposes of cross-examination

- — Repair or minimize damage
- — Enhance your case
- — Detract from their case
- — Establish foundation
- — Discredit direct testimony
- — Discredit witness
- — Reflect on credibility of another

— Organization of cross-examination

- — No need to start strong
- — Use topical organization
- — Give details first
- — Scatter inferential or circumstantial evidence
- — Save a zinger for the end

— A classic format for cross-examination

- — Friendly information
- — Affirmative information
- — Incontrovertible information
- — Challenging information
- — Hostile information
- — Zinger

— Questioning Technique

— Use short, leading, propositional questions

— Use questions that achieve control

 — Use incremental questions

 — Use sequenced questions for impact

 — Use sequenced questions for indirection

 — Use sequenced questions for commitment

 — Create a "conceptual corral"

 — Avoid ultimate questions

 — Listen to the witness and insist on an answer

— Avoid questions that lose control

 — Avoid nonleading questions

— Avoid "why" questions

— Avoid "fishing" questions

— Avoid long questions

— Avoid "gap" questions

— Avoid "you testified" questions

— Avoid characterization questions

5) Impeachment

— Tactical considerations

 — Impeach witness only on significant matters

 — Impeach only on true inconsistencies

 — Impeach only when success is likely

 — Do not impeach favorable information

 — Consider "rule of completeness"

 — Consider refreshing witness's recollection

— Procedure for impeaching a witness with a prior inconsistent statement

 — Recommit witness

 — Validate prior statement

- — Confront witness with prior statement
- — Impeachment with other prior inconsistencies
  - — By omission or silence
  - — By prior inconsistent actions
- — Character impeachment
  - — Conviction of crime
  - — Past untruthfulness and other bad acts
  - — Impaired perception or recollection
- — "Case data" impeachment
  - — Personal interest
  - — Motive
  - — Bias or prejudice

6) Expert Testimony

- — Direct examination of expert witness
  - — Humanize the expert witness
  - — Use plain language
  - — Avoid narrative
  - — Use examples and analogies
  - — Use visual aids
  - — Use internal summaries
  - — Use concept of consensus
  - — Use leading questions as necessary
  - — Encourage powerful language
  - — Use enumeration
  - — Consider inoculation
  - — Don't stretch witness's expertise
- — Cross-examination of expert witness
  - — Challenge the witness's credentials

— Voir dire on credentials

— Cross-examine on credentials

— Limit scope of witness's expertise

— Stress missing credentials

— Contrast your expert's credentials

— Obtain favorable information

— Affirm your own expert

— Elicit areas of agreement

— Criticize opposing party's conduct

— Use learned treatises

— Challenge witness's impartiality

— Fees

— Relationship with party or counsel

— Positional bias

— Point out omissions

— Substitute information

— Change assumptions

— Vary the facts

— Challenge expert's degree of certainty

— Challenge factual underpinnings of opinion

— Challenge technique or theory

7) Foundations for Evidence

— General requirements

— Relevance

— Authenticity

— Specific requirements depending on nature of evidence

— Foundations for testimonial evidence

— Conversations

            — Date, time, and place of conversation
            — Persons present
        — Telephone conversations and voice identification
            — Same as for conversations, plus
            — Voice identification
        — Prior identification
            — Witness made prior identification
            — After perceiving the person identified
        — Habit and routine
            — Witness with personal knowledge of the regular conduct of the person or organization involved
            — Asserted conduct was, in fact, of a consistently repeated nature
    — Foundations for oral hearsay statement exceptions
        — Foundation for oral opposing party statements
            — Witness can authenticate the statement
            — Statement was made by the party against whom it is offered
    — Foundation for oral (or written) statements of an agent or employee of party
        — Same as for party above, plus
            — Declarant was an agent or employee of the opposing party at the time that the statement was made
        — Statement concerned a matter that was within the scope of the agency or employment
    — Foundation for present sense impression
        — Declarant perceived an event
        — Declarant described the event
        — Description was given while the event occurred or immediately afterwards
    — Foundation for excited utterance
        — Declarant perceived a startling event or experienced a stressful condition

- — Declarant made a statement concerning the event or condition
- — Statement was made while the declarant was under the stress of the event or condition

— Foundation for state of mind

- — Statement actually probative of declarant's mental, emotional, or physical condition
- — Statement made during the existence of such condition
- — Date and time statement was made
- — Where it was made
- — Who was present
- — What was said

— Foundation for medical treatment

- — Declarant made a statement for purpose of obtaining medical care or diagnosis
- — Statement that includes medical history or past symptoms relates to a then-present bodily condition

— Foundation for dying declaration

- — Declarant made a statement while believing that their death was imminent
- — Statement concerned what they believed to be the cause of death

— Foundations for documents

- — General foundation requirements
  - — Authentication
    - — Handwriting and signature
    - — Circumstantial evidence of authorship and origin
    - — Mailing or transmission
  - — Original writing (or "best evidence") rule

— Foundations for documentary hearsay exceptions

- — Foundation for business records and computer printouts
  - — Documents are records kept in the course of a regularly conducted business activity

— made at or near the time of a transaction or event

— made by, or based on information transmitted from, a person with knowledge

— made as a part of the regular practice of that business activity

— Foundation for summaries

— Original documents are so voluminous that they cannot be conveniently examined in the arbitration hearing

— Witness has examined the original data

— Witness is qualified to produce a summary of the information

— Exhibit is a fair and accurate summary of the underlying information

— Foundation for recorded recollection

— Witness once had personal knowledge of the relevant acts or events

— Witness cannot currently recall the events fully and accurately

— Witness previously made an accurate memorandum or record of the facts at a time when the events were fresh in their memory

— Foundation for public records

*Note:* most government records are self-authenticating, not requiring a government witness to testify.

— Document must be made by a public office or agency

— Set forth the activities of the office or agency, or

— Set forth matters observed pursuant to a duty imposed by law, or

— Set forth, in limited circumstances, certain investigative findings, or

— Set forth officially required records of vital statistics

— Foundation for absence of public record

*Note:* this evidence may be offered by certification from the appropriate official, in which case no witness needs to be called. The evidence may also be offered via testimony.

— Certain events, occurrences or matters were regularly recorded in some form by a public office or agency

— A diligent search has failed to disclose a record of a particular fact or event

— Foundation for previous testimony

  — Declarant is currently "unavailable" to testify

  — Testimony was given under oath in court or at a deposition

  — Party against whom the testimony is being offered had a fair opportunity to examine the witness when the testimony was originally given

— Foundation for written statements of an opposing party

  — Same as for oral opposing party statements, above

  — Proof that writing was made or adopted by the party against whom it is being offered, or by an agent, servant, or employee of such party

— Foundations for real and demonstrative evidence

  — Foundation for real evidence/tangible objects

    — Recognition of exhibit

      — Witness was familiar with the object at the time of the underlying events

      — Witness is able to recognize the exhibit as that very same object

    — Chain of custody

      — Location, handling, and care of an object between the time of its recovery and the time of trial

      — Needed where

        — Object is not uniquely recognizable and has not been marked, or

        — Object's physical properties are in issue.

— Foundations for photography and other recording devices

  — Foundation for still photographs

    — Photograph "fairly and accurately" portrays the scene shown

    — Witness may be photographer or any person who is familiar with the scene as it appeared at a relevant time

— Foundation for motion pictures and videotapes

  — Similar to requirements for photographs

        — Operator of the camera needs to be called only if special features were employed, or if the date of the filming is in issue

    — Foundation for audiotapes

        — Depends upon the purpose for which it is offered

        — Voice exemplar: witness who is able to recognize the voices of the various speakers

        — Recorded music: witness who is familiar with the material recorded

    — Foundation for X-rays and similar images

        — Qualified witness testifies that X-ray, CAT scan, or MRI image is a fair representation of internal structure of the patient's body

        — Witness testifies to identifying marks on film to demonstrate it is a business record of the hospital or clinic

    — Foundations for demonstrative evidence

        — Foundation for map, charts, or other diagrams

            — Similar to photograph

            — Witness must be familiar with the scene, location, or structure as it appeared at a relevant time, and

            — Witness must testify that exhibit constitutes a fair representation

    — Foundation for models and reproductions

        — Similar to photograph

        — Witness must be familiar with the real location or object, and must testify to the model's accuracy

    — Foundation for illustrative aids

        — Exhibit is accurate

        — Exhibit will assist witness in explaining their testimony

8) Common Objections

    — Form of question objections

    — Leading question

    — Compound question

    — Vague question

— Argumentative question

— Narrative question

— Asked and answered

— Assuming facts not in evidence

— Nonresponsive answer to question

— Substantive objections

— Hearsay objection

— Irrelevant

— Unfair prejudice

— Improper character evidence

— Lack of personal knowledge

— Improper lay opinion

— Speculation or conjecture

— Authenticity

— Lack of foundation

— Best evidence

— Privilege

— Subsequent remedial measures

— Settlement offers

9) Final Argument

— Structure

— Topical organization

— Chronological organization

— Other organizing tools

— Start and end strong

— Claimant should advance affirmative case first

— Cluster circumstantial evidence and accumulate details

— Bury your concessions

        — Weave in witness credibility
        — Carefully consider how to approach damages

— Content
    — Tell a persuasive story
    — What happened?
    — Why did it happen?
    — How can we be sure?
        — Is it plausible?
    — Tie up cross-examinations
    — Comment on promises
    — Resolve problems and weaknesses
    — Discuss damages
    — Thank arbitrator(s)

# • Appendix F •

## Exhibit Log

| Date | Ex. No. | Description | ID | Offered | Offer of Proof | Admit | Ruling Reserve | Reason | Party Admit. Agnst. |
|---|---|---|---|---|---|---|---|---|---|
| | | | | | | | | | |
| | | | | | | | | | |
| | | | | | | | | | |
| | | | | | | | | | |
| | | | | | | | | | |
| | | | | | | | | | |
| | | | | | | | | | |
| | | | | | | | | | |
| | | | | | | | | | |

# • Appendix G •

## Post-Hearing Advocacy Checklist

1) Drafting Post-Hearing Briefs
   - — Think like an arbitrator
   - — Format and language
     - — Reader-friendly
     - — Well organized
     - — Divided by headings and subheadings
     - — Avoid using unnecessary words and legalese
     - — Avoid bluster and self-important style
     - — Avoid harping on technicalities
     - — Use simple and direct writing style

2) Challenging Awards in Court
   - — Rarely successful
   - — Bases for challenge
     - — Contract
       - — No written agreement to arbitrate
       - — Party breached part of agreement to arbitrate
       - — Arbitration agreement is invalid
       - — Arbitration was demanded after contract or statutory limitation
     - — Hearing
       - — Arbitrator conducted hearing contrary to the arbitration statute or rules

— Party committed fraud in the arbitration

— Arbitrator refused to consider material facts

— Parties agreed to reopen the hearing because of the discovery of new evidence, but the arbitrator refused

— Arbitrator

— Arbitrator displayed bias and partiality

— Arbitrator failed to disclose a serious conflict of interest

— Arbitrator was corrupt

— Arbitrator refused to postpone hearing when good cause was shown

— Arbitrator exceeded authority

— Award

— Arbitrator decided nonarbitrable matters

— Arbitrators failed to make a mutual, final, and definite award

— Award was procured by corruption, fraud, or undue means

— Award was not timely rendered, despite party's protest

— Evident material miscalculation of figures in the award

— Evident material mistake in the description of a person, thing, or property referred to in the award

— Award is contrary to public policy

# • Appendix H •

## Organizations Offering ADR Services

| ORGANIZATION | LOCATION AND CONTACT INFORMATION | TYPES OF DISPUTES |
|---|---|---|
| ADR Systems of America, LLC | www.adrsystems.com<br>Chicago, IL | Personal Injury<br>Commercial<br>Family Law |
| American Arbitration Association | www.adr.org<br>Nationwide | Commercial<br>Construction<br>Employment<br>International<br>Labor<br>Government<br>Consumer |
| Arbitration Forums Inc. | https://home.arbfile.org<br>Tampa, FL | Insurance claims |
| CDR Associates | www.cdrassociates.org<br>Boulder, CO | Commercial government |
| Chicago International Dispute Resolution Association (CIDRA) | www.cidra.org<br>Chicago, IL | International business |
| International Centre for Settlement of Investment Disputes (Public International Organization) | https://icsid.worldbank.org<br>Washington, DC | International investment |
| JAMS Mediation, Arbitration, and ADR Services | www.jamsadr.com<br>Nationwide | General civil |

| | | |
|---|---|---|
| Judicial Arbiter Group, Inc. | www.jaginc.com<br>Denver, CO | General civil |
| Judicial Dispute Resolution, Inc. | https://www.jdr4adr.com/<br>Costa Mesa, CA | General civil |
| Washington Arbitration & Mediation Service | www.usamwa.com<br>Seattle and Tacoma, Washington | Commercial<br>Tort |
| World Wildlife Fund | www.worldwildlife.org<br>Washington, DC | Environmental, Natural resources |

**NONPROFIT ORGANIZATIONS THAT STUDY AND PROMOTE ADR**

| ORGANIZATION | CONTACT INFORMATION | PRINCIPAL SERVICES |
|---|---|---|
| ABA Section of Dispute Resolution | https://www.americanbar.org/groups/dispute_resolution/ | ADR services to ABA members and general public |
| Association for Conflict Resolution | https://acrnet.org | Enhance the practice and public understanding of conflict resolution |
| CPR Institute for Dispute Resolution | www.cpradr.org | Promotes ADR through corporate policy statements |
| American Arbitration Association | www.adr.org | ADR publications, training, meetings, and seminars |
| Center for Conflict Resolution | https://www.ccrchicago.org | ADR training and mediation center |

# • Appendix I •

## Organizations Offering Online Dispute Resolution Services

| ODR ORGANIZATIONS | PRINCIPAL TYPE OF DISPUTE(S) | WEBPAGE | COMMENTS |
|---|---|---|---|
| American Arbitration Association (AAA) | All disputes | https://www.adr.org/ | U.S. not-for-profit organization that provides extensive arbitration regulations and services, as well as limited online arbitration services called "Virtual Hearing Managed Services." |
| Arbitration Resolution Services Inc. | Consumer disputes; commercial disputes | https://www.arbresolutions.com/ | United States (U.S.)-based company which seeks to provide online arbitration and mediation services in "business to business" and "business to individual" disputes involving consumer, financial, commercial, and real-estate disputes. |

| | | | |
|---|---|---|---|
| Better Business Bureau Online | Consumer disputes | https://www.bbb.org | U.S.-based nonprofit industry association to promote relationship between businesses and consumers worldwide. |
| CPR Institute for Dispute Resolution | Domain-name disputes | https://www.cpradr.org | U.S.-based alliance of 500 counsel of corporations and lawyers seeking to promote ADR. |
| FairClaims | All disputes ranging from $10,000–$25,000 | https://www.fairclaims.com/ | U.S.-based business providing ODR software and arbitration services regarding matters valued at $10,000–$25,000. FairClaims facilitates online arbitration hearings and payment to the prevailing party. |
| International Chamber of Commerce | Commercial disputes | https://iccwbo.org/dispute-resolution/ | France-based international commerce organization offering virtual arbitration hearings for commercial and trade disputes. |

| | | | |
|---|---|---|---|
| Internet Corporation for Assigned Names and Numbers (ICANN) | Domain-name disputes | https://www.icann.org/resources/pages/dispute-resolution-2012-02-25-en | U.S.-based nonprofit organization that manages internet data and facilitates online dispute resolution for domain-name and trademark infringement disputes. |
| Matterhorn | All disputes | https://getmatterhorn.com/ | U.S.-based private business that provides ODR software solutions within the courts, including small claims, family court compliance, traffic court, civil infractions, and misdemeanors. Software is effective for facilitating easy payment of fines and online arbitration. |
| MODRON Spaces | All disputes | https://www.f6s.com/company/modron/ | Australian-based software company providing virtual dispute resolution software, known as "spaces," which contain video communication software and the ability to share files and payment. |

| ODR.com | All disputes | https://odr<br>.com/ | Formerly India-based company, CREK ODR, and now part of AAA, offering ODR technology solutions to mediators and arbitrators to facilitate dispute resolution. Such solutions include diagnosis, automated negotiation, negotiation and mediation evaluation/adjudication/arbitration. Its workflow and rules engine, private and joint caucus (discussions/chats including video), collaborative editing of awards and settlement agreements, time, scheduling, and notes help parties arrive at a fair resolution. CREK mainly assists asynchronous text-based mediation and arbitration and is available in a variety of languages. |
|---|---|---|---|

| | | | |
|---|---|---|---|
| Rapid Ruling | All disputes | https://rapidruling.com/ | U.S.-based company specializing in online arbitration in specific industries and areas such as fintech, construction, freelancers, e-commerce, and family law. |
| Trokt | Commercial disputes | https://www.trokt.org/ | U.S.-based software company with collaboration products that help facilitate virtual mediation and arbitration. |
| World Intellectual Property Organization (WIPO) | Commercial disputes, domain-name disputes | https://www.wipo.int/amc/en/index.html | United Nations specialized agency that promotes and protects intellectual property and offers virtual dispute resolution for I.P. and technology disputes. Approved by ICANN and applies the UDRP and its own supplemental rules. |

# • Appendix J •

## Arguments to Support Rulings on Various Motions and Objections During Arbitration Proceedings

### Introduction

This appendix is an idea generator. Its principal purpose is to provide the arbitration advocate, claimant and respondent alike, with a kaleidoscope of ideas for arguments to advance in order to prevail on various oral motions and objections made during the course of an arbitration. It can also be used by the arbitration advocate as a resource to focus legal research in connection with preparing written motions and responses prior to, during, or after an arbitration hearing. In some situations, a single argument will be sufficient independently to provide support for an arbitrator's ruling on a particular motion or objection; in others, several arguments may be combined to provide such support.

#### *Index of Motions and Objections*

#### *Support for Orders and Rulings Entered Prior to Arbitration Hearing*

1. Motion to Dismiss Based on Failure of Party to Timely Initiate Arbitration
2. Motion to Dismiss Claim Because of Lack of Arbitrability
3. Motion to Dismiss for Failure to State a Claim
4. Motion to Dismiss Based on Res Judicata, Collateral Estoppel, or Waiver
5. Motion to Dismiss for Failure to Prosecute Claim
6. Motion for Entry of Default Award for Failure to Defend
7. Motion to Dismiss or to Join a Party
8. Motion to Sever Claim or Cause of Action
9. Motion for More Definite Statement
10. Motion for Entry of an Award on the Pleadings

11. Motion to Strike Pleadings
12. Motion for Summary Judgment
13. Motion to Compel Discovery
14. Motions for Restraining Orders or Injunctions
15. Motion for Continuance
16. Motion for Bifurcated Discovery and/or Arbitration Hearing
17. Motion for Disqualification of Attorney

### *Support for Orders and Rulings Entered During the Course of Arbitration Hearing*

18. Objection to Opening Statement
19. Motion for Arbitrator to Take Judicial Notice
20. Motion to Exclude Evidence on Relevance Grounds
21. Objection to Character Evidence
22. Objection to Evidence of Habit, Custom, or Common Practice
23. Objection to Evidence of Subsequent Remedial Measures
24. Objection to Evidence Based on Assertion of Privilege
25. Objection to Scope of Direct Examination
26. Objection to Scope of Cross-Examination
27. Objection to Scope of Redirect Examination
28. Objection to Scope of Recross-Examination
29. Objection to Questioning Procedure or to Substance of Testimony on Direct Examination
30. Objection to Questioning Procedure or to Substance of Testimony on Cross-Examination
31. Objection to Expert Testimony
32. Objection to Hearsay Evidence
33. Assertion of Exception to Hearsay Rule—Opposing Party Statement and Admissions

## Support for Orders and Rulings Entered After Arbitration Hearing

# Support for Orders and Rulings Entered Prior to Arbitration Hearing

## 1. Motion to Dismiss Based on Failure of Party to Timely Initiate Arbitration

| ORDER DENYING DISMISSAL OF ARBITRATION PROCEEDINGS | ORDER GRANTING DISMISSAL OF ARBITRATION PROCEEDINGS |
|---|---|
| POSSIBLE SUPPORTING ARGUMENTS | POSSIBLE SUPPORTING ARGUMENTS |
| 1. Tolling of time limits | 1. Tolling inapplicable |
| 2. Moving party waived right to object | 2. Moving party's waiver of right to object was ineffective |
| 3. Moving party fraudulently concealed evidence of breach of agreement | 3. Nonmoving party lacked diligence in complying with initiation clause |
| 4. Moving party is estopped to complain because of its prior statements or conduct | 4. Moving party's silence did not constitute acquiescence in untimely initiation |
| 5. Moving party relied on wrong clause/statute/rule | 5. Nonmoving party relied on wrong clause/statute/rule |
| 6. Sufficient evidence of prior acknowledgment by moving party that initiation was timely | 6. Insufficient evidence of moving party's prior acknowledgment of timeliness |

## 2. Motion to Dismiss Claim Because of Lack of Arbitrability

| ORDER DENYING DISMISSAL | ORDER GRANTING DISMISSAL |
|---|---|
| POSSIBLE SUPPORTING ARGUMENTS | POSSIBLE SUPPORTING ARGUMENTS |
| 1. Arbitrability founded in case law | 1. Nonmoving party waived right to arbitrate claim |

| | |
|---|---|
| 2. Statute/rule permits or requires arbitration of claim | 2. Nonmoving party is estopped from arbitrating claim |
| 3. Parties agreed to arbitrate claim | 3. Parties did not agree to arbitrate claim |

### 3. Motion to Dismiss for Failure to State a Claim

| ORDER DENYING DISMISSAL | ORDER GRANTING DISMISSAL |
|---|---|
| POSSIBLE SUPPORTING ARGUMENTS | POSSIBLE SUPPORTING ARGUMENTS |
| 1. Allegations sufficient | 1. Allegations insufficient and not remediable |
| 2. Errors in statement of claim correctable | 2. Allegations consist of legal conclusions |
| 3. Statement of claim is amendable | 3. Uncontradicted evidence of affirmative defense obviates nonmoving party's ability to state claim |
| 4. Motion to dismiss is insufficiently specific | 4. Statement of claim fails to comply with provisions of the arbitration rules |

### 4. Motion to Dismiss Based on Res Judicata, Collateral Estoppel, or Waiver

| ORDER DENYING RES JUDICATA OR COLLATERAL ESTOPPEL EFFECT | ORDER BARRING ACTION OR RELITIGATION OF AN ISSUE |
|---|---|
| POSSIBLE SUPPORTING ARGUMENTS | POSSIBLE SUPPORTING ARGUMENTS |
| 1. Lack of final judgment on merits | 1. Prerequisites for res judicata met |
| 2. Prior judgment is null and void | 2. Prior judgment is valid |
| 3. Lack of identity of parties or privity | 3. Matters that could have been litigated are barred by res judicata (not collateral estoppel) |

| | |
|---|---|
| 4. Different cause of action | 4. Failure to plead compulsory counterclaim constitutes waiver and res judicata doctrine bars later suit on such claim |
| 5. Waiver | 5. Collateral estoppel bars claim where party had full and fair opportunity to litigate it in prior action |
| 6. Lack of mutuality as required by collateral estoppel doctrine | 6. Negligence in litigating prior action is not a defense to the application of collateral estoppel |
| 7. Lack of full and fair opportunity to litigate as required by collateral estoppel doctrine | 7. Statute or rule provision specifically bars relitigation of cause of action or claim |

## 5. Motion to Dismiss for Failure to Prosecute Claim

| ORDER DENYING DISMISSAL | ORDER GRANTING DISMISSAL |
|---|---|
| POSSIBLE SUPPORTING ARGUMENTS | POSSIBLE SUPPORTING ARGUMENTS |
| 1. No abandonment | 1. Prejudice to defendant |
| 2. Complicated nature of case | 2. Abuse of process |
| 3. Illness | 3. Negligence of complainant or counsel |
| 4. Attorney error | 4. Noncompliance with arbitrator's orders |
| 5. Delay due to defendant | 5. Complainant's specific intent to delay proceedings |

## 6. Motion for Entry of Default Award for Failure to Defend

| ORDER REFUSING DEFAULT AWARD | ORDER GRANTING DEFAULT AWARD |
|---|---|
| **POSSIBLE SUPPORTING ARGUMENTS** | **POSSIBLE SUPPORTING ARGUMENTS** |
| 1. Compliance with statutes and rules | 1. Mandatory statutory provision |
| 2. Nonarbitrability | 2. Mandatory rule provision |
| 3. Sufficient appearance | 3. Arbitration clause provision |
| 4. Waiver by moving party | 4. Nonmoving party waived right to object to entry of default award |
| 5. Moving party's defective pleadings | 5. Nonmoving party estopped from objecting to entry of default award |
| 6. Improper or inadequate notice | 6. Proper notice served on nonmoving party |
| 7. Inadequate proof of liability (if jurisdiction requires proof of all elements of claims) | 7. Moving party presents adequate proof of liability (if required) and damages |
| 8. Inadequate proof of damages | 8. Nonmoving party's failure to comply with arbitrator's orders or rulings |

## 7. Motion to Dismiss or to Join a Party

| ORDER DENYING DISMISSAL OF PARTY (OR GRANTING MOTION TO JOIN PARTY) | ORDER GRANTING DISMISSAL OF PARTY (OR DENYING MOTION TO JOIN PARTY) |
|---|---|
| **POSSIBLE SUPPORTING ARGUMENTS** | **POSSIBLE SUPPORTING ARGUMENTS** |
| 1. Statutory, rule, or contract provision | 1. Statutory or rule provision |
| 2. Untimely motion | 2. Not a party to arbitration agreement |
| 3. Other waiver | 3. Party has no interest or involvement in subject matter of arbitration |

## 8. Motion to Sever Claim or Cause of Action

| ORDER DENYING SEVERANCE OF CAUSE OF ACTION | ORDER GRANTING SEVERANCE OF CAUSE OF ACTION |
|---|---|
| POSSIBLE SUPPORTING ARGUMENTS | POSSIBLE SUPPORTING ARGUMENTS |
| 1. Complete relief otherwise unattainable | 1. Fairness, convenience, or certain prejudice to moving party if there is a single hearing |
| 2. Causes of action/claims interwoven and covered by arbitration clause | 2. Avoidance of confusion |
| 3. Prejudice to defendant who would be required to defend in two separate arbitrations | 3. Cause of action or claim not covered by arbitration clause or non-moving party waived right to object to severance |

## 9. Motion for More Definite Statement

| ORDER DENYING MOTION FOR MORE DEFINITE STATEMENT | ORDER GRANTING MOTION FOR MORE DEFINITE STATEMENT |
|---|---|
| POSSIBLE SUPPORTING ARGUMENTS | POSSIBLE SUPPORTING ARGUMENTS |
| 1. Pleading is acceptable | 1. Ambiguous and/or vague pleadings |
| 2. Moving party is seeking opponent's contentions rather than factual allegations | 2. Moving party is unable to formulate a response on the basis of the information provided and will be prejudiced |
| 3. Motion is inadequate, unclear, or incomplete | 3. Pleading fails to state a claim for relief |

## 10. Motion for Entry of an Award on the Pleadings

| ORDER DENYING MOTION FOR AWARD ON THE PLEADINGS | ORDER GRANTING MOTION FOR AWARD ON THE PLEADINGS |
|---|---|
| POSSIBLE SUPPORTING ARGUMENTS | POSSIBLE SUPPORTING ARGUMENTS |
| 1. Pleading attacked is not fatally defective and can be amended | 1. Pleading is fatally defective and defect cannot be cured |
| 2. Resolving all doubts in favor of the nonmovant, there is an issue of fact which requires determination | 2. No issues of fact are in dispute and only an issue or issues of law need to be resolved |
| 3. Movant waived right to move for judgment on the pleadings by its conduct | 3. Nonmoving party elects not to respond to motion, thereby waiving right to object to an award on the pleadings |
| 4. Motion is premature | 4. Nonmovant admitted allegations of pleadings in answers to requests to admit or in answers to interrogatories |

## 11. Motion to Strike Pleadings

| ORDER DENYING MOTION TO STRIKE PLEADINGS | ORDER GRANTING MOTION TO STRIKE PLEADINGS |
|---|---|
| POSSIBLE SUPPORTING ARGUMENTS | POSSIBLE SUPPORTING ARGUMENTS |
| 1. Pleadings are sufficient | 1. Pleadings are insufficient and vague |
| 2. Granting motion to strike would leave pleadings ambiguous | 2. Pleadings are irrelevant, frivolous, or redundant |
| 3. No prejudice to moving party if motion is denied | 3. Pleadings are scandalous, impertinent, or a sham |
| 4. Movant waived right to move to strike by prior conduct | 4. Denying motion to strike would materially prejudice movant in presenting case |

## 12. Motion for Summary Judgment

| ORDER DENYING MOTION FOR SUMMARY JUDGMENT | ORDER GRANTING MOTION FOR SUMMARY JUDGMENT |
|---|---|
| POSSIBLE SUPPORTING ARGUMENTS | POSSIBLE SUPPORTING ARGUMENTS |
| 1. Fact in issue is genuine | 1. No genuine issue of material fact |
| 2. Fact in issue is material | 2. Lack of counter-affidavits or other responding materials |
| 3. Movant failed to comply with statute or rule regarding inclusion of affidavits, transcripts, or other supporting materials | 3. Movant prevails on the issues of law raised |

## 13. Motion to Compel Discovery

| ORDER DENYING MOTION TO COMPEL DISCOVERY | ORDER GRANTING MOTION TO COMPEL DISCOVERY |
|---|---|
| POSSIBLE SUPPORTING ARGUMENTS | POSSIBLE SUPPORTING ARGUMENTS |
| 1. Information sought is privileged or otherwise immune from production | 1. Information sought is reasonably calculated to lead to the discovery of admissible evidence |
| 2. Motion is made to embarrass or harass a party, or for purposes of delay | 2. Asserted privilege is nonexistent or inapplicable |
| 3. Discovery request is overbroad or burdensome | 3. Scope of discovery request is reasonable and procedures can be prescribed which facilitate production and lessens its cost |

### 14. Motions for Restraining Orders or Injunctions

| ORDER DENYING MOTION FOR TRO, INJUNCTION, OR OTHER INTERIM RELIEF | ORDER GRANTING MOTION FOR TRO, INJUNCTION, OR OTHER INTERIM RELIEF |
|---|---|
| POSSIBLE SUPPORTING ARGUMENTS | POSSIBLE SUPPORTING ARGUMENTS |
| 1. Movant has adequate legal remedy | 1. Irreparable injury will occur if interim relief is denied |
| 2. Order granting interim relief would restrain nonmovant from exercising legal or constitutional rights | 2. Movant has no adequate remedy at law |
| 3. Movant lacks clean hands in connection with the matter for which they seek relief | 3. Movant is likely to succeed on the merits of their claims in the arbitration hearing |
| 4. Movant is guilty of laches or has acquiesced in nonmovant's acts | 4. Statute or rule authorizes interim relief to be granted on the specific facts presented |
| 5. Any order entered would be overly broad or vague and incapable of compliance | 5. Public will not suffer substantial harm if interim relief is granted |
| 6. Movant will not likely succeed on the merits of their claims in the arbitration proceeding | 6. Substantial public harm will occur if interim relief is not granted |

### 15. Motion for Continuance

| ORDER DENYING MOTION FOR CONTINUANCE | ORDER GRANTING MOTION FOR CONTINUANCE |
|---|---|
| POSSIBLE SUPPORTING ARGUMENTS | POSSIBLE SUPPORTING ARGUMENTS |
| 1. Reasons for continuance are inconsequential, frivolous, or not convincing | 1. Movant would suffer significant prejudice in presenting case if motion were denied |

| | |
|---|---|
| 2. Movant has shown lack of due diligence | 2. Movant has shown due diligence |
| 3. Movant has failed to show that evidence which would be unavailable if continuance is denied is material and not merely cumulative | 3. Statute or rule specifically requires a continuance be granted in circumstances presented |

## 16. Motion for Bifurcated Discovery and/or Arbitration Hearing

| ORDER DENYING BIFURCATED DISCOVERY AND/OR TRIAL | ORDER GRANTING BIFURCATED DISCOVERY AND/OR TRIAL |
|---|---|
| POSSIBLE SUPPORTING ARGUMENTS | POSSIBLE SUPPORTING ARGUMENTS |
| 1. Issues of liability and damages are intertwined | 1. Evidence on liability and damages is significantly different |
| 2. Multiple hearings would be overly duplicative and would require recalling of several witnesses | 2. Bifurcation would expedite arbitration proceedings and lessen their overall cost |
| 3. Bifurcation would add time and expense with no counterbalancing advantages | 3. Bifurcation would be more convenient for the parties, the arbitrators, and the witnesses |
| 4. Issues in case are relatively simple and straight forward | 4. Parties consent to bifurcation |

## 17. Motion for Disqualification of Attorney

| ORDER DENYING DISQUALIFICATION OF ATTORNEY | ORDER GRANTING DISQUALIFICATION OF ATTORNEY |
|---|---|
| POSSIBLE SUPPORTING ARGUMENTS | POSSIBLE SUPPORTING ARGUMENTS |
| 1. Attorney's client consents to representation after full disclosure of apparent or actual conflict of interest | 1. Attorney's conflict of interest which client has not waived or cannot waive |

| | |
|---|---|
| 2. Disqualification would work a substantial hardship to the attorney's client | 2. Attorney's representation of a party in a present matter adverse to the interests of a former client if there is a substantial relationship between the subject matters of the present and former representations |
| 3. Moving party failed to promptly object | 3. Attorney or another attorney in their law firm will be called as a witness on behalf of the attorney's client |
| 4. Moving party would not be prejudiced if disqualification is denied | 4. Attorney is senile, mentally incompetent, or under the influence of drugs or alcohol |

## Support for Orders and Rulings Entered During the Course of Arbitration Hearing

### 18. Objection to Opening Statement

| ORDER SUSTAINING OBJECTION TO OPENING STATEMENT | ORDER OVERRULING OBJECTION TO OPENING STATEMENT |
|---|---|
| POSSIBLE SUPPORTING ARGUMENTS | POSSIBLE SUPPORTING ARGUMENTS |
| 1. Attorney is presenting legal arguments | 1. Attorney may refer briefly to applicable statute or rule in opening statement |
| 2. Attorney is presenting personal opinion, touting own credibility, or asserting personal knowledge of facts | 2. Attorney is not presenting personal opinion, touting own credibility, or asserting personal knowledge of facts |
| 3. Attorney is raising matters outside scope of pleadings | 3. Attorney is referring to matters within scope of pleadings |
| 4. Attorney is discussing excluded or inadmissible evidence | 4. No ruling has been made with regard to the challenged evidence |

| | |
|---|---|
| 5. Attorney's comments are demeaning to opponent's client or witnesses | 5. Attorney's references to opposing party's behavior is within the bounds of permissible comment |
| 6. Attorney is exceeding time limits for opening statement | 6. Objecting party may have additional time to respond if it desires |

## 19. Motion for Arbitrator to Take Judicial Notice

| JUDICIAL NOTICE REFUSED | JUDICIAL NOTICE TAKEN |
|---|---|
| POSSIBLE SUPPORTING ARGUMENTS: | POSSIBLE SUPPORTING ARGUMENTS: |
| 1. Facts sought to be judicially noticed are uncertain or doubtful | 1. Facts sought to be judicially noticed are well known in the jurisdiction |
| 2. Facts are known to judge personally, but are not common knowledge | 2. Judicial notice of certain facts is required by statute or rule |

## 20. Motion to Exclude Evidence on Relevance Grounds

| ORDER SUSTAINING OBJECTION TO RELEVANCE (EVIDENCE EXCLUDED) | ORDER OVERRULING OBJECTION TO RELEVANCE (EVIDENCE ADMITTED) |
|---|---|
| POSSIBLE SUPPORTING ARGUMENTS | POSSIBLE SUPPORTING ARGUMENTS |
| 1. Evidence does not tend to prove or disprove issues in case | 1. Evidence tends to prove or disprove issues in case |
| 2. Evidence does not render a fact more or less probable | 2. Objection is untimely and right to object is therefore waived |
| 3. Evidence is not logically linked to other evidence to aid arbitrator in determining a fact in issue | 3. Evidence that is weak, incomplete, or slightly prejudicial does not require exclusion on ground of irrelevance |

## 21. Objection to Character Evidence

| ORDER SUSTAINING OBJECTION TO EVIDENCE OF CHARACTER (EVIDENCE EXCLUDED) | ORDER OVERRULING OBJECTION TO EVIDENCE OF CHARACTER (EVIDENCE ADMITTED) |
|---|---|
| **POSSIBLE SUPPORTING ARGUMENTS** | **POSSIBLE SUPPORTING ARGUMENTS** |
| 1. Character of party is not at issue | 1. Character of party is at issue |
| 2. Unless witness's character has been attacked, character evidence is inadmissible to enhance witness's credibility | 2. Evidence of witness's bad reputation for truthfulness or veracity is admissible for impeachment purposes |
| 3. Improper evidence of character is offered (specific acts or personal opinion of witness instead of general reputation of witness in the community) | 3. Evidence of a witness's good character or reputation for truthfulness or honesty is admissible to rebut impeaching evidence |

## 22. Objection to Evidence of Habit, Custom, or Common Practice

| ORDER SUSTAINING OBJECTION TO ADMISSIBILITY (EVIDENCE EXCLUDED) | ORDER OVERRULING OBJECTION TO ADMISSIBILITY (EVIDENCE ADMITTED) |
|---|---|
| **POSSIBLE SUPPORTING ARGUMENTS** | **POSSIBLE SUPPORTING ARGUMENTS** |
| 1. In some jurisdictions, evidence of habit is not admissible to show that a person acted in a particular way at a particular time | 1. The Federal Rules of Evidence and some jurisdictions allow evidence of habit to be used to prove an act or a specific occurrence, if the habit is sufficiently regular and uniform, particularly if there are no eyewitnesses available to testify |
| 2. Evidence of habit is not sufficiently regular or uniform | 2. Evidence of habit or customary practices of business organizations (as opposed to individuals) is routinely admissible |

| | |
|---|---|
| 3. Evidence of habit is not sufficiently routine | 3. Except in cases of negligence per se, or inherently dangerous activities, or dissimilar circumstances, evidence of habit of normally prudent people in performing an act or using an instrument is admissible to permit the arbitrator to decide if the particular use which caused an injury was or was not negligent under the circumstances of its use |

## 23. Objection to Evidence of Subsequent Remedial Measures

| ORDER SUSTAINING OBJECTION TO EVIDENCE OF SUBSEQUENT REMEDIAL MEASURES (EVIDENCE EXCLUDED) | ORDER OVERRULING OBJECTION TO EVIDENCE OF SUBSEQUENT REMEDIAL MEASURES (EVIDENCE ADMITTED) |
|---|---|
| POSSIBLE SUPPORTING ARGUMENTS | POSSIBLE SUPPORTING ARGUMENTS |
| 1. Evidence of subsequent remedial measures is inadmissible to prove negligence | 1. Evidence of subsequent remedial measures is admissible to show that such measures are feasible, if feasibility of remedial measures is an issue in case |
| 2. Control of premises is not an issue in the case | 2. Evidence is admissible to show control of premises or object, if control is a matter in dispute |
| 3. Physical condition at time of accident is not an issue in the case | 3. Evidence is admissible to establish physical conditions existing at time of accident |
| 4. Evidence is not being offered to impeach credibility of witness | 4. Evidence may be admitted to impeach credibility of a witness |
| 5. This is not a strict products liability case | 5. Evidence is admissible in strict products liability case |

## 24. Objection to Evidence Based on Assertion of Privilege

| ORDER SUSTAINING OBJECTION BASED ON ASSERTION OF PRIVILEGE (EVIDENCE EXCLUDED) | ORDER OVERRULING OBJECTION BASED ON ASSERTION OF PRIVILEGE (EVIDENCE ADMITTED) |
|---|---|
| POSSIBLE SUPPORTING ARGUMENTS | POSSIBLE SUPPORTING ARGUMENTS |
| 1. Communication is privileged on basis of common law | 1. No common law privilege exists in jurisdiction |
| 2. Communication is privileged on basis of statute | 2. No statutory privilege exists in jurisdiction |
| 3. Communication is privileged by prior agreement of the parties | 3. Objector has no right to claim privilege because no requisite privileged relationship existed or because of some other technical noncompliance with case law or statute |
| 4. Privilege was not waived, or if waived, waiver was timely withdrawn | 4. Objector waived privilege by word or action, such as failure to timely object, or by voluntary disclosure of privileged matter in discovery or privately to third persons |

## 25. Objection to Scope of Direct Examination

| RULING EXCLUDING TESTIMONY | RULING ALLOWING TESTIMONY |
|---|---|
| POSSIBLE SUPPORTING ARGUMENTS | POSSIBLE SUPPORTING ARGUMENTS |
| 1. Evidence is irrelevant | 1. Evidence is relevant and material |
| 2. Evidence is immaterial | 2. Evidence relates to background of witness |

## 26. Objection to Scope of Cross-Examination

| RULING EXCLUDING TESTIMONY | RULING ALLOWING TESTIMONY |
|---|---|
| POSSIBLE SUPPORTING ARGUMENTS | POSSIBLE SUPPORTING ARGUMENTS |
| 1. Questions seek evidence beyond scope of direct examination | 1. Questions seek evidence within scope of direct examination |
| 2. Cross-examiner is attempting to impeach witness on a collateral matter | 2. Questions seek evidence relating to credibility witness |

## 27. Objection to Scope of Redirect Examination

| RULING EXCLUDING TESTIMONY | RULING ALLOWING TESTIMONY |
|---|---|
| POSSIBLE SUPPORTING ARGUMENTS | POSSIBLE SUPPORTING ARGUMENTS |
| 1. Questions seek to elicit information unrelated to any issue yet raised by either party | 1. Questions seek to elicit testimony clarifying the subject matter of the direct examination or any new matters brought out by cross-examination |
| 2. Questions do not seek information designed to rehabilitate witness | 2. Questions seek information designed to rehabilitate witness, by bringing forth matters rebutting or explaining unfavorable inferences raised on cross-examination |

## 28. Objection to Scope of Recross-Examination

| RULING EXCLUDING TESTIMONY | RULING ALLOWING TESTIMONY |
|---|---|
| POSSIBLE SUPPORTING ARGUMENTS | POSSIBLE SUPPORTING ARGUMENTS |
| 1. Questions seek information that is cumulative or not within scope of redirect examination | 1. Questions seek information responsive to new matters arising on recross-examination |

## 29. Objection to Questioning Procedure or to Substance of Testimony on Direct Examination

| ORDER SUSTAINING OBJECTION (EVIDENCE EXCLUDED) | ORDER OVERRULING OBJECTION (EVIDENCE ADMITTED) |
|---|---|
| **POSSIBLE SUPPORTING ARGUMENTS** | **POSSIBLE SUPPORTING ARGUMENTS** |
| 1. Examiner has asked a leading question, not satisfying a permitted exception to the rule against leading questions on direct examination | 1. Leading question on direct examination is appropriate where witness is hostile or where answers of the witness have surprised direct examiner<br>Or<br>Leading questions are addressed to preliminary or background matters not in dispute, or they seek to direct witness to a particular subject<br>Or<br>Leading questions are permissible where direct examiner has difficulty obtaining intelligible answers because the witness is a child, is timid or ignorant, or has difficulty understanding English |
| 2. Questions seek cumulative information or are repetitious | 2. Cumulative questioning is permissible where a witness does not understand the question, or gives unclear testimony, or where the witness's answer is incomplete |
| 3. Questions seek information not based on witness's firsthand knowledge or opportunity to observe | 3. Witness must testify from personal knowledge or observation, but the opportunity to observe may be limited, attention may be imprecise, and the recall of witness need not be absolutely certain |

| | |
|---|---|
| 4. In some jurisdictions, it is improper to allow witness to use a memorandum to refresh past recollection where no past recollection is revived if the memorandum is not made at or about the time the events were fresh in the witness's | 4. Most jurisdictions allow witness to refresh memory by use of a written memorandum, whether written by witness, or someone else, and whether the document is an original or a copy. |
| 5. In some jurisdictions, it is improper for witness to use a writing to refresh recollection if no proper foundation is laid for the use of the writing or if adversary is denied opportunity to inspect the writing | 5. Most jurisdictions allow a witness's recollection to be refreshed by a photograph, report, record, an object, any document, or even a leading question |
| 6. Traditionally, lay witness may not give opinion testimony, particularly when the opinion will prejudice, confuse, or mislead the factfinder | 6. Lay witness may give opinion evidence as a matter of convenience, if it would be difficult or impossible for the witness to provide actual and accurate details, or if the witness is more knowledgeable about the particular subject than the average factfinder |
| 7. Lay witness may not express an opinion about an ultimate fact or issue or how a case ought to be decided | |
| 8. Lay witness may not give an opinion on conclusions of law | |

## 30. Objection to Questioning Procedure or to Substance of Testimony on Cross-Examination

| ORDER SUSTAINING OBJECTION TO TESTIMONY ON CROSS-EXAMINATION (EVIDENCE EXCLUDED) | ORDER OVERRULING OBJECTION TO TESTIMONY ON CROSS-EXAMINATION (EVIDENCE ADMITTED) |
|---|---|
| **POSSIBLE SUPPORTING ARGUMENTS** | **POSSIBLE SUPPORTING ARGUMENTS** |
| 1. Question asked by cross-examiner is improper in that it is insulting, harassing, repetitive, argumentative, or causes undue embarrassment | 1. Question seeks information showing that witness made a prior inconsistent statement (or made a prior statement with an omission) that is materially inconsistent with witness's current testimony |
| 2. Question seeks information that is not impeaching in that witness's prior statement is not in fact inconsistent with witness's present testimony | 2. Question seeks information showing that witness's credibility is impeached because their mind or memory is impaired in such a way that the witness's capacity to perceive, remember, or describe correctly is affected |
| 3. Question seeks to impeach witness by eliciting a witness's prior statement without laying a proper foundation for the prior statement | 3. Question seeks information showing that the witness's credibility is impeached because the witness is biased, prejudiced, or has an interest in the outcome of the arbitration |
| 4. In some jurisdictions, questions seeking information that would impeach a witness's testimony only on a collateral matter are improper | 4. Question seeks information showing that the witness's credibility is impeached because they have been convicted of a crime. (In some jurisdictions, the crime must be punishable by imprisonment of more than one year, involve dishonesty, involve moral turpitude, and the conviction must predate the current testimony by a certain limited time period) |

| | |
|---|---|
| 5. Question seeks information regarding an arrest, accusation, or prosecution of witness, where no conviction can be proved | 5. Question seeks information that witness's credibility is impeached because of the witness's character or reputation for lack of truthfulness |
| 6. Question seeks information regarding witness's drug use solely for the purpose of showing witness is generally unreliable or lacks truthfulness | 6. Question seeks information to show that witness is currently under the influence of drugs while testifying or that the witness was under the influence of drugs at the time of the occurrence at issue |

## 31. Objection to Expert Testimony

| ORDER SUSTAINING OBJECTION TO EXPERT TESTIMONY (EVIDENCE EXCLUDED) | ORDER OVERRULING OBJECTION TO EXPERT TESTIMONY (EVIDENCE ADMITTED) |
|---|---|
| POSSIBLE SUPPORTING ARGUMENTS | POSSIBLE SUPPORTING ARGUMENTS |
| 1. Expert's testimony is not limited to matters within their expertise | 1. Expert is testifying within area of expertise |
| 2. Witness was not properly qualified as expert | 2. Expert opinion may be based, in part, on hearsay evidence |
| 3. In some jurisdictions, expert may not give an opinion on an improper hypothetical question | 3. Expert witness is properly qualified to testify on the basis of experience, education, and training |
| 4. In some jurisdictions, an expert may not state an opinion based on facts and data not in evidence | 4. Some jurisdictions allow expert to give opinion on an ultimate issue in the case |
| 5. In some jurisdictions, expert may not give opinion testimony when the subject matter of the testimony is within the understanding of the average factfinder | 5. Expert may testify as to the particular hypothetical question asked |

| | |
|---|---|
| 6. Ordinarily, an expert may not testify to a conclusion of law | 6. Expert's prior relationship with party or counsel is insufficient to render testimony nonprobative |
| 7. Expert failed to disclose report prior to hearing | 7. Error in expert's list of credentials is insufficient to bar testimony |

## 32. Objection to Hearsay Evidence

| ORDER SUSTAINING OBJECTION TO HEARSAY GENERALLY (EVIDENCE EXCLUDED) | ORDER OVERRULING OBJECTION TO HEARSAY GENERALLY (EVIDENCE ADMITTED) |
|---|---|
| POSSIBLE SUPPORTING ARGUMENTS | POSSIBLE SUPPORTING ARGUMENTS |
| 1. The statement is other than one made by the declarant while testifying at a trial or hearing and it is being offered in evidence to prove the truth of the matter asserted | 1. Objection is untimely |
| 2. The witness's own previous out-of-arbitration statement may constitute hearsay | 2. Statement is not offered to prove the truth of the matter asserted, but rather the effect on the hearer of the statement |
| 3. Conduct which was intended as an assertion may be considered as a "statement" excluded by the rule against hearsay | 3. The witness's own prior statement is not hearsay because it was given under oath and it is inconsistent with the witness's current testimony, or it is consistent with current testimony and it is offered to rebut a charge of recent fabrication, or it is a statement of past identification, or it is an admission against interest and offered against that party as such |
| 4. The statement does not satisfy any exception to the rule against hearsay (see below) | 4. The statement satisfies one of the exceptions to the rule against hearsay (see below) |

### 33. Assertion of Exception to Hearsay Rule—Opposing Party Statement and Admissions

| RULING EXCLUDING EVIDENCE (EXCEPTION DOES NOT APPLY) | RULING ADMITTING EVIDENCE (EXCEPTION APPLIES) |
|---|---|
| **POSSIBLE SUPPORTING ARGUMENTS** | **POSSIBLE SUPPORTING ARGUMENTS** |
| 1. Person making admission lacks capacity to make an admission | 1. A written or oral statement of a party or their representative is admissible as substantive evidence of the fact admitted even if it is not against interest when made and even if it is opinion or legal conclusion |
| 2. Inconsistent statements in pleadings or pleadings in the alternative are not considered to be admissions | 2. An admission in a pleading can be considered a judicial admission which waives production of evidence and removes the admitted fact from controversy |
| 3. An admission by an agent or employee should not be received into evidence if the employment or agency relationship was terminated before the statement was made, or if the statement was not made within the scope of agency or employment | 3. A statement by an agent or employee of a party may constitute the party's statement if the statement was made within the scope of the agent's or employee's duties and if it was made while the agency or employment was still in effect |
| 4. Declarant was not in privity with the party to whom admission is to be attributed | 4. An admission can be by conduct or by express adoption of another's statement |
| 5. Silence in face of an oral statement may not be considered an admission if the silent person did not hear or understand it, has physical or emotional impediments to responding, had a relationship with speaker such that a denial was difficult or unlikely, or reasonably thought the oral statement did not call for a response | 5. Silence can constitute an admission where there is a failure to deny or object to an oral or written statement calling for a response or denial |

| | |
|---|---|
| 6. Subsequent remedial measures, offers to compromise a claim, or offers to pay medical expenses ordinarily do not constitute admissions | 6. An admission may be received into evidence if made by someone in privity with the party against whom the declaration is offered as long as the declaration relates to the interest in property and is made when the declarant has an interest in the property |

## 34. Assertion of Exception to Hearsay Rule—Prior Statement of Witness

| RULING EXCLUDING EVIDENCE (EXCEPTION DOES NOT APPLY) | RULING ADMITTING EVIDENCE (EXCEPTION APPLIES) |
|---|---|
| POSSIBLE SUPPORTING ARGUMENTS | POSSIBLE SUPPORTING ARGUMENTS |
| 1. In some jurisdictions, prior statements are only admissible for the limited purpose of impeachment and may not be used as substantive evidence unless they fall within another recognized exception to the hearsay rule | 1. The witness admits in present testimony that the prior inconsistent statement is true |
| 2. In some jurisdictions, no inconsistency can exist where the witness's present testimony is strictly "I don't remember" | 2. "Inconsistent" means any material variation between the prior statement and the present testimony of the witness, including omission from the prior statement of a material fact that the witness includes in present testimony |
| 3. A consistent statement made after the source of bias, interest, influence, or incapacity arose is irrelevant and inadmissible | 3. A consistent statement made soon after the event testified to transpired is admissible to counter allegations that the witness's memory at trial is impaired or that the present testimony is a recent fabrication |

| | |
|---|---|
| 4. Consistent statements cannot be used to counter impeachment by prior inconsistent statements since the inconsistency remains despite any statement to the contrary | 4. Some jurisdictions admit prior consistent statements to rebut any form of impeachment, including prior inconsistent statements |
| 5. Assertion of exception to hearsay rule is untimely or was waived | 5. Assertion of exception to hearsay rule has not been waived |

### 35. Assertion of Exception to Hearsay Rule—Excited Utterance

| RULING EXCLUDING EVIDENCE (EXCEPTION DOES NOT APPLY) | RULING ADMITTING EVIDENCE (EXCEPTION APPLIES) |
|---|---|
| POSSIBLE SUPPORTING ARGUMENTS | POSSIBLE SUPPORTING ARGUMENTS |
| 1. Proponent of evidence failed to put forward sufficient independent evidence to support a finding that a startling event occurred and that the declarant actually witnessed it | 1. An excited utterance is admissible regardless of whether the statement explains or illuminates the event which provoked it |
| 2. The utterance was not reasonably contemporaneous with the event to which it relates | 2. The only tests of competency applying to a declarant of an excited utterance is the ability to observe and communicate |
| 3. Present sense impression was not contemporaneous with event it described | 3. Declarant's emotional condition compensated for and explained the considerable length of time between the excited utterance and the preceding event to which it related |
| 4. Declarant's statement was self-serving and declarant had time to reflect and fabricate before speaking | 4. Even though declarant's statement was not an excited utterance, it qualifies for admission as a present sense impression |
| 5. Assertion of exception to the hearsay rule is untimely or was waived | 5. Even though there was a substantial time lapse between the event and the declarant's present sense impression, there is substantial circumstantial evidence corroborating the accuracy of the statement |

## 36. Assertion of Exception to Hearsay Rule—State of Mind: Emotional or Mental State

| RULING EXCLUDING EVIDENCE (EXCEPTION DOES NOT APPLY) | RULING ADMITTING EVIDENCE (EXCEPTION APPLIES) |
|---|---|
| POSSIBLE SUPPORTING ARGUMENTS | POSSIBLE SUPPORTING ARGUMENTS |
| 1. Statement of witness's belief is inadmissible to prove a fact | 1. Statement of intent to perform a certain act is admissible as circumstantial evidence that the declarant acted according to their stated intent |
| 2. Declarant's mental or emotional condition did not exist at the time statement was made | 2. In some jurisdictions, a declaration of intent by one person to prove that another person acted accordingly is admissible |
| 3. Statement by one person as to the mental or emotional condition of another is inadmissible under the state of mind exception | 3. In some jurisdictions, all statements of a deceased declarant, made in good faith with personal knowledge before the litigation commenced, are admissible |
| 4. A declaration of mental or emotional condition is inadmissible because the declarant's state of mind is not an issue in the case | 4. Mental or emotional condition of the declarant is the key fact on which an element of the case depends |

## 37. Assertion of Exception to Hearsay Rule—Statement of Physical Condition or for Medical Diagnosis

| RULING EXCLUDING EVIDENCE (EXCEPTION DOES NOT APPLY) | RULING ADMITTING EVIDENCE (EXCEPTION APPLIES) |
|---|---|
| POSSIBLE SUPPORTING ARGUMENTS | POSSIBLE SUPPORTING ARGUMENTS |
| 1. Statements of medical history, past pain, symptoms, or causation do not fall within hearsay exception for physical condition | 1. In some jurisdictions, a spontaneous statement of physical condition is admissible even though it was made to a nonphysician, and Federal Rules of Evidence extend the rule to statements of medical history, past or present symptoms, pain sensations, or general causation, if the statement was made for the purpose of medical diagnosis or treatment |
| 2. In some jurisdictions (not under the Federal Rules of Evidence), statements were made for the purpose of preparing a physician to testify on declarant's behalf | 2. Nonspontaneous statement regarding physical condition was made to a physician for the purpose of obtaining their testimony, but the declarant had a significant treatment motive in consulting the physician, and evidence that the declarant followed the physician's advice is highly probative of treatment motive |
| 3. In some jurisdictions, statements made to physician related to fault are not admissible under the physical condition exception | 3. Under the Federal Rules of Evidence, all statements on which a nontreating physician relied in forming their opinion are admissible as substantive evidence |
| 4. Assertion of the exception is untimely or was waived | 4. Declaration of someone other than the patient is admissible because it was made for the purpose of obtaining medical treatment |

### 38. Assertion of Exception to Hearsay Rule—Private, Published, and Institutional Records

| RULING EXCLUDING EVIDENCE (EXCEPTION DOES NOT APPLY) | RULING ADMITTING EVIDENCE (EXCEPTION APPLIES) |
|---|---|
| POSSIBLE SUPPORTING ARGUMENTS | POSSIBLE SUPPORTING ARGUMENTS |
| 1. Proponent of evidence has not shown that the private record was made when the facts were still fresh in the declarant's mind and that the information in the private record was true and accurate when the private record was made | 1. Under the Federal Rules of Evidence, total loss of memory is not required as a prerequisite to admission of past recollection recorded |
| 2. Business record is inadmissible where the informant had no business duty to report the information to the author | 2. "Business record" is liberally construed and "business" consists of almost any regularly conducted, organized activity for purposes of the exception |
| 3. Record was prepared with a view toward litigation and not in the regular course of business | 3. Computer printouts, results of psychological tests, desk calendars, notes of conversations, photographs, and shorthand notes have qualified for admissibility under the business records exception |
| 4. Too much time elapsed between the event and the recording to allow record to be admitted under the business records exception | 4. Party has not waived right to assert the exception |

## 39. Assertion of Exception to Hearsay Rule—Public Records

| RULING EXCLUDING EVIDENCE (EXCEPTION DOES NOT APPLY) | RULING ADMITTING EVIDENCE (EXCEPTION APPLIES) |
|---|---|
| **POSSIBLE SUPPORTING ARGUMENTS** | **POSSIBLE SUPPORTING ARGUMENTS** |
| 1. Record contains information given to the author by another person, and the informant's statements do not fall within an exception to the hearsay rule | 1. Investigatory records of public agencies are admissible if they involve "factual findings," findings of law, and conclusions based on disputed factual information supplied to the author by other persons |
| 2. The broader business records exception cannot be used to justify admissibility of investigatory records of public agencies | 2. The public records exception does not exclude investigatory records of a public agency on the ground that they were primarily prepared with a view to litigation |
| 3. Source of information contained in public record lacks trustworthiness | 3. A report made to a public agency by one with a professional duty is admissible under the public records exception |
| 4. Declarations of remote cause in death certificates, as opposed to immediate cause, are inadmissible because such statements were made to the examining physician by another person | 4. Judgment of a foreign court in a criminal matter qualifies for admission under the public records exception if the foreign proceedings were conducted according to standards of civilized jurisprudence |
| 5. Mere fact that report is required by law does not satisfy admissibility requirement that declarant have an official or professional duty to report | 5. Evidence of prior conviction is admissible in the present proceeding to prove a fact that was a necessary element of the criminal offense |
| 6. Evidence of a prior conviction is inadmissible to prove facts that were not essential to sustain the judgment | 6. Party did not waive right to assert exception to hearsay rule |

## 40. Assertion of Exception to Hearsay Rule—Declarant Unavailable

| RULING EXCLUDING EVIDENCE (EXCEPTION DOES NOT APPLY) | RULING ADMITTING EVIDENCE (EXCEPTION APPLIES) |
|---|---|
| **POSSIBLE SUPPORTING ARGUMENTS** | **POSSIBLE SUPPORTING ARGUMENTS** |
| 1. Advantages of proceeding with hearing without declarant's live testimony do not outweigh need for granting a postponement | 1. Declarant's testimony is unavailable when declarant is dead, sick, insane, beyond reach of process, invokes a privilege against testifying, or refuses to testify |
| 2. Proponent of evidence failed to show that they exhausted all reasonable means to obtain the testimony by making a good-faith effort to locate missing declarant and by taking all reasonable steps necessary to subpoena declarant to ensure presence at hearing | 2. In some jurisdictions, when the declarant is beyond reach of process, proponent need not make an effort to secure declarant's voluntary testimony |
| 3. Prior testimony of unavailable declarant is inadmissible because party against whom the testimony is offered did not have an adequate opportunity and similar motive to examine the declarant when the testimony was taken | 3. Prior testimony is admissible because party against whom it is being offered (or predecessor in interest) had an opportunity and similar motive to develop the testimony during the former proceedings |
| 4. Declaration against interest was not against declarant's interest at the time the statement was made | 4. Declarations against interest include statements against proprietary, pecuniary, penal, and social interests. |
| 5. Declaration against interest is inadmissible because, at the time the statement was made, the declarant would not have been competent to testify | 5. Unlike an admission, which may only be used against the party who made it or their privies in interest, a declaration against interest may be introduced in evidence by or against anyone |

| | |
|---|---|
| 6. Assertion of exception to hearsay rule is untimely or was waived | 6. Many of the traditional restrictions on use of a dying declaration have been abandoned; it is now usually admissible in civil cases; where declarant believed death was imminent though they later recovered, and statements are not necessarily restricted to the cause or circumstances of death. |

## 41. Objection to Evidence Based on Lack of Foundation

| RULING EXCLUDING EVIDENCE (FOUNDATION INADEQUATE) | RULING ADMITTING EVIDENCE (FOUNDATION ADEQUATE) |
|---|---|
| POSSIBLE SUPPORTING ARGUMENTS | POSSIBLE SUPPORTING ARGUMENTS |
| 1. Proponent of evidence has not advanced sufficient admissible evidence to support a finding of authenticity | 1. Question of whether the proponent of evidence has proved an adequate chain of custody goes to weight rather than to the admissibility of the evidence |
| 2. Lay witness may not authenticate genuineness of handwriting if they are familiar with the handwriting by making only a single comparison with another sample for purposes of adversary proceedings | 2. Methods of authentication may be used alone or in combination to build a prima facie case of authenticity |
| 3. Fact that telephone caller identified themselves is insufficient in itself to authenticate the identity of the caller | 3. A privately maintained document is properly authenticated by the testimony of a witness with knowledge of either a direct or circumstantial nature, and answers to interrogatories are properly considered as testimony for purposes of authentication |

| | |
|---|---|
| 4. Proponent of evidence failed to authenticate specimen | 4. Authenticity may be proven by showing that the document contains information only the purported author was likely to know, that the appearance of the document suggests a single source, that the document was a reply to another authenticated communication, or that the document reflects the special linguistic characteristics of its author |
| 5. Proponent of computer-generated evidence failed to authenticate it by testimony that describes the process or system and proves that it produces accurate results | 5. In some jurisdictions, certain documents are presumed authentic—i.e., are self-authenticating—newspapers, periodicals, trade inscriptions, commercial papers, and certified copies of public documents including judgments of conviction |

## 42. Objection to Evidence Based on Best Evidence Rule

| RULING EXCLUDING SECONDARY EVIDENCE | RULING ADMITTING SECONDARY EVIDENCE |
|---|---|
| POSSIBLE SUPPORTING ARGUMENTS | POSSIBLE SUPPORTING ARGUMENTS |
| 1. Secondary evidence is inadmissible where there is an insufficient showing that the original could not be produced | 1. Best evidence rule does not apply where a writing is not offered to prove its contents, such as instances where a witness testifies about an event that was only incidentally memorialized in writing, where a writing is used to refresh a witness's recollection or to illustrate their testimony, or where a witness testifies that records do not contain a particular entry |

| | |
|---|---|
| 2. Best evidence rule may be applied to exclude the testimony of a witness concerning the identity, rather than the contents, of a writing if the witness had to take note of the contents in order to make the identification | 2. A duplicate is admissible to the same extent as an original unless a genuine question is raised concerning the authenticity of the original or it would be unfair to admit the duplicate in lieu of the original |
| 3. Original of a photograph or recording must be produced to prove its contents | 3. Secondary evidence is admissible to prove contents of original if there is proof that the original was lost or destroyed but not in bad faith, the original is outside the reach of the process, or the writing is collateral to a material issue |
| 4. Photocopies are secondary evidence and inadmissible unless production of the original is excused | 4. Secondary evidence is admissible where original was destroyed by accident or mistake or in the ordinary course of business |
| 5. Duplicate document is inadmissible because it is incomplete or illegible, or evidence shows that the original document may have been intentionally destroyed thereby producing an inference of fraud | 5. Contents of a public record may be proven by a certified copy |
| 6. Proponent's request to offer secondary evidence is untimely | 6. Objector waived right to require best evidence |

### 43. Objection Relating to Closing Argument

| ORDER OVERRULING OBJECTION TO SCOPE AND CONTENT OF CLOSING ARGUMENT | ORDER SUSTAINING OBJECTION TO SCOPE AND CONTENT OF CLOSING ARGUMENT |
|---|---|
| **POSSIBLE SUPPORTING ARGUMENTS** | **POSSIBLE SUPPORTING ARGUMENTS** |
| 1. Comment on discrepancy between pleading and proof is proper in closing argument | 1. Scope of closing argument is properly confined to the record |
| 2. Counsel may argue law in closing argument | 2. Counsel refers to facts not in evidence or misstates the evidence in the record |
| 3. Counsel is allowed wide latitude to make emotional argument in closing | 3. Counsel's overly emotional appeals are improper |
| 4. Counsel may legitimately comment on failure of opponent to call an available witness | 4. Counsel may not express their personal belief in the justness of the client's cause or the credibility of the witnesses, nor assert their personal knowledge of the facts in issue |

## Support for Orders and Rulings Entered After Arbitration Hearing

### 44. Motion for Reconsideration or for Order for Additional or Amended Findings

| ORDER DENYING RECONSIDERATION OR ADDITIONAL OR AMENDED FINDINGS | ORDER GRANTING RECONSIDERATION OR ADDITIONAL OR AMENDED FINDINGS |
|---|---|
| **POSSIBLE SUPPORTING ARGUMENTS** | **POSSIBLE SUPPORTING ARGUMENTS** |
| 1. Movant's request is untimely | 1. Case issued after the close of the evidence but before ruling should be considered by the arbitration panel |

| | |
|---|---|
| 2. Movant's request for reconsider-ation is without merit | 2. Reconsideration of quality or quantity of evidence pertaining to a critical aspect of claim or defense is proper |
| 3. Movant had access to evidence they now wish to present to the ar-bitration panel as "newly discovered evidence" | 3. Additional findings are neces-sary to effectuate the arbitration award |

## 45. Objection Relating to Interest on Award

| ORDER REFUSING TO AWARD INTEREST OR REDUCING THE AMOUNT OF INTEREST AWARDED | ORDER AWARDING INTEREST |
|---|---|
| **POSSIBLE SUPPORTING ARGUMENTS** | **POSSIBLE SUPPORTING ARGUMENTS** |
| 1. Party was not deprived of use of money for the period during which interest was awarded | 1. Statute requires award of interest |
| 2. No interest may be imposed where money is not part of award, such as an award in rem | 2. Rule requires award of interest |
| 3. Statute does not allow an award of interest | 3. Agreement requires award of interest |
| 4. By statute, interest is not due on a lump sum payable in installments | 4. Case law requires award of interest |
| 5. Wrong date used to begin interest computation | 5. Law permits pre-award interest |
| 6. Improper method used to com-pute interest | 6. Additional interest is awardable because of error in computation |

## 46. Objection Relating to Award of Costs

| ORDER REFUSING TO ALLOW COSTS | ORDER ALLOWING COSTS |
|---|---|
| **POSSIBLE SUPPORTING ARGUMENTS** | **POSSIBLE SUPPORTING ARGUMENTS** |
| 1. No statute or rule expressly provides for the awarding of costs | 1. Statute or rule makes the award of costs mandatory |
| 2. Party requesting costs is not a "prevailing party" within the meaning of the statute or rule | 2. Costs may be assessed against a party for misconduct of its attorney such as for filing untrue pleadings, or for unduly delaying proceedings |
| 3. Prevailing plaintiff is not entitled to costs because defendant offered a sum to settle before hearing pursuant to rule, and plaintiff is being awarded an amount less than that sum | 3. Defendant offered an amount in judgment prior to arbitration and plaintiff proceeded to trial and recovered less than the amount offered |
| 4. Entity requesting costs is not technically a party to the arbitration | 4. Party requesting costs was prevailing party |
| 5. Party failed to submit a bill of costs in accordance with the pertinent statute or rule | 5. Party requesting costs is a bona fide party to the arbitration |
| 6. Party's request for costs is premature; it must await outcome of arbitration of consolidated case | 6. Party's request for costs is timely |
| 7. Party waived its right to request costs prior to the hearing | 7. Party has not waived its right to request costs |

## 47. Objection Relating to Award of Attorney Fees

| ORDER REFUSING ATTORNEY'S FEES | ORDER ALLOWING ATTORNEY'S FEES |
|---|---|
| POSSIBLE SUPPORTING ARGUMENTS | POSSIBLE SUPPORTING ARGUMENTS |
| 1. No statute, rule, or contract provision provides for an award of attorney fees | 1. Statute or rule specifically provides for an award of attorney fees |
| 2. Party requesting fees is not a prevailing party | 2. Successful litigant sued on behalf of a class and provided a common benefit |
| 3. Party requesting fees did not actually incur the expenses of an attorney | 3. Party seeks attorney fees because opposing party acted in bad faith |
| 4. Prevailing party acted for themselves and there is no common benefit | 4. Party seeks attorney fees because opposing party conducted the arbitration vexatiously, oppressively, or unreasonably |
| 5. Prevailing party is not entitled to attorney fees under the bad-faith exception to the rule precluding them when the opposing attorney merely litigates a claim in an unsettled area of the law and loses | 5. Party seeks attorney fees because opposing party willfully abused the judicial process |
| 6. Attorney fees may be reduced if the award is based on an improper method of calculation | 6. Party seeks attorney fees because opposing party perpetrated a fraud on the court |
| 7. Party waived right to request attorney fees | 7. Party did not waive right to request attorney fees |

## 48. Motion to Reopen Arbitration Hearing

| ORDER REFUSING TO REOPEN ARBITRATION HEARING | ORDER ALLOWING REOPENING OF ARBITRATION HEARING |
|---|---|
| POSSIBLE SUPPORTING ARGUMENTS | POSSIBLE SUPPORTING ARGUMENTS |
| 1. Motion to reopen hearing is untimely | 1. Motion to reopen hearing is timely made |
| 2. Movant failed to comply with requirements of statute or rule | 2. Newly discovered evidence came to light after the arbitration hearing, the party discovering the evidence was not negligent in failing to discover it prior to the hearing, the evidence is material and not merely cumulative, the evidence is such that it is reasonably probable that it would change the result of the arbitration |
| 3. Movant failed to specify grounds for reopening hearing | 3. Movant would be greatly prejudiced if hearing were not reopened |
| 4. Offer of proof, if admitted as evidence, would not change arbitrator's decision | 4. Arbitrator reopens hearing on their own motion to take additional evidence |
| 5. No just cause exists for reopening hearing | 5. Hearing is reopened to permit counsel to argue applicability of recent Supreme Court decision to the facts of this case |
| 6. Movant waived their right to request reopening of hearing | 6. Movant did not waive their right to request reopening of hearing |

# • INDEX •

## D